Growing Democracy in Japan

Growing Democracy in Japan

The Parliamentary
Cabinet System
since 1868

BRIAN WOODALL

UNIVERSITY PRESS OF KENTUCKY

Editorial and Sales Offices: The University Press of Kentucky
663 South Limestone Street, Lexington, Kentucky 40508-4008
www.kentuckypress.com

Library of Congress Cataloging-in-Publication Data

Woodall, Brian.
  Growing democracy in Japan : the parliamentary cabinet system since 1868 /
Brian Woodall.
     pages cm.
  Includes bibliographical references and index.
  ISBN 978-0-8131-4501-3 (hardcover : alk. paper) — ISBN 978-0-8131-4502-0 (pdf)
  — ISBN 978-0-8131-4503-7 (epub)
  1. Cabinet system—Japan. 2. Legislative bodies—Japan—History.
3. Democracy—Japan. 4. Japan—Politics and government—1868-   I. Title.
JQ1642.W66 2014
320.952—dc23   2014010370

This book is printed on acid-free paper meeting
the requirements of the American National Standard
for Permanence in Paper for Printed Library Materials.

∞

Manufactured in the United States of America.

Member of the Association of
American University Presses

To my mother
and
the memory of my father

Contents

Abbreviations
and Japanese Terms

AMA	Administrative Management Agency
Anpo	Japan-U.S. Mutual Security Treaty
ARC	Administrative Reform Council
AVM	Administrative Vice Minister
CEFP	Council on Economic and Fiscal Policy
CLB	Cabinet Legislation Bureau
CLO	Central Liaison Office
daimyō	feudal lord
DLP	Democratic Liberal Party
DPJ	Democratic Party of Japan
FEC	Far Eastern Commission
G2	Counterintelligence Section (U.S. occupation)
genrō	elder statesman
hanbatsu	leaders from the main outside domains (Satsuma, Chōshū, Tosa, and Hizen)
GHQ	General Headquarters (U.S. occupation)
GS	Government Section (U.S. occupation)
IRAPA	Imperial Rule Assistance Political Association
JCCM	Japanese Cabinets and Cabinet Ministers Database
JCP	Japan Communist Party
JSP	Japan Socialist Party
jūshin	senior statesman
kantei	Official Residence of the Prime Minister (equivalent to the U.S. White House)
"KY"	"unable to read the air" (*kūki yomenai*), clueless
LDP	Liberal Democratic Party
LKPS	Lord Keeper of the Privy Seal
MCI	Ministry of Commerce and Industry
METI	Ministry of Economy, Trade, and Industry

MITI	Ministry of International Trade and Industry
MP	Member of Parliament (elected member of the National Diet)
MPT	Ministry of Posts and Telecommunications
NDL	National Diet Library
OECD	Organization for Economic Cooperation and Development
OPEC	Organization of the Petroleum Exporting Countries
PARC	Policy Affairs Research Council
PMO	Prime Minister's Office
Rinchō	Second Ad Hoc Commission on Administrative Reform
SACO	Special Action Committee on Okinawa
Sat-Chō cabal	post-Meiji Restoration leaders from Satsuma and Chōshū domains
SDF	Self-Defense Forces
Seiyūkai	Friends of Constitutional Government (political party)
SWNCC	State-War-Navy Coordinating Committee
Tōdai	Tokyo University
tozama	"outside lord" (certain powerful *daimyō*)
zoku	policy tribe
zoku giin	policy specialist

Note on Conventions

Throughout the text, Japanese personal names are given in the common Japanese manner, with the surname followed by the given name. The main exception to this rule is made in the case of Japanese writers whose works are well known to Western readers. The names of cabinets (for example, the Kuroda cabinet, second Ōhira cabinet, etc.) follow the system employed on the website of the Prime Minister and His Cabinet (http://www.kantei .go.jp/jp/rekidai/index.html). Macron marks are used except in cases where the word in question is widely familiar to Western readers, such as Tokyo and Osaka instead of Tōkyō and Ōsaka.

Introduction

After being in Government one realizes that Parliament has a somewhat more peripheral role to perform. . . . Parliament is, in fact, not the centre of government. *The centre of Government is the Cabinet.*
—British cabinet minister quoted in Donald D. Searing,
Westminster's World (1994), 329 (italics added)

I must have attended nearly ninety Cabinet meetings. They lasted an average of ten minutes and all I did was sign documents.
—Former health minister and future prime minister Kan Naoto, quoted in Aurelia George Mulgan,
Japan's Failed Revolution (2003a), 156

System Failure

On the afternoon of March 11, 2011, an apprehensive nation looked to Prime Minister Kan Naoto and his cabinet for leadership and reassurance in the aftermath of a series of cascading disasters. Unleashed by the most powerful temblor ever to hit the quake-prone country, the catastrophe began with the Eastern Japan Great Earthquake, one of the five strongest in recorded history. Hundreds of aftershocks followed, and millions of households and businesses were left without electrical power. The earthquake produced an enormous tsunami that propelled a lethal wall of water ten kilometers inland. Nearly twenty thousand people died and more than three hundred thousand were displaced. Hundreds of thousands of homes, buildings, roads, bridges, railway lines, and other elements of critical infrastructure were destroyed or damaged. In addition, the earthquake and tsunami disabled the cooling systems at the Fukushima Daiichi Nuclear Power Plant, resulting in hydrogen explosions and visible damage to three reactors. These natural and man-made disasters produced a vast, heart-wrenching humanitarian crisis that was painstakingly reported by the domestic and international media. The survivors desperately needed shelter, drinking water and food, bathroom facilities, and medical care. And, with a late winter storm approaching, no time could be wasted before

1

launching a large-scale, coordinated rescue and recovery effort. Government spokespeople called on citizens to remain calm and downplayed reports of a nuclear catastrophe.

But the leadership displayed by Kan and his cabinet was ridiculed by the mass media. One day after the earthquake, Kan assessed the stricken nuclear power plant from a helicopter (evoking criticism that his visit delayed crucial venting at the plant) and reportedly asked officials on the scene, "What the hell is going on?" (*Guardian*, November 2, 2011). Then, for the next few days Kan and his government's spokespeople more or less read from a script written by the Tokyo Electric Power Company, the utility company that operates the plant. The Kan government repeatedly assured the nation that the situation was under control, even after the order was issued to evacuate tens of thousands of people living within a twelve-mile radius of the plant. The Kan government was also criticized for its humanitarian response. "It's been a week, and there's still been no government help," said a resident of one of the hardest hit areas, expressing the exasperation of many victims (*Los Angeles Times*, March 18, 2011). In response, Chief Cabinet Secretary Edano Yukio conceded, "In hindsight, we could have moved a little quicker in assessing the situation and coordinating all that information and provided it faster" (*Bloomberg BusinessWeek*, March 18, 2011).

The fears of a distrustful public were substantiated when dangerous levels of radioactivity began to appear in milk and vegetables produced in the Fukushima area, and when the media reported that beef cattle fed contaminated hay had been shipped around the country. Then, one month into the crisis, Japan's nuclear safety agency retroactively raised the event at Fukushima Daiichi from "Level 5" to "Level 7," putting it on par with the Chernobyl catastrophe (*Energy News*, April 11, 2011). In the weeks that followed, opinion surveys showed that most citizens wished to do away with nuclear power. Meanwhile, Kan and various cabinet officials repeatedly contradicted themselves by calling for "de-nuclearization" and then asserting that the country could not do without nuclear energy. On August 30, with a sub-20 percent approval rating, Kan and his ministers resigned en masse amid criticism of the inept handling of the multiple disasters.

The first question raised by these events is this: Why did Prime Minister Kan and his cabinet ministers fail to use their powers to galvanize and reassure the nation following the catastrophic sequence of events? Indeed, the

Kan cabinet's inept handling of the March 11 triple disaster is surprising, given the fact that the cabinet's disaster management machinery had been bolstered following the Murayama cabinet's bungled response to the 1995 Kōbe earthquake that claimed nearly sixty-five hundred lives.[1] A similar question could be posed concerning the succession of Japanese prime ministers and their cabinets who failed to lead Japan out of the "lost decades" (*ushinawareta jūnen*) that followed the bursting of the bubble economy.[2] In fact, the Constitution of Japan vests executive power in the cabinet, and even a cursory reading of the historical record reveals that this "supreme law of the nation"—which, ironically, was authored in large measure by Americans who knew little about parliamentary democracy—aimed to establish a parliamentary cabinet system inspired by Britain's "Westminster" model (Ward 1956, 1000; Stockwin 1999, 38; McNelly 2000, 65–66). Moreover, as we shall see, the executive leaders of the Japanese polity do, in fact, possess powers and prerogatives that are similar to those of their counterparts in other advanced parliamentary democracies.

It is tempting to blame Kan's leadership for the flawed response to the calamities of March 11, which is exactly what the mass media did. Yet the scope and complexity of the disasters were unprecedented and would have proved a daunting challenge for any leader. The case can be made, therefore, that the flawed response was the result of failure of the cabinet *system,* not shoddy prime ministerial leadership. This draws attention to two additional puzzles. Why, after more than six and a half decades of parliamentary democracy, has cabinet government failed to set root in Japan? And what forces conspired to give Japan's cabinet system its characteristic form and function, unflatteringly described as an "un-Westminster" system commanded by prime ministers who are "among the weakest democratic leaders in the world" (George Mulgan 2003a, 140; Krauss and Pekkanen 2010, 280)?

To solve these puzzles, we must trace the development of Japan's parliamentary cabinet system. In this introductory chapter, I survey the analytical topography and introduce the conceptual framework that informs this study. I draw upon concepts derived from institutionalization theory and historical institutionalism to create a unique lens through which to assess the process by which Japan's cabinet system evolved and the factors that molded its distinctive form and functions. I contend that Japan's cabinet system was transformed at eight historical junctures. In prewar times, significant changes followed the 1868 Meiji Restoration, the advent of party-led cabinets in 1898, and their violent demise in 1932. In postwar times, the Allied occupation produced a dramatic reconfiguration, while significant changes followed the emergence of the "1955 system" that ushered in the Liberal Democratic Party's (LDP) protracted hegemony, the "shocks" of the early 1970s, the advent of coalition cabinets in 1993, and the emergence of Twisted Diets following the 2007 House of Councillors elections. The substantive chapters of this book trace the evolution of Japan's cabinet system and, in so doing, "deal at length with history, and with time in history" (Braudel 1982, 26). Through this discussion, it will become clear that the present system is the product of a developmental process that has resulted in Japan's inability to establish a properly functioning system of cabinet government.

ORGANIZATION OF THE NATIONAL EXECUTIVE

The executive branch of the modern democratic polity is organized in one of three broad forms—presidential, semi-presidential, and parliamentary. In a presidential system, legislative and executive powers are separated, while the symbolic and political functions of the executive are fused in a single office. Among the thirty-four advanced industrialized polities that make up the Organization for Economic Cooperation and Development (OECD), the United States, Mexico, the Republic of Korea, and Chile are governed under presidential systems. Ministers in America's presidential system go by the title of "secretary" and are appointed by the president with the consent of the Senate. But the U.S. cabinet has no formal constitutional role; rather, it is an informal, extra-constitutional advisory organ that is not directly responsible to the legislature. The cabinet is responsible to the president, and, as is the case with cabinets in most presidential systems, it is a relatively weak organ. Indeed, as the authors of a popular U.S. government textbook observe, "unlike in England and many other parliamentary countries, where the cabinet *is* the government, the American cabinet is not a collective body. It meets but makes no decisions as a group. . . . The cabinet is made up of directors, but it is not a board of directors" (Lowi and Ginsburg 1998, 242–243). For this reason, meetings of America's cabinet have been described as "vapid non-events in which there has been a deliberate non-exchange of information as part of a process of mutual non-consultation" (Weisband and Franck, quoted in Cronin 1980, 253). Hence, the U.S. cabinet is not a "formally integrated institution," but "more a collection of a dozen or so secretaries who sometimes meet together in sessions called by the president, and at his whim" (Cohen 1988, 23).

In a semi-presidential system, executive powers are divided between a popularly elected president and a prime minister. The president is endowed with considerable constitutional authority, while the prime minister also wields substantial power and is subject to the confidence of Parliament (Shugart 2005, 324). Semi-presidential systems can be subdivided into two types, premier-presidential and president-parliamentary. The French Fifth Republic (1956 to the present) is the best known and most widely emulated premier-presidential model, but somewhat similar systems also can be found in Portugal, Poland, Lithuania, and the Ukraine. The classic example of a president-parliamentary system was that of Germany's Weimar Republic (1918 to 1933), and this type of executive system is found in Russia, the Republic of China (Taiwan), Georgia, Armenia, Peru, and Mozambique. Among OECD countries, only France, Portugal, and Poland are governed under semi-presidential systems.

In a parliamentary system, the executive's symbolic and political functions are carried out by separate officeholders. The symbolic functions are the domain of a "head of state," in effect a ceremonial figurehead, as is the case with the hereditary monarchs in Britain, Sweden, and elsewhere, as well as with India's president.[3] The political functions are entrusted to a "head of government." In Britain's widely emulated "Westminster system," the head of government, known as the "prime minister," is the leader of the majority party or coalition in a popularly elected Parliament. This officeholder is selected by the Parliament, not through direct popular elections. Executive power is concentrated in the prime minister and "cabinet," in essence a committee composed of "ministers" who head up the major departments of public administration. With few exceptions, ministers are recruited from the ranks of elected members of Parliament. The expectation that ministers should be elected MPs helps to ensure a "democratic character" to the cabinet, whose members are "accountable to the people's elected representatives" (House of Commons 2010, 6). Because a single party or coalition controls Parliament as well as the executive, centralized and disciplined party control under strong prime ministerial leadership becomes the norm. Parliamentary cabinets make decisions as a collectivity, and their members are collectively responsible to the legislature. The prime minister and the cabinet serve at the pleasure of Parliament, which at any time can remove them by passing a non-confidence resolution or rejecting a confidence resolution.

All together, twenty-seven of the thirty-four OECD countries can be classified as parliamentary democracies: the United Kingdom, Australia, New Zealand, Canada, Ireland, Belgium, the Netherlands, Luxembourg, Denmark, Norway, Sweden, Finland, Estonia, Iceland, Germany, Austria, Switzerland, Italy, Spain, the Czech Republic, Slovakia, Hungary, Slovenia, Israel, Greece, Turkey, and Japan. Indeed, since 1947 Japan has been governed under a parliamentary system, although the emergence of "party cabinets" in the 1920s and 1930s appeared "to be bringing a relationship between the Diet and the executive which resembles that of the British parliament to the cabinet" (Quigley 1932, 199). Although Japan's brief prewar drift toward democracy ended in disaster, the postwar polity is founded on the institutions of parliamentary democracy.

JAPAN'S CABINET SYSTEM

Japan boasts all of the classic features of a parliamentary democracy. The head of state is the emperor, who as "the symbol of the State" performs certain ceremonial duties (Constitution of Japan, Article 1). The head of government is the prime minister, who must be an elected member of the Diet, as is also the case with a majority of cabinet ministers (Articles 67 and 68). The prime minister as well as all cabinet ministers must be "civilian" (Article 66). In the event that the cabinet fails to retain the Diet's confidence, the cabinet must resign en masse unless the House of Representatives is dissolved within ten days (Article 66). The prime minister and cabinet are collectively responsible to the Diet in the exercise of executive power, which has been interpreted to mean that all cabinet decisions should be unanimous (Article 66; Administrative Management Bureau 2007, 117; Tanaka 1976, 41). To secure unanimity, the prime minister is empowered to appoint and dismiss ministers (Article 68). To facilitate the candid expression of views, no official public minutes are kept at cabinet meetings, which only state ministers and three designated government officials—two deputy cabinet secretaries and the director general of the Cabinet Legislation Bureau—are allowed to attend.[4]

The cabinet is responsible for performing a variety of functions. It administers the law, supervises the government bureaucracy, manages foreign affairs, concludes treaties (with subsequent approval of the Diet), prepares and presents the budget to the Diet, enacts cabinet orders, and decides on amnesty, commutation of punishment, reprieve, and restoration of rights (Constitution of Japan, Articles 72 and 73). All laws and cabinet orders must be signed by the relevant ministers and countersigned by the prime minister to signify that they have assumed responsibility for the faithful implementation of those decisions (Article 74). A cabinet minister is the supreme authority within each government ministry and agency, supervising the agency's officials, submitting bills and government ordinances to the cabinet for approval, and approving all significant departures in agency policy and procedure. The minister is empowered to appoint and dismiss agency officials below a certain rank (Park 1986, 1). The prime minister and cabinet occupy the apex of the central executive, and are tasked with coordinating and securing administrative uniformity among the various organs of government and bearing ultimate responsibility for all executive activities of the state (Administrative Management Bureau 2007, 116–117). The powers and perquisites that go along with ministerial appointment exude an irresistible appeal for Japanese MPs, which has given rise to the term "minister disease" (*daijinbyō*) to describe the phenomenon (Kuroda and Miyagawa 1990, 6). The celebrity status accorded ministers is attested to by the "tent villages" (*tento mura*) that the press corps sets up outside the Prime Minister's Official Residence whenever a new cabinet is formed.[5]

The official view of the Japanese government is that "the Cabinet, Ministries, Agencies, and public corporations function as one organization, *at the top of which exists the Cabinet*. . . . Consequently, it is natural that the agencies and corporations which take care of national administration should be *systematically organized under the Cabinet*" (Administrative Management Bureau 2007, 116; italics added). While the ministers attract the lion's share of media attention, these busy leaders could not perform their multifarious functions without the assistance of a large, professional support staff. Indeed, a minister must simultaneously don multiple hats—those of government representative, public agency head, front-bench party leader, and member of Parliament. The Cabinet Office assists with overall administrative coordination and a variety of other concerns, including the handling of official documents. The Cabinet Secretariat arranges cabinet meetings, provides safekeeping for official seals, and supports the chief cabinet secretary in sundry other ways. The Cabi-

```
┌─────────────────────────────────────────┐
│                 Cabinet                   │
├───────────────────────────────────────────┤
│              Prime Minister               │
├───────────────────────────────────────────┤
│          Chief Cabinet Secretary          │
├───────────────────────────────────────────┤
│ Minister of State for:                    │
│ ▪Finance                                  │
│ ▪Internal Affairs and Communications      │
│ ▪Justice                                  │
│ ▪Foreign Affairs                          │
│ ▪Education, Sports, S&T, and Culture      │
│ ▪Health, Welfare, and Labor               │
│ ▪Agriculture, Forestry, and Fisheries     │
│ ▪Economy, Trade, and Industry             │
│ ▪Land, Infrastructure, and Transport      │
│ ▪Environment                              │
│ ▪Defense                                  │
│ ▪National Public Safety                   │
│ ▪Reconstruction                           │
│ ▪Special Missions (four)                  │
└───────────────────────────────────────────┘
```

Senior Parliamentary Vice Ministers

Parliamentary Secretaries

| Security Council of Japan | Cabinet Secretariat | Cabinet Office | Cabinet Legislation Bureau |

Cabinet Councils

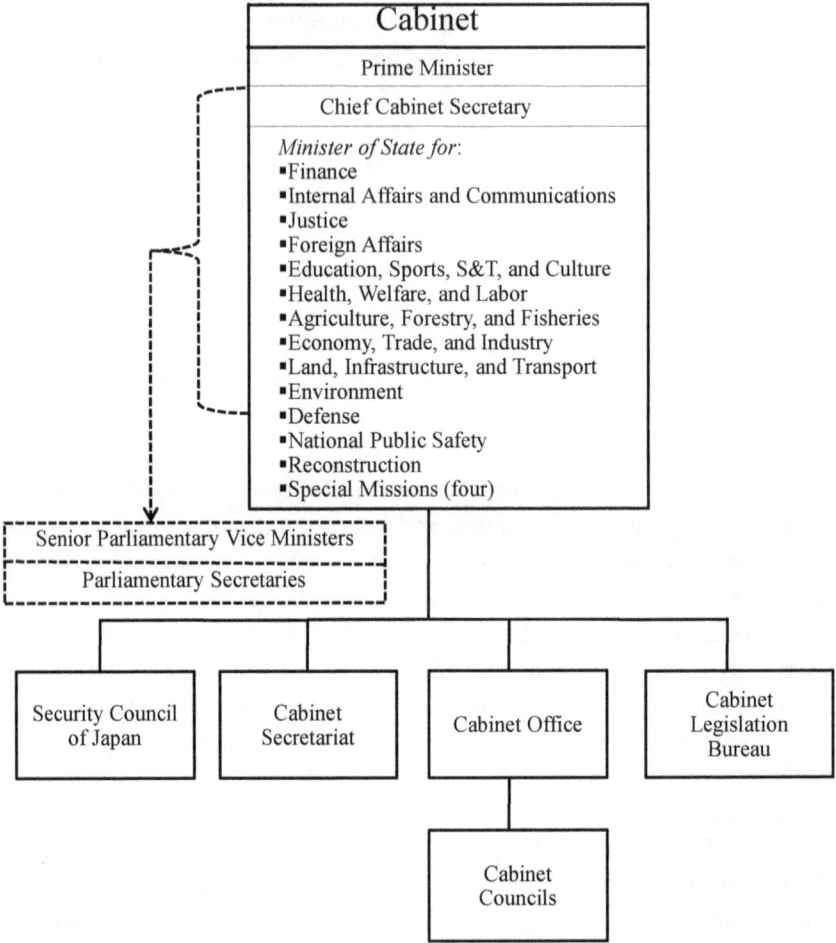

Figure I.1. Japan's Cabinet System (2nd Abe Cabinet, December 26, 2012)

net Legislation Bureau (*Naikaku hōsei kyoku*, or CLB)—staffed entirely by elite career officials seconded by government ministries—offers legal opinions and assists in drafting legislative bills, cabinet orders, and proposed treaties (*Asahi Shimbun Globe*, June 14, 2010). In addition, the Security Council of Japan and other cabinet-related councils and committees provide for focused policy deliberation. Taken together, these organs—and their mutually supportive and interdependent interactions—constitute Japan's cabinet system.[6]

THE COMPARATIVE PERSPECTIVE

Cross-national comparisons help us understand the extent to which Japan's premiers and cabinet ministers are adequately equipped to shoulder their weighty administrative burdens. As noted earlier, Japan's cabinet serves at the pleasure of the Diet, which can topple it with a simple majority vote in support of a non-confidence resolution or by rejecting a confidence resolution. Similar constitutional conventions are in place in Britain, Canada, and Australia. By way of contrast, a majority of German legislators must first elect a successor before the *Bundestag* can dismiss a chancellor (Kommers 1997, 191; Lancaster 1997, 317). In the Japanese case, non-confidence resolutions have succeeded on only four occasions, most recently in 1993 when the Miyazawa cabinet was ousted, injecting a brief hiatus in the LDP's legislative hegemony.[7] Likewise, Japan is one of many advanced countries that require or permit cabinet ministers to be recruited from the ranks of elected members of Parliament.[8] Except for the occasional non-MP appointed to a ministerial post, Japanese cabinet ministers are entitled to hold a seat and to vote in Parliament, as is the case in Britain, the Commonwealth countries, and elsewhere.[9] Such is not the case in Holland and Norway, where ministers are obliged to relinquish their parliamentary seats, nor in Sweden, where ministers may hold parliamentary seats but cannot vote (Andeweg and Bakema 1994, 66; Strom 1994, 43; and Larsson 1994, 172).

The Japanese prime minister's formal powers are comparable to those of heads of government in other established parliamentary democracies. As noted earlier, Japan's prime minister is empowered to appoint and remove cabinet ministers, which also holds true for the British, Danish, Icelandic, Irish, and Swedish heads of government. In contrast, the Dutch, Finnish, and Norwegian heads of state lack the power to select or sack cabinet ministers unilaterally (Andeweg and Bakema 1994, 59; Nouisiainen 1994, 98–99). Unlike the British prime minister, Japan's prime minister is not empowered to create departments of state, as this requires Diet legislation. However, as part of the 2001 central government restructuring, the Japanese premier is now able to create ministerial portfolios known as "minister of state for special missions" (*tokumei tantō daijin*) (Headquarters for the Administrative Reform of the Central Government 2000). Nevertheless, while there has been some evidence of "presidentialization" of the prime minister's role or the emergence of a "*kantei*" (the Japanese equivalent of the White House) style of diplomacy, few, if any, would argue that the actual influence of the Japanese premier even remotely compares to that exercised by the British prime minister (Krauss and Nyblade 2005, 368; Shinoda 2007; Thayer 1996, 71).

Japan's cabinets are similar in size to those in other parliamentary democracies.[10] The Cabinet Law specifies that the number of ministers of state shall not exceed fourteen, except under special circumstances, in which no more than four additional ministers may be appointed. Including the prime minister, therefore, the maximum number of ministers in a Japanese cabinet is eighteen. In December 2010, the average membership size of the twenty-nine OECD member countries governed under parliamentary systems was just under nineteen members (Central Intelligence Agency 2010). The Israeli and Canadian cabinets were the largest, with thirty-five and thirty ministers, respectively, while the smallest were the Icelandic (twelve ministers) and Hungarian (eleven ministers) cabinets. Meanwhile, the Swiss Federal Council—which is not responsible to the elected assembly, and, therefore, not a parliamentary cabinet—was composed of just seven members. As Klimek and his colleagues discovered, there is a high significance of negative correlation between a cabinet's size and its performance.[11] With a few exceptions, cabinets that number more than around twenty members surpass the critical "Coefficient of Inefficiency," resulting in poorer performance as measured by the United Nations Development Program's Human Development Indicator (Klimek et al. 2008).

By law, Japan's cabinet performs its functions through "cabinet meetings" (*kakugi*) that are presided over by the prime minister, who sets the agenda for discussion, during which each minister is allowed to pose questions (Cabinet Law, Article 4). Three main types of cabinet meetings have come to exist. The bulk of cabinet-related business is conducted in biweekly "regular cabinet meetings" (*teirei kakugi*), while "special cabinet meetings" (*rinji kakugi*) are convened whenever necessary. When an immediate cabinet decision is required, officials of the Cabinet Secretariat are dispatched to secure signatures (*kaō*) from each minister in what are referred to as "revolving cabinet meetings" (*mochimawari kakugi*), even though face-to-face meetings do not occur.[12] Cabinet meetings take place in a special room in the Prime Minister's Official Residence, with ministers seated around a round wooden table in a predetermined order.[13] The prime minister's seat is considered the center of the table, with the chief cabinet secretary on the right and the holders of senior posts—generally beginning with the foreign or finance ministers—seated in alternating right-left order around the table. This arrangement is somewhat similar to that of the British cabinet, whose seating is arranged hierarchically, with the cabinet secretary on the prime minister's immediate right and holders of senior posts on his or her left or across the table (Kavanaugh 2000, 247).

If time spent in cabinet meetings is any indication, Japan's ministers are about as busy as their counterparts in other parliamentary democracies. Regular cabinet meetings are generally held each Tuesday and Friday at 10:00 A.M., but when the Diet is in session the meetings are convened at 9:00 A.M. in a special room in the National Diet Building. By way of comparison, the Irish cabinet also meets biweekly, but ministers are required to attend an annual retreat lasting two or three days. The British cabinet normally meets for about two hours each Thursday morning at Whitehall when Parliament is in session, although under Tony Blair cabinet meetings were said to last about an hour (ibid., 247). Cabinets in Australia, Austria, Belgium, the Czech Republic, and Denmark also meet once weekly. The Norwegian cabinet generally meets on Monday and Thursday, and again briefly in the presence of the monarch on Friday. Meanwhile, the Swedish cabinet meets weekly when the *Riksdag* is in session, but ministers who are in Stockholm are expected to meet each weekday for "lunch deliberations." In addition, Swedish ministers are expected to attend a weekly lunch deliberation as well as a short annual retreat (Larsson 1994, 173–174).

Japanese cabinets endure about as long as their counterparts in other countries. According to the government's official system, the thirty-two individuals who held the premiership from May 1946 (first Yoshida cabinet) through December 2012 (second Abe cabinet) formed a total of ninety-three cabinets, or just under three cabinets per government. The average life expectancy of these governments was 760 days, meaning that prime ministers rotated about every two years.[14] In contrast, a study of government duration in nineteen Western countries from 1945 to 1999 found the Finnish (399 days), Italian (350 days), and Portuguese (327 days) cabinets to be the most ephemeral, while the Canadian (945 days), British (995 days), and Luxembourgian (1,122 days) cabinets were the longest-lived (Huber and Martinez-Gallardo 2004). Viewed in comparative context, therefore, Japan's governments find themselves in the middle of the pack when it comes to life expectancy.

Beginning in the early 1970s, a hierarchy of ministerial portfolios emerged in Japanese cabinets that bears a close likeness to those found in other parliamentary democracies. Because the Japanese prime minister is the head of government and something more than *primus inter pares* in cabinet decision-making, it is natural that that portfolio would be accorded high esteem. In addition, the holders of the finance, foreign, and international trade and industry portfolios are regarded as the crème de la crème of departmental ministers (Kato and Laver 1998; Ono 2012). In this regard, the ministerial pecking order in Japanese cabinets corresponds with the results of an expert survey of twenty-three countries, which found that the finance and foreign affairs portfolios ranked no lower than third among all portfolios, while the economy/industry portfolio also ranked near the top (Laver and Hunt 1992, 133–316).

Of course, a permanent, professional staff is essential to assist ministers in shouldering the onerous executive burden they are called upon to bear. In Japan, the Cabinet Office, Cabinet Secretariat, and Cabinet Legislation Bureau provide a large measure of this administrative support. In 2012, the Cabinet Office boasted a full-time staff of 2,202 national government employees, while the respective staffs posted to the Secretariat and CLB numbered 338 and 72 employees (Ministry of Internal Affairs and Communications 2012b). On the surface, the permanent staff supporting Japan's cabinet—nearly 3,000 employees—would appear to be considerably larger than that employed in the British Cabinet Office, with its staff of 1,230 employees (Office for National Statistics 2010). However, if the employees posted to Britain's other cabinet-related agencies are included—in other words, the Central Office of Information (970 staffers), National School of Government (250 staffers), and Office of the Parliamentary Counsel (80 staffers)—the difference is not significant.

At least on the surface, therefore, Japan's premiers and cabinet ministers appear to be amply empowered, sufficiently supported, and similar in form and function to their counterparts in other advanced parliamentary democracies. In other words, it seems that Japan's foremost executive leaders possess the requisite formal authority and resources to carry out the functions tasked to them by the Constitution and related laws. Why, then, did the Kan cabinet fail to provide strong, effective leadership after the disasters of March 11? And why did a succession of prime ministers and cabinets who occupied the executive helm throughout the "lost decades" fail to muster those powers to right the ship? Is this the result of flawed leadership or of the failure of the cabinet system?

INSTITUTIONALIZATION

A theoretical guide is necessary to understand the process by which Japan's cabinet system came to be what it is. The question to begin with is this: To what extent has cabinet government become *institutionalized* in the Japanese context? Institutionalization is a ubiquitous process that has been observed in a variety of national, subnational, and supranational political organizations around the world (Meyer and Rowan 1977; Tolbert and Zucker 1996). It employs parsimonious concepts to explain a universal process not bound by geography, culture, time, or regime type.

Institutionalization is the process whereby an organization becomes well established and, in so doing, acquires value and stability as an end in itself (Huntington 1965, 394; Ragsdale and Thies 1997, 1282). An organization's value is enhanced as it develops a distinctive identity, functions, and mode of operation. The degree of institutionalization is determined by the organization's progression along four dimensions: complexity, coherence, autonomy, and adaptability (Huntington 1965). *Complexity* is reflected in the emergence of an increasingly intricate organizational structure, division of labor, and growth of specialized units. *Coherence* involves the establishment of boundaries that distinguish the organization and its human element from all other people and groups. *Autonomy,* in the case of a political organization, is the quality of being relatively free of constraint such that the organization has "authoritative control over policy outcomes, acceded to by those in other organizations" (Ragsdale and Thies 1997, 1282). *Adaptability* refers to the ability of an organization to perpetuate its existence through leadership succession and modification of its roles, functions, and procedures in response to external and internal challenges. Complexity and coherence relate to the organization's *internal* dynamics, while autonomy and adaptability relate to its interactions with the *external* environment. An organization is not fully institutionalized until it has achieved high and enduring levels of development in each of these four measures.

There is no agreement concerning institutionalization's causes. Perhaps the earliest formulation was Durkheim's "density theorem," which holds that "the division of labor varies in direct proportion to the volume and density of societies, and if it progresses in a continuous manner over the course of social development, it is because societies become regularly more dense and generally more voluminous" ([1893] 1984, 205; Polsby 1968, 164). This is implicit in Weber's thesis that large, highly differentiated bureaucracies, whose power derives from rational-legal authority, emerged as a consequence of the development of market economies and centralized states (Weber 1946, 204–209). It is also evident in Michels's study of Germany's Social Democratic Party, from which he derived his famous "iron law" that holds, "who says organization, says oligarchy" (Michels [1911] 1962). In fact, the expansion of the role of government has been a persistent theme in countries around the world since the nineteenth century, as reflected in the rise of the "Administrative State" and the "Welfare State" (for example, Ashford 1986). Hence, as a larger portion of the nation's life came under the sway of centrally made decisions, "the agencies of the national government institutionalized" (Polsby 1968, 164).

Yet institutionalization is also driven by human choice and ambition. This is seen in Parkinson's observations concerning increases in staff size and paperwork generated in Britain's Colonial Office even as the overseas empire was contracting, and, therefore, should have resulted in the opposite. Indeed, Parkinson's "laws"—officials "multiply subordinates, not rivals" and "make work for each other"—derive from the rational self-interested actions of bureaucratic actors rather than abstract organizational forces (Parkinson 1955). As Ragsdale and Thies observe, individuals affiliated with the organization employ their energies and seek to amass "resources to establish the organization, bolster its persistence, and make their activities more routine. The environment creates conditions for the organization to be taken for granted as it conducts specialized activities upon which other units grow to depend" (1997, 1283; also Zucker 1991, 105). As Searing found in his study of political roles in Britain's Westminster system, the principal incentives that attracted ministerial aspirants were ambition, status, stimulation, and power (1994, 356–357). Ministers—the vast majority of whom are, after all, professional politicians—seldom see their careers advance when their agencies shrink in budget, staff size, or policy significance. Such is also the case with career bureaucrats, who have a vested interest in seeing their agencies grow.

Institutionalization theory provides conceptual tools with which to explain how Japan's cabinet system developed. It draws attention to the frequently uneven progress of development along the dimensions of institutionalization and the consequences that follow. For example, the battle to privatize Japan's postal system pitted the Koizumi cabinet against the "postal family," a deeply entrenched subgovernment composed of influential LDP lawmakers, government officials, and postmasters that epitomized Japan's rigidly fragmented political structure. To adapt government policy to restore economic prosperity, it was necessary for the Koizumi cabinet to declare war on a traditional pillar of support for the ruling party that gave birth to the cabinet. "When institutions are better at holding the line than responding to change," explains Kesselman, "political constraint and overinstitutionalization can occur" (1970, 25; Reed 1991). I explore the implications of uneven institutional development in the substantive chapters of this book, but for now it is necessary to ask how to identify a well-established cabinet system. Specifically, what would such a system look like in the Japanese context? On this score, the logical comparison is to Britain's widely emulated Westminster system.

The Westminster Ideal

An established Westminster system is characterized by high and enduring levels of development in each of the four measures of institutionalization. Because ministerial appointment bestows prestige, power, and perquisites, cabinet portfolios are highly coveted and almost exclusively reserved for ruling party lawmakers who possess the requisite level of seniority and ambition. Because prime ministers believe that "parliamentary apprentice-ships are prerequisites for understanding ministerial roles and perform-ing them successfully," they will distribute few if any portfolios to "lateral entrants" or insufficiently senior MPs (Searing 1994, 362; Rose 1971, 401). British ministers tend to serve nearly fifteen years in Parliament before entering the cabinet, and a similarly lengthy parliamentary apprenticeship seems reasonable to expect of Japanese ministerial aspirants (Searing 1994, 348; Heasman 1962b, 318). Assuming that elections are held every three years, novice ministers would be in their fifth terms. It follows that the majority of ministers will embark upon political careers by the time they reach their mid-forties and will emerge from "occupations of a kind that facilitate the pursuit of politics as a serious career," such as law, media, aca-demia, parliamentary staffer, and local elective politics (King 1981, 262–263). Few young people possess the "name brand," established campaign organizations, or riches required to launch and sustain a parliamentary career. This puts the offspring or close relatives of MPs in a position of comparative advantage. And because "the only significant path to the top of the polity passes through the university," cabinet ministers will tend to be well educated (Aberbach et al. 1981, 51).

Complexity is a defining characteristic of an established Westminster system. The British system began as a small, nominal cabinet within the Privy Council and evolved into an expansive and specialized network of executive organs, multiple levels of ministerial roles, and a "pecking order within the Cabinet that is very well recognized by Ministers" (Searing 1994, 283–284). I would expect those at the top of the ministerial hierarchy to possess the basic attributes required of a cabinet minister mentioned in the previous paragraph, albeit in more concentrated dosages.[15] It is reasonable to assume that the high-status ministers will have been elected to at least seven parliamentary terms in the dominant chamber of Parliament, amassed more than two decades of service as MPs, and previously held ministerial posts. In other words, the highest-status portfolios will not be given as gold watches simply to reward many years of faithful service. Also, the lion's share of prestigious portfolios likely will be reserved for men— alas, "women have been found to hold fewer cabinet positions, and where they have been appointed, to be mainly allocated portfolios with 'feminine' characteristics and lower levels of prestige" (Krook and O'Brien 2012, 1). While the British cabinet evolved with little external influence, Japan's modern cabinet system incorporated elements of foreign models. Thus, even though the postwar cabinet system did not materialize out of thin air, I would expect advancement toward institutionalization to be reflected in increasingly differentiated organizational structures and ministerial roles (Searing 1994, 344). This does not necessarily mean that cabinets will become larger and larger. On the contrary, I would expect that lawmakers would, through intuition or trial and error, discover that, as "Parkinson's Law" and empirical assessment have shown, cabinets of more than around twenty members perform poorly (Klimek et al. 2008).

An established Westminster-style cabinet is the most powerful executive organ, and as such it should be able to act with relative autonomy vis-à-vis the legislature, government bureaucracy, and other potential competitors for executive primacy (Lijphart 1999, 10). The cabinet sets the general course for government policy, acts as the ultimate coordinator and arbiter of last resort in executive affairs, and oversees the various departments of government. In the words of a former British cabinet minister, the cabinet is at the "centre of the web" (Searing 1994, 366). The cabinet sets the agenda for legislative deliberation and sponsors the largest share of policies that are enacted into law. In addition, the cabinet oversees the government bureaucracy, referees inter-ministerial disputes, and reviews and authorizes all major policy decisions (Kavanaugh 2000, 239). Ministers are the supreme authorities within their departments, over which they are individually responsible. At the same time, all ministers are subordinate to the cabinet, which, as a team, possesses powers that are greater than the sum of its parts. The prime minister has the power to appoint and dismiss ministers and, of necessity, plays a role that exceeds that of first among equals. Yet the cabinet's "consent to major initiatives usually must be obtained, and not even the most determined Prime Minister could prevail against the opposition of his or her colleagues for long" (Thomas 1998, 12). In sum, a Westminster-style cabinet should be firmly entrenched in the center of the central state executive.

Finally, a well-established Westminster-style system is the product of an evolutionary process that requires "the capacity to respond to the challenges of time and changing environment; the dropping of old tasks and taking on of new ones and the resolution of succession problems" (Dominguez and Mitchell 1977, 173). For this reason, I perceive organizational age and iterated leadership succession as simple indicators of durability. Indeed, a defining feature of the Westminster system is the broadly embraced legitimacy and irregularity by which prime ministers and cabinet members assume their executive posts, only to be replaced by new prime ministers and cabinets. To endure and continue to fulfill their core functions, cabinets must adapt to the challenges posed by protracted economic downturns, mushrooming government deficits, public health concerns, environmental problems, demographic changes, and natural and manmade disasters. In addition, they must deftly respond to international structural changes (for example, the end of the Cold War), tension in foreign relations, territorial conflicts and challenges to national sovereignty, and homegrown as well as international terrorism. Likewise, they must effectively respond to structural changes or challenges in the political order (such as the advent of coalition governments) and major corruption scandals.

In sum, a well-established Westminster system boasts high and enduring levels of development in each of the four dimensions of institutionalization. The complexity and coherence dimensions relate to the cabinet system's *internal* orientation, while the autonomy and adaptability dimensions relate to its *external* orientation. A Westminster system presumes the existence of competitive legislative parties whose members are sufficiently disciplined and fearful of punishment at the hands of party leaders that their votes seldom deviate from government proposals. To carry out its functions, the cabinet must exhibit a high degree of *cohesiveness,* as reflected in well-developed criteria for recruiting members and promoting leaders, collectivity norms, and highly differentiated organizational structures. It is important to keep in mind that the cabinet is a collective body whose members jointly make decisions for which they are "equally and jointly responsible," while allowing "all departmental perspectives and competing claims to be filtered through the specific issue being debated" (James 2002, 6; Buckley 2006, 4; also Rhodes et al. 2009, 120–132). As the foremost executive organ of government, the cabinet must be endowed with sufficient powers and resources to operate with relative autonomy in conducting executive affairs and in adapting to environmental challenges. In its external orientation, therefore, the cabinet system must be capable of effecting *strategic choice* in executive decision-making (Hrebiniak and Joyce 1985, 340). By distilling the dimensions of institutionalization into two synthetic variables—*cohesiveness* (coherence + complexity) and *strategic choice* (autonomy + adaptability)—we can derive a typology of cabinet forms.

Four types of parliamentary cabinet systems emerge, *corporatist, confederate, figurehead,* and *Westminster.* The *corporatist* cabinet exerts a high degree of strategic choice, although it lacks cohesiveness as a result of internal divisions or an inability to control the ruling party or coalition. The *confederate* cabinet presents a cohesive executive, but its degree of freedom in effecting strategic choice is constrained by a fragmented or unstable policy-making environment. The lack of cohesion on the part of the corporatist cabinet and the fragmented or unstable policy-making environment that confronts the confederate cabinet effectively rule out the possibility of cabinet government in either case. On the other hand, as the foremost organ of executive decision-making, the *Westminster* cabinet is endowed with sufficient powers and prerogatives to enable it to respond flexibly and tactically to virtually any challenge that may arise. In addition, because its ministers double as leaders of a centralized and disciplined majority party, "it can confidently count on staying in office and getting its legislative proposals approved" (Lijphart 1999, 12). In contrast, the *figurehead* cabinet clearly is not the most powerful organ of government, even if laws and conventions say that this should be so; it functions mainly to rubber-stamp decisions made elsewhere. Moreover, because the strategic choice of the prime minister and cabinet is constrained—owing to a coalition arrange-

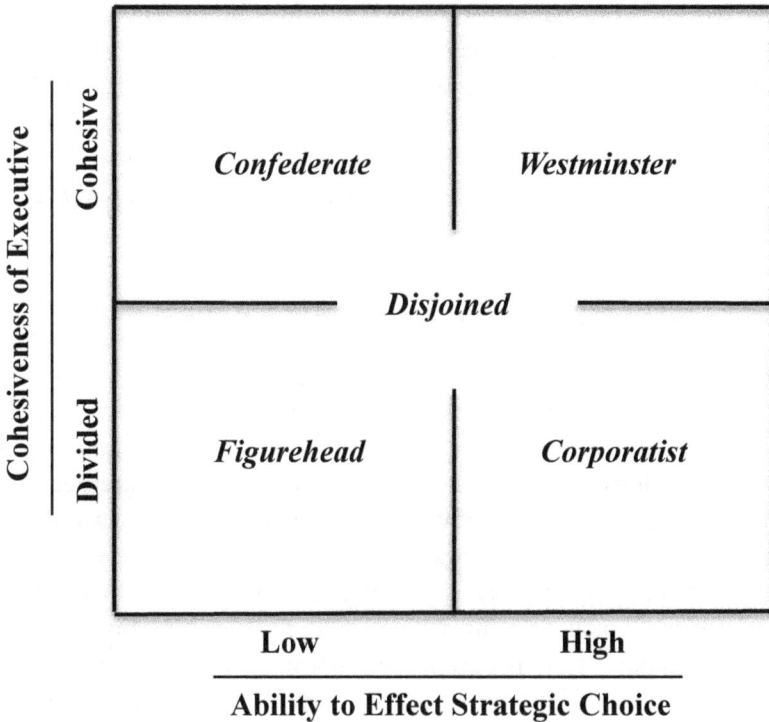

Figure I.2. Typology of Parliamentary Cabinet Systems

ment or to a decentralized dominant party—these cabinets cannot count on staying in office or getting their legislative proposals approved. These handicaps severely constrain the cabinet's adaptive capabilities in response to external or internal challenges.

I argue that a transitional fifth type—a *disjoined* cabinet—stood at Japan's executive helm from 1993 through 2013. This is not a distinct cabinet type, but, rather, reflects the chaotic and unsettled state of Japan's cabinet system since the structural changes and political reforms of 1993 and 1994. While, on occasion, the disjoined cabinet exhibits forceful, coherent executive leadership (for example, the Koizumi cabinet's campaign to privatize the postal system), just as often its actions are inconsistent and ineffective (such as the Kan cabinet's handling of the Fukushima Daiichi crisis). The hopes of the citizenry, whose expectations had been elevated by the 2001 government restructuring and the changes promised by the

Democratic Party of Japan (DPJ) when it became the party in power, were dashed by the inability of the disjoined cabinets to provide forceful leadership under coalition arrangements and Twisted Diets. While Japan's cabinet system has assumed different forms during different historical periods, it has never developed into a fully functional Westminster-style cabinet system despite meaningful steps in this direction (Estevez-Abe 2006; Krauss 2007; Mochizuki 2007).

EXPLAINING INSTITUTIONAL CHANGE

While institutionalization theory helps to explain *how* Japan's cabinet system evolved, it cannot explain *why* it came to assume its characteristic form and function. Indeed, since institutionalization is a ubiquitous process, we might logically expect all parliamentary systems patterned after the Westminster model to exhibit similar organizational forms and performance levels. Yet, despite outward similarities, Japan has never evolved a fully functioning Westminster-style cabinet system. I argue that the distinctive organizational structures, roles, and relationships that together form Japan's cabinet system were forged in a matrix of laws, ordinances, political structures, and unwritten codes of conduct. But where do institutions come from? The answer is found in the spurts of institutional innovation that cluster around critical junctures in history when "institutional configurations are upended and replaced by fundamentally new ones" as well as in the gradual evolution of established institutions (Mahoney and Thelen 2010, 2).

North's definition of the term *institution*—a "humanly devised constraint" that structures behavior—provides a foundation upon which to build a conceptual framework (1990, 3). *Formal institutions* are embodied in rules, laws, and constitutions (ibid., 4). In the case of Japan's cabinet system, important formal institutions include the Constitution, Cabinet Law, National Government Organization Law, and the political party system. During the half-century of LDP dominance, intraparty politics and cabinet decision-making became so intimately intertwined that it was impossible to say where one began and the other ended (Laver and Shepsle 1994b, 7; also Calder 1988, 446). A consequence of the failure of the opposition to oust the LDP was the systematic exclusion of organized labor and environmental, women's rights, anti-nuclear, and other interest groups that tended to support the opposition (Steinhoff 1989). Of course, this situation could have been remedied had the opposition unseated the LDP, but this did not occur from 1955 until 2009. *Informal institutions* are embodied in behavioral norms, conventions, and unwritten codes of conduct, such as the seniority system for ministerial aspirants and the unanimity rule in cabinet decision-making (North 1990, 4; Rose 1971, 401, 411). Taken together, these formal and informal "rules of the game" constitute what North terms the "interdependent web of an *institutional matrix*" that patterns behavior and molds organizational forms (North 1990, 3, 95; italics added).

While the Northian definition explains the static effects of institutions, it does not account for their dynamic aspect. Institutions should be viewed as political instruments that are "fraught with tensions because they invariably raise resource considerations and invariably have distributional consequences" (Mahoney and Thelen 2010, 8). In other words, "dynamic tensions and pressure for change are built into institutions," which embody "political legacies of historical struggles" that invariably dictate an unequal distribution of resources and produce cleavages that later form coalitions for change (ibid., 7, 14; Pierson 2000, 258–259). Those interests that are disadvantaged by existing arrangements represent potential change agents that will constantly be on the lookout for opportunities to redress their grievances. As Mahoney and Thelen explain, "where institutions represent compromises or relatively durable but still contested settlements based on specific coalitional dynamics, they are always vulnerable to shifts" (Mahoney and Thelen 2010, 8). For these reasons, I define an *institution* as *a humanly devised constraint that structures behavior and carries power-distributional consequences.*

While much attention focuses on the abrupt bursts of institutional innovation that cluster around critical junctures, most institutional change is gradual and incremental. A critical juncture is a watershed event, or "key choice point," that leads to the reconfiguration of institutional arrangements or structural patterns (Mahoney 2001, 6–7). It can appear as an immediate response to an external shock, such as the Great Depression or the Second World War. It can also result from a primarily internal stimulus, such as the Iranian Revolution that overthrew the Pahlavi regime in 1979 or the toppling of long-standing dictatorships in Tunisia and Egypt in the "Arab Spring." But such exogenous shocks occur only rarely, while institutions constantly undergo incremental change. For example, the electoral realignment in the United States that began in 1932—when FDR's Democratic Party took control of the executive and legislative branches, and, more or less, maintained its dominance for the next three decades—facilitated a succession of incremental changes that fundamentally transformed American politics. In this way, the cumulative effects of gradual changes, as well as the occasional exogenous shock, create openings for disadvantaged interests to seek to improve their situation by pressing for change.

Mahoney and Thelen propose a framework for identifying and explaining the different forms of institutional change. Four types of institutional change are identified, *displacement* ("the removal of existing rules and the introduction of new ones"), *layering* ("the introduction of new rules on top of or alongside existing ones"), *drift* ("the changed impact of existing rules due to shifts in the environment"), and *conversion* ("the changed enactment of existing rules due to their strategic redeployment") (Mahoney and Thelen 2010, 15–18). Each type of change can be produced gradually, but displacement episodes are also associated with shocks that result in abrupt institutional reconfigurations that produce path-dependent legacies. Particular types of change agents tend to be associated with particular types of change: *insurrectionaries* are associated with displacement, *subversives* with layering, *renegades* with drift, and *opportunists* with conversion (ibid., 22–27).[16]

Building upon this framework, I argue that Japan's cabinet system was significantly recast at eight historical junctures. Two of these resulted in reconfigurations of institutional and structural arrangements. The 1868 Meiji Restoration and the American-led Allied occupation of Japan (1945–1952) were exogenous shocks that resulted in the displacement and recasting of a broad array of political institutions and socioeconomic structures. The six remaining tipping points were precipitated by the accumulation of gradual changes and structural shifts. The changes that followed the establishment of Prime Minister Ōkuma Shigenobu's "party cabinet" in 1898 and the advent of coalition cabinets following the LDP's brief fall from grace in 1993 reflect drift, in the sense that existing rules were changed in response to environmental shifts. Similarly, the changes that followed the 1932 assassination of Prime Minister Inukai Tsuyoshi and the "shocks" of the early 1970s—precipitated by actions or threats on the part of U.S. president Richard M. Nixon and the Organization of the Petroleum Exporting Countries (OPEC)—resulted in the layering of new rules on top of or alongside existing ones. The changes that followed the emergence of the "1955 system," during which the LDP enjoyed parliamentary dominance, can be understood as the conversion of existing rules to serve the needs of

Table I.1. Institutional Change in Japan's Cabinet System, 1868 to 2013

Event (Year)	Source of Change	Change Agent	Institutional Change	Cabinet Type
Meiji Restoration (1868)	Exogenous	Insurrectionary	Displacement	Cabal
Ōkuma's "Party Cabinet" (1898)	Endogenous	Renegade	Drift	Quasi-Party
"May 15th Incident" (1932)	Endogenous	Subversive	Layering	Techno-Fascist
Defeat & Occupation (1945)	Exogenous	Insurrectionary	Displacement	Comprador
Creation of "1955 System" (1955)	Endogenous	Opportunist	Conversion	Corporatist
Nixon & OPEC "Shocks" (1971-)	Endogenous	Subversive	Layering	Confederate
Coalition Governments (1993)	Endogenous	Renegade	Drift	Disjoined-1
"Twisted Diets" (2007)	Endogenous	Opportunist	Conversion	Disjoined-2

the perpetually ruling party. A somewhat similar state of affairs has accompanied the changes that emerged in the post-2007 era of "Twisted Diets," in which the ruling party in the lower house does not hold a majority in the upper house.

In sum, my approach brings together conceptual tools from political sociology and historical institutionalism. I believe that analytical eclecticism is necessary to explain how Japan's cabinet system evolved, why it came to assume its characteristic form and functions, and what consequences this holds for Japan's system of democratic governance and its foreign relations. As Katzenstein and Okawara explain, "theory and policy are both served better by eclecticism, not parsimony" (2001/2002, 185). By combining different paradigms, I am knowingly jumping headfirst into what Evans approvingly describes as the "eclectic messy" center of comparative politics, where *getting it right* is the analyst's primary objective (Evans 1996, 2). My central argument is that Japan's cabinet system was forged through an ongoing *process* of institutionalization filtered through and interacting with a *matrix* of key institutions that were periodically transformed as a result of gradual change and the occasional shock.

THE CONTEXT OF THIS STUDY

In recent years, Japan's cabinet system has begun to attract scholarly attention. Thayer identifies three "archetypes" in the evolution of Japan's cabinet system—"the imperial cabinet, the predominant party cabinet, and the coalition cabinet" (1996, 71). Assessing Japan's 2001 government restructuring, Shinoda sees little meaningful change with regard to the functions of the cabinet, which continues to play an insignificant role, while "actual decisions are made at regularly scheduled meetings of the top career officials of ministries and agencies and then rubber-stamped at subsequent cabinet meetings" (2005, 805). George Mulgan argues that "Japan does not have cabinet government; it has party-bureaucratic government," by which she means that the cabinet is subordinate to the long-ruling LDP and government officialdom (2003a, 129). Krauss and Pekkanen argue that the LDP never became the strong, centralized ruling party required in a Westminster system. This is because vote mobilization was in the hands of the candidate-support organizations (*kōenkai*) of party backbenchers, the distribution of offices was the domain of the bosses of the intraparty factions, and the party's Policy Affairs Research Council performed the role of veto player in policy-making (Krauss and Pekkanen 2010, 5–6, 279–280; also Krauss 1989, 51–52).

While most pundits doubt that cabinet government will arrive on the Japanese scene, at least anytime soon, some offer reasons for hope. Shimizu maintains that the changes made under the Koizumi government ensure the eventual emergence of cabinet government (2005, 404). Estevez-Abe shares this view, pointing out that Koizumi's bold decision to obtain a popular referendum on his postal privatization bills "cast the die in favor of a Westminster system that centralizes power in the hands of the party leadership and prime minister" (2006, 633). She concedes that, historically, Japan's cabinet "simply rubber-stamped decisions made by others," but argues that an "increasingly centralized party structure of the LDP and the strengthening of the Cabinet will push Japan in the direction of a British-style parliamentary democracy" with a "Westminster system" (ibid., 633, 651). Krauss argues that, as a result of the institutional changes following the LDP's brief hiatus from power in 1993, "Japan has moved somewhat closer to the British model" (2007). Of course, these scholars were writing before the LDP's temporary expulsion from the helm in 2009, and much of the progress toward enhancing the cabinet's role taken under the Koizumi cabinet was reversed by the LDP- and DPJ-led governments that followed. For these reasons, it is time to take a hard look at the nature, capabilities, and limitations of Japan's parliamentary cabinet system—which is what this book is about.

Rival Approaches

Theories purporting to explain who rules the roost in the affairs of Japan's central state executive fall into three broad categories, dominant actor theories, fragmented state theories, and core executive theories. To date, the debate among learned observers has primarily focused on which political actor dominates executive decision-making. Laver and Shepsle identify six general models of executive decision-making—bureaucratic government, legislative government, prime ministerial government, party government, ministerial government, and cabinet government (1994b, 5–8). Each of these models has attracted advocates among students of Japanese executive-making.

Bureaucratic government holds that "the elite bureaucracy . . . makes most major decisions, drafts virtually all legislation, controls the national budget, and is the source of all major policy innovations in the system" (Johnson 1982, 20; also Pempel 1974, Campbell 1977, Inoguchi 1983, Amyx 2004, and Vogel 1996). This view is bolstered by the image of a Japanese cabinet minister as a mere "figurehead who [is] manipulated and controlled by the career officials" (Park 1986, 8). In addition to being a traditional elite, Japan's career civil servants carry out their duties under the oversight of, at most, six political appointees per ministry. Because ministers rely on bureaucrats for policy expertise, they are prone to become the bureaucrats' "lap dogs" (Takenaka 2008, 51, 81; Iio 2007). Bureaucratic influence is ensured by the Supreme Court-like role of the Cabinet Legislation Bureau, which examines all draft bills, treaties, and cabinet orders, and whose opinions are regarded as authoritative and difficult to overturn. As Samuels argues, "No administrative agency of the Japanese state enjoys higher prestige or greater independence than the CLB" (2004, 2). Bureaucratic influence is further ensured through the deputy chief cabinet secretary for administrative affairs (*Naikaku kanbō fukuchōkan*), a senior ex-bureaucrat who chairs the biweekly meetings of administrative vice ministers (*jimujikan*) from each ministry at which the agenda for cabinet meetings is set (Johnson 1995b, 221; Tanaka 2000, 5). Yet the bureaucracy's relative influence has diminished in recent years as a result of liberalization, privatization, scandal, and the fact that fewer ex-officials are opting to pursue "second careers" as MPs.

Party government presumes the existence of a strong executive whose members are "subject to the discipline of well-organized political parties" (Laver and Shepsle 1994b, 7). This model found fruitful application in the works of rational choice theorists, who posit that "real bureaucrats . . . administer in the shadow of the LDP," by which they mean that through a series of delegations LDP backbenchers strummed the tune to which cabinet ministers obligingly danced (quotation is from Ramseyer and Rosenbluth 1993, 120; also McCubbins and Noble 1995). Beginning in the early 1960s, the LDP began requiring that all policy proposals be submitted to its Policy Affairs Research Council for "prior approval" before being sent on to the cabinet and then to the Diet (Krauss and Pekkanen 2010, 20; also George Mulgan 2003a, 140; Holliday and Shinoda 2002, 101). Yet, because of the LDP's essentially decentralized structure, this veto role actually served to undermine the relative influence of the prime minister (who doubled as party president) and central party leadership, and, in so doing, impeded the emergence of a Westminster-style cabinet system (Krauss and Pekkanen 2010, 279–280).

The four remaining models can be accounted for succinctly. *Ministerial government* denotes a system in which "individual ministers . . . are able to have a significant impact on policy in areas that fall under their jurisdiction" (Laver and Shepsle 1994b, 8). This thesis echoes in Campbell's discovery that, in the politics of Japanese budgetary policy, "if collectively the Cabinet is not an important . . . actor, individual ministers have often assumed prominent parts" (1977, 151). *Prime ministerial government* posits that "the cabinet is a mainly residual organization" in policy-making, ministers are "agents of the . . . prime minister's will," and bureaucrats are "confined to implementing rather than making policy" (Elgie 1997, 222–223). While recent reforms and the increasing importance of television have enhanced the prime minister's role, Japan's premiers continue to be regarded as passive leaders who serve mainly as "consensus articulators" (Hayao 1993, 202; Angel 1988–1989, 600; Iio 2007). *Legislative government* assumes that the cabinet mechanically implements policies made by the legislature (Laver and Shepsle 1994b, 6). The policy gridlock and rapid turnover in governments dictated by the post-2007 Twisted Diets provides fodder for advocates of this model.

Finally, *cabinet government* denotes a parliamentary system with a strong executive that provides tactical direction to government policy, and whose leaders are chosen by Parliament from among its members and bound together by norms of collective responsibility and solidarity. While this viewpoint has attracted a few advocates—including an ex-bureaucrat who opined that the cabinet is now "the main battle ground for policy-making" (quoted in *Asahi Shimbun Globe,* May 31, 2002)—most observers believe that the cabinet is "more an aggregation than a real institution, its membership turns every year or so . . . and ministers are normally more concerned with their individual political affairs than with advancing the Cabinet as such" (Campbell 1977, 151).

While they provide insights, these generic models do not account for factors specific to the Japanese case. For example, what about the role of the "policy tribes" (*zoku*) in shaping executive decision-making? The influential MPs who are members of the various tribes exercise considerable sway over policy outcomes in agriculture, postal affairs, public works, and so on (Muramatsu and Krauss 1984 and 1987; Satō and Matsuzaki 1986; Inoguchi and Iwai 1987; Schoppa 1991; Krauss and Pekkanen 2010). While service as a cabinet minister often affords entrée to a policy tribe, not all *zoku* politicians are incumbent ministers. The influence of these policy tribes contributed to the "political capture" that afflicted policy-making, especially in the latter years of the LDP's hegemonic reign (Samuels 2013, 181). And what about the role of the LDP's intraparty faction bosses in allocating ministerial posts? In fact, factional "balance" was a critical concern in the allocation of portfolios under the "1955 system" (Thayer 1969, 31–35; Curtis 1988, 86–87; Krauss and Pekkanen 2010, 132–134). This diminished the prime minister's leadership role, and on occasion produced cabinets that seemed to be under the "remote control" of faction bosses. Finally, how do we account for the external pressure (*gaiatsu*) applied by the United States, which, after all, remains the guarantor of Japan's national security and a major destination for its exports? It goes without saying that American views strongly influenced Japanese executive decision-making during the occupation period (Dower 1999). Much like the proverbial elephant in the room, explicit or implicit pressure from the United States is difficult for Japanese policy-makers to ignore, especially when it comes to bilateral trade and security issues (Schoppa 1997; Pyle et al. 2010; Woodall 1996, 129–132).

Fragmented state theories come in a variety of forms. The most extreme variant, the "stateless nation" thesis, argues that "there is no supreme institution with ultimate policy-making jurisdiction. Hence there is no place where . . . the buck stops. In Japan, the buck keeps circulating" (van Wolferen 1989, 26, 5). "Hollow state" theory holds that "government is becoming so fragmented that pulling business together at the centre is now an almost impossible task" (Holliday and Shinoda 2002, 108). Various case studies confirm the fragmented nature of Japanese executive decision-making, especially during the 1990s. In his research on Japanese budgetary politics, Campbell observed signs of fragmentation in the 1960s in the form of "subgovernments made up of agencies, specialized LDP politicians, and interest groups—sometimes in alliance, sometimes with much internal division" (Campbell and Scheiner 2008, 99; also Campbell 1977 and 1984). Subsequent studies drew attention to the ways in which a fragmented political structure shaped policy outcomes in a variety of arenas, including education policy, tax reform, public works, postal services, and the response to the banking crisis (for example, Hayao 1993; Schoppa 1993; Kato 1994; Woodall 1996; MacLachlan 2004; and Amyx 2004).

Finally, *core executive* theories focus on the organs and structures that "pull together and integrate central government policies, or act as final arbiters within the executive of conflicts between different elements of the government machine" (Dunleavy and Rhodes 1990, 4; also Holliday and Shinoda 2002; and Krauss 2007). This approach explicitly recognizes the multiplicity of actors that, of necessity, must be involved in executive decision-making in an advanced parliamentary democracy. In a study comparing the core executives of Britain and Japan, Holliday and Shinoda argue that the cabinet is not a "key player" in the core executive of either country. They posit that Japan's core executive is composed of the "Prime Minister, the Chief Cabinet Secretary and his three deputies in the Cabinet Secretariat, the key leaders of the LDP, plus top officials in the supporting offices. Those offices are the Prime Minister's Office, the Ministry of Finance and the Ministry of Foreign Affairs" (2002, 98).

While there is merit in each of these explanations, I have come to see things in my own way. As I demonstrate in the substantive chapters of this book, the relative influence of specific actors has varied over time in response to domestic and external crises, institutional change, and tectonic shifts in political, economic, and social structures. Moreover, I argue that by the early 1990s a fragmented policy-making environment severely limited the options that prime ministers and cabinets could pursue in attempting to guide the country out of the gloom and policy lethargy that defined the "lost decades." While core executive theory draws attention to power relations among a number of actors, I believe that its most fruitful application is as a conceptual device for assessing shifts over time in that power balance.

Summary

By focusing on the evolution of Japan's cabinet system, the core chapters of this book highlight the capabilities and limitations of a crucial component of Japanese parliamentary democracy. Throughout this book, I seek to solve two central puzzles. First, why has cabinet government failed to take root in Japan? This is puzzling because postwar Japan has been governed under Westminster-style parliamentary institutions and yet has not managed to nurture cabinet government. In other words, why has Japan failed to produce cabinet government *in practice* despite having a parliamentary system *in form*? Focusing on the manner and degree to which the cabinet system has become institutionalized reveals much about the capacity of Japan's political executive—what it can and cannot do, as well as how it lives up to and falls short of its intended place in a parliamentary system. In this regard, the Westminster ideal provides benchmarks against which to assess the degree to which the Japanese cabinet system has progressed toward institutionalization.

This calls attention to a second puzzle. Why has Japan's cabinet system assumed its characteristic form and function? Since institutionalization is a ubiquitous process, why is the Japanese cabinet system distinctive? The question draws attention to the shaping influence of institutions, which requires that we "take time seriously" by accounting for the significant roles played by context and history in determining institutional change in the *"longue durée"* (Pierson and Skocpol 2002, 685; Braudel 1982, 25–54). It also highlights the distributional consequences of institutions and the role of critical junctures and tipping points as strategic openings for institutional reconfiguration.

While the domestic implications should be obvious, understanding Japan's cabinet system is relevant to academics, policy-makers, and business leaders in other countries. For one thing, the findings presented in this book illuminate the dimly understood inner workings of the cabinet system of an important non-Western parliamentary democracy. Perhaps this intensive analysis of the Japanese case might offer lessons for reformers in Japan as well as for those who seek to build democratic institutions in countries such as Iraq and Afghanistan. Or, perhaps someday the Japanese experience may help to guide the establishment of democratic regimes in Cuba, Nigeria, China, and the new regimes born during the Arab Spring. At the very least, Japan's struggles with this fundamental component of parliamentary governance should serve as a cautionary tale for those who believe that parliamentary institutions *in form* equate to parliamentary government *in practice.* In fact, growing democracy is *not* easy, and in this regard the Japanese case offers crucial lessons for understanding the challenges and disappointments that confront today's developing countries.

1

The Anti-Westminsterian Roots of Japan's Parliamentary Cabinet System, 1868–1946

The cabinet, in a word, is a board of control chosen by the legislature, out of persons it trusts and knows, to rule the nation.
—Walter Bagehot, *The English Constitution* ([1867] 1925), 14

In England a party cabinet is headed by the leader of the party commanding the majority in the House of Commons; but not so under the imperial constitution of Japan. To insist on such a principle is to encroach on the sovereign power of the emperor.
—Prime Minister Terauchi Masatake, quoted in T. Iyenaga, "Parties and the Cabinet System in Japan" (1917), 382

INHOSPITABLE ROOTS

The modern cabinet system that was established in 1885 did not materialize out of thin air. In fact, it inherited organizational structures, institutions, and experienced administrators from the "Grand Council," an administrative system that was originally imported from China during the eighth century and was resurrected as part of the Meiji Restoration, an institutional reconfiguration initiated in 1868. The Chinese characters that combine to form the Japanese term for "cabinet"—*nai* and *kaku*—translate to mean "inner palace."[1] From 1868 until 1898, Japan's central state executive was dominated by a cabal composed of leaders from Satsuma and Chōshū, two feudal domains that played the protagonist's role in bringing about the Restoration. When a schism in the Meiji government gave impetus to

31

a "freedom and popular rights movement," the *Sat-Chō* cabal responded by granting a constitution that vested sovereignty in a divine-right monarch and erected steep barriers to prevent popularly elected representatives from having meaningful influence on national policy. Although the Sat-Chō cabal went to great lengths to control all of the major executive organs, including the military branches, the "people's parties" and elected members of Parliament managed to claw their way into the inner sanctum of policy-making. So it was that the era of "cabal cabinets" gave way to a brief period in which "party cabinets" wielded influence. When party government became synonymous with political corruption and pusillanimous diplomacy, technocratic government bureaucrats and military officers joined forces with the leaders of fascist-inspired groups in establishing a "new structure" of domestic institutions and a "new order" in East Asia. This ushered in an era of "*techno-fascist* cabinets."

Japan's current parliamentary cabinet system inherited important legacies from the authoritarian prewar order. In fact, the organizational genealogy of many of today's cabinet-related agencies can be traced to organs established in prewar times. Just as prewar cabinets never played more than a subordinate executive role, postwar cabinets have not played the expected role of imparting strategic direction to government policy. For instance, the decision made by American occupation authorities to indirectly govern a defeated Japan through the existing civil bureaucracy perpetuated a state of affairs in which the primary purpose of cabinet meetings was to ratify decisions made by elite career civil servants. Likewise, the absence of a robust collective solidarity norm that undermines contemporary cabinets is the offspring of a system in which prewar ministers were individually responsible to a divine-right sovereign and were in no way responsible to Parliament. Then there is the human bridge embodied in the twenty-six prewar cabinet ministers—including five prime ministers—who held portfolios in postwar cabinets.[2] To understand these legacies, it is necessary to examine the historical process through which an *anti*-Westminsterian prewar cabinet system evolved.

THE MEIJI RESTORATION

On July 8, 1853, Commodore Matthew C. Perry led a squadron of "black ships" (*kurobune*)—so known because two of the four American vessels were smoke-belching steam frigates—into Edo Bay. He brushed off attempts to get him to make his appeal at Deshima in faraway Kyūshū, as was required of foreign emissaries. Instead, Perry demanded to present a letter from President Millard Fillmore to the Japanese emperor proposing to open bilateral trade. Perry's request was denied, and he departed peacefully and vowed to return the following year.

Despite the small size of Perry's squadron, Japanese officials recognized that it packed sufficient firepower to outgun Edo's meager shore defenses (Ravina 2004, 55). This created a quandary for Japan's supreme political leader, the *shōgun,* who ruled the country from Edo Castle. In fact, well before Perry's uninvited visit, nationalist thinkers had begun questioning the legitimacy of a shōgun who ruled while a divine-right emperor merely reigned from the Imperial Palace in Kyoto (Pyle 1996b, 51). In an unprecedented move, the shōgun's chief adviser asked for written input from the local lords—known as *daimyō*—on how to respond to the American demands (ibid., 62–63). When Perry returned the following February— this time in command of a seven-ship flotilla—the shōgun's agents meekly acquiesced and signed the Treaty of Peace and Amity (*Nichibei Washin Jōyaku*). By the terms of the treaty, an American "diplomatic agent"—a role performed by Townshend Harris—was permitted to reside in Japan. Harris negotiated the 1858 U.S.-Japan Treaty of Amity and Commerce, the first of a series of "unequal treaties" with the Western powers that imposed a semi-colonial status by denying tariff autonomy and granting extraterritoriality to Westerners in Japan (Gordon 2003, 50).

The arrival of Perry's ships turned what had been a "chronic low-grade crisis into an acute, reactionary situation" (ibid., 46). When the domestic powder keg finally exploded in 1867, the shōgun was Tokugawa Yoshinobu, fifteenth in a family dynasty that had ruled Japan through relative peace for 264 years. In essence, the Tokugawa shōgunate governed through a system of "centralized feudalism," whereby ruling power was based in Edo while some 250-odd daimyō enjoyed substantial autonomy in administering their regional domains (Craig 1961, 3). Some of these daimyō were blood relatives (*shinpan daimyō*) or hereditary vassals (*fudai daimyō*) of the Tokugawa. But certain "outside lords" (*tozama daimyō*) were never fully trusted—and for good reason, as we shall see—as they had to be forced to submit to Tokugawa domination yet were too powerful to be removed.

Thus, the shōgunate ensured that tozama daimyō governed domains far from Edo and that they and all daimyō spent alternate years in the shōgunal capital, while their wives and heirs remained there as hostages. This "alternate attendance" (*sankin kōtai*) system consumed up to half the time and revenue of the daimyō "in the purely ceremonial functions of attending the shōgun's court and traveling in stately procession between Edo and their fiefs" (Vlastos 1990, 6). Some of the tozama daimyō—such as Mori of Chōshū, whose castle had to be relocated because the Tokugawa substantially reduced the area of domain—continued to harbor animosity toward the shōgunate two and a half centuries later (Hackett 1971, 6–7). By the time of Perry's visit, certain powerful tozama daimyō were contravening shōgunal prohibitions by engaging in foreign trade, setting up Western-style factories, and building strong local militaries (Pyle 1996b, 70–71). It was difficult for the shōgunate to police and punish such acts of insubordination because of the distance of these domains from Edo. With Tokugawa influence waning, some tozama daimyō began pressing for the creation of a council of lords in Kyoto, in which the Tokugawa shōgun would be first among equals, to grant them greater voice in national politics.

If the tozama daimyō felt constrained by the shōgunate's stifling controls, low-ranking samurai were incensed at a social order that placed them in perpetual subordination to superiors who "had been corrupted by inherited rank beyond the possibility of . . . redemption" (Smith 1988, 11). They were also outraged that a shōgunal official coerced the emperor into consenting to the inequitable Harris Treaty that invited "the threat of barbarian domination and debauchment" (ibid., 159). For the most part, these "men of spirit" (*shishi*) were angry young samurai who lived on modest incomes, if not in real poverty, and deeply resented the fact that they were denied access to important offices of government by a rigid hereditary system (ibid., 136, 139–40; Jansen 2002, 338). After Perry's uncongenial visit, shishi emerged from domains across the country and converged upon Kyoto. When Tokugawa forces sought to squelch the mounting intrigue in the imperial capital, many of these young hotheads fled to Chōshū, where they were joined by a handful of refugee allies from the Imperial Court (Beasley 1995, 48). Although there was no specific unifying ideology, these firebrands shared a belief that action, not mere words, was necessary to destroy an incurably corrupt shōgunate, restore ruling power to the emperor, and cast out the Western barbarians. In retrospect, the temperament of these shishi is reflected in the violent ends they met. Indeed, seven of the ten leading figures in the defeat of the

Figure 1.1. Major Outside Domains. Map by Dick Gilbreath, University of Kentucky cartography lab

shōgunate and establishment of the new regime were assassinated, committed suicide, or were executed.[3]

The Tokugawa rulers attempted to turn back the insurrection through various reforms. In 1862, the shōgunate modified the alternate attendance system to require daimyō to reside in Edo only one hundred days every three years and permitted family hostages to leave. The ban on the construction of oceangoing vessels was lifted, and, in a move that had not occurred in two hundred years, the shōgun traveled to Kyoto to consult with the emperor (Pyle 1996b, 66–67; Duus 1998, 76). Meanwhile, the shōgunate retained a French mission to advise in military modernization, and considered adopting a Western-style cabinet system with functional ministries (Cullen 2003, 196). This was too late and too little. In 1863, loyalists convinced the emperor to order the shōgun to expel the Western barbarians, and a deadline of 25 June was agreed to, even though the shōgunate knew that it could not enforce this order (Gordon 2003, 55).

When the Edo authorities failed to act, Chōshū hotheads took matters into their own hands and fired on Western ships passing through the Strait of Shimonoseki, eliciting a retaliatory bombardment by British, Dutch, French, and American warships. Around the same time, Satsuma, another powerful tozama domain, was shelled by British warships for refusing to make reparations for the assassination of an English businessman by samurai retainers of its daimyō. In 1864, extremist samurai from Chōshū and elsewhere marched on Kyoto to rescue the emperor, but Tokugawa and Satsuma troops drove them out (Gordon 2003, 56). The shōgunate dispatched a punitive mission to Chōshū, which saw to it that the leaders of the failed coup were executed. In January 1866, officials from Tosa, another important tozama domain, brokered a secret alliance between Satsuma and Chōshū in the cause of toppling the shōgunate. When the shōgunate dispatched a second punitive mission to Chōshū in June, Satsuma and other domains refused to supply troops (ibid., 57).

So it was that the curtain came down on two and a half centuries of Pax Tokugawa. In November 1867, after coming to believe that he would remain first among peers in a governing council of daimyō, Shōgun Tokugawa Yoshinobu agreed to "return" power to the emperor and withdrew to his castle in Osaka. But leaders from Satsuma and Chōshū engineered the issuance on January 3, 1868, of an imperial rescript officially declaring the shōgunate defunct and "restoring" ruling power to the Emperor Meiji, then a fifteen-year-old boy. Yoshinobu responded by dispatching a sizable army to Kyoto to deliver a message protesting his ouster, but a small defensive force from Chōshū, Satsuma, and Tosa easily prevailed. After Edo Castle was bloodlessly surrendered to a combined Satsuma-Chōshū army in April 1868, the defeat of the Tokugawa shōgunate was complete, save for a few scattered pockets of resistance that held out for another year. The Boshin War was a small-scale civil war in which an undermanned "imperial" army soundly defeated forces loyal to Yoshinobu, who was sent into confinement. The conflict's final battles were fought to suppress Enomoto Takeaki and his followers, the last remaining band of rebels, who had commandeered some of the shōgunate's naval vessels and sailed off to Hokkaidō to carry on the fight. By the time Enomoto's forces were finally defeated in July of 1869, the emperor had been relocated to Edo, now known as Tokyo or "eastern capital." In the meantime, the powerful outside lords symbolically returned control of their domains to the emperor in 1871; soon, virtually all daimyō had followed suit and were appointed governors of their former fiefs, now known as "prefectures."

Out of this foment emerged the Meiji Restoration (*Meiji ishin*), a dramatic reconfiguration of institutional and structural arrangements amid a "generation of sweeping and breathless change such as history had rarely seen" (Smith 1988, 134). Yet, in reality, an oligarchy composed largely of young ex-samurai primarily from Satsuma and Chōshū—with supporting roles played by similarly spirited men from Tosa and Hizen, another powerful tozama domain—replaced the Tokugawa shōgunate as the actual rulers of a new regime that continued to govern behind the façade of imperial rule. This marks the genesis of the era of "*hanbatsu* (domain clique) politics"—during which time a "*Sat-Chō-To-Hi* alliance" (*Sat-Chō-To-Hi dōmei*)—supposedly ruled the roost (Large 2009, 156). However, the real power brokers in this arrangement were oligarchs from Chōshū and Satsuma, who were at pains to establish institutions that enabled them to maintain an iron grip on political power and the distribution of policy benefits. From 1871 until 1898, this Sat-Chō cabal controlled all of the key positions in government, including the most coveted and powerful ministerial portfolios. This did not go unnoticed by leaders from Tosa and Hizen, a number of whom would soon leave their positions in government and become renegade agents of change.

Cabinet Forms and Structures

Japan's first cabinets emerged three and a half years after the Meiji Restoration and were cobbled together out of preexisting organizational structures and staffed in large measure by members of the traditional administrative elite. Having vanquished the shōgunate and, at least on paper, returned ruling power to the emperor, the victorious insurrectionaries had to establish an administrative system through which to govern the country. To reinforce their "Restoration" message, they resurrected a long moribund governmental system fashioned after a model imported from T'ang China during the eighth century.[4] Out of the Grand Council of State, as that administrative system was known, emerged what were, in effect, Japan's first proto-cabinets. These proto-cabinets arose spontaneously within the group of relatively youthful officials appointed to serve as imperial councilors (*sangi*), whose membership bore testimony to Sat-Chō dominance. This oligarchic control continued even after the establishment of a modern cabinet system in 1885, and would persist for nearly a decade and a half thereafter.

Chinese Roots of Japan's Cabinet System

China was the natural place for the Emperor Meiji's distant predecessors to look for inspiration in designing administrative structures to facilitate centralized control over all of Japan. As Korean priests who appeared at the Japanese Court in A.D. 623 reported, "The Land of Great T'ang is an admirable country whose laws are complete and fixed. Constant communications should be kept up with it" (Asakawa 1903, 150, 253). Japan's rulers dispatched numerous missions across the treacherous seas separating Japan from the Asian mainland (ibid., 148–150). Some Japanese emissaries remained in China for decades. In 649, the Japanese government enlisted several returnees from missions to T'ang China to advise in the design of governmental institutions (Varley 1974b, 27).[5] Their input led to the creation of an administrative system based on a Department of Rites (*Jingikan*) and a Department of State (*Dajōkan*). The Department of Rites oversaw matters involving religious and court rituals, yet enjoyed little real power (Varley 1974a, 34). The Department of State—also known as the Grand Council—administered secular affairs. In theory, the council was under a leadership triumvirate consisting of a grand minister of state (*dajōdaijin*), minister of the left (*sadaijin*), and minister of the right (*udaijin*). However, in practice the grand minister had no specific duties other than to advise the emperor, and the post generally remained vacant. The council was divided into eight functional ministries: Central Administration, Ceremonial, Civil Affairs, People's Affairs, Military Affairs, Justice, Finance, and Imperial Household (Varley 1974a, 34).[6]

Over time, the Grand Council's administrative powers dissipated. By the mid-ninth century, the Fujiwara family, through its monopolization of the positions of regent (*sesshō*) and chief councilor (*kanpaku*), was able to effectively manipulate a succession of emperors. With the establishment of the Kamakura *Bakufu* (1185–1333)—literally "tent government"—the Grand Council was relegated to figurehead status. This marks the beginning of a separation of authority and power that would characterize Japanese political life for centuries. Even as an emperor reigned from his palace in Kyoto, a "barbarian-subjugating generalissimo" (*seii taishōgun* or, simply, shōgun) ruled from his warrior castle. This state of affairs continued as the Kamakura *Bakufu* gave way to the Ashikaga shōgunate (1336–1573), although virtually any semblance of centralized authority ceased to exist during the "warring states period" (*sengoku jidai*) that extended from the mid-1400s until the early 1600s. In 1603, Tokugawa Ieyasu established control over the entire country under a dynastic shōgunate that would persist until 1867. Centrally, the Tokugawa shōgunate monopolized contact with the Imperial Court and ruled through an elaborate administrative network based in Edo. Locally, the 250-odd daimyō were allowed to exercise substantial autonomy over affairs in their fiefs while being kept in check through the system of alternate attendance and other controls.

The Emergence of Cabal Cabinets

The Meiji government articulated its basic policies and established a central state executive in the Five-Article Oath (*Gokajō no seimon*), issued on April 6, 1868.[7] It called for the establishment of an assembly of daimyō to decide matters of state through open discussion, unity of social classes in carrying out administration, freedom for all in pursuing their respective callings, discarding evil practices of the past, and the quest for "knowledge throughout the world so as to strengthen the foundation of imperial rule" (Lu 1973, 36). This was given concrete expression in the "Document of the Form of Government" (*Seitaisho*), issued on June 11, which called for the establishment of an assembly composed of "qualified men" selected by "each great city, *han* [domain], and prefecture." It set a four-year term for government officers, but allowed for "a few additional years" to be added to the terms of officials who were "well accepted by the public" and "difficult to replace" (ibid., 37). It called for the establishment of a three-way separation of governing power within the Grand Council (ibid., 36–37). The Department of Legislation (*Giseikan*)—subdivided into an Upper Bureau (*Jōkyoku*) and Lower Bureau (*Gekyoku*)—was given charge of lawmaking, bureaucratic appointments, and the ratification of treaties, while the Department of Justice (*Keihōkan*) handled juridical matters. Executive affairs came under the Department of Administration (*Gyōseikan*), which was organized into six subdepartments, subsequently renamed "ministries" (*shō*), for Religious Shrines and Rituals, Finance, Foreign Relations, Military, Judicial, and Civil Affairs.

In July 1871, the most important executive posts—grand minister of state, cabinet adviser (*Naikaku komon*), and imperial councilor (sangi)—

were placed under a Central Board (*Sei-in*), which became "the focal point of the politics of the time" (Ishii 1980, 101). Sanjō Sanetomi, one of the disaffected court nobles who sided with the anti-Tokugawa forces, was appointed grand minister, a post he held until 1885. Leaders from Satsuma and Chōshū alternated as cabinet adviser, a post sometimes left unfilled, while young officials from the four main tozama domains all but monopolized the imperial councilor posts. In retrospect, the significance of the councilor appointment is evident in the fact that the first four post-1885 prime ministers had, at some point, served in the post. In fact, twenty-two of the twenty-three councilors hailed from one of the four main tozama domains. Satsuma claimed the most (nine), followed by Chōshū and Tosa (with five each), and Hizen (three).[8] In 1873, councilors received the title of "state minister" (*kyō*) and were given charge of administrative and policy affairs as officials of the cabinet. This is the first time that the term "cabinet"—described as "the core governing body in which the councilors review legislative and administrative affairs on behalf of the Emperor"—was invoked in an official proclamation ("Naikaku seido to rekidai naikaku," accessed March 20, 2013). With this, the imperial councilors became a proto-cabinet "which decided all important governmental questions collegially" (Ishii 1980, 102).

As part of this reform effort, the government departments were recast into ministries (*shō*) of Finance, Foreign Affairs, Justice, Military Affairs, Education, Industry, and Imperial Household.[9] While court nobles and feudal lords were placed in supervisory positions in each ministry, youthful vice ministers—many of whom were young ex-samurai from the main tozama domains—wielded power over day-to-day administrative activities (Beasley 1989, 641). This state of affairs continued until 1873, when ex-samurai replaced the nobles and former daimyō as administrative heads of the ministries (Silberman 1993, 159). In May 1872, the Ministry of Military Affairs was subdivided into an Army Ministry (*Rikugunshō*) and Navy Ministry (*Kaigunshō*), and in 1873 the Home Ministry (*Naimushō*) was established and given broad powers over local administration, internal security, public works, and elections. In February 1875, the Legislation Bureau (*Hōsei kyoku*)—the forerunner of the Cabinet Legislation Bureau—was established within the Grand Council to advise government and to review all laws, treaties, and imperial ordinances (Naikaku Hōsei Kyoku 1985, 2). This was followed in 1881 by the establishment of the Ministry of Agriculture and Commerce (*Nōshōmushō*). The only other ministerial agency created during this period was the Colonization Board (*Kaita-kushi*), which, during its brief existence from 1869 to 1882, promoted Japanese settlement of Hokkaidō and Sakhalin Island to guard against Russian expansion.

From Council to Cabinet

On December 22, 1885, Grand Council Order No. 69 (*Dajōkan tasshi Dai-69-go*) established a modern cabinet system based on a prime minister and ministers of state. With this, the Grand Council orchestrated itself into

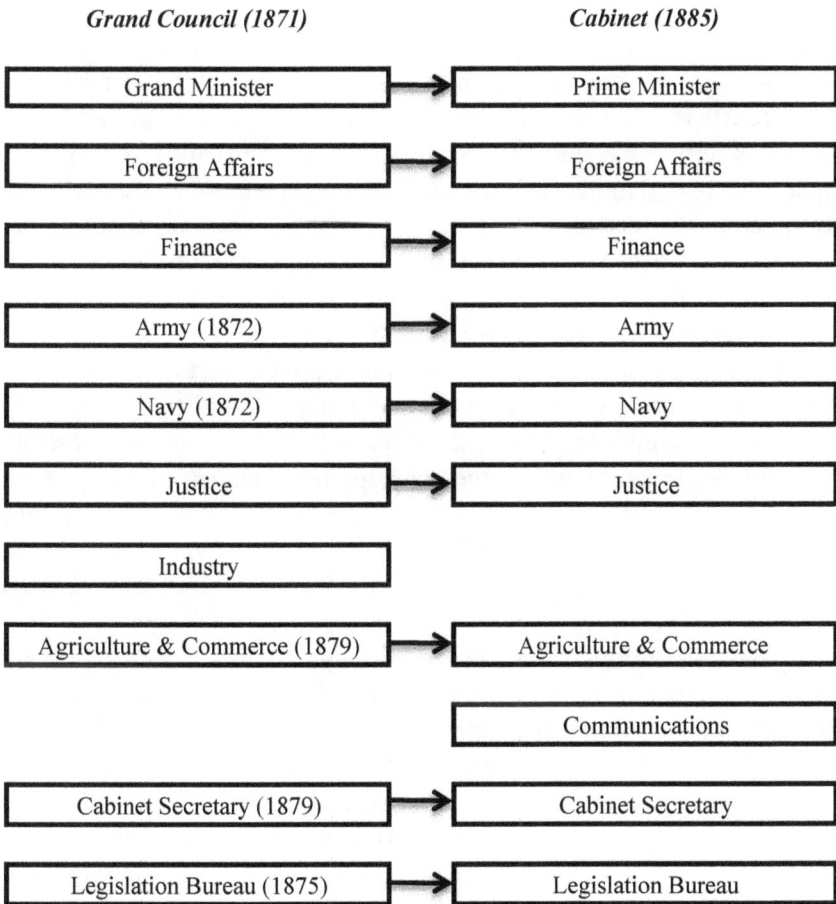

Grand Council (1871)	Cabinet (1885)
Grand Minister	→ Prime Minister
Foreign Affairs	→ Foreign Affairs
Finance	→ Finance
Army (1872)	→ Army
Navy (1872)	→ Navy
Justice	→ Justice
Industry	
Agriculture & Commerce (1879)	→ Agriculture & Commerce
	Communications
Cabinet Secretary (1879)	→ Cabinet Secretary
Legislation Bureau (1875)	→ Legislation Bureau

Figure 1.2. Ministerial Portfolios under the Grand Council and Cabinet System

extinction, and, in so doing, provided the legal foundation to transform what had been a "hodgepodge of councilors" into "ministers with a cabinet" (Samuels 2003, 56). In other words, it transformed proto-cabinets into true cabinets. The order abolished the positions of grand minister, left minister, right minister, imperial councilor, and state minister, and established the posts of prime minister (*sōri daijin*) and ministers of state (*daijin*) for foreign affairs, home, finance, army, navy, justice, education, agriculture and commerce, and communications.

The cabinet's primary function was to advise the emperor and to oversee the affairs of the government ministries. Lord Keeper of the Privy Seal Sanjō Sanetomi counseled the emperor that "the cabinet should be made a supreme council of Ministers with authority to communicate directly with Your Majesty . . . [and] should serve as the hands and feet, the ears and eyes of Your Majesty" (cited in Beckmann 1957, 75). Guidelines were given in a seven-article ordinance entitled "Official Powers of the Cabinet" (*Naikaku shokken*). It specified the responsibilities of the prime minister, who, "as a chief among ministers" (*kakudaijin no shuhan to shite*), was to report to the emperor, receive his instruction, direct the enactment and implementation of policies, and supervise the various executive organs of government. Ministers were *individually* responsible for their portfolios, but were required to report to the prime minister. As Uyehara explained, "each minister is not responsible for the action of the Cabinet as a whole, and the Cabinet is not responsible for the action of each minister" (1910, 137). However, the establishment of the Privy Council eliminated any possibility that the cabinet might become the emperor's foremost advisory organ. As Itō explained in his *Commentaries on the Constitution of the Empire of Japan* (1889, 84, 98), the Privy Councilors and state ministers "are the Emperor's most eminent assistants" and "the highest body of the Emperor's constitutional advisers."

From 1885 through 1898, approximately 550 government officials—about 1 percent of all government employees—were assigned to staff positions in support of the cabinet and its auxiliary organs.[10] The most important of the auxiliary organs were the Office of the Cabinet Secretariat (*Naikaku shokikan*) and the Legislation Bureau. Their directors, referred to as the cabinet's "chief clerks" (*ryō bantō*), received imperial appointments and participated in cabinet meetings (Naikaku Hōsei Kyoku 1985, 56). The main functions of the Secretariat, originally founded in 1879, were to promulgate laws and imperial edicts as well as to provide administrative support for the cabinet. The Legislation Bureau was tasked with providing guidance and interpretation in the drafting of legislative bills. In addition, bureaus were established under the cabinet to administer finance, records, the official gazette, pensions, and statistics. In May 1891, the cabinet's responsibilities were strengthened and clarified, and a Political Department was set up within the Secretariat to draft cabinet policy as well as to oversee interactions with the press and foreign governments.[11]

The Cabinet's Cabalistic Roots

Leaders from Satsuma and Chōshū dominated the proto-cabinets and cabinets formed between 1871 and 1898, monopolizing the premiership and seizing the lion's share of the coveted foreign, home, and finance portfolios. With the exception of a court noble who served as grand minister from 1871 until 1885 (and briefly headed a caretaker cabinet), all of the premiers appointed during the period were Sat-Chō leaders.[12] The Sat-Chō cabal ensured that its members grabbed more than half of the foreign and finance minister portfolios (respectively, 53 and 56 percent), and three-quarters of the home minister portfolios (76 percent). In sum, ministers from Satsuma or Chōshū controlled two-thirds (65 percent) of these key portfolios. If the military minister portfolios are included, the cabal's dominance is even more obvious. Indeed, Sat-Chō figures occupied three-quarters of the naval minister portfolios (73 percent) and all of the army minister portfolios. In addition, Sat-Chō leaders accounted for 62 percent of the imperial councilor (sangi) appointees. By dominating the key positions in government, the Sat-Chō cabal was able to have its way in dictating policy outcomes that ensured a happily inequitable distribution of benefits. Not surprisingly, this produced deep-seated resentment of *hanbatsu* favoritism, especially on the part of former government insiders from Tosa and Hizen.

Yet the cabalistic roots of Japan's cabinet system are not unique. In fact, rulers around the world have for centuries turned to small groups of advisers for counsel in making decisions of momentous and trivial importance. Often, when a small group of advisers acquires the favor of the sovereign, it is perceived as a "cabal," which connotes "secret artifices or machinations of a few persons united in a close design," which invariably connotes secretive, sinister motives and intrigue (*Webster's New International Dictionary*). British political history is rife with such cabals, the most famous of which arose during the reign of Charles II (1660 to 1685), when a five-member group of imperial advisers in the "Committee for Foreign Affairs" of the king's Privy Council came to control the conduct of domestic and foreign affairs. This "ministry of the cabal"—or "cabal cabinet"—became "the dominant force in English affairs" from 1667 until 1674 (Abbott 1906, 46–47; Lee 1965, 1). By coincidence, the first letter in the last names of its members—Sir Thomas Clifford, The Lord Arlington, The Duke of Buckingham, The Lord Ashley, and The Earl of Lauderdale—form the word "cabal," thus contributing to the atmosphere of intrigue. Yet while the respective ancestries of the Japanese and British cabinets can be traced to cabals, the similarities end there. The Cabal Cabinet that arose during the reign of Charles II held together for only half a dozen years, and a parliamentary system with a strong, responsible cabinet gradually emerged to take its place. In contrast, cabal cabinets were the rule in Japan for nearly three decades, and their influence continued to be felt many years later. Thus, England's Cabal Cabinet eventually gave rise to the Westminster system, while the Sat-Chō cabal produced an *anti*-Westminster system.

The Emergence of Parties and a Constitution

The most vexing domestic challenge faced by Japan's cabal cabinets came from ex-samurai angered by the loss of traditional privilege as a result of the government's reforms. These privileges were taken away one by one, beginning with government edicts that permitted commoners to have surnames and to travel on horseback. Later on, interclass marriage was allowed, and the exclusive right of samurai to bear arms and hold office was taken away (Samuels 2003, 50). In 1873, the Grand Council issued the Universal Conscription Law (*Chōheirei*) requiring all able-bodied Japanese men of twenty years of age to serve three years on active duty, followed by four years on reserve status. This was distasteful for the samurai, who believed that warriors were born, not made. The crowning blow came in 1876, when the government announced cancellation of the annual rice stipends (*kuramai*) that sustained the warrior class. As loyal retainers of the daimyō, ever willing to lay down their lives in their masters' service, the samurai were not expected to produce their own sustenance. By this plan, ex-samurai were to be paid off with government bonds, the amount of which was a multiple of their annual rice stipend. The bonds were redeemable in twenty years, after which the ex-samurai could make no claim on the national treasury (Smith 1988, 142). As the course of events would reveal, samurai discontent found its most violent expression in those southwestern provinces where traditional values remained strong. Not coincidentally, those same provinces were the native domains of disenchanted ex-leaders of the Meiji government.

In the midst of these reforms, a group that included about half the Sat-Chō oligarchs departed on a twenty-one-month mission to the United States and Europe. The mission's purposes were to obtain revision of the unequal treaties, promote goodwill, and observe Western institutions. The Iwakura mission (*Iwakura shisetsudan*), led by court noble Iwakura Tomomi, set sail from Yokohama on December 23, 1871.[13] While Iwakura and his colleagues were schmoozing with foreign leaders, such as President Ulysses S. Grant and Queen Victoria, the oligarchs who remained in Tokyo were seething at the insult given by the Korean Court in refusing to accept the credentials of the Meiji government's emissary. In August 1873, it was decided that Saigō Takamori, the acting head of the caretaker government, would be dispatched to Korea on the assumption that he would be assassinated, which would serve as the perfect pretext for a Japanese invasion.[14] But, having caught wind of this, the Iwakura mission rushed home, arriving on September 13, and Iwakura and Ōkubo Toshimichi succeeded in reversing the emperor's approval of Saigō's proposed posting to Korea. Saigō resigned his government posts and returned to Satsuma. Meanwhile, Itagaki Taisuke, Gotō Shōjirō, Etō Shinpei, and Soejima Taneomi also parted ways with the Meiji government and returned to their native provinces.

Five years later, Saigō was dead, having committed ritual suicide after leading an abortive rebellion against the Meiji government. But the intra-elite schism created by the "Invade Korea debate" (*seikanron*) gave birth to the "freedom and popular rights movement" (*jiyū minken undō*). In January 1874, Itagaki and Gotō founded the Aikoku Kōtō (Public Party of Patriots) in Tosa, and shortly thereafter Etō founded a branch of this anti-government protest group in Hizen. This threesome then added their signatures to a petition imploring the emperor to create a popularly elected assembly. But Etō was not content to express his discontent merely through peaceful protest. In 1874, he led a large mob of discontented ex-samurai in attacking government offices in Saga, the capital of the former Hizen domain (Gordon 2003, 85–86). Government forces easily suppressed the Saga Rebellion (*Saga no ran*), capturing and executing Etō and a co-leader.

As a warning to anyone else who might have been contemplating rebellious action, Etō's severed head was placed on a pike and put on public display (Ravina 2004, 192). While the Meiji government suppressed the Saga Rebellion and similar uprisings of ex-samurai and peasants, the Sat-Chō oligarchs understood that something must be done to defuse a potentially revolutionary situation.

To this end, Ōkubo, Itō, and Inoue Kaoru met with Itagaki and Kido Kōin in Osaka in January 1875. Kido had resigned as imperial councilor in April 1874 to protest what he perceived to be a dangerously provocative military mission dispatched by the Meiji government to punish Taiwanese aborigines for murdering Ryūkyū Islands fishermen (Fraser 1967, 590–591). The Osaka Conference led to an agreement between the representatives of the Meiji government and key leaders of the popular rights movement on a fundamental restructuring of government, the basic design of which was captured in a simple flow chart drawn by Kido (NDL "Modern" 1-10). In it, the sovereign emperor is placed above a central executive composed of a "cabinet [with a] grand minister and councilors" (*naikaku dajōdaijin sangi*) in between a minister of the left and minister of the right. Below are the three branches of government as represented in a legislative advisory board (*Genrōin*), a supreme court (*Taishinin*), and the government ministries (*Gyōsei*). Although the *Genrōin* and the proposed cabinet structure did not amount to much, this conciliatory gesture bought the Sat-Chō oligarchs a breathing space during which to craft a constitution and other institutions that would not easily bend to the fickle winds of representative democracy. An important consequence of the Osaka Conference was that it induced Itagaki and Kido to return to the Meiji government as imperial councilors.

The "1881 political crisis" (*Meiji jūyonen no seihen*) drove another wedge into the oligarchy. It was sparked by a chorus of demands for a representative assembly that, by December 1879, had grown sufficiently boisterous to prompt Minister of the Right Iwakura Tomomi to command each of the seven imperial councilors to present their views on the subject of constitutional government. By the end of 1880, six had responded. Itō Hirobumi, Yamagata Aritomo, Kuroda Kiyotaka, Yamada Akiyoshi, Inoue Kaoru, and Ōki Takato submitted opinions suggesting that constitutional government should be established, albeit gradually, and in such a way that the powers of Parliament were carefully circumscribed (Saikō hōki 2003, 14). Itō wanted to ensure that the constitution take the form of an "imperial document" (*chokusho*), presented as a gift to the people from their benevolent divine-right emperor (Furuya 1991, 10). Ōkuma Shigenobu, the lone holdout, finally submitted his memorial in March with the proviso that it not be shown to the other councilors. As a Hizen native in a group of imperial councilors dominated by a Sat-Chō cabal, Ōkuma was convinced that the best way to break the cabal's stranglehold on political power was through establishing a British-style system with a prime minister and cabinet selected by the majority party in Parliament (Lebra 1959, 482; Saikō hōki 2003, 19).[15] When Ōkuma's views became known, Itō had him ousted from his government posts. Not willing to go quietly, Ōkuma lent his insider voice to that of the partisan newspapers in attacking Kuroda for using his influence as director of the Hokkaidō Colonization Board to propose a plan by which government properties in Hokkaidō were to be sold to a Satsuma businessman on extremely generous terms. Ōkuma argued that creation of a parliamentary system would eliminate *hanbatsu* favoritism, to which Itō countered that it would require at least a decade of tutelary governance under transcendental cabinets to prepare the citizenry for parliamentary democracy. On October 12, 1881, the day Ōkuma and fifteen other officials submitted their resignations, the Meiji government announced that it had suspended the plan to sell the Hokkaidō properties and, more importantly, that a constitution and national assembly would be granted by 1890 (Lebra 1959, 486).

Now that the emperor had promised a constitution, it was necessary to determine its content. In an imperial order dated March 3, 1882, His Imperial Highness commanded Itō to investigate the various constitutional systems of the European countries. A separate document listed thirty-one items to be studied, including each country's constitution, imperial family, Parliament, peerage, judiciary, budget, and local administration. Among those items, Itō was specifically tasked with studying the organization, powers, and appointment of the European cabinets, as well as the nature of the relationship between cabinets and Parliament (Saikō hōki 2003, 30). The Itō mission departed on March 14 and spent the next fourteen months touring Italy, Germany, France, Holland, Belgium, England, and Russia.

Much of the Itō mission's time was spent imbibing the wisdom of Prussian legal scholars. One of them, Rudolph von Gneist, suggested that *if* the Meiji government were to choose to grant a constitution, budgetary power should not be given over to Parliament. In addition, the mission received forty-four lectures from scholar Albert Mosse on topics ranging from Prussian constitutional history to the monarch's powers and citizens' rights (Saikō hōki 2003, 30). Lorenz von Stein emphasized the benefits of a system whereby cabinet ministers are appointed by the monarch, rather than at the whim of the majority in Parliament. Stein also echoed Gneist's view that parliament's budgetary powers should be carefully constrained (ibid., 32–33). Members of the mission were quick to perceive the benefits of the Prussian system, with its limited parliamentary powers and safeguards to ensure effective governance under cabinets whose ministers were individually responsible to a sovereign emperor (Quo 1972, 24). As Itō observed in a letter to Iwakura, "the tendency of our country is to erroneously believe in the works of British, French, and American liberals and radicals as if they were Golden Rules, and thereby lead virtually to the overthrow of the State. I have found principle and means of combating this trend" (Beckmann 1957, 72, n. 17).

In March 1884, Itō was appointed director general of the Systems Investigation Bureau (*Seido torishirabe kyoku*). Four months later he secured issuance of the Peerage Ordinance (*Kazoku rei*), which created a five-rank nobility and a ready-made supply of personnel for an unelected upper house of Parliament. Peerage titles were given to imperial family members, court nobility, former daimyō, noted scholars, wealthy taxpayers, and, later on, even a few exemplary subjects from Japan's colonies. A strong Sat-Chō presence was ensured by giving titles to important government officials and "individuals who made major contributions to the Restoration" (*ishin no kōrōsha*) (Saikō hōki 2003, 34). In November of 1886, Itō and his working group began working on a draft constitution, and less than five months later they submitted the proposed constitution for review by the Privy Council. Naturally, Itō was the Council's inaugural president. Itō presented the completed constitution to the emperor on April 27, 1888 (ibid., 38).

The Emperor Meiji promulgated the Constitution of the Empire of Japan (*Dainippon teikoku kenpō*) at a grand ceremony on February 11, 1889. Although the Meiji Constitution created a national assembly—a bicameral Imperial Diet (*Teikoku kokkai*) composed of an elected House of Representatives (*Shūgiin*) and an unelected House of Peers (*Kizokuin*)—it was founded on the premise that the emperor was "sacred and inviolable," and, as head of the empire, combined "in himself the rights of sovereignty." Itō and his fellow founding fathers were at pains to constrain the powers of the Imperial Diet. The three hundred-member House of Representatives would be elected by a franchise composed of male citizens over twenty-five years of age who paid ¥15 in direct national taxes. This meant that a mere 1.3 percent of the populace was empowered to elect lower house MPs. Moreover, because the Diet's two houses were independent of one another and equal in power, the conservative unelected upper house could be expected to restrain any liberalizing initiatives from the popularly elected lower house (Gordon 2003, 126). Moreover, parliamentary sessions were limited to three months of the year, leaving government bureaucrats in charge of the nation's governance for the remainder of the time (Pempel 1986, 113). Parliament's budgetary powers were constrained by a provision stating that "when the Imperial Diet has not voted on the Budget, or when the Budget has not been brought into actual existence, the Government shall carry out the Budget of the preceding year" (Meiji Constitution, Article 71; Beckmann 1957).

Naturally, Itō and the other architects of the Meiji Constitution "had no intention of introducing the system of unified Cabinet control" and ensured that the cabinet would *not* be collectively responsible to the Diet (McGovern 1920, 107). In fact, the term "cabinet" (*naikaku*) does not appear in the Meiji Constitution, and its existence is merely implied in the lone article in which the "respective ministers of state" are instructed to "give their advice to the Emperor and be responsible for it." It goes on to dictate that "all laws, imperial ordinances, and imperial rescripts of whatever kind that relate to the affairs of the state, require the countersignature of a Minister of State" (Article 55). An equal amount of verbiage is given to the role of the Privy Councilors (*Sūmitsu komon*), who "shall, in accordance with the provisions for the organization of the Privy Council, deliberate upon important matters of State when they have been consulted by the Emperor" (Article 56). In his *Commentaries,* Itō observed that "the appointment and dismissal of [ministers] having been included by the Constitution in the sovereign power of the Emperor, it is only a legitimate consequence, that the power of deciding as to the responsibility of Ministers, is withheld from the Diet" (Itō 1889, 102). He added that "in some countries, the Cabinet is regarded as constituting a corporate body, the Ministers are not held to take part in the conduct of the government each one in an individual capacity, but joint responsibility is the rule. The evil of such a system is, that the power of party combination will ultimately overrule the supreme power of the Sovereign" (ibid., 104).

The duties of the cabinet and its ministers were set forth in the Cabinet Ordinance (*Naikaku kansei kōfu*), issued on December 24, 1889. It authorized the prime minister to report affairs of state to the emperor and to exercise general administrative control over the various administrative branches. Nevertheless, each minister was given the right to "submit any matter whatsoever for the cabinet's consideration through the prime minister." And each minister was individually responsible for giving advice to the emperor concerning the affairs of his ministry. This reduced the relative status of the prime minister to that of first among equals within the cabinet. At the same time, not all ministers were created equal, as the military ministers were allowed to report directly to the emperor on matters concerning the armed forces.

The Sat-Chō Cabal

The social origins of the five men who held the prime ministership between 1871 and 1898 reflect the forces that propelled the Meiji Restoration. Sanjō Sanetomi, who served as grand minister of state in the proto-cabinets that prevailed from 1871 until 1885, was one of seven court nobles who fled to Chōshū in 1863 when the shōgunate attempted to muzzle dissent in Kyoto (Craig 1961, 190; Gordon 2003, 56). From 1885 through 1898, the premiership alternated between Chōshū and Satsuma leaders, each of whom emerged from low-ranking samurai households and had been groomed as imperial councilors in the Grand Council. Itō Hirobumi and Yamagata Aritomo, the Chōshū leaders, were the most important political figures of the Meiji era. Itō's "great talent and natural flair for political life" propelled him through virtually every major position in the Meiji government (Hackett 1971, 146). Yet his most significant contribution to the development of the cabinet system was in forging the Meiji Constitution, which limited popular influence and created a façade of imperial authority, behind which the Sat-Chō cabal wielded actual, and nearly absolute, power. Regarded as the "father of the modern Japanese army," Yamagata established military branches that were immune to control by civilian governments (Samuels 2003, 65). He once observed that "power is indispensible, so I do my best to maintain mine" (Najita 1967, 7; Hackett 1971, 145–146). Kuroda Kiyotaka—who carried a reputation for drunken misbehavior and an unsubstantiated rumor that he murdered his wife during an intoxicated rage—became leader of the Satsuma clique as a result of the deaths of Saigō Takamori and Ōkubo Toshimichi (Koyama 1979, 12; Baxter 1994, 158).

Table 1.1. The Cabal Cabinets, 1871 to 1898

Cabinet	Prime Minister	Established	Dissolved	PM's Domain
Grand Council	Sanjō Sanetomi	7/29/1871	12/22/1885	Kyoto
1st Itō Cabinet	Itō Hirobumi	12/22/1885	4/30/1888	Chōshū
Kuroda Cabinet	Kuroda Kiyotaka	4/30/1888	10/25/1889	Satsuma
1st Yamagata Cabinet	Yamagata Aritomo	12/24/1889	5/6/1891	Chōshū
1st Matsukata Cabinet	Matsukata Masayoshi	5/6/1891	8/8/1892	Satsuma
2nd Itō Cabinet	Itō Hirobumi	8/8/1892	8/31/1896	Chōshū
2nd Matsukata Cabinet	Matsukata Masayoshi	9/18/1896	1/12/1898	Satsuma
3rd Itō Cabinet	Itō Hirobumi	1/12/1898	6/30/1898	Chōshū

Source: JCCM Database (Appendix A).

Likewise, Matsukata Masayoshi became the Satsuma leader by default, although he gained fame as a financial wizard who pressed deflationary policies during a lengthy stint as finance minister (Bailey 1983, 104).

Including the five prime ministers, a total of sixty-eight individuals held ministerial portfolios in the cabal cabinets.[16] Not surprisingly, the composite profile of this first generation of cabinet ministers bears little resemblance to that of ministers associated with a Westminster system. In fact, the modal minister in the earliest cabinets was a youthful ex-samurai male from Satsuma or Chōshū who had risen through the ranks of the new government's civil or military bureaucracies. In the unlikely event that this modal minister had any connection to the Imperial Diet that was established in 1890, it was as a member of the nonelected House of Peers.

Young ex-samurai from the main tozama domains were well represented in the ministerial rosters of the cabal cabinets. In a society steeped in a Confucianist respect for seniority, it is surprising that the average minister was less than forty-four years of age upon initial appointment to a cabinet post. For example, Itō Hirobumi had just celebrated his thirty-first birthday when he was appointed imperial councilor in a proto-cabinet headed by thirty-four-year-old Grand Minister Sanjō Sanetomi. Yet the fact that 90 percent of ministers emerged from samurai households is to be expected, given the fact that, over the course of two and a half centuries of Pax Tokugawa, the samurai were transformed from a warrior class into well-educated urban bureaucrats (Duus 1969, 100). In this regard, ex-samurai possessed elite social status and represented the best available administrative talent with which to staff the key posts of the new Meiji government. Meanwhile, two-thirds of all ministers appointed to the cabal cabinets originated in the main tozama domains, with five ministers hailing from Hizen, nine from Tosa, fourteen from Chōshū, and seventeen from Satsuma. Overall, ministers from Satsuma and Chōshū commanded 54 percent of portfolios in the cabal cabinets and held the lion's share of the most prestigious portfolios, including prime minister (70 percent), army (100 percent), navy, (73 percent), home (76 percent), and finance (56 percent).

Nearly three-quarters of all ministers ascended through the ranks of the Meiji government's civil bureaucracy en route to their ministerial appointments, and nearly all of the rest emerged from the officer corps of the Imperial Army or Imperial Navy.[17] For example, Yamagata rose to the rank of field marshal in the Imperial Japanese Army before assuming a succession of cabinet-level posts that included war minister and premier. Although few held university diplomas (which is not surprising, given the paucity of Japanese universities at the time), a number of them studied in Europe or the United States. For example, Inoue Kaoru (who served in a variety of posts, including minister of foreign affairs, industry, agriculture and commerce, justice, and finance) and Yamao Yōzō (industry minister) were among five young Chōshū samurai—along with Itō Hirobumi—sent to study in England in 1863 in violation of the shōgunate's ban on overseas travel. Others—such as Yamagata and Saigō Tsugumichi—were sent to Europe to study military affairs. At least ten incumbent or future ministers visited Washington, D.C., and the major Western European capitals with the Iwakura mission.[18]

Throughout the period, only 1 percent of ministers were recruited from the ranks of elected MPs. In fact, only *three* elected MPs held portfolios in the cabal cabinets. They were Mutsu Munemitsu, Suematsu Kenchō, and Kōmuchi Tomotsune. This tells us that the system of ministerial recruitment functioned as it was designed to do—that is, to ensure that Sat-Chō interests prevailed and that popularly elected politicians and the "people's parties" (*mintō*) had little influence in shaping national policy.

Core Executive Actors

The cabal cabinets never played more than a supporting role in executive affairs. In fact, the Sat-Chō oligarchs wielded significant influence, if not outright control, over prime ministers and their cabinets, the government bureaucracy, the Privy Council, elder statesmen, military supreme command, and even the emperor and his "private palace cabinet" (Byas 1942, 106). The only actors with any meaningful influence over executive affairs *not* under the cabal's control were the people's parties and their legions of lower house MPs.

From 1868 until the opening of the Diet in 1890, the central state bureaucracy and government were one and the same (Silberman 1967, 84). Because many government bureaucrats emerged from samurai backgrounds, they brought with them the prestige of a traditionally elite warrior class that had been transformed into an administrative class during the period of Pax Tokugawa. The leaders of the Sat-Chō cabal controlled the bureaucracy by seeing to it that their supporters occupied up to 40 percent of upper administrative posts in the central government (Silberman 1993, 182). Tokyo Imperial University (*Tōkyō teikoku daigaku*) was established in 1886 to train career civil servants, and, over time, alumni of this prestigious institution came to dominate the upper echelons of the bureaucracy. Beginning in 1887, a Higher Civil Service Examination (*Kōtō bunkan shiken*) determined appointment to all central government positions with the exception of the two highest ranks, which were occupied by imperial appointees (Silberman 1970, 349; Koyama 1979, 11). From 1893 on, officials who passed the examination were given priority in appointments to all central bureaucratic postings (Beasley 1989, 668).[19]

Bureaucrats were in charge of drafting cabinet ordinances (*seirei*) and imperial ordinances (*chokurei*), neither of which required Diet approval. Even after the establishment of the Diet, the bureaucracy issued nine ordinances for every enacted law (*hōritsu*), providing "an important extralegal channel for direct bureaucratic control over wide areas of public policymaking, a control that carried the important legitimacy provided by the imperial seal" (Pempel 1982, 218).[20] Government bureaucrats set the agenda for cabinet deliberations through the ritualized weekly meetings of top career officials from each of the ministries (van Wolferen 2001, 4). These meetings, which were initiated in 1886 at Yamagata's urging, would continue for the next 123 years, when they were temporarily suspended.

The Privy Council (*Sūmitsuin*) was established on April 30, 1888, to review the draft constitutions being prepared by Itō Hirobumi and his working group. Of the Council's thirty-one original members, twenty-one (67 percent) hailed from the four main tozama domains, with the Sat-

Chō contingent alone accounting for thirteen of them (Saikō hōki 2003, 44). Three of the four Privy Council presidents who served between 1888 and 1898—Itō, Yamagata, and Kuroda—were Sat-Chō leaders and former or future prime ministers.[21] In theory, the council was an impartial body whose purpose was to protect the constitution, curb the "arrogance of the Diet," and control the "autocracy of the ministers of state" (Colegrove 1931a, 594; Harada 1968, 302). In rationalizing the council's existence, Itō explained that Japan's well-being depended on effectuating "new enactments" and "far-sighted schemes of statecraft" that necessitated the creation of a "special institution made up of men of wide experience and of profound erudition" (Itō 1889, 109). In reality, the Privy Council was "a 'watchdog' (bannin) to protect oligarchic power from popular encroachment" and served as the "supreme board of advisers on all questions of special importance" (Samuels 2003, 57; Colegrove 1931a, 589; Nitobe 1931, 193). As "the palladium of the Constitution and of the law," the Privy Council was to Japan's prewar political system what the Supreme Court is to the president and Congress in the United States (Colegrove 1936a, 920; Nitobe 1931, 192). Under the Meiji Constitution, the council was authorized to deliberate on "important matters of state," which meant, in effect, that it became a potential veto player in executive and legislative affairs (Nitobe 1931, 193; Colegrove 1931a, 598; and Quigley 1932, 92). The council frequently requested modifications of treaties, cabinet draft proposals, and imperial ordinances, and recommended rejection in the event that the desired amendments were not made (Colegrove 1931a, 609).[22]

By the late 1890s, an extra-constitutional council of elder statesmen, known as the *genrō*, emerged to become, arguably, the "ultimate executive power" in the Meiji government (Hackett 1974, 192; Beasley 1995, 133). As confidential, self-appointed imperial advisers, the genrō were core members of a cabal that collectively made decisions in the name of the emperor. The original members of this exclusive fraternity were those Sat-Chō leaders who, through "their brilliancy and experience in statesmanship, guided the new Japan through the perplexities of its first years" (Iwasaki 1921, 31). During the period of cabal cabinets, the members of the genrō included all four Sat-Chō ex-prime ministers—Itō, Kuroda, Yamagata, and Matsukata—as well as Saigō Tsugumichi, a senior figure in the Satsuma clique. At one time or another, these five figures held virtually every major position in the Meiji government (Silberman 1993, 188). The genrō played an important role in shaping long-range policy and in solving leadership crises, particularly when it came to recommending prime ministerial candidates (ibid., 189; Colegrove 1936a, 907).

The military supreme command—the army and navy ministers, chiefs of staff, field marshals, and fleet admirals—represented a "distinct executive agency" (Quigley 1932, 89). An 1871 ordinance dictated that only active-duty officers holding the rank of major general (shōshō) or above could fill the military ministerships. While this requirement was relaxed in 1886, in practice those appointed to the posts continued to be career military officers.[23] Simultaneously state ministers *and* members of the supreme command, the army and navy ministers had the authority to bypass the cabinet in reporting military matters directly to the emperor (iaku jōsō). The military branches could topple cabinets or dictate their composition by refusing to appoint a minister. Of the ten men who held military portfolios under the cabal cabinets, eight traced their roots to Satsuma or Chōshū.[24] This state of affairs gave rise to the expression "Army of the Chōshū clique, Navy of the Satsuma clique" (Riku no Chō-batsu, Kai no Satsu-batsu). In a cabinet system in which the prime minister was merely *primus inter pares,* the special powers accorded the supreme command made it an "independent—indeed paramount—force in government" (Samuels 2003, 60).

Historically, Japan's emperors had been figureheads who remained aloof from mundane political concerns. But the Emperor Meiji (who reigned from 1868 to 1911) was known as a "hands-on ruler making decisions in all affairs of state" (Bix 2000, 8). As the "sacred and inviolable" sovereign, the monarch wielded expansive legislative and administrative powers. Under the 1890 Constitution, the emperor was empowered to appoint and dismiss government officials and to determine the organization of the administrative branches and salaries for civil and military officials. In performing his duties, the emperor was assisted by a palace entourage—a "private palace cabinet"—whose core members included the lord keeper of the privy seal, the grand chamberlain, and the imperial household minister. This "enclave of privilege and the nucleus of the Japanese elite" acted as the monarch's closest advisers and as gatekeepers controlling all access to the sovereign (ibid., 178). While the emperor himself seldom overtly meddled in political matters, the palace entourage ensured "that his purposes were incorporated into decisions of the cabinets" and the selection of prime ministers (ibid., 180; Colegrove 1936a, 907). Yet the Sat-Chō cabal had means to manipulate the emperor and his private palace cabinet. Itō drafted both the Imperial Household Law and the peerage ordinance, and he served as imperial household minister from December 1885 through September 1887. And Yamagata maintained a network of loyal followers that extended into virtually every major political and military organ, including the Imperial Household Ministry (Samuels 2003, 59).

The only executive actors *not* under the thumb of the Sat-Chō cabal were the people's parties. After the establishment of the Diet in 1890, the parties battled with a succession of governments over issues involving the national budget, foreign policy, and so forth. The Sat-Chō oligarchs employed a variety of legal and extralegal devices, including Diet dissolution (exercised on five occasions), bribery, intimidation, and violence, to have their way with the political parties. Moreover, the oligarchs could count on the House of Peers to put the brakes on any undesired policy departures that might emerge from the party-dominated lower house. Coequal in power to the lower house, "the upper house enjoyed the additional prestige of comprising the body of men with the highest social status the nation could bestow—titles of nobility" (Berger 1974, 460). Yet the people's parties were able to harass, annoy, and otherwise embarrass a succession of Sat-Chō governments. Because the oligarchs desperately wanted to avoid parliamentary discord that would cast doubt on the image of democratic civility they wished to project to the outside world, they were vulnerable to blackmail by the political parties (Akita 1967, 78, 176). The leaders of the political parties perceived this and seldom missed an opportunity to reject or delay objectionable government proposals. In the thirteen Diets convened from November 1890 through June 1898, the lower house rejected nearly 40 percent of all government bills.

THE DECAY OF THE CABAL

Despite numerous and imposing obstacles, the people's parties in the Diet's lower house did, in fact, become the nightmare that the architects of the Meiji state had so painstakingly endeavored to avoid. In response to popular pressure, the Sat-Chō cabal crafted a Prussian-inspired Constitution intended to appease anti-government protest while denying the despised people's parties influence over the national budget and foreign policy. Nevertheless, the parties were able to exploit a flaw in the Meiji Constitution to force a succession of "transcendental" (*chōzen*) governments, ones that were "above politics," to take heed of their budgetary demands. Even though it was not until 1918 that the leader of the largest party in the Diet's lower house would become prime minister, the days of Sat-Chō dominance were numbered. In fact, the seedlings of the cabal's demise were nurtured within those same carefully crafted institutions that had been designed to establish and perpetuate its rule. Looking ahead, it was clear that the people's parties—the myopic and capricious agents of popular rights—would manage to force their way into the inner sanctum of executive decision-making. Nevertheless, dire consequences accompanied Japan's first attempt at parliamentary democracy.

THE FLEETING AGE OF QUASI-PARTY CABINETS, 1898–1932

On June 30, 1898, Ōkuma Shigenobu became prime minister of Japan. This was a milestone event, because Ōkuma was the first modern premier who did not hail from the former feudal domains of Chōshū or Satsuma (he was from Hizen), and, more importantly, he was the leader of a political party. For supporters of the long-suffering party movement, the appointment of one of its own to the premiership and the awarding of ministerial portfolios to a handful of elected members of Parliament heralded the advent of an age of "party cabinets." Indeed, by the late 1920s party participation in cabinets had become the rule. This abruptly changed on May 15, 1932, when, after paying their respect to Japan's war dead at Yasukuni Shrine, eleven young Imperial Navy officers made an uninvited visit to the Prime Minister's Official Residence. Wearing their officers' uniforms, they had little difficulty making their way to the premier's private apartment, where they gunned down Prime Minister Inukai Tsuyoshi. During his trial, the ringleader of the attack admitted to having no personal grudge against Inukai. Instead, he orchestrated the murderous plot to "overthrow the Premier, who was also the president of a political party; in other words *to overthrow the very center of government*" (Byas 1942, 29; italics added). The plotters also contemplated bombing the House of Representatives and assassinating two American diplomats and comedian Charlie Chaplin, who had been invited to tea at the Prime Minister's Residence. In the end, Inukai was the only murder victim of the "May 15th Incident" (*goichigo jiken*).

What happened during the three decades between the founding of Ōkuma's "party cabinet" and the murder of Inukai? Although the age of party cabinets—actually, as we shall see, *quasi*-party cabinets—overlaps the reigns of the emperors Meiji (1868–1911) and Shōwa (1926–1989), it is associated with the era of "Taishō democracy" (*Taishō demokurashii*).

Unlike the father who preceded and the son who succeeded him, the Emperor Taishō (1912–1926) was unable to be a hands-on monarch because of brain disease and poor health (Hara 2008a, 213; Hara 2008b, 227; Bix 2000, 12). A famous, possibly apocryphal story told of the Emperor Taishō portrays him using a scroll as a telescope through which to peer at bewildered lawmakers at an opening session of the Imperial Diet (Hara 2008b, 227). Yet the reign of this infirm monarch occurred in the midst of an amazing three-decade period during which political parties gained entrée to the "star chamber" of policy-making, party leaders from the popularly elected House of Representatives organized cabinets, and the franchise was gradually extended to all male citizens over twenty-five years of age (Murai 2005, 14). Still, the reign of the Emperor Taishō, who unwittingly presided over many of these developments, can be seen as a metaphor for the structurally unsound and incomplete experiment with democracy that took place between the establishment of Ōkuma's "party cabinet" and Inukai's assassination.

Drifting into Party Cabinets

Prime Minister Inukai was collateral damage in a holy war to put an end to party cabinets. In the minds of the eleven young naval officers and a grow-ing number of radical nationalists, party politicians such as Inukai were traitors to the "rich country, strong military" (fukoku kyōhei) cause, which had served as the mantra for Japan's forced-march program of industri-alization and the quest for national security through creating a colonial empire. Despite the painstaking efforts of the Sat-Chō cabal, political par-ties had come to occupy—at least in the minds of some, including the young naval officers—the "very center of government." The institutional barriers erected by the Sat-Chō cabal included a constitution in which ministers of state were individually responsible to a sovereign emperor and bore no responsibility to the bicameral Diet. In addition, while lower house MPs were elected by a razor-thin franchise of male taxpayers (which expanded after the introduction of universal manhood suffrage in 1925), their coun-terparts in the unelected upper house possessed equal powers and could be counted on to veto excessively "liberal" proposals. The Constitution's Prussian-inspired Article 71 was designed to deny the Diet ultimate con-trol over the nation's budget by automatically carrying forward the previ-ous year's budget in the easily imagined event that the Diet could not agree on a bill. Moreover, the Imperial Army and Navy were not subject to civilian control, and an assortment of constitutional and extra-constitutional actors possessed the wherewithal to veto undesired policies proposed by party-led cabinets.

Despite the barriers put in their way—not to mention the violence, intimidation, and vote-buying by government authorities to thwart their rise—the people's parties (*mintō*) refused to back down. The Diet's lower house became a battleground in which the parties jousted with a succession of cabal cabinets over the national budget and issues of domestic and foreign policy. Indeed, parties in the Diet quickly perceived that they could use Article 71 to *block* government budget proposals calling for increased expenditures to pay for wars and enhanced arsenals (Akita 1967, 76–89; Banno 1992, xiii–xiv, 49–50). By 1898, the two leading figures in the Sat-Chō cabal—Itō Hirobumi and Yamagata Aritomo—were at odds over how to deal with the obstreperous parties. Itō gradually came to favor accommodation and, in January 1892, recommended this strategy in a memorial to the Emperor Meiji. Itō's idea was to create a large government-friendly party that could control the Diet. But Yamagata regarded that as a first step down the slippery slope leading to a British-style parliamentary system (Sims 2001, 74). For the next six years, Yamagata's view held sway among the elder statesmen who represented the Sat-Chō cabal's dominant position. But, on June 22, 1898, the two largest people's parties merged to form the *Kenseitō* (Constitutional Government Party), which controlled an overwhelming majority of lower house seats. This made Yamagata's nightmare come to pass; the oligarchs were obliged to hand the reins of government to the *Kenseitō*'s leaders, Ōkuma Shigenobu and Itagaki Taisuke.

Although the birth of the first Ōkuma cabinet was heralded as the genesis of an "age of party government," its effects were far less dramatic than the institutional reconfiguration set in motion four and a half decades earlier by Commodore Perry's uninvited visit. Indeed, by the time of Perry' s visit, the shōgunate was no longer able to police and punish insurrectionary acts, especially those committed in the distant domains of powerful outside lords. In contrast, the people's parties operated in an environment dominated by a Sat-Chō cabal that possessed a panoply of institutional and extra-institutional means of blocking unwanted change. Moreover, the Sat-Chō oligarchs enjoyed considerable discretion in enforcing their dictates, which had not been the case with an enervated shōgunate. The change agents in the drama that unfolded between 1898 and 1932 were former insiders, led by ex-government officials from the former domains of Hizen and Tosa and their followers. These renegades formed anti-government protest groups that evolved into the people's parties that became a perpetual irritant for Sat-Chō oligarchs. The result was *drift* from transcendental cabinets to cabinets in which parties and elected politicians played a visible, if not dominant, role in executive affairs.

The Central State Executive

When the first Ōkuma cabinet was formed, eleven ministers were allocated twelve portfolios. In addition to the premiership, these included portfolios for foreign affairs, home, army, navy, justice, education, agriculture and commerce, and communications. In addition, the directors general of the Cabinet Secretariat and Legislation Bureau continued to participate in cabinet meetings, and the occupants of those posts were regarded as de facto cabinet ministers (Quigley 1932, 130). By the time the ill-fated Inukai cabinet took office, the number of portfolios had expanded to fifteen, distributed among fourteen ministers. Part of this expansion was owed to the decision taken in 1925 to split the Ministry of Agriculture and Commerce into a Ministry of Agriculture and a Ministry of Commerce and Industry. In 1920, a Ministry of Railways was founded to oversee a rapidly expanding national railway system, which already employed nearly ninety thousand personnel and claimed jurisdiction over eighty-two hundred kilometers of track. Nine years later, the Ministry of Colonial Affairs was established to manage Japan's expanding empire, which, by the time of Inukai's assassination, included control over Taiwan, the southern half of Sakhalin Island, and Korea, as well as a "protectorate" over Germany's holdings in China (Jiaozhou Bay in Shandong Province) and in the northern Pacific (the Marshall Islands, the Carolines and Marianas, and the Palau Islands).[25]

The cabinet also got into the business of managing economic planning and industrial mobilization. In 1918, the Munitions Bureau (*Gunju kyoku*) was established as a cabinet organ and staffed with military officers and statisticians who formulated economic plans, gathered statistical data, and administered the recently enacted Munitions Industries Mobilization Law (Johnson 1982, 117). This is an early indication of the rising influence of technocrats in Japan's civil and military bureaucracies. In 1927 the Resources Bureau (*Shigen kyoku*) was established under the cabinet and given charge of formulating the "materials mobilization plans" (ibid., 118).

Cabinets normally met weekly in the Prime Minister's Official Residence, except when Parliament was in session, when they met in the cabinet chamber of the National Diet Building. The proceedings of cabinet meetings were kept secret, although it is known that efforts were made to give the appearance of cabinet unity whenever votes were taken (Takeuchi 1967, 24). In addition, the Cabinet Secretariat, Legislation Bureau, and other agencies supported the activities of the prime ministers and their cabinets. At the turn of the century the professional staff posted to cabinet-related agencies numbered around 700 government employees; by 1922 that number had more than doubled to 1,521 staffers. Although the number of government employees was cut following the 1923 Great Kantō Earthquake, by 1932 some 1,269 staffers were working in cabinet-related agencies. Still, the cabinet's support staff never accounted for more than 1 percent of government employees.

Party Cabinet Ministers

Between June 1898 and May 1932, twenty-two cabinets were formed under sixteen prime ministers. They included nine ex-bureaucrats and seven military men, while only the ill-fated Inukai Tsuyoshi could be described as a "career politician." The ex-bureaucrats were Itō Hirobumi, Ōkuma Shigenobu, Saionji Kinmochi, Hara Kei (who also worked as a newspaper reporter), Takahashi Korekiyo, Kiyoura Keigō, Katō Takaaki, Wakatsuki Reijirō, and Hamaguchi Osachi. Yamagata Aritomo, Katsura Tarō, Terauchi Masatake, Kiyoura Keigo, and Tanaka Giichi were army generals, while Yamamoto Gonbei and Katō Tomosaburō were admirals. Inukai was a newspaper reporter before winning a Diet seat in the 1890 election. He was serving his seventeenth consecutive lower house term when he assumed the premiership, having acquired the moniker of "god of constitutional government" (*kensei no kamisama*) despite his traitorous willingness to assume portfolios in transcendental cabinets (Shiota 2011, 100).

While the appointment of Ōkuma, a Hizen man, brought an end to the Sat-Chō monopoly on the premiership, six of those who held the foremost executive post originated in Chōshū or Satsuma. Yamagata, Itō, Katsura, Terauchi, and Tanaka traced their roots to Chōshū, while Yamamoto was a Satsuma man.[26] From June 1898 on, Yamagata and Itō were at odds over Itō's decision to become president of the *Seiyūkai* (Friends of Constitutional Government). Yamagata viewed political parties as divisive elements, and

Table 1.2. The Quasi-party Cabinets, 1898 to 1932

Cabinet	Prime Minister	Established	Dissolved	MPs[a]	Cabinet Type
1st Ōkuma Cabinet	Ōkuma Shigenobu	6/30/1898	11/8/1898	0.50	Party
2nd Yamagata Cabinet	Yamagata Aritōmo	11/8/1898	10/19/1900	0	Transcendental
4th Itō Cabinet	Itō Hirobumi	10/19/1900	5/10/1901	0.13	Semi-Transcendental
1st Katsura Cabinet	Katsura Tarō	6/2/1901	1/7/1906	0	Transcendental
1st Saionji Cabinet	Saionji Kinmochi	1/7/1906	7/14/1908	0.13	Semi-Transcendental
2nd Katsura Cabinet	Katsura Tarō	7/14/1908	8/30/1911	0	Transcendental
2nd Saionji Cabinet	Saionji Kinmochi	8/30/1911	12/21/1912	0.23	Semi-Party
3rd Katsura Cabinet	Katsura Tarō	12/21/1912	2/20/1913	0	Transcendental
1st Yamamoto Cabinet	Yamamoto Gonbei	2/20/1913	4/16/1914	0.27	Semi-Party
2nd Ōkuma Cabinet	Ōkuma Shigenobu	4/16/1914	10/9/1916	0.24	Semi-Party
Terauchi Cabinet	Terauchi Masatake	10/9/1916	9/29/1918	0	Transcendental
Hara Cabinet	Hara Kei	9/29/1918	11/4/1921	0.50	Party
Takahashi Cabinet	Takahashi Korekiyo	11/13/1921	6/12/1922	0.46	Semi-Party
Katō (Tomosaburō) Cabinet	Katō Tomosaburō	6/12/1922	9/2/1923	0.07	Semi-Transcendental
2nd Yamamoto Cabinet	Yamamoto Gonbei	9/2/1923	1/7/1924	0.08	Semi-Transcendental
Kiyoura Cabinet	Kiyoura Keigo	1/7/1924	6/11/1924	0.08	Semi-Transcendental
Katō (Takaaki) Cabinet	Katō Takaaki	6/11/1924	1/30/1926	0.50	Party
1st Wakatsuki Cabinet	Wakatsuki Reijirō	1/30/1926	4/20/1927	0.41	Semi-Party
Tanaka (Giichi) Cabinet	Tanaka Giichi	4/20/1927	7/2/1929	0.50	Party
Hamaguchi Cabinet	Hamaguchi Osachi	7/2/1929	4/14/1931	0.50	Party
2nd Wakatsuki Cabinet	Wakatsuki Reijirō	4/14/1931	12/13/1931	0.50	Party
Inukai Cabinet	Inukai Tsuyoshi	12/13/1931	5/16/1932	0.63	Party

[a] Percentage of ministers who held seats in the House of Representatives.
Source: JCCM Database (Appendix A).

he viewed Itō's action as tantamount to treason. The Yamagata-Itō rivalry lived on in their respective protégés, Katsura Tarō and Saionji Kinmochi, who alternated as prime minister from 1901 through 1913.

Including the prime ministers, 156 individuals held ministerial portfolios in the quasi-party cabinets. The modal minister was a fifty-six-year-old male (making him nearly nine years older than his cabal cabinet counterpart) who originated in less urbanized regions of Kyūshū or southwestern Honshū. He very well may have served as an upper-level government official or as a military officer prior to being appointed to a cabinet post, and there was a better than fifty-fifty chance he attended university. Indeed, from around the time of the First World War on, a majority of ministerial appointees had received a university education. For two-thirds of those who did attend university, Tokyo Imperial University (*Tokyo teikoku daigaku*, or simply *Tōdai*) was their alma mater. Yet even in this age of party cabinets, the modal minister was *not* an elected MP. In fact, elected representatives accounted for only one-quarter of ministers, and represented half or more of ministers in only seven of the twenty-two cabinets formed during this period. As noted earlier, only three of the sixteen prime ministers held seats in the Diet's lower house.

Taken together, the career civil service and imperial armed forces produced nearly three-quarters of all those who held ministerial portfolios. More than half emerged from the central state bureaucracy, and better than four in five of these ex-bureaucrats (sixty-four of seventy-eight) had ascended to the rank of bureau chief or above. This explains the prominence of Tōdai alumni among the ministerial elite, as the purpose in founding the Imperial University was to train upper civil servants. Slightly over 20 percent of ministerships were given to retired or active officers in the imperial armed forces, with soldiers outnumbering sailors almost two to one. Nearly half of these soldier-ministers hailed from Chōshū, which wielded enormous sway over that branch of the armed services. Chōshū men who held the post of army minister included Kodama Gentarō, Oka Ichinosuke, and future premiers Yamagata, Katsura, Tanaka, and Terauchi. Despite Satsuma's strong influence over the navy, only two of its native sons—Saigō Tsugumichi and Yamamoto Gonbei—held the navy ministerial portfolio.

Ministers from the predominantly rural and politically conservative southwestern areas were disproportionately represented in the party cabinets. In particular, the Chūgoku, Kyūshū, and Shikoku regions—which, uncoincidentally, included the former "outside domains" of Chōshū, Satsuma, Hizen, and Tosa—accounted for 55 percent of all ministers, despite being home to less than 30 percent of the country's population.[27] And, by themselves, ministers from Chūgoku (southwestern Honshū) and Kyūshū garnered more than half of all portfolios allocated. Although men from Chōshū (which had become Yamaguchi Prefecture) and Satsuma (Kagoshima Prefecture) had accounted for more than half of all cabal cabinet ministers, these two former feudal domains produced only 22 percent of ministers in the party cabinets.

While elected MPs assumed a more visible presence in cabinet meetings, the "age of party cabinets" (seitō naikaku jidai) is a misnomer. In fact, only one in four ministers appointed during the period held seats in the Diet's lower house, and five cabinets were "transcendental" (chōzen), which is to say that they included exactly zero elected MPs. Furthermore, five cabinets can be labeled "semi-transcendental," with elected MPs making up less than a quarter of the ministers, while another five could be classified as "semi-party" cabinets, in which elected MPs accounted for between one-quarter and one-half of the ministerial roster. This means that elected MPs accounted for half or more ministers in only seven "party cabinets," and it was not until the establishment of the Katō (Takaaki) cabinet on June 11, 1924, that such cabinets became the rule. This is shown in table 1.2. It is worth pointing out that MPs who held portfolios in the six cabinets formed between June 1924 and May 1932 had been elected to an average number of 6.5 lower house terms. This is the first clear sign that a seniority system for cabinet ministers was beginning to take root.

Power Relations in Executive Affairs

As Colegrove observed, the cabinet "never enjoyed the unrivaled direction of administration as found in many parliamentary democracies" (1936a, 903). Indeed, despite all the hype about "party cabinets" and "Taishō democracy" (Taishō demokurashii), the government bureaucracy, the Privy Council, elder statesmen, the emperor and the palace entourage, and the military supreme command continued to dominate the core executive. Nonetheless, the people's parties and elected MPs managed to gain a precarious place at the "high table" of executive decision-making.

The government bureaucracy wielded considerable influence in executive affairs (Iwasaki 1921, 51). Whereas the approval of both Diet chambers was required to enact new laws, the bureaucracy was empowered to issue imperial ordinances, which did not require Diet approval. In fact, for every law passed by the Diet from 1898 until 1932, the bureaucracy issued nearly seven ordinances. When Ōkuma established his "party cabinet" in 1898, he employed the spoils system to install his followers in upper posts in the government officialdom. Of course, this is exactly what the Sat-Chō oligarchs had done for their followers, but they were not about to allow party leaders to do it. So the oligarchs modified the Civil Service Appointment Ordinance (*Bunkan nin'yō rei*) to require that the highest bureaucratic posts be reserved for those who passed the Upper Civil Service Examination (Silberman 1970, 349).[28] Under the second Ōkuma cabinet, parliamentary undersecretary (*sanseikan*) and deputy parliamentary undersecretary (*fuku-sanseikan*) posts were established in each ministry and staffed with political appointees. Henceforth, each ministry would be supervised by only three politically appointed officials—a minister and two undersecretaries—while the ministry's day-to-day operations and all of its career and noncareer civil servants were supervised by a hierarchy of bureaucratically appointed officials under the direction of an administrative vice minister.[29]

As "the highest body of the emperor's constitutional advisers," the Privy Council wielded "an immense and sometimes overpowering influence" (Itō 1889, 98; Nitobe 1931, 192). Supposedly "impartial, with no leanings to this or that party," in reality the council sided with the Sat-Chō oligarchs in decisions concerning major legislative bills, proposed treaties, and imperial ordinances (Itō 1889, 98). Under Yamagata's influence, the council's role expanded to include the appointment of upper civil servants and the "reform and organization of Government offices" (Nitobe 1931, 193; Quigley 1932, 92). Yamagata made the Privy Council into a "citadel of reaction" and a "check upon the cabinet, which [had] come more and more under the representative branch of government" (Nitobe 1931, 193; Colegrove 1931a, 590). As an observer of the time pointed out, "when we remember that the average age of Councilors is threescore and ten, we can easily understand the resentment of a cabinet of busy, energetic and progressive younger men at having to run to the Council for approval of their every move" (Quigley 1931, 502). The Privy Council vetoed cabinet proposals on several occasions, most famously in the decision taken in 1927 to reject the Wakatsuki cabinet's proposed rescue plan for the financially troubled Bank of Taiwan (Colegrove 1931b, 885–888).

Although the influence of the genrō waxed and, mostly, waned over time, these elder statesmen continued to represent a potent executive force, especially when it came to selecting candidates for a vacant prime ministership (Kitazawa 1929, 52–53; Quigley 1931, 503; Murai 2002, 22–23). With the exception of Saionji—who was born into a family of Kyoto court nobles but became Itō's protégé—all of the genrō hailed from Satsuma or Chōshū. After the Emperor Meiji's death in 1911, the influence of the genrō increased as the mentally and physically feeble Emperor Taishō sat upon the Chrysanthemum Throne.[30] As premier-to-be Yamamoto Gonbei observed to elder statesman Matsukata Masayoshi, the present emperor "is not [of the same caliber] as the previous emperor. In my view, it is loyal not to obey the [Taishō] emperor's word if we deem it to be disadvantageous to the state" (Bix 2000, 40). So it was that the elder statesmen did not find it necessary to consult the emperor in the selection of Takahashi Korekiyo to form a cabinet in November 1921 (ibid., 123).

"Upon the fall of a ministry," an observer of the time noted, "it is customary for the Emperor to ask the . . . lord keeper of the privy seal, for advice upon the selection of a prime minister. Invariably the [lord keeper of the privy seal] proposes that the *Genrō* be consulted, and invariably the Emperor follows the advice of the *Genrō*" (Colegrove 1936a, 907). In fact, beginning around 1927, there is reason to believe that this private palace cabinet decided on a candidate for the premiership and then dispatched a messenger to secure the rubber-stamped approval of Saionji, the last of the genrō (Bix 2000, 174). Yet it is difficult to know exactly how much influence the emperor and the palace entourage wielded. Although supposedly a mere "figurehead dressed in Imperial robes" (Byas 1942, 113), the Meiji emperor was known to be a "power wielder," and the Shōwa emperor acted "energetically behind the scenes," influencing the conduct of prime ministers, hastening the collapse of party cabinets, and shaping policy (Bix 2000, 39–40, 11–12). Further, "Imperial displeasure" could bring the resignation of a ministry (McGovern 1920, 109).

The military branches had the power to topple or transform cabinets and appeal directly and independently to the emperor, and they were in no way compelled to bow to civilian authority. In 1900, the Yamagata cabinet issued an imperial ordinance stipulating that only active-duty military officers could hold the army minister or navy minister portfolio (Colegrove 1936a, 917). This meant that if one branch of the military refused to recommend a replacement for a vacant ministerial portfolio, the cabinet would collapse, and any attempt to form a new government would have to pay heed to the wishes of the aggrieved branch. That is exactly what happened in 1912, when the Saionji cabinet refused to provide funding for two new army divisions. In response, the army minister resigned and the army refused to nominate an active-duty officer to replace him (Koyama 1979, 33). Saionji and his ministers had no choice but to throw in the towel, and Katsura Tarō, an army general who could be counted on to pursue pro-army policies, was tapped to form a new cabinet (Gordon 2003, 130). The extraordinary power of the military branches meant that Japan was ruled under a system of "dual government" (*nijū seifu*) (Colegrove 1936a, 917).

Despite the numerous barriers erected by the Sat-Chō oligarchy to stem their rise—including the creation in 1900 of a system for electing MPs through a single nontransferable vote in multimember constituencies—the people's parties were able to influence executive affairs.[31] One source of influence was a loophole in the Meiji Constitution, by which the budget for the previous year automatically carried forward in the event that the Diet could not agree on a budget. This inadvertently granted influence to the Diet in the event that the government's proposal called for *increased* expenditures. In addition, parties employed non-confidence motions to embarrass and annoy governments, but these motions carried no force, since ministers were *individually* responsible to the emperor and cabinets were not *collectively* responsible to the Diet. Nevertheless, the establishment of the Hara cabinet on June 29, 1918, was seen as a hopeful sign. Dubbed the "commoner prime minister" (*heimin saishō*), Hara distributed ministerial portfolios to eight *Seiyūkai* MPs. Leaders of the *Seiyūkai* (Tanaka and Wakatsuki) and *Minseitō* (Hamaguchi and Inukai)—the two largest parties of the day—alternated in the premiership in the four cabinets formed between April 1927 and May 1932. In this way, the task of forming a new cabinet came to be entrusted to the leader of the largest political party as the "normal course of constitutional governance" (Duus 1998, 178–179; Murai 2002, 34). Unfortunately, all three of the "commoner" prime ministers—Hara, Hamaguchi, and Inukai—fell victim to assassins' bullets.

Killing the "Party Cabinet System"

What started out to be a wondrous age of party cabinets ended with the bloody May 15th Incident.[32] Indeed, it was not until the late 1920s that elected MPs consistently accounted for even half of cabinet ministers, and tapping the leader of the largest party in the lower house to be prime minister never became firmly established. More fundamentally, cabinets and ministers remained *individually* responsible to a sovereign emperor, meaning there was no requirement of *collective* responsibility to the Diet. Despite the fact that governments that ran afoul of the elected representatives in the lower house tended to collapse, there was no real connection—no electoral mandate—between cabinets and lower house elections.[33] Even the authors of an almanac of the day were forced to concede that "the representative system of government in this country has not developed to such a stage as to make the cabinet ministers necessarily responsible to the Diet" (*Japan Times Year Book* 1933, 37). In fact, cabinet decisions were subject to potential, and often actual, veto by the Privy Council or the genrō, while members of the Imperial Court influenced executive affairs from the shadow of the Chrysanthemum Throne. Meanwhile, a dozen or so transitory cabinet ministers were expected to monitor a vast government bureaucracy staffed by elite career civil servants who regarded themselves as "servants of the emperor." Most critically, the military branches openly demonstrated that they were not subject to civilian control and that they were able and willing to topple uncooperative governments.

THE TECHNO-FASCIST CABINETS AND THE TOTAL STATE, 1932–1946

On May 26, 1932, a week and a half after Inukai's assassination, Admiral Saitō Makoto formed a "national unity cabinet" (*kyokoku itchi naikaku*) (Shiota 2011, 103). The appointment of Saitō ushered in an era in which "reform bureaucrats" and "control officers" were given free rein to engage in rational planning that employed all of the country's resources as well as those of its expanding colonial empire. Together with their industrialist allies, these technocrats went about their work under the umbrella of a "total state" that permitted little interference from the elected MPs who had briefly occupied a position of executive influence. Yet this rational planning took place in a context punctuated by seemingly irrational acts of terror, both at home and abroad. After exiting the premiership, Saitō himself was felled by an assassin's bullet in a bloody putsch that also claimed the lives of the finance minister, an imperial adviser, and a member of the army's supreme command. Others, including two future premiers, narrowly escaped assassination, and it required an order from the emperor to bring an end to the attempted coup. Meanwhile, on the Asian mainland, the Imperial Army was making foreign policy by the sword and delivering *faits accompli* to the civilian governments in Tokyo. Government leaders concluded that declaring war against an objectively mightier United States and its allies was somehow worth the risk.

The misguided policies and corruption of the "party cabinets" gave rise to subversive individuals and groups determined to rectify Japan's malfunctioning domestic institutions and an international order that they believed denied the country its rightful place in world affairs. They included government officials, military officers, and industrialists who articulated a strategy of economic autarchy pursued through rational state planning and the efficient mobilization of all of the empire's resources. These technocrats were impressed by the Soviet Union's experiments with central planning, and many of them honed their planning skills during postings to Japan's puppet state in Manchuria (Mimura 2011, 14; Barnhart 1987, 270). They joined forces with nationalist leaders such as Hiranuma Kiichirō and Konoe Fumimaro, who espoused a vision inspired by the models of Fascist Italy and Nazi Germany that incorporated the homegrown ideas of Nakano Seigō, Tosaka Jun, Kita Ikki, and others. This produced a polythetic vision that called for a "Shōwa Restoration" and stressed the sanctity of the mystical concept of "kokutai," the traditional national essence based on the centrality of a divine-right emperor in the body politic (Tansman 2009, 11). Thus, by the outset of the 1940s Japan's central state executive was dominated by techno-fascists who "spoke a language close to that of European fascist thinkers and promoted a political structure akin to that found in Italy and Germany" (ibid.).[34]

The Techno-Fascists Take Charge

On the home front, the techno-fascists set about destroying the institutional foundations of parliamentary democracy and laissez-faire capitalism. They blamed "party cabinets" for the Great Depression, the effects of which were especially painful to the rural populace that was directly impacted by the collapse of the world silk market in 1930. The techno-fascists associated party cabinets with a succession of high-profile corruption scandals involving politicians, industrialists, and government officials (Mitchell 1996). They criticized party cabinets for seeking to enhance civilian control of the military, for undermining military capabilities, and for the undisciplined management of the nation's labor force and its natural resources. Following Inukai's assassination, the practice of tapping the leader of the largest party in the Diet's elective chamber ceased, as the premiership was given over to a succession of admirals and generals, with a right-wing ex-diplomat and a pair of fascist ideologues sprinkled in. Naturally, elected MPs were allowed only a token presence among ministers in these techno-fascist cabinets. With almost religious fervor, these change agents enacted mobilization laws and created "superagencies" to enhance state control over economic planning, labor activities, corporate profiteering, and the use of strategic resources.

On the international front, the techno-fascists took aim at the institutions of the "Versailles-Washington System," which were, they believed, rigged to favor American and British interests to the detriment of Japanese interests.[35] They were outraged that the mission sent to the 1919 Versailles Conference by "commoner prime minister" Hara Kei and his "party cabinet" failed to secure Japan's main demands. These unfulfilled demands included the cession to Japan of German concessions in China and the north Pacific, as well as the inclusion of an anti-racial-discrimination clause in the League of Nations charter. In addition, the change agents were incensed at the pusillanimous compromises made by diplomats dispatched by Takahashi Korekiyo's semi-party cabinet to the Washington Conference on Naval Limitation in 1921–1922. That conference produced a Five-Power Treaty that permitted Japan to maintain only 60 percent as many large warships as were possessed by the United States and the United Kingdom, and a Four-Power Treaty in which the Anglo-American powers, France, and Japan agreed to preserve the status quo in the Pacific. Meanwhile, the Nine-Power Treaty affirmed the sanctity of an "open door" policy in China that denied Japan the opportunity to create a sphere of influence in the same way the Western imperialist countries had done. Further, Japan's assent to the 1928 Kellogg-Briand Pact meant that the country waived the right to employ military force to acquire territory. A young Konoe Fumimaro expressed the view of many Japanese malcontents in arguing that, under the Versailles-Washington System, Japan "would be left forever a backward country" (quoted in Hata 1989, 283).

The party cabinets, which had never become firmly established, were powerless in the face of the techno-fascist assault. Domestically, the techno-fascists engineered the New Structure Movement (*Shin taisei undō*), which, among other things, led to the dissolution of political parties and interest groups and their recombination under the government's monolithic "official" party. Internationally, the efforts of the techno-fascists culminated in the creation of a "New Order in East Asia" superimposed over an expansive Japanese empire. As time would tell, Japan's response to these domestic and international challenges led to total war, complete defeat, and institutional reconfiguration under a foreign military occupation.

The Techno-Fascist Institutions

New ministerial portfolios and supra-ministerial agencies were created to assist in planning and mobilizing all of Japan's resources, as well as those of its expanding empire, in preparation for total war. At the time of its formation on May 26, 1932, the Saitō cabinet was composed of fourteen ministers holding fifteen portfolios. By the time the Tōjō cabinet assumed office just over nine years later, twenty portfolios were distributed among seventeen ministers.

Five new ministerial portfolios were created under the techno-fascist cabinets. The Ministry of Health and Welfare (*Kōseishō*) was established in January 1938 at the urging of the Imperial Army, which was concerned about the poor health of its recruits (Anderson 1993, 50). Prior to this, the nation's health had been the administrative concern of the powerful Home Ministry. The Ministry of Greater East Asia (*Dai Tō-a Shō*) was created in November 1942 and given responsibility for administering all of Japan's colonies and occupied territories except Taiwan, Korea, and Karafuto (Sakhalin) (Peattie 1984, 124). Three new ministries were established on November 1, 1943. The Ministry of Transportation and Communications (*Un'yu teishin shō*) was born from the merger of the Ministry of Communications and the Ministry of Railways. Meanwhile, the Ministry of Munitions (*Gunjushō*) and Ministry of Agriculture and Commerce (*Nōshōmushō*) were forged through splitting the Ministry of Commerce and Industry. With the establishment of the Munitions Ministry, the functions of industrial planning, electric power, and airplane manufacture were, for the first time, brought together under the administrative control of a single ministry (Johnson 1982, 169).

When Hiranuma replaced Konoe as prime minister in January 1939, the two swapped seats as Privy Council president and prime minister, but Konoe was allowed to stay on in the cabinet as "*Hanretsu*," a de facto minister without portfolio. Upon reassuming the premiership in December

1940, Konoe established the position of minister of state without port-folio (*muninsho daijin*) in his cabinet (Uzawa 1981, 103). This enabled Konoe and his successors to bestow "state minister" (*kokumu daijin*) sta-tus on directors of important governmental agencies—such as the Cabi-net Planning Board and the Cabinet Information Bureau—that had not been accorded formal ministerial status. Hiranuma Kiichirō and Hoshino Naoki became the first ministers without portfolio. Hoshino's appointment was significant in that it brought the president of the Cabinet Planning Board into the Konoe cabinet, thus underscoring the board's importance as the cockpit of the "new structure movement" (discussed below). Simi-larly, Prime Minister Koiso Kuniaki's appointment of Ogata Taketora as minister without portfolio and director of the Cabinet Information Bureau signaled the importance of that organ in his government. Ministers with-out portfolio were appointed in every cabinet formed through the end of the Pacific War.

Supra-Ministerial Agencies

Beginning in the mid-1920s, cabinet-level "superagencies" were estab-lished to enhance state control over planning and mobilization (Samuels 2003, 144). Although technically under the cabinet's control, some of these superagencies were created at the urging of the Imperial Army and behaved accordingly. In addition, cabinets got into the propaganda and censorship business with the establishment of high-level deliberative organs to coordi-nate the views of leading figures in matters pertaining to national security and foreign policy.

One of the first of the superagencies was the Resources Bureau (*Shi-gen kyoku*), established in 1927 to assess the nature and capabilities of the country's workforce, control labor action and corporate profits, and super-vise production facilities of all kinds (Barnhart 1987, 25).[36] The bureau was a civilian agency staffed by elite bureaucrats and special appointees from the officer corps of the armed forces (Mimura 2011, 20). In 1935, the Cab-inet Research Bureau (*Naikaku chōsa kyoku*) was founded with Yoshida Shigeru, a Home Ministry bureaucrat and leading figure among the "new bureaucrats," as its director. Two years later, the army succeeded in gaining establishment of the Cabinet Planning Board (*Kikaku-in*), which produced the "materials mobilization" laws of the late 1930s that aimed to improve the means and methods of production to enhance efficiency in industries deemed pivotal to the war effort (Uzawa 1981, 94; Johnson 1982, 120). The board's founding director was Taki Masao, a lower house MP and former director of the Legislation Bureau. Other noteworthy Planning Board presidents or vice presidents included Aoki Kazuo and Hoshino Naoki (ex-Finance Ministry bureaucrats), Suzuki Teiichi (an Imperial Army general), and Abe Genki (former director of the dreaded Special Higher Police—the so-called "thought police"—under the Home Ministry) (Johnson 1982, 138). Not long after Japanese forces invaded China proper in July 1937, the Konoe government created the post of cabinet councilor (*naikaku sangi*) and appointed generals, admirals, bureaucrats, and industrialists to advise the cabinet in its planning functions (Uzawa 1981, 94; Falk 1961, 513–514). This was a "return to the old tradition" of the role played by "imperial councilors" (*sangi*) under the Meiji government (Sekiguchi 1938, 7).

In September 1932, military officials and bureaucrats from the Foreign Affairs, Education, Home, and Communications Ministries began meeting informally to coordinate the gathering and dissemination of information (Awaya 1993, 292–293). These discussions led to the creation four years later of the Dōmei Tsūshinsha, the ancestor of today's Kyodo News and Jiji Press agencies. In September of that same year, a Cabinet Information Department (*Naikaku jōhō bu*) was established and given broad enforcement powers and functional jurisdiction that included administrative supervision of the National Spirit Mobilization Movement (*Kokumin seishin sōdōin un'dō*). One of the movement's mottos was "luxury is our enemy," which, among other things, aimed to discourage the wearing of Western-style permanent-waved hair-dos by Japanese women (Sodei 2001, 248). In 1937, state authorities moved to "defer" publication of a number of works deemed excessively critical of government policy. Tokyo Imperial University economist Yanaihara Tadao—who was fired for questioning Japan's aggressive policies in Manchuria—was among those whose writings were blacklisted (Ienaga 1978, 116). On December 6, 1940, the Cabinet Information Bureau (*Naikaku jōhō kyoku*) was created to keep a watchful eye on newspapers, print publications, and radio transmissions. It brought together the intelligence-gathering units of the army and navy, as well as relevant units of the Foreign, Home, and Communications Ministries.

Two important high-level deliberative councils were established to coordinate views concerning matters of foreign, national security, and economic policy. The Five Ministers' Conference (*Goshō kaigi*), created in 1933, brought together the prime minister and the army, navy, finance, and foreign affairs ministers. In 1935, the Cabinet Deliberation Council (*Naikaku shingikai*) was established to advise the government of important matters of economic administration. Founded under the Okada cabinet, the fifteen-member council included "senior statesmen" (*jūshin*), peers, political party leaders, and ex-bureaucrats (Johnson 1982, 123; Colegrove 1936b, 65).

Techno-Fascist Ministers

Between May 1932 and May 1946, fifteen cabinets were formed under thirteen prime ministers. Three of these premiers emerged from high-ranking positions in the career civil service, nine were high-ranking military officers, and one was a hereditary aristocrat. The three ex-government officials—Hirota Kōki, Shidehara Kijūrō, and Hiranuma Kiichirō—had risen to senior posts in the Foreign and Justice Ministries. Saitō Makoto, Okada Keisuke, Yonai Mitsumasa, and Suzuki Kantarō were navy admirals, while Hayashi Senjurō, Abe Nobuyuki, Tōjō Hideki, Koiso Kuniaki, and Higashikuni Naruhiko were army generals. The most important of the military figures, Tōjō, earned the sobriquet "Razor-sharp Tōjō" (*Kamisori Tōjō*) for being "quick and decisive and impatient with those who were not" (Butow 1969, 7). Konoe Fumimaro, the hereditary aristocrat, was a descendent of the aristocratic Fujiwara family and acquired the title of "prince" at the age of fourteen.

Including the thirteen prime ministers, 166 individuals held ministerial portfolios in the techno-fascist cabinets. The modal minister was a fifty-eight-year-old male who had emerged from the upper echelons of the civil bureaucracy or was a general or admiral in the military branches. In other words, he was a technocrat who "advocated a new activist, goal-oriented approach toward government and paved the way for unprecedented state control of politics, private industry, and public services based on their vision of the 'managerial state'" (Mimura 2011, 9). Technocrats eschewed the undisciplined allocation of resources under a laissez-faire capitalist order, preferring state planning and a rational mobilization of labor, capital, and resources. Chances are the modal minister was an alumnus of Tokyo Imperial University. He was *not* an elected MP, and therefore had no meaningful connection to a political party, and very possibly originated in Japan's conservative and less-urbanized southwestern regions.

Ministers in the techno-fascist cabinets were a bit older and better edu-

Table 1.3. The Techno-Fascist Cabinets, 1932 to 1946

Cabinet	Prime Minister	Established	Dissolved	PM's Background
Saitō Cabinet	Saitō Makoto	5/26/1932	7/8/1934	Navy Admiral
Okada Cabinet	Okada Keisuke	7/8/1934	3/9/1936	Navy Admiral
Hirota Cabinet	Hirota Kōki	3/9/1936	2/2/1937	Diplomat
Hayashi Cabinet	Hayashi Senjurō	2/2/1937	6/4/1937	Army General
1st Konoe Cabinet	Konoe Fumimaro	6/4/1937	1/5/1939	Imperial Prince
Hiranuma Cabinet	Hiranuma Kiichirō	1/5/1939	8/30/1939	Nationalist Leader
Abe Cabinet	Abe Nobuyuki	8/30/1939	1/16/1940	Army General
Yonai Cabinet	Yonai Mitsumasa	1/16/1940	7/22/1940	Navy Admiral
2nd Konoe Cabinet	Konoe Fumimaro	7/22/1940	7/18/1941	Imperial Prince
3rd Konoe Cabinet	"	7/18/1941	10/18/1941	"
Tōjō Cabinet	Tōjō Hideki	10/18/1941	7/22/1944	Army General
Koiso Cabinet	Koiso Kuniaki	7/22/1944	4/7/1945	Army General
Suzuki (Kantarō) Cabinet	Suzuki Kantarō	4/7/1945	8/17/1945	Navy Admiral
Higashikuni Cabinet	Higashikuni Naruhiko	8/17/1945	10/9/1945	Army General
Shidehara Cabinet	Shidehara Kijurō	10/9/1945	5/22/1946	Diplomat

Source: JCCM Database (Appendix A).

cated than their predecessors. Novice ministers averaged fifty-six years of age, making them three years older than the previous ministerial cohort. Ninety-five percent of techno-fascist cabinet ministers were university educated, as opposed to only 60 percent of ministers in the party cabinets. Tokyo Imperial University was the alma mater to better than half of all ministers, while alumni of Kyoto University and Hitotsubashi University also began appearing on ministerial rosters. Together these three elite public universities educated more than 90 percent of the ex-career civil servants who held ministerial portfolios. Meanwhile, graduates of prominent private institutions, such as Waseda, Chūō, and Keiō universities began populating the cabinet elite, accounting for 9 percent of all ministers.

Former government officials and military officers accounted for three-quarters of the ministers. More than half of those who held portfolios were former government officials, the vast majority of whom (81 percent) shifted from upper bureaucratic posts into ministerial posts. A large number of ex-government officials fit the description of "reform bureaucrats," and many of them were groomed in the Home Ministry. They included Gotō Fumio, Yoshida Shigeru (not to be confused with the diplomat and post-war premier of the same name), Yasui Eiji, and Abe Genki. Aoki Kazuo, Hoshino Naoki, and Sakomizu Hisatsune emerged from the Finance Ministry, while Kishi Nobusuke and Ishiguro Tadaatsu were officials of the Ministry of Agriculture and Commerce. One-quarter of all ministers were products of the armed services, including twenty-one army men and eighteen navy men. Naturally, only generals or admirals were permitted to hold the respective army and navy ministers' portfolios, but this did not disqualify them from holding other "civilian" portfolios.

Elected MPs accounted for only 16 percent of ministers. This contrasts starkly with the state of affairs under the last four "party cabinets" (those that were formed between April 1927 and May 1932), in which elected MPs accounted for half of all ministers. While most techno-fascist cabinets boasted a few token MPs, the third Konoe cabinet included none. In other cases, the apparent presence of elected lawmakers holding ministerial portfolios is misleading. For example, the Seiyūkai expelled Tokonami Takejirō, Yamazaki Tatsunosuke, Uchida Shin'ya, and Mochizuki Keisuke for their willingness to assume ministerial posts in the Okada cabinet. Thus, only two of the twenty-two individuals who held portfolios in the Okada cabinet actually retained ties to political parties (Kanechika 1979, 80).

Competition in the Core

The techno-fascist cabinets operated in a core executive whose central actors included the elder statesmen, Emperor Hirohito and his chief advisers, the Privy Council, "reform bureaucrats," and "control officers." "The Cabinet, and hence the civil government," observed former prime minister Konoe Fumimaro in his memoirs, "were manipulated like puppets by the Supreme Command and amounted to little more than weak fixtures" (Maxon 1957, 182). Despite the gains they made during the era of quasi-party cabinets, the relative influence of the political parties and elected MPs declined.

Following Inukai's assassination, the status of political parties plummeted from that of "full-fledged members of the 'political establishment'" to that of organizations holding only a "feeble but persistent role in the

Diet" (Berger 1977, vii; Colegrove 1936b, 58). Beginning in 1940, political parties dissolved themselves and were absorbed into the monolithic
government-sponsored Imperial Rule Assistance Parliamentarians League
(*Yokusan giin dōmei*), which was supplanted in April 1942 by the Imperial
Rule Assistance Political Association (*Taisei yokusan seiji kai,* or IRAPA).
As a result of the 1942 general elections, 381 of 466 IRAPA-endorsed candidates were elected. One of those who dared to go against the flow was
future prime minister Hatoyama Ichirō, who was reelected as an independent. (Unfortunately for Hatoyama, this did not absolve him from the
right-wing purge carried out under the U.S. occupation in 1946.) In this
climate, aspiring cabinet ministers had little choice but to abandon sometimes long-standing partisan allegiances to jump on the IRAPA's bandwagon.[37] Indeed, from this point on, the primary *raison d'être* of parties
was to support unanimously any and all cabinet-sponsored bills (Berger
1977, 351). In the minds of many Japanese citizens, party cabinets were
synonymous with corruption, government immobilism, and dangerously
misguided policies.

Extra-constitutional imperial advisers and the Privy Council continued to shape executive affairs. As the elder statesmen (*genrō*) passed away,
they were replaced by a group of "senior statesmen" (*jūshin*). Indeed, after
1924, only one genrō, Saionji Kinmochi, remained. Like the genrō, the
jūshin were an extra-constitutional and self-appointed group whose major
function was to recommend candidates for the premiership (Tomita et al.
1981, 236). The senior statesmen included former prime ministers, the
Privy Council president, and the lord keeper of the privy seal. Although
Saionji—the last of the genrō—was consulted in prime ministerial selec-
tions until he passed away in 1940, his influence began to wane in the late
1920s, and prime ministerial candidates generally were selected through
jūshin consultations (Bix 2000, 174). Meanwhile, Privy Council approval
was required for any major departure in legislation, diplomacy, or modification of the organization or powers of the government (Samuels 2003,
57). In addition, appointments made by imperial ordinance required the
council's stamp of approval (Quigley 1932, 92). Three of the Privy Council's
seven presidents who served from 1932 through 1947—Hiranuma, Konoe,
and Suzuki—went on to become prime ministers (Kanechika 1979; Uzawa
1981).

As divine-right sovereign and commander in chief of the armed forces,
the Shōwa emperor was, at least in theory, Japan's supreme executive officer.

Hirohito was twenty-five years old when he assumed the Chrysanthemum Throne, yet he had been the de facto monarch since 1921, when he became regent to his mentally and physically infirm father. Because of the shroud of secrecy surrounding the imperial institution, it is unlikely that we will ever know the full extent of the emperor's involvement in executive affairs or that of his closest imperial court advisers. Yet it is known that Hirohito was involved in the appointment of at least three prime ministers— Saitō, Yonai, and Tōjō—and made his feelings known in other ministerial appointments and executive decisions (Bix 2000, 253, 355, 418). Members of the private palace cabinet—in particular the lord keeper of the privy seal (*Naidaijin*)—influenced executive affairs (Byas 1942, 106). Beginning with the selection of Konoe to succeed Hayashi as premier in June 1937, the lord keeper of the privy seal assumed the role of "ever-vigilant attendant" (*tsunemachi hōhistu*) in soliciting the views of the genrō and, later, the jūshin in selecting candidates for the premiership (Uzawa 1981, 92).

A new breed of government official—the "reform bureaucrat" (*kakushin kanryō*) or "new bureaucrat" (*shinkanryō*)—emerged. Many of these technocrats honed their planning skills in postings to the Cabinet Planning Board or as colonial administrators to the puppet state of Manchukuo. Their leaders included the aforementioned Kishi Nobusuke and Hoshino Naoki, as well as Ayukawa Yoshisuke (Nissan *zaibatsu*), Matsuoka Yōsuke (Foreign Affairs Ministry), and General Tōjō Hideki (Mimura 2011, 3, 14; Lu 2002, 123–125). The reform bureaucrats—who began to assume ministerial portfolios as early as July 1934 with the formation of the Okada cabinet—used the Cabinet Planning Board and other superagencies to impose their will in economic planning and to force the Diet to ratify their policies (Mimura 2011, 20; Shiota 2011, 106). In fact, 98 percent (1,031) of the 1,048 laws enacted between 1933 and 1946 originated as cabinet-sponsored bills, which were initiated and drafted by government bureaucrats. For five consecutive years beginning in 1939, the Diet dutifully passed every cabinet-sponsored bill submitted to it. In addition, bureaucrats continued to incrementally shape policy through the issuance of imperial ordinances, which did not require Diet approval. From 1933 through 1946, more than ten thousand such ordinances were issued.

Finally, the military branches represented a "state within a state," and the "high command was, in effect, the government of Japan" (Lederer 1934, 377; Falk 1961, 505). In the words of a Japanese journalist of the day, "Our soldiers of the sea, land, and air forces stand outside the pale of contemptible politics. They are responsible directly to the Emperor, in no sense obligated to heed the barkings of the Diet or the snobberies of the Administration" (Akimoto 1933, 25). The army and navy ministers continued to enjoy the right of "direct access" to the throne, and only active-duty generals and admirals were permitted to hold the military portfolios. This meant that the respective service branches, *not* the prime minister, were responsible for appointing their ministers. This gave the armed forces a life-and-death hold over any cabinet, and, as noted by a Japanese observer of the day, "when military circles, the Army in particular, come to the conclusion that a Ministry should go, it goes" (Sekiguchi 1938, 10; also Colegrove 1936b, 23).

Yet the Imperial Army was factionalized. In fact, the rise of the reform bureaucrats had been paralleled by the emergence of "reform officers" (*kakushin bakuryō*), who believed that military power was a function of the industrial capacity of a nation to produce the weapons and supplies required by a mechanized army (Crowley 1962, 325–326; Mimura 2011, 17). Many of them served tours of duty in Manchuria, where they came to understand economic planning and the need to cooperate with the government and the *zaibatsu*, the industrial and financial conglomerates that controlled significant parts of the prewar and wartime economy (Johnson 1982, 124; Mimura 2011, 16, 55). They tended to gravitate to the "Control faction" (*tōsei-ha*)—or "Staff Officers' faction" (*bakuryō-ha*)—which looked to Nazi Germany for inspiration. In contrast, the "Imperial Way faction" (*kōdō-ha*) "religiously espoused the principles of *kokutai*" and emphasized the "spiritual power" of Japanese military culture over mechanization, mass mobilization, and economic planning (Crowley 1962, 310, 314; Bix 2000, 244).

This factionalism came to its most violent expression in the February 26, 1936, uprising, in which young officers with ties to the Imperial Way faction led fourteen hundred troops in seizing the National Diet Building and other government offices.[38] They assassinated the finance minister, the lord keeper of the privy seal, and the inspector general of military education. Prime Minister Okada narrowly escaped the death squad, which mistakenly murdered his look-alike brother-in-law instead. The rebels refused to stand down until the emperor ordered them to do so three days later (Shillony 1973, 184–185). Death sentences were delivered to seventeen conspirators, and prison terms to fifty-one others, while eighteen high-ranking generals—the core leaders of the Imperial Way faction—were forced to resign their posts to atone for the serious breach of military discipline (Shillony 1973, 51; Crowley 1962, 324–325). This created a power vacuum that members of the Control faction filled.

The Consequences of the Failed Gamble

The technocrats and fascists who assumed the executive helm following Inukai's assassination were convinced that Japan's future was best ensured through centralized planning, the rational mobilization of resources, and concerted efforts to enhance the unique national essence. To construct this total state, the techno-fascists endeavored to stifle dissent and eradicate parliamentary institutions that bred divisiveness, greed, corruption, and misguided policies. As a result, the once obstreperous people's parties meekly dissolved themselves and melded into the monolithic Imperial Rule Assistance Parliamentarians League. At the same time, new superagencies such as the Cabinet Planning Board brought together reform bureaucrats and control officers in the cause of central state planning, which further marginalized elected politicians (Samuels 2003, 144). The techno-fascist cabinets were part of a corporatist state structure dominated by senior statesmen, the Privy Council, the emperor and his private palace cabinet, and, especially, the career civil service and the military high command. These captains of the state forged "mobilization" laws, enforced "thought control" to ensure compliance, and turned a blind eye as the Kwantung Army unilaterally made foreign policy by the sword.

The decision taken in February 1933 to walk out of the League of Nations when that body refused to recognize Japanese control of Manchuria symbolized the rejection of an international institutional order that served to maintain the dominant—and, in the minds of the techno-fascists, hypocritical—position of the Western imperialist powers. In response, Japan set up puppet states and otherwise endeavored to impede the unification of China, while establishing a zone of control that eventually extended southward until it crashed into French, Dutch, and British colonies. When the Americans called for an embargo of fuel and critical raw materials, Japan's supposedly rational techno-fascist political leaders took the risky gamble of launching a surprise attack on the United States and establishing an empire across a vast expanse of East Asia and the Pacific. Less than four years after the raid on Pearl Harbor, the Japanese war machine and most of its major cities had been reduced to ashes.

FINDINGS

The uninvited visit of a small American naval squadron set the stage for the Meiji Restoration, a critical juncture in the evolution of Japan's central state executive. As early as 1871, proto-cabinets emerged within the Grand Council, which provided a ready-made set of organizational structures, institutions, and personnel to staff the central state executive. The Sat-Chō oligarchs who dominated the core executive had a strong preference for transcendental cabinets and a deep disdain for political parties and popular democracy. Because cabinets and state ministers were not responsible to the Diet, there was no norm of collective responsibility. On the contrary, ministers were *individually* responsible to a sovereign emperor, who was under no obligation to heed the advice they proffered. In sum, the Sat-Chō cabal went to great lengths to design a central state executive that was *anti-*Westminsterian.

At the outset of the 1920s, an American scholar observed that the cabinet seemed headed toward becoming responsible to the lower house, at least inasmuch as "the incessant and marked dislike of the lower house to a particular ministry . . . usually resulted in the long run in its downfall" (McGovern 1920, 109). Indeed, by the late 1920s it seemed that this first attempt at parliamentary democracy was about to bear fruit. As Princeton-educated diplomat and future MP Kitazawa Naokichi optimistically observed, while "the Constitution expressly provides for the individual responsibility of Cabinet Ministers . . . the establishment of a quasi-party Cabinet system or pure party Cabinet system" had progressed to a point at which "the collective responsibility of the Cabinet . . . is almost established" (1929, 54).

The techno-fascist cabinets that took charge in the aftermath of the May 15th Incident reinforced the structures of the *anti-*Westminster system. Under pressure from a mushrooming ultranationalist movement with a fascist coloration, the once-active political parties dissolved themselves and melded into the monolithic "official" government party. Naturally, the techno-fascist cabinets bore no responsibility to the Diet, collective or otherwise, and ministers remained individually responsible to the divine-right emperor. While these cabinets responded with alacrity to the challenges of mobilizing for total war and building a "new structure" at home and a "new order" in East Asia, the end result was total defeat, unconditional surrender, and military occupation.

So it was that the stage was set for the arrival of an American-led military occupation. General Douglas MacArthur became the "indisputable overlord of occupied Japan, and his underlings functioned as petty viceroys" (Dower 1999, 205). The shock of total defeat, unconditional surrender, and occupation by a foreign army created conditions for a dramatic institutional reconfiguration. In fact, the reforms enacted under the American occupation proved to be every bit as sweeping as those brought forth by the Meiji Restoration (ibid., 205). Nevertheless, the "old" was not entirely swept away by the "new," as institutions, structures, leaders, and ideas forged under the techno-fascist cabinets carried on and shaped the Westminster-style system erected under the American occupation.

2

Comprador Cabinets and Democracy by the Sword, 1946–1955

The national government of Great Britain today is controlled by the
Cabinet, who, indeed, are His Majesty's servants, but for all normal
purposes servants whose advice the King must accept, and readily does
accept.
—Arthur Berriedale Keith, *The British Cabinet System,*
1830–1938 (1939), 1

For all practical purposes, General MacArthur's supergovernment relied
on the Japanese bureaucracy to carry out its directives, creating in effect
a two-tiered mandarinate.
—John W. Dower, *Embracing Defeat* (1999), 27

DEMOCRACY IMPOSED

When the Shidehara cabinet resigned on May 22, 1946, it was expected
that Hatoyama Ichirō, leader of the largest party in the House of Representatives, would become prime minister. But as Hatoyama was preparing
to make his way to the Imperial Palace to receive his appointment, word
arrived that he had been purged on orders from General Headquarters,
which was carrying out the American-led occupation's policy of removing
former militarists from public office. Hatoyama turned over the reins of
party leadership to Yoshida Shigeru, a retired career diplomat, who promised to vacate the party's leadership position upon Hatoyama's eventual
return to public office. But Yoshida occupied the premiership for the better part of the next eight and a half years, during which time he acquired

the sobriquet "One-Man Yoshida" (*wan man Yoshida*) for his autocratic leadership style. Even when Hatoyama returned to public life and won a seat in the October 1952 general elections, Yoshida refused to step aside. So Hatoyama took the helm of a rival party, and for the next two years the rivalry between the two men played itself out on Japan's political stage. Finally, on December 10, 1954, when a corruption scandal forced Yoshida to resign, Hatoyama's dream of becoming prime minister came true.

The period from May 1946 through November 1955 witnessed an institutional reconfiguration as sweeping as Japan's 1868 Meiji Restoration. During much of this time Japan was governed by an American-led military dictatorship. To assess the extent to which cabinet government became established during the period, I examine the background characteristics of the first cohort of postwar prime ministers and cabinet ministers. Because they acted as intermediaries between the occupation authorities and the Japanese body politic, these ministers played a role similar to that of the nineteenth-century comprador merchants who served as "indispensible go-betweens" between Chinese and foreigners (Hsu 1983, 146).[1] The Chinese compradors played a variety of roles, including that of on-the-ground managers for foreign firms, middlemen in the company's dealings with the Chinese, and negotiators in talks with foreign powers. Some compradors became extremely wealthy and influential (Hao 1970, 446, 454). Because of his ability to communicate with and sometimes manipulate the American military occupiers, Yoshida Shigeru was the quintessential comprador prime minister (Pyle 1996b, 21).[2] As a former U.S. occupation official observed many years later, "to be the sole Japanese source of information on MacArthur's views was a powerful weapon in Yoshida's hands, which he used often and effectively" (Finn 1992, 212). In addition, diplomats posted to the Central Liaison Office played a critical role in intermediating between the Japanese government and occupation authorities.

I then assess the major institutional changes wrought under the comprador cabinets and seek to determine whether or not cabinets came to play their expected role as the foremost executive organ in a parliamentary system of governance. Afterward, I evaluate the ability of cabinets to adapt to important internal and external challenges. But I begin by surveying the efforts of the American occupiers—the foreign mandarinate—who dictated, encouraged, and inspired an array of institutional changes, including some revolutionary departures.

Planning for Occupation

In reality, the "Allied occupation" of Japan was an American operation. It began on August 28, 1945, with the deplaning of forty-two hundred paratroopers of the U.S. 11th Airborne Division at Atsugi Airfield. It ended on April 28, 1952, with the formal restoration of sovereignty according to the terms of the San Francisco Peace Treaty. From start to finish, the occupation lasted 2,435 days—more than six years and eight months—and it had been under way for nearly nine months when Yoshida formed his first cabinet. American planning for the anticipated occupation of a defeated Japan had begun in early 1942, even as Japanese forces continued to rack up victories on the battlefield. The initial planning was undertaken by a small group of diplomats and academic specialists in the State Department, but, as the tide of the war turned in favor of the Allied side, the group expanded to include officials from the Navy and War Departments. This planning group evolved into the State-War-Navy Coordinating Committee (SWNCC, pronounced "swink"), which began meeting in December 1944.

While SWNCC's planners plotted policy for postwar Japan, U.S. president Harry S. Truman, British prime minister Winston Churchill (later replaced by Clement Attlee), and Soviet leader Joseph Stalin met at Potsdam, a suburb of Berlin, to decide on the terms of surrender. On July 26, 1945, Chinese leader Ch'iang Kai-shek joined Truman and Churchill in issuing the Potsdam Declaration, which demanded Japan's unconditional surrender and called on its government to "remove all obstacles to the revival and strengthening of democratic tendencies among the Japanese people." Failure to do so, the declaration assured, would result in Japan's "prompt and utter destruction." The declaration drew heavily on a paper written a year earlier by George H. Blakeslee and Hugh Borton, a pair of State Department officials who were members of SWNCC (McNelly 1959, 176). Blakeslee, a Harvard-trained professor of history and international relations at Clark University, was regarded as one of America's foremost authorities on the foreign relations of East Asia (Janssens 1995, 65).[3] Borton was a historian at Columbia University who spoke Japanese and had lived in Tokyo during some tumultuous times in the late 1920s and 1930s (Borton 2002, 18, 43, 68).

SWNCC's Subcommittee on the Far East was tasked with drawing up a comprehensive statement of America's postwar policy for Japan. After various iterations and amendments, "SWNCC 228" was finalized on

November 27 and forwarded to the Joint Chiefs of Staff for comment. The document was drafted primarily by Borton, who later described the project as the "most important single undertaking" of his life (Borton 2002, 163). SWNCC 228 states that "though the ultimate form of government in Japan is to be established by the freely expressed will of the Japanese people, the retention of the Emperor institution in its present form is not considered consistent with [Allied] objectives." In the event that the Japanese people were to choose to retain the emperor, therefore, certain safeguards would be required. According to SWNCC 228, such safeguards would include constitutional provisions that (1) cabinet ministers must be civilian and chosen with the advice and consent of a democratically elected legislature to which the cabinet would be collectively responsible; (2) a cabinet must either resign or appeal to the electorate when it loses the confidence of the representative legislative body; and (3) the emperor would be deprived of all military authority and would act only on the advice of the cabinet. The authors of SWNCC 228 advised that it should appear that the Japanese themselves had taken the lead in these reforms, "as the knowledge that they had been imposed by the Allies would materially reduce the possibility of their acceptance and support by the Japanese people for the future."

SWNCC 228 became the party line at the State Department and GHQ. On October 4, George Atcheson, a State Department "China hand" dispatched to Tokyo to advise MacArthur, telegraphed Washington asking for guidance in revising Japan's constitution. Secretary of State James F. Byrnes responded with an outline of specific constitutional safeguards organized into two groups, depending on whether or not the imperial institution was to be retained (Borton 1966, 206; McNelly 1959, 179–180). Atcheson pressed the message in a series of conversations with former premier Konoe Fumimaro, at the time a minister without portfolio in the Higashikuni cabinet, who was sounding out occupation officials prior to proposing his own draft constitution (McNelly 1959, 178–179; Masumi 1985, 48). Likewise, on December 6, Lieutenant Colonel Milo Rowell, an official in GHQ's Government Section, submitted his "Report of Preliminary Studies and Recommendations of Constitution." Among other things, Rowell called for the elimination of extra-constitutional bodies having access to the emperor and proposed "that the cabinet, being the ministers of state and responsible heads of the various executive departments, must be composed of elected representatives; must be answerable to the house and dissolve on vote of no confidence" (NDL "Birth" 3-5). In other words, the American planners proposed to create a Westminster-style cabinet system.

GHOSTWRITTEN CONSTITUTION

On September 18, a little more than two weeks after Japan's formal surrender, Prime Minister Higashikuni Naruhiko told foreign press correspondents that his cabinet had more pressing concerns to worry about than writing a new constitution.[4] Regardless, the Higashikuni cabinet did not survive long enough to take any meaningful action even if it had wanted to. Higashikuni's replacement, Shidehara Kijūrō, met with General MacArthur on October 11 and attempted to convince the Supreme Commander that democracy could be achieved without revising the 1890 Meiji Constitution (McNelly 1959, 182; Amakawa 1995, 21). MacArthur strongly disagreed, and two days later Shidehara obligingly appointed Matsumoto Jōji as minister of state with responsibility for investigating the *possibility* of constitutional revision. Matsumoto would chair the Constitutional Problems Investigation Committee (*Kenpō mondai chōsakai*), whose name was intentionally chosen to avoid mention of "revision" or "amendment" (Dower 1999, 351). Matsumoto spoke openly about the deficiencies of "government by the people" (Borton 1955, 402).

The Matsumoto committee was composed of academicians, Privy Council officers, and officials of the Legislation Bureau. In addition to Matsumoto himself, the academic specialists included Minobe Tatsukichi, Nomura Junji, Miyazawa Tsuyoshi, Kiyomiya Shirō, Kawamura Matasuke, Gyōbu Tadashi, and Satō Isao. All of the academics had ties to Tokyo Imperial University except Kiyomiya (Tōhoku Imperial University) and Kawamura (Kyūshū Imperial University). Interestingly, Matsumoto was an expert in commercial law, not constitutional law, as might be expected, and had served as a high-ranking official in the South Manchuria Railway Company and as director general of the organizational predecessor of the Legislation Bureau. Minobe was a constitutional law theorist who, in 1935, had been fired from his university professorship and driven from his seat in the House of Peers for suggesting that the divine-right emperor was merely an "organ" of the state. Yet Minobe shared Matsumoto's view that there was no need to rush to revise the Meiji Constitution, especially while the country was under a foreign military occupation, or to feel any compulsion to alter the status of the "sacred and inviolable" emperor (Dower 1999, 355). Two committee members, Shimizu Tōru and Ishiguro Takeshige, were recruited from the Privy Council, an extra-constitutional body with veto power over major legislative proposals, treaties, and proposed changes in the structure or powers of government. The remaining members were Legislation Bureau officials Narahashi Wataru, Irie Toshio, and Satō Tatsuo.

The Matsumoto committee met for the first time on October 27 and held a total of twenty-two confidential meetings over the course of the next three months (Dower 1999, 352). On January 31 the committee completed work on a draft document entitled "Outline for a Revised Constitution" (*kenpō kaisei yōkō*). In fact, this "Matsumoto draft" (*Matsumoto shian*) was the more liberal of two drafts the committee was preparing. On that day, Nishiyama Ryūzō, a reporter for *Mainichi Shimbun,* noticed an open door to the room in which the committee was holding its secret meeting. Venturing inside, he discovered that committee members had departed for lunch but had left binders containing the draft constitution on the table. Nishiyama "borrowed" one of the binders, scurried back to his office to have it hand-copied, and was able to return it to the meeting room before the committee reconvened (ibid., 359). The following day, the *Mainichi Shimbun* published the Matsumoto draft verbatim under the headline "Establishing Monarchism" (*kunshushugi o kakuritsu*). This touched off speculation that the newspaper's scoop was in reality a "trial balloon" sent up by Foreign Minister Yoshida Shigeru to gauge reaction to a revised constitution (ibid.). As it turned out, the story behind the newspaper scoop remained a mystery for nearly half a century, until Nishiyama confessed to his stealthy reporting (Inoue 1991, 12 n. 3).

American occupation officials were flabbergasted to learn that the Matsumoto committee proposed to construct a new, "democratic" Japan on a foundation of warmed-over imperial sovereignty.[5] Brigadier General Courtney Whitney, chief of the GHQ's Government Section (GS), sent a translation of the Matsumoto draft to MacArthur. In an accompanying memorandum, Whitney commented that "the draft is extremely conservative in character and leaves substantially unchanged the status of the Emperor, with all the rights of sovereignty vested in him" (NDL "Birth" 3-7). The warmed-over nature of the Matsumoto draft leaps out in various articles, including those that set forth the powers and responsibilities of the cabinet. For example, much of the language in Article 55 had been cut and pasted from the Meiji Constitution—specifically, the clauses stating that "every minister of state shall give his advice to the Emperor and be responsible for it" and that "all Laws, Imperial Ordinances, and Imperial Rescripts of whatever kind, that relate to the affairs of the state, require the countersignature of a Minister of State."

MacArthur was displeased with the Matsumoto committee's efforts. Anticipating a negative response from the Supreme Commander, Whitney had taken the liberty of rescheduling a meeting set with Foreign Minister Yoshida. In a memo to MacArthur, Whitney explained, "I could foresee the reactionary group carrying the ball on constitutional reform were way off the beam to what you could agree to." Whitney reasoned that it was "better strategy to orient them [the Shidehara cabinet] before the formal submission of a draft than to wait and force them to start from scratch once an unacceptable draft had been submitted and to which they were committed." MacArthur ordered Whitney to produce a document to serve as a model for the Japanese side. To assist in its preparation, the Supreme Commander provided a memorandum listing three basic points: (1) that the "Emperor is at the head of state," but that his duties and powers will be exercised according to the Constitution and the "basic will" of the people; (2) "war as a sovereign right of the nation is abolished"; and (3) "the feudal system of Japan will cease," meaning that other than those of the Imperial family, the privileges of peerage would no longer exist. At the bottom of the memorandum, unnumbered and without commentary, the Supreme Commander inserted the cryptic phrase "pattern budget after British system" (NDL "Birth" 3-10).

On February 5, 1946, Whitney assembled a group of twenty-five American military officers, civilian attachés, researchers, secretaries, and interpreters and tasked them with drafting a model constitution for Japan (Gibney 1996). He informed the group that a draft should be ready for review by MacArthur by February 12 (Dower 1999, 361). The rush job was necessary to deliver a *fait accompli* to the Far Eastern Commission (discussed below), which would give control of the occupation to America's allies (Buckley 1978, 566). Colonel Charles L. Kades was placed in charge of the Constitution Steering Committee, the cockpit of this "constitutional convention," which held its meetings "under the cover of absolute secrecy" in the ballroom of the Dai-Ichi Mutual Life Insurance Building. A Harvard Law graduate, Kades worked as private practice attorney and as assistant general counsel to two U.S. government agencies before being called to active military duty. The Constitution Steering Committee's other members included Lieutenant Milo E. Rowell, Commander Alfred R. Hussey, and Ruth Ellerman. Rowell was a Stanford-trained lawyer who fought in the Philippines before becoming chief of the Judicial Affairs Office at GHQ, Hussey was a University of Virginia Law School graduate who worked as a lawyer and judge before joining the navy, and Ellerman was the committee's scribe (Koseki 1997, 81–82; Moore and Robinson 2002, 96–97).

"Before I arrived," Kades later confessed, "I knew nothing about Japan except that which one would glean from a local American newspaper." He added, "I don't think any of us had any idea what the British [budget] system was" and any resemblance GHQ's draft articles had to it could only have been "purely coincidental" (Gibney 1996). For inspiration, the GS team studied the Constitution of the United States and various European constitutions, copies of which had been stealthily gathered from various Tokyo area libraries so as to not attract attention. In addition, the GS team took special account of SWNCC 228, MacArthur's three basic principles, and a document that had been prepared by the Constitution Investigation Association, a private Japanese group (NDL "Birth" 3-10 and 2-16).[6]

Whitney divided his GS team into seven committees, with responsibilities for drafting specific articles on civil rights, local government, finance, and the roles and responsibilities of the emperor, legislature, judiciary, and executive. Cyrus H. Peake was tapped to chair the executive committee, whose members included Jacob I. Miller and First Lieutenant Milton J. Esman. As it turned out, members of the committee did not always see eye to eye, and a disagreement between Peake and Esman threatened to delay completion of the draft. Peake was a professor of Chinese history at Columbia University, where he and Hugh Borton had coedited the *Far Eastern Quarterly*, while Esman had just earned a Ph.D. in politics from Princeton University before service in the army led him to a post as a civil affairs officer in GHQ's Government Section. The two butted heads on the question of whether or not the prime minister should have the authority to dissolve the Diet. Peake believed that the prime minister should not be empowered to dissolve except when the Diet passed a no-confidence vote or rejected a vote of confidence. Esman argued that the prime minister should also be empowered to dissolve the Diet when it defeated the government's "major legislation." He feared that Peake's proposal, which was supported by the Constitution Steering Committee, would reproduce "the very weakest feature of French experience" by inducing the prime minister to resign "while denying him any bargaining power in cases of disagreement with the Diet" (NDL "Birth" 3-14). In the end, only Peake affixed his signature to the committee's draft report, while Esman and Miller expressed their dissenting views in an attached memorandum.[7] Both documents were forwarded to the Constitution Steering Committee.

On February 10, GHQ's "constitutional convention" produced a draft that was warmly received by MacArthur. Three days later, Whitney—accompanied by Constitution Steering Committee members Kades, Rowell, and Hussey—set off for the rescheduled meeting with Yoshida, who, along with Matsumoto, welcomed them at the foreign minister's official residence. When the American entourage arrived, it was apparent that the Japanese officials had been poring over the Matsumoto draft, which was, Whitley wasted no time in saying, "wholly unacceptable to the Supreme Commander as a document of freedom and democracy" (Dower 1999, 374). He refused to accept the Matsumoto draft and asked Yoshida and Matsumoto to examine and discuss the GHQ draft, a copy of which he handed them. Whitney and his aides then retired to the garden while Matsumoto and Yoshida scrutinized the document. About fifteen minutes later, Shirasu Jirō, Yoshida's aide and an adviser to the Central Liaison Office, ventured into the garden and apologized for keeping the Americans waiting, to which Whitney replied, "We are out here enjoying the warmth of atomic energy" (NDL "Birth" 3-16). As Whitney later recalled, "at that moment, with what could not have been better timing, a big B-29 came roaring over us" (Whitney 1956, 251).

After returning to the patio where Matsumoto and Yoshida were waiting, Whitney explained that prompt acceptance of the GHQ draft was the only hope for the "conservative group, considered by many to be reactionary," to remain in power (NDL "Birth" Hussey Paper-2). He went on, "The Supreme Commander is determined that the people of Japan shall be free to choose between this Constitution and any form of Constitution which does not embody these principles" (NDL "Birth" 3-16). Three weeks later, on February 26, the Shidehara cabinet decided to draft a revised constitution based on the basic principles laid out in the GHQ draft. Matsumoto was given charge of the project.

Cabinet-Related Provisions

A provisional draft constitution was completed on March 2. While the draft clearly drew heavily on the handiwork of General Whitney's "constitutional convention," the Japanese side was able to obtain modifications. As time would tell, perhaps the most important of these was the Japanese side's insistence on a bicameral Diet instead of the unicameral body called for in the GHQ draft (Yoshida 1962, 134; Dower 1999, 378). By requiring that both chambers approve all laws and treaties as well as the national budget and prime ministerial appointments, Matsumoto and his colleagues were, presumably unwittingly, laying the foundation for the Twisted Diets (*nejire kokkai*) that would produce policy stalemate decades later. The repercussions of a Diet in which the ruling party in the lower house did not control the upper house are discussed beginning in chapter 4.

On March 6, the Shidehara cabinet announced the "Outline of a Draft for a Revised Constitution" (*Kenpō kaisei soan*), which was subsequently rewritten in language that the average Japanese citizen could understand. Beginning in early April, Irie Toshio and Satō Tatsuo—the director and deputy director of the Legislation Bureau—and Katō Ren of the Central Liaison Office took the lead in consulting with GHQ officials to determine the extent to which the Americans would permit modifications. In the meantime, GHQ brushed aside the demands of the Far Eastern Commission—theoretically the supreme organ for supervision of occupation policy—that it be allowed to approve the proposed constitution. On April 22, the draft constitution was submitted to the Privy Council for review; a little less than two months later, the Council sent it on to the Imperial Diet. As a result of discussion in the Diet, about thirty additional modifications were incorporated into a final draft constitution (Dower 1999, 392). On October 7, the Diet approved the Constitution of Japan, which was promulgated on November 3 and went into effect in May 1947.

It is instructive to compare the cabinet-related provisions of the GHQ draft with those of the 1947 Constitution. Both documents are subdivided into eleven chapters, with the fifth chapter devoted to matters specifically related to "The Cabinet." Chapter 5 in the GHQ draft is subdivided into eight articles, while the corresponding chapter in the Constitution is made up of eleven articles. Twenty-one articles in the GHQ draft mention the "cabinet," "prime minister," and "ministers of state," while twenty-three articles in the Constitution do so. These cabinet-related articles appear under the same chapter rubrics in each document—"The Emperor" (chapter 1), "The Diet" (4), "The Cabinet" (5), "Judiciary" (6), and "Finance" (7).

Eighteen of the twenty-three cabinet-related articles in the Constitution were essentially cut and pasted from the GHQ draft. In fact, fourteen of the cabinet-related articles in the Constitution are almost verbatim reproductions of material in the GHQ draft. For example, Article 60 of the GHQ draft states that "Executive power shall be vested in the Cabinet," while Article 65 in the Constitution simply substitutes "is" for "shall be."[8] Article 73 of the Constitution lists the same seven "other administrative functions" to be performed by the cabinet in the precise order given in Article 65 of the GHQ draft—that is, to administer the law, manage foreign affairs, conclude treaties, administer the civil service, prepare the budget, enact cabinet orders, and decide on general amnesty. In addition, two articles in the Constitution involve minor revisions to the emperor's ceremonial powers. Article 6 of the Constitution grants the emperor power to "appoint the Chief Judge of the Supreme Court as designated by the Cabinet" (this ceremonial power is not granted in the GHQ draft), while Article 7 gives the monarch power to attest to the "instruments of ratification and other diplomatic documents as provided for by law" (the GHQ draft is mute on this matter). In other words, it is fair to say that three-quarters of the cabinet-related articles in the Constitution were essentially lifted from the GHQ draft.[9]

Significant revisions were made to six cabinet-related articles. Article 53 of the Constitution specifies that the cabinet may call a special session of the Diet on petition of at least *one-quarter* of the members of either House chamber, as opposed to Article 48 of the GHQ draft, which requires the petition of not less than *20 percent* of MPs. Likewise, Article 54 permits the cabinet to convene a session of the House of Councillors in times of "national emergency," which, of course, would not have been necessary with the unicameral Diet envisioned in the GHQ draft. Article 67 stipulates that the designee of the lower house for the prime minister's post will be the decision of the Diet in the event that the two houses cannot agree on a prime minister and a joint committee is unable to resolve the matter. Even though the primacy of the lower house decision is made clear, this provision allows the upper house to impose a ten-day delay on the appointment of the lower house's designee for the prime ministership. Article 69 states that, in the event that the lower house passes a no-confidence motion or rejects a confidence motion, the cabinet will resign en masse unless the lower house is dissolved within ten days.

Three articles deal with the qualifications of the prime minister and ministers of state. Article 67 specifies that the prime minister "shall be designated from among the members of the Diet," while Article 68 specifies that a majority of cabinet ministers must be MPs. In this case, the authors of the GHQ draft seem to have assumed that these characteristic features of a Westminster-style parliamentary system could be taken for granted. An early version of the GHQ draft contains a passage in which it is stated that the prime minister is to be "the leader of the Majority party in the Diet or, failing a Majority party, such member of the Diet as is able to command a majority therein . . ." (NDL "Birth" 3-14). The MP qualification does not appear in either the GS subcommittee's proposal or the final version of the GHQ draft. A passage in Ellerman's notes states that "The Prime Minister, in turn, will select his Cabinet from either the majority party or a coalition of parties" (NDL "Birth" Hussey Papers-2). This seems to indicate that Kades and some GS officials assumed that the Diet would select the leader of the ruling party to be prime minister, and, therefore, it need not be specified in the Constitution.

Finally, the famous "civilian clause" in Article 66 was included as a result of pressure from America's allies. Despite the fact that the occupation was an American production, overall policy was, in theory, placed in the hands of the Far Eastern Commission (FEC), composed of delegates from the United States, the United Kingdom, the Soviet Union, China, Australia, New Zealand, Canada, the Netherlands, France, India, and the Philippines.[10] The FEC began meeting on February 26, 1946, and was almost immediately broadsided by the Shidehara cabinet's publication, on March 6, of the "Outline of a Draft for a Revised Constitution." FEC delegates believed that MacArthur had exceeded his authority in pressing the cabinet to produce a revised constitution and, in a letter dated March 20, made this known to Secretary of State Byrnes, who was instructed to relay the message to the Supreme Commander. On July 2, 1946, the FEC approved a document entitled "Basic Principles for a New Japanese Constitution," which included a provision stating that the prime minister and all members of the cabinet "shall be civilians" (NDL "Birth" 4-6). On August 19, Prime Minister Yoshida asked for and received MacArthur's permission to remove the provision on the grounds that Article 9, the "no war" clause, obviated the need to spell this out.[11] At an FEC meeting on September 21, the Chinese delegate, Dr. S. H. Tan, raised the possibility that the Diet might someday reinterpret Article 9 to permit the maintenance of land, sea, and air forces. The FEC members were not persuaded by the assurances of Hugh Borton, who served on the subcommittee charged with looking into the matter, that Article 9 provided a safeguard against the return of military figures to ministerial posts (NDL "Birth" 4-11; Stratton 1948, 8).[12]

In fact, a preliminary version of the GHQ draft stipulated that "the Ministers of State and Ministers without Portfolio . . . shall at all times be civilians" (NDL "Birth" 3-14). This qualification had been spelled out in SWNCC 228, Borton's handiwork, which stated that "although the authority and influence of the military in Japan's governmental structure will presumably disappear with the abolition of the Japanese armed forces, formal action permanently subordinating the military services to the civilian government by requiring that the ministers of state or members of the cabinet must, in all cases, be civilians would be advisable" (NDL "Birth" 3-2).

On September 25, the FEC requested a provision calling for all ministers of state to be civilians. General Whitney explained this to Yoshida, and the civilian clause was dutifully inserted into the constitution sent to the House of Peers subcommittee deliberating on the draft. However, there was a problem—no Japanese equivalent could be found for the term "civilian." After considering several options, the Peers invented a word, "*bunmin*" (literally, "person of letters"), to distinguish those whose primary tool of trade is the writing brush as opposed to the sword, and Article 66 came to state that "The Prime Minister and other Ministers of State must be civilians" (Lu 1997, 471).

THE COMPRADORS

The comprador cabinet minister was a new breed. Gone were the generals, admirals, and ultranationalist leaders who lorded over the techno-fascist cabinets. From this point on, each and every prime minister would be the leader of the largest party or ruling coalition in the Diet's lower house, and the vast majority of ministers would be elected MPs as well. In other words, precisely as the Westminster model prescribes, popularly elected representatives would almost monopolize ministerial appointments. Nevertheless, many comprador ministers would be retired government bureaucrats who had been fast-tracked into coveted ministerial posts, and a significant number of them were veterans of techno-fascist cabinets or other institutions of the totalitarian prewar order.

Prime Ministers and the Overlord

Yoshida Shigeru, Katayama Tetsu, Ashida Hitoshi, and Hatoyama Ichirō held the premiership in the twelve cabinets formed between May 1946 and

November 1955. The fifth Yoshida cabinet (which survived for 568 days) was the longest-lived of the comprador cabinets, while the first Hatoyama cabinet (99 days) was the era's most short-lived. Yoshida was prime minister in eight cabinet reshufflings over the course of seven years, while Katayama and Ashida headed up short-lived coalition cabinets. Hatoyama returned to political life to organize three cabinets, the third of which was formed after the creation of the Liberal Democratic Party. Nevertheless, while these Japanese premiers exercised governing authority from the Prime Minister's Official Residence, for five and a half years General Douglas MacArthur wielded sovereign power from his headquarters in the Dai-Ichi Mutual Life Insurance Building, reveling in his role as American overlord.

Yoshida Shigeru was a career diplomat whose most obvious qualifications for the premiership were his English language skills and the fact that he was arrested for opposing the wartime government. The son-in-law of prewar "senior statesman" Makino Nobuaki, Yoshida joined the Foreign Ministry after graduating from Tokyo Imperial University. His diplomatic postings took him to Manchuria, the Paris Peace Conference, Korea, Italy, and Great Britain. In February 1945, Yoshida was arrested by the "Thought Police" and briefly jailed for suggesting that Japan sue for peace to avoid a Communist revolution (Yoshida 1962, 24–30). The American occupiers viewed this as evidence that Yoshida was anti-militarist, and they were not troubled by his advanced age. In fact, Yoshida was sixty-seven years old at the time of Japan's surrender and had retired nearly a decade earlier. GHQ's decision to purge Hatoyama opened the door for Yoshida, who insisted on three conditions for assuming the premiership: that he not be required to raise campaign funds, that he could freely select cabinet ministers, and that he be allowed to quit anytime he wanted (ibid., 75; Itoh 2003, 105).[13] Despite the fact that Yoshida was not an elected MP when he became prime minister, he was given a significant leadership post in the Liberal Party and quickly became its president. Yoshida was elected to the lower house in May 1947, and his cabinet presided over the acceptance of the GHQ draft constitution. He was obliged to step down following the 1947 election, but returned to serve as prime minister from October 1948 until December 1954.

Katayama Tetsu and Ashida Hitoshi presided over coalition governments. Katayama was a Tokyo Imperial University-trained attorney who became interested in social democracy during the 1920s. He won election

Table 2.1. The Comprador Cabinets, 1946 to 1955

Cabinet	Prime Minister	Established	Dissolved	PM's Background
1st Yoshida Cabinet	Yoshida Shigeru	5/22/1946	5/24/1947	Ambassador to UK
Katayama Cabinet	Katayama Tetsu	5/24/1947	3/10/1948	Attorney; Christian
Ashida Cabinet	Ashida Hitoshi	3/10/1948	10/15/1948	Diplomat
2nd Yoshida Cabinet	Yoshida Shigeru	10/15/1948	2/16/1949	Ambassador to UK
3rd Yoshida Cabinet	"	2/16/1949	6/28/1950	"
Reorg'ed 3rd Yoshida (1) Cabinet	"	6/28/1950	7/4/1951	"
Reorg'ed 3rd Yoshida (2) Cabinet	"	7/4/1951	12/26/1951	"
Reorg'ed 3rd Yoshida (3) Cabinet	"	12/26/1951	10/30/1952	"
4th Yoshida Cabinet	"	10/30/1952	5/21/1953	"
5th Yoshida Cabinet	"	5/21/1953	12/10/1954	"
1st Hatoyama Cabinet	Hatoyama Ichirō	12/10/1954	3/19/1955	Career Politician
2nd Hatoyama Cabinet	"	3/19/1955	11/22/1955	"

Source: JCCM Database (Appendix A).

to the lower house in 1932, but was forced to vacate his seat in 1940 for refusing to vote to sanction fellow MP Saitō Takao, who criticized Japan's "holy war" in China in an address to the Diet. After the war, Katayama returned to the Diet and, when his Japan Socialist Party (*Nihon shakaitō,* or JSP) emerged from the 1946 lower house elections with a plurality of seats in that chamber, unexpectedly found himself in the position of having to put together a governing coalition. The Katayama cabinet was founded on a three-way coalition between the JSP, Democratic Party, and People's Cooperative Party. General MacArthur found spiritual implications in Katayama's selection, observing that "for the first time in its history, Japan is led by a Christian leader—one who throughout his life has been a member of the Presbyterian Church. It reflects the complete religious freedom which now dominates the Japanese mind and the complete religious freedom which exists throughout this land" (NDL "Modern" 5-9-2).[14]

Ashida Hitoshi, too, was a *Tōdai* alumnus, whose first career as a diplomat included postings to Russia, France, Turkey, and elsewhere. He resigned from the diplomatic corps in 1932 to protest the Japanese occupation of Manchuria and immediately launched a second career in elective politics (Duus and Hasegawa 2011, 92; Finn 1992, 148). After the war, Ashida became president of the Democratic Party and held important portfolios in the Katayama cabinet. In October 1948, after only seven months in office, the Ashida cabinet was brought down by the Shōwa Denkō bribery scandal (discussed below) and Ashida's implication in unrelated corruption charges. Ashida's ouster opened the door to the return of Yoshida, who occupied the premiership for the next six years.

Hatoyama Ichirō replaced Yoshida as prime minister in December 1954. The son of a former speaker of the House of Representatives, Hatoyama graduated from Tokyo Imperial University and practiced law before winning election to the Tokyo City Council in 1911. Four years later, he was elected to the first of fifteen lower house terms, and held portfolios in three prewar cabinets. In 1933, as education minister in the Saitō cabinet, Hatoyama fatefully ordered Takigawa Yukitoki to resign his law professorship at Kyoto Imperial University for espousing "leftist" views in two legal textbooks (Itoh 2003, 62). Hatoyama was one of a relatively small number of candidates to emerge victorious from the 1942 general elections *without* the endorsement of the Imperial Rule Assistance Political Association, the government's "official" party (ibid., 68). After the war, Hatoyama became president of the Japan Liberal Party and, in May 1946, was preparing to replace Shidehara as prime minister when GHQ designated him an "undesirable person." In addition to his actions as prewar education minister, Hatoyama earned the disapproval of occupation authorities for praising Hitler and Mussolini in a book he published after touring Europe in 1937 and 1938 (Yamamuro 1995, 95; Shiota 2011, 176). After his rehabilitation, Hatoyama won a lower house seat in the 1952 election, and, when Yoshida refused to step aside, became president of the rival Japan Democratic Party.

Prime ministers came and went, but General Douglas MacArthur remained the decisive actor from August 29, 1945, to April 11, 1951 (Finn 1992, 211). MacArthur was sixty-five years old, a recipient of the Congressional Medal of Honor, and a five-star general at the time of his appointment as Supreme Commander. The top graduate of his class at West Point, MacArthur was appointed Army Chief of Staff at fifty years of age, and, as a result of having spent a number of years in the Philippines, was convinced that he possessed unique insights into the "oriental mind." He arrived at

Atsugi Air Base on August 30, 1945, two days after U.S. troops alighted there, and set up a temporary headquarters in Yokohama. After receiving Japan's surrender on the USS *Missouri*, MacArthur moved his headquarters to the Dai-Ichi Mutual Life Insurance Building, a stone's throw from the Imperial Palace. By insisting that the emperor call on him rather than the other way around, the Supreme Commander ensured his absolute authority as the American viceroy. MacArthur would later become commander of United Nations forces during the Korean War, but would run afoul of U.S. president Harry S. Truman for making provocative statements about taking the war to China. MacArthur left Japan to a hero's departure on April 16, 1945, and was replaced by the less flamboyant General Matthew Ridgway.

Departmental Ministers

One hundred and twenty-four individuals held portfolios in the comprador cabinets. The modal minister was a fifty-nine-year-old lower house MP who represented a district outside the densely populated areas around Tokyo, Osaka, and Nagoya. There is a nine-in-ten chance that this modal minister attended university, most likely Tokyo Imperial University or Kyoto Imperial University. By constitutional dictate, this modal minister emerged from a "civilian" background, in contrast to the numerous generals and admirals who populated ministerial rosters in the techno-fascist cabinets. There is a good chance that *he*—alas, even though the 1947 Constitution gave women the right to vote and hold public office, the ministerial elite remained an exclusively male world—was a former high-ranking civil servant.

With the exception of the first Yoshida cabinet, whose ministers took up their portfolios before the 1947 Constitution went into effect, the vast majority of ministers were elected MPs. In contrast to the tiny fraction of techno-fascist cabinet ministers recruited from the prewar Diet's elective chamber, nine of every ten comprador cabinet ministers were elected MPs, and more than three-quarters of them occupied lower house seats. The average comprador minister had been elected to four lower house terms and had amassed a decade of parliamentary service, which indicates that a seniority system for cabinet ministers had yet to become established. This is the logical result of the influx of new faces in the Diet, and also of Yoshida's effort to fast-track (*batteki*) ex-bureaucrats and the occasional corporate figure into ministerial posts. For example, in October 1948 Yoshida suddenly summoned Izumiyama Sanroku, an ex-Mitsui Bank officer, to meet with him. Yoshida smiled and said little, but as Izumiyama was leaving Chief Cabinet Secretary Satō Eisaku whispered, "Yoshida is saying that he would like to organize a cabinet around you" (Masumi 1985, 279). The next evening Izumiyama learned he would become finance minister in the second Yoshida cabinet.[15]

Ex-bureaucrats accounted for 37 percent of ministers in the comprador cabinets. In fact, former bureaucrats were about the only experienced administrators in a setting in which nearly every prewar cabinet minister and senior military officer was deemed ineligible to hold public office. Among the former bureaucrats were Prime Ministers Shidehara, Yoshida, and Ashida, while others—such as Okazaki Katsuo (who left the vice minister post at the Ministry of Foreign Affairs for a succession of cabinet posts) and Ōhashi Takeo (an ex-upper official at the Home Ministry who went on to direct the "red purge" as justice minister in the fourth Yoshida cabinet)—assumed coveted portfolios. At the same time, "career politicians" such as Hatoyama, who approached elective politics as a lifelong calling, represented only about one-quarter of cabinet ministers. In fact, only about one in five comprador ministers emerged from local elective office or from positions as MPs' staff assistants, the traditional pathways for aspiring grassroots politicians.

ORGANIZATIONAL UPHEAVAL

The organizational structure of the cabinet system was transformed under the comprador cabinets. Twenty-seven new cabinet-level ministries and agencies were created, while twenty-two others were abolished. On the day it left office, the Shidehara cabinet was composed of fourteen ministers holding a total of fifteen portfolios. By the time the second Hatoyama cabinet exited the stage nine and a half years later, twenty portfolios were distributed among eighteen ministers. This represents the most dramatic period of institutional reconfiguration since the modern cabinet system was established in 1885. The most enduring changes involved the dismantling of the mighty Home Ministry, whose multifarious functions were transferred to a number of new and reconstituted ministries and agencies. Yet, when the dust settled on this breathtaking burst of institutional reconfiguration, the legacy of the undemocratic prewar order continued to be evident.

Some changes were temporary or cosmetic. In December 1945, the First and Second Demobilization Ministries were established and tasked with overseeing the disarmament and repatriation of more than 7 million armed forces personnel. Six months later, the two ministries consolidated into the Demobilization Agency, which functioned until the San Francisco Peace Treaty went into effect on April 28, 1952. In February 1948, a Reparations Agency was created to oversee the payment of retribution to countries that had suffered under Japanese aggression. Although the agency was abolished three years later, it oversaw the first installments of Japan's "official development assistance." Similarly, in August 1945 the splitting up of the Ministry of Agriculture and Commerce resulted in the creation of an agriculture portfolio (to oversee the Ministry of Agriculture, Forestry, and Fisheries) and a commerce and industry portfolio (to oversee the Ministry of Commerce and Industry, which, in May 1949, became the Ministry of International Trade and Industry). The Ministry of Communications, established in July 1946, almost immediately subdivided into the Ministry of Posts and Telecommunications (MPT) and the Ministry of Electric Communications. The Legislation Bureau was abolished in February 1948 and placed under the Ministry of Justice, but Prime Minister Yoshida resurrected the bureau in August 1952, shortly after the restoration of sovereignty (Naikaku Hōsei Kyoku 1985, 136–148, 158–162; Samuels 2004, 2).

Not surprisingly, GHQ insisted on the abolition of the Home Ministry, which had housed the dreaded "Thought Police" (*Tokubetsu kōtō keisatsu*) and other repressive organs. One of the first actions taken under the American occupation was to purge the home minister and the head of the national police, and more than two-thirds of the relatively few purged civilian bureaucrats were Home Ministry officials (Dower 1999, 81; Johnson 1982, 41–42).[16] The administrative bailiwick of the Home Ministry had included public works, local administration, elections, censorship of dangerous publications, labor relations, business licensing, disease prevention, social welfare, immigration, oversight of temples and shrines, and the development of Hokkaidō and Sakhalin. On December 31, 1947, the ministry was abolished and its functions were parceled out to a variety of new and existing organs, resulting in the creation of new ministerial portfolios. The ministry's supervisory powers over elections and local finance were given to the National Election Management Committee (*Zenkoku senkyo kanri iinkai*) and the Regional Finance Committee (*Chihō zaisei iinkai*), which later merged to form the Local Autonomy Agency (*Jichichō*).

Responsibility for public works administration was transferred to the Construction Board (*Kensetsuin*), which shortly thereafter became the Ministry of Construction. In July 1954, oversight of the National Police Agency was given over to the National Public Safety Commission (*Kokka kōan iinkai*). In addition, some of the Home Ministry's other functions were transferred to the Ministry of Health and Welfare and the newly established Labor Ministry.

Meanwhile, new portfolios were created for economic planning, administrative management, and national defense. In August 1946, the cabinet-level Economic Stabilization Headquarters and Price Stabilization Agency were established to bring inflation under control. Two years later, these organs folded into the Central Economic Assessment Agency, which became the Economic Deliberation Agency and eventually morphed into the Economic Planning Agency. Similarly, the Administrative Evaluation Department, established in October 1946, eventually became the Administrative Management Agency (AMA). As it turned out, the AMA's inaugural director general was seventy-six-year-old Saitō Takao, who in March 1940 had been expelled from the Diet for questioning Japan's belligerent actions in China. In June 1950, a ministerial portfolio was created to supervise the Hokkaidō Development Agency (*Hokkaidō kaihatsu chō*), which was charged with overseeing resource development, agricultural production, and public works projects on the northernmost of Japan's main islands. In August 1952, a cabinet-level Security Agency (*Hōanchō*) was created, with Prime Minister Yoshida himself holding the portfolio. Two years later, the Security Agency changed its name to the Defense Agency (*Bōeichō*), while the National Police Reserve became the Japan Self-Defense Forces (*Jieitai*).[17]

Other structural changes followed. In June 1949, the Prime Minister's Agency (*Sōrichō*) became the Prime Minister's Office (*Sōrifu*, or PMO) and was placed in charge of the Imperial Household Agency, the National Police Agency (under the National Public Safety Commission), and the Japan Fair Trade Commission. In addition, the PMO oversaw the Special Procurements Agency, established in June 1949 to handle supply requisitions from occupation forces, which increased dramatically following the outbreak of the Korean War. The PMO was also given supervisory powers over the National Personnel Authority (*Jinji-in*), created in 1948 as an independent organ to administer matters relating to the recruitment, training, and post-retirement employment of national government employees. In addition, the Cabinet Secretariat was stripped of its information-gathering duties, while the supra-ministerial Cabinet Research Bureau was abolished. Finally, in May 1947, the name of the Cabinet Secretariat was changed from *Naikaku shokikan* (which sounds like an office housing clerical staff) to the more dignified-sounding *Naikaku kanbōchōkan*.

The organizational changes required a rethinking of cabinet procedures. For example, while the 1947 Cabinet Law states that "the Cabinet shall perform its functions through Cabinet Meetings" (*kakugi*), it makes no mention of how cabinet meetings are to be conducted. An obvious issue involved the seating arrangement for cabinet ministers. Beginning in 1948, under the second Yoshida cabinet, the chief cabinet secretary (who, technically, did not become an official minister of state until 1966) was seated to the prime minister's right. Ministers were seated in right-left sequence depending on the date their respective ministries were established, while the directors of the various cabinet-level agencies were seated in left-right sequence according to the Japanese alphabetization of their names.[18] In fact, although the agency directors were accorded ministerial status, the title of "director general" (*chōkan*) carried less prestige than that of "minister" (*daijin*). Meanwhile, the director general of the Cabinet Legislation Bureau and the two vice directors of the Cabinet Secretariat were seated at a separate square table to the prime minister's right (Naikaku seido 1995, 96–97). Naturally, the proceedings of cabinet meetings remained confidential.

RIVALS FOR EXECUTIVE PRIMACY

The 1947 Constitution established the institutional framework for a Westminster-style parliamentary system. Henceforth, executive power was vested in a cabinet that was collectively responsible to a democratically elected Diet, while the military supreme command, Privy Council, elder statesmen, and House of Peers were abolished and the divine-right emperor and his private palace cabinet relegated to ceremonial roles. Yet, while *in theory* the cabinet was the paramount executive organ, *in reality* government bureaucrats and American occupation authorities were the dominant actors in the spheres of executive influence.

Diet and Parties

The 1947 Constitution enhanced the ability of the Diet and political parties to influence executive affairs. This is evident in the greater salience of MP-sponsored bills, which accounted for 20 percent of enacted laws under the comprador cabinets, as opposed to only 2 percent under the techno-fascist cabinets. In addition, political parties that had been outlawed or persecuted in prewar times were allowed to participate in policy-making. This became clear in the April 1947 general elections, from which the Japan Socialist Party emerged as the largest party in the lower house. Having secured a place at the table, the JSP wasted no time in pressing for passage of a law to nationalize the coal industry, which, to the surprise of many, was not opposed by MacArthur and GHQ. After considerable debate—including fistfights between members of the JSP's left and right wings—a watered-down version of the State Coal Control Bill was enacted in December 1947 (Hein 1990, 142). Although the new law subordinated the interests of organized labor to those of economic productivity, passage of such a law would have been unimaginable in prewar times (Watanabe, ed. 1995, 69–70; Shiratori 1981, 144).

No-confidence motions now carried constitutional force—in contrast to the symbolic acts of the prewar lower house—as was demonstrated on two occasions involving Prime Minister Yoshida. Article 69 of the Constitution specifies that the cabinet must resign or call new elections if the lower house approves a no-confidence motion or rejects a confidence motion. In December 1948, this parliamentary institution was given a road test as a result of the controversy sparked by Yoshida's decision to involve the emperor in dissolving the Diet and calling new elections. Yoshida maintained that the emperor was constitutionally empowered to dissolve the lower house and proclaim a general election "with the advice and approval of the Cabinet" (Article 7). But the opposition argued that dissolution must be preceded by passage of a no-confidence motion or rejection of a confidence motion (Yoshida 1962, 89). Ultimately, Justin Williams, an official in GHQ's Legislative Division, proposed a compromise whereby the opposition would agree to approve a supplementary budget before passing the non-confidence motion (Masumi 1985, 177; Finn 1992, 214). Consequently, on December 23, the lower house approved the supplementary budget and then voted 227 to 130 in favor of a non-confidence measure against the Yoshida cabinet. As it turned out, however, the "conspiracy dissolution" (*nareai kaisan*) gave Yoshida exactly what he desired all along: the supplementary budget proposed by his cabinet and a landslide victory for his Democratic Liberal Party in the general elections of January 1949.

The second non-confidence motion was precipitated by Yoshida's reference to Socialist MP Nishimura Eiichi as a "fool" (*bakayarō*) during February 1953 Budget Committee interpellations. Yoshida refused to apologize, and the opposition seized upon the indiscretion in voting to censure the prime minister. The motion's passage was ensured by the strategic absence of Hatoyama Ichirō and his followers, who were convinced that Yoshida had played a role in delaying Hatoyama's depurging (Masumi 1985, 280; Itoh 2003, 114–115). The opposition then proposed a nonconfidence motion against the Yoshida cabinet, which was approved on March 14 in a 229 to 218 vote. This time, Hatoyama and his followers voted along with the majority in approving the motion. This left the Yoshida cabinet with the choice of resigning en masse or dissolving the Diet and calling new elections. The cabinet opted to dissolve the Diet, and the April 1953 general election resulted in a stinging defeat for Yoshida's Liberal Party, which managed to win control of only 43 percent of the lower house seats. To hang on to power, Yoshida forged a coalition with the Reformist Party (*Kaishintō*).

Homegrown Mandarinate

The American decision to "indirectly" occupy a defeated Japan unwittingly enhanced the influence of an already mighty civil bureaucracy. Indeed, GHQ opted to purge relatively few career civil bureaucrats, while declaring almost all senior military officials and most prewar cabinet ministers ineligible for public office. In fact, the decision to exempt the majority of civil bureaucrats from the purge permitted the American occupiers to govern with a much smaller force than would have been the case if Allied officials had been required to fill all of the key administrative posts in national and local government. MacArthur reckoned that the occupation force would have required several hundred thousand additional officials had a "direct" occupation been pursued (Dower 1999, 325). Absent that, civil bureaucrats represented the best and largest source of experienced administrative talent from which to staff the central state executive. As pointed out above, the majority of civil bureaucrats singled out for removal were Home Ministry officials who held positions in its repressive police apparatus. As a consequence, many of the same technocrats who were in charge of economic planning in prewar times remained at their desks and continued to guide the development of the postwar economy (Johnson 1982, 40–41; Pempel 1986, 123).

An ex-bureaucrat himself, Yoshida could appreciate the policy expertise and elite status of government officials. With the leadership void created by GHQ's right-wing purge, Yoshida proceeded to "fast-track" high-ranking former officials into ministerial posts. Among the distinguished alumni of the so-called "Yoshida School" were future prime ministers Satō Eisaku and Ikeda Hayato, both of whom had risen to the administrative vice minister post in their respective ministries (Masumi 1985, 279).[19] Satō had just retired from the Transport Ministry and had yet to be elected to the Diet when Yoshida tapped him to serve as chief cabinet secretary. Yoshida rewarded Ikeda with the coveted finance minister's portfolio not long after Ikeda resigned his post at the Finance Ministry and just three weeks after he had won election to the Diet (Satō et al. 1990, 122). In addition, Yoshida fast-tracked Sudō Hideo, an ex-Agriculture Ministry official, into the post of secretary general of the Liberal Party and then handed him the agriculture portfolio. Okazaki Katsuo (Foreign Affairs), Ōhashi Takeo (Home), Noda Uichi (Foreign Affairs), Yoshitake Eiichi (Labor), and Aichi Kiichi (Finance) were among the ex-bureaucrats who benefited from Yoshida's tutelage. As it turned out, Yoshida School alumni went on to play crucial roles in executive affairs for the next three decades.

The Central Liaison Office (*Shūsen renraku chūō jimukyoku,* or CLO) played an important role in intermediating between the Japanese government and GHQ. Established on August 26, 1945, as an external organ of the Foreign Ministry, the CLO was staffed by English-speaking diplomats such as Okazaki Katsuo, Shirasu Jirō, and Suzuki Tadakatsu (Takemae 2002, 113). Okazaki, the CLO's inaugural director, was a rising star in the diplomatic corps, with experience in China and India and in important internal posts in the Foreign Ministry. Later on he was fast-tracked into the foreign minister's post and held portfolios in several cabinets. Shirasu, it will be recalled, was the recipient of General Whitney's "atomic energy" remark at the meeting with Yoshida and Matsumoto. Described as "Yoshida's alter ego in dealing with the Americans" and a "slippery character," the Cambridge-educated Shirasu was able to bypass GHQ's Government Section—the fountainhead of the occupation's most utopian reforms—in seeking support for the conservative cause from General C. A. Willoughby, MacArthur's anti-leftist chief of intelligence (Finn 1992, 124; Gayn [1946] 1973, 21). As head of the local CLO branch in Yokohama, Suzuki had a close working relationship with General Robert L. Eichelberger, commanding general of the 8th Army, which helped in defusing potential tension arising from crimes by U.S. servicemen (Finn 1992, 38). These CLO officials served as the main channel for relaying directives from GHQ to local authorities while helping to deflect or roll back overly zealous American proposals.

Alien Mandarinate

Japan's homegrown mandarins understood that they had to dance to the tune played by GHQ. For instance, General Whitney's "atomic energy" quip as a B-29 flew overhead helped the Shidehara cabinet perceive the wisdom in swiftly accepting the GHQ draft of the constitution *and* claiming authorship of it.[20] In addition, the influence of the foreign mandarinate can be seen in the "Dodge Line" and the Shoup mission's recommendations, as well as in a purge of rightists and intrusion into prime ministerial selection.

The "Dodge Line" refers to the strict economic stabilization measures recommended by Detroit banker Joseph Dodge, whom Truman dispatched to Tokyo in February 1949 (Calder 1988, 79). Dodge's "nine-point stabilization plan" included a tax hike to enable balanced budgets, steep cuts in the size of the governmental workforce, and a fixed exchange rate (Pempel 1998, 104). Dodge made it clear that the U.S. taxpayer was no longer willing to pay "hundreds of millions of dollars" each year to subsidize an inefficient Japanese economy (Nishi 2004, 76). He bluntly told senior Japanese officials, "The budget will have to be balanced. Unpopular steps will have to be taken. Austerity will have to be the basis for a series of economic measures" (quoted in Finn 1992, 222). Despite the risks entailed (for example, a steep jump in unemployment, cuts in public works spending, and an unpopular tax increase), the Yoshida cabinet dutifully accepted the Dodge Line (Masumi 1985, 187).

In May 1949, MacArthur invited Carl S. Shoup, a Columbia University economist, to visit Tokyo with a group of American tax experts to study the Japanese tax system. Despite the fact that virtually every group in Japanese society found something distasteful about the Shoup mission's proposed reforms—which included a progressive and broadly based income tax, tax equity, and emphasis on "local autonomy"—MacArthur made it known to Yoshida that he wanted to see them enacted "at the earliest possible time" (Cohen 1949, 311, 307). "Reflecting this support from the *highest authorities*," observes Ishi Hiromitsu, an authority on Japan's tax system, "the Japanese government and the Diet acted with vigor in accepting nearly all the proposals" (1989, 31; italics added). It should be noted that, despite these and other examples of obeisance, there were many instances when the Japanese side cleverly "pretended to obey while secretly disobeying" (*menjū fukuhai*) (Johnson 1982, 43).

The American mandarinate reshuffled Japan's political leadership through a right-wing purge. On January 4, 1946, GHQ issued a directive entitled "Removal and Exclusion of Undesirable Personnel from Public Office." It ordered the purge from public office of all individuals who were (1) "active exponents of militaristic nationalism and aggression"; (2) "influential members of any Japanese ultra-nationalistic, terroristic, or secret patriotic society, its agencies or affiliates"; or (3) "influential in the activities of the Imperial Rule Assistance Association, the Imperial Rule Assistance Political Society or the Political Association of Great Japan." This right-wing purge was implemented in stages and disqualified large numbers of experienced parliamentarians, government officials, and industrialists from holding public office. This had the effect of almost decimating several political parties, notably the Progressive Party; only fourteen of its 274 founding members were exempted from the purge (Masumi 1985, 96). Of course, the most famous casualty of the purge was Hatoyama, but a number of cabinet ministers also got axed. Five members of the Shidehara cabinet—Home Minister Horiki Zenjirō, Education Minister Maeda Tamon, Agriculture Minister Matsumura Kenzō, Transport Minister Tanaka Takeo, and Chief Cabinet Secretary and Minister without Portfolio Tsugita Daisaburō—were deemed unfit for public office. Later on, three members of the first Yoshida cabinet—Finance Minister Ishibashi Tanzan, Justice Minister Kimura Tokutarō, and Commerce and Industry Minister Ishii Mitsujirō—were purged, as was Kawai Yoshinari, who days earlier had resigned as Minister of Foreign Affairs. In all, around two hundred thousand persons with some sort of connection to the war effort were disqualified from holding public office.

Behind the scenes, GHQ meddled in prime ministerial selection. At the time of the Ashida cabinet's resignation in October 1948, Yoshida's Democratic Liberal Party (DLP) was the largest party in the Diet, controlling 152 lower house and 46 upper house seats (Fukui 1984, 481). Even though the DLP did not command a majority, its leader should have been the logical choice to form a new cabinet. But certain GHQ officials regarded Yoshida as "reactionary" and likely to revive undemocratic practices. This led MacArthur and Whitney to approach Miki Takeo (head of the centrist National Cooperative Party), who politely suggested that the premiership should go to the leader of the largest party (Finn 1992, 211). At the same time, GS officials were encouraging the candidacy of DLP secretary general Yamazaki Takeshi. Not surprisingly, Yoshida was enraged to learn that the secretary general of his own party was involved in GHQ-led "plot politics" (ibid., 212). The previous week, Yoshida had met with MacArthur, and, although no records of the meeting were kept, he later implied that the Supreme Commander supported his candidacy. Yamazaki subsequently withdrew and resigned his seat in the Diet (although he was reelected in January 1949), and on October 4 the lower house voted to approve Yoshida's selection as prime minister.

THE CHALLENGES OF A "NEW JAPAN"

The comprador cabinets confronted a host of challenges, beginning with the complex problem of rebuilding Japan's devastated economy and infrastructure. This offered an opportunity for the cabinet to assume the executive role envisioned for it in the new Constitution, and to demonstrate that party-led cabinets and elected MPs were capable of placing the nation's interests above partisan interests and personal greed. The comprador cabinets also had to cope with an American military dictatorship that displayed bipolar, mutually contradictory tendencies. Although the Yoshida government was obliged to make certain concessions to secure the San Francisco Peace Treaty, it was quick to roll back many unpalatable reforms after the U.S. occupiers permitted the reversion of sovereignty and returned home.

The Irresistible Temptation

In the public's mind, the party cabinets of the late 1920s and early 1930s were synonymous with corruption, scandal, and misguided policies (Sekiguchi 1938, 14; Scalapino 1953, 393; Buckley 1978, 564). As a result, many postwar Japanese citizens held the view that elected MPs were incapable of subordinating their greed and narrow partisan interests in pursuing the national interest (Tanaka 1976, 652). For this reason, the success of the postwar efforts to establish cabinet government depended on severing the perceived link between parliamentary institutions and political corruption. Of course, the comprador cabinets would have to account for their policies in a more transparent setting—in other words, in interpellations before a democratically elected Diet without the benefit of a government-censored mass media.

Unfortunately, it did not take long for cabinet ministers to discover the rewards of influence peddling. One of the first corruption scandals of the postwar era arose in July 1947, when several ministers in the Katayama cabinet were accused of hoarding military goods and government materiel that had been released to individuals and companies on the eve of Japan's surrender (Mitchell 1996, 96). While the "hoarded goods scandal" was minor in comparison to the succession of scandals that followed, it helped to establish structural corruption as "one foundation stone of the postwar political economy" (Dower 1999, 117).[21]

The Shōwa Denkō scandal was the first large-scale corruption incident of the postwar era. At its heart were allegations that members of the Ashida cabinet and government bureaucrats had peddled their influence in steering government funds to the Showa Denkō Company, a fertilizer manufacturer. The scandal erupted on June 23, 1948, when the company's president was charged with bribing an official of the Ministry of Commerce and Industry in the hope of securing Reconstruction Finance Bank loans. Implicated in the mushrooming scandal were a number of MPs—including cabinet minister Kurusu Takeo and former vice premier Nishio Suehiro—as well as bureaucrats in the Commerce and Industry, Finance, and Agriculture Ministries and several leading bankers. Future premier Fukuda Takeo, then head of the Finance Ministry's Budget Bureau, was one of the government officials charged in the investigation. Although charges were brought against thirty-four individuals, in the end only Kurusu, MP Shigemasa Seishi, and Showa Denkō's president were convicted. While Ashida himself was not directly involved, he was arrested on unrelated charges of tax evasion and accepting a bribe from a construction company (Mitchell 1996, 100–106). On October 15, Ashida (who had been found innocent of the bribery charges) and his ministers resigned to take responsibility for the massive scandal.

The most damaging corruption incident of the early postwar era was the Shipbuilding scandal. On February 16, 1954, special investigators obtained permission to arrest Arita Jirō, deputy secretary general of the Liberal Party, on charges that he accepted bribes from shipbuilding companies wishing to acquire Japan Development Bank loans. In addition, four other MPs and several Transport Ministry officials were arrested, and investigators began tracing evidence linking Satō Eisaku, secretary general of the Liberal Party, to the expanding scandal. On April 21, as prosecutors were closing the net on Satō, Yoshida ordered Justice Minister Inukai Takeru to exercise the "right of command" (*shikiken*) to block the arrest of a "prized pupil" of the Yoshida School (Hayashi and Tsuji 1981, 5:271). Inukai complied, and the opposition immediately demanded his resignation, which was granted one month later. In the end, more than fifty politicians, businessmen, and government officials were implicated in the scandal, which prompted talk of a non-confidence motion in the lower house and led to the defection of a large number of MPs from Yoshida's Liberal Party (Shiratori 1981, 163–164). The scandal exacerbated factional rifts among Liberal Party MPs and led corporate donors to insinuate that campaign contributions might stop flowing (Mitchell 1996, xvi, 113; Hayashi and Tsuji 1981, 5:272). In the end, the Shipbuilding scandal brought down the curtain on Yoshida's protracted run as prime minister and set the stage for the establishment of the Liberal Democratic Party.

A Bipolar Occupation

At the time of Japan's surrender, some feared that the occupation might go on indefinitely and that the Americans would radically recast Japanese political, economic, and social institutions to suit their alien tastes. Indeed, these fears seemed to be confirmed by the utopian reforms undertaken in the occupation's early stages. Yet, by the time the occupation ended, all of the most radical reforms—save for the Constitution's "no war" clause—had been rolled back. Moreover, sovereignty was restored far more swiftly than almost anyone had imagined, and on terms that were relatively favorable to Japanese interests. In large measure, this U-turn in occupation policy came in response to the new realities of the Cold War, in which U.S. policymakers came to believe that a politically stable and economically robust Japan was essential to contain "creeping Communism." But the stubborn persistence and cleverness of the Japanese compradors—most notably Prime Minister Yoshida—also played a role in the change of direction in occupation policy.

Japan's political leaders performed abysmally in some of their initial encounters with the American occupiers. The obtuseness of the Japanese leaders was readily apparent in their initial attitude toward constitutional revision. It should have been abundantly clear from the Potsdam Declaration that the Americans and their allies were dead serious about ensuring that the Japanese adopted democratic institutions. Yet the Shidehara cabinet was clueless. "The [Matsumoto] Committee does not necessarily aim at the revision of the constitution," Shidehara explained; its purpose was to "determine whether any amendment may be necessary, and, if so, what are the points to be amended" (quoted in Tanaka 1976, 656). Years later, Matsumoto admitted that he and members of his committee "thought we could handle the matter as we pleased. We even thought it might be all right to leave [the existing constitution] as it was" (quoted in Dower 1999, 351). Obviously, this was not "all right" to MacArthur and the Americans, and, as a result, Japan ended up with a ghostwritten constitution.

Yoshida and other Japanese leaders deftly played different factions at GHQ against one another. It soon became apparent that the views of the Government Section (GS) clashed with those of the Counterintelligence Section (commonly known as G2). GS was under the command of General Whitney, a conservative Republican and MacArthur's personal friend. Whitney delegated considerable authority to his chief aide, Colonel Charles L. Kades, a self-described "thorough New Dealer" who had held posts in the Roosevelt administration (Itoh 2003). Meanwhile, G2 was under the leadership of General Charles Willoughby, the German-born son of a Prussian baron and his American wife (whose maiden name was Willoughby) (Campbell 1998, 1). Willoughby—whom MacArthur referred to as "my pet fascist"—doubted that American-inspired reforms could make Japan into a democracy, and his skepticism permeated GHQ's military intelligence arm (Gordon 2003, 239). GS was given the reins in formulating the early occupation-sponsored reforms. With the onset of the U-turn in occupation policy, however, the divergent views of GS and G2 came to the surface. Reflecting on this many decades later, Hans Baerwald, a linguist attached to GS, recalled that when it came to political reforms during the early stages of the occupation, GS was "on the side of the angels most of the time," while G2 and Willoughby "epitomized our ideological enemy" (Baerwald 2003). Mark Gayn, an American journalist posted to Tokyo, described the state of relations between GS and G2 as "warring camps" (Gayn 1981, 42).

As the right-wing purge was in progress, GHQ encouraged the expansion of labor unions and applauded the participation of leftist parties in coalition governments. In particular, officials at GS were convinced that a unionized labor force would promote democracy and that leftist parties would serve to check the likely efforts of conservative interests to revive undemocratic practices and institutions. The Labor Union Law, which guaranteed the right of collective bargaining, was enacted in December 1945, and the share of unionized laborers as a percentage of the nation's workforce skyrocketed, as did the number of labor disputes and strikes. Even though MacArthur appeared to adopt an anti-labor stance in ordering a halt to a general strike planned for February 1, 1947, his real objective was to maintain public order while pressuring Yoshida to call elections before the new Constitution went into effect. Besides, as noted earlier, officials at GS were pleased with the progressive reforms pressed forward by the Katayama and Ashida cabinets, each of which boasted socialist participation.

In late 1948, occupation policy began to take its U-turn, ushering in what came to be known as the "reverse course." By this time GHQ had become weary of the demands of unionized labor and the increasing militancy of the leftist parties, especially the Japan Communist Party (JCP). In May 1950, MacArthur suggested that it would be a good idea if the JCP were to be outlawed, although, in this case, the Supreme Commander's suggestion was not acted upon. Then, on June 5, 1950, less than three weeks before the outbreak of the Korean War, GHQ ordered the purge of twenty-four members of the JCP's Central Committee. Soon thereafter, seventeen members of the editorial board of *Akahata,* the party's print organ, were also purged. This marked the beginning of the "red purge," which ultimately resulted in the removal and exclusion of thousands of private- and public-sector workers, many of whom had only vague ties to the Communist movement. It was accompanied by the staged rehabilitation of the previously purged rightists, many of whom returned to reassume their Diet seats and leadership posts in the political parties and government. For example, the three ministers who were purged in the last days of the first Yoshida cabinet—Ishibashi, Kimura, and Ishii—quickly resumed their political careers and went on to hold important party and cabinet posts, with Ishibashi eventually becoming prime minister. Of course, Hatoyama returned to political life to assume the premiership.

Findings

As Ward observed, "the Allied Occupation of Japan was perhaps the single most exhaustively planned operation of massive and externally directed change in world history" (1987, 401). A major part of this operation was to get the Japanese to adopt a democratic constitution. Japanese authorities were reluctant to revise the Meiji Constitution, so the task fell to a secretive "constitutional convention" held in the ballroom of the Dai-Ichi Mutual Life Insurance Building. In just six breathless days, GHQ officials produced a draft constitution that would, with Japanese and Allied input, evolve into the Constitution of Japan that laid the foundation for parliamentary democracy with a "British-style cabinet system" at its heart (Dower 1999, 370).

Yet despite the establishment of a Westminster system *in form,* cabinet government *in practice* failed to take root. Yoshida's fast-tracking of high-ranking ex-bureaucrats demonstrated that parliamentary seniority mattered little in the recruitment of ministers, and helped to account for the paucity of "career politicians" among the ministerial elite. Moreover, the cabinet failed to assume its expected role as the foremost organ of executive influence; instead it remained a loose collection of individual ministers acting as advocates for the interests of their respective ministries. As Dower points out, "from 1945 to 1952, Japan was essentially ruled by an American military dictatorship that, for simple reasons of expediency, governed . . . through a bureaucratic system that remained essentially intact from the war years" (1999, 7). Although the Japanese compradors sometimes got what they wanted by dragging their feet or exploiting factional differences within GHQ, at the end of the day they danced to an American tune. Meanwhile, corruption scandals brought down ministers, toppled cabinets, and confirmed the popular perception that parliamentary democracy and political corruption go hand in hand. Indeed, the inability of this first cohort of postwar cabinet ministers to resist the forbidden fruit of influence peddling laid the foundation for an enduring system of structural corruption.

By the time the Hatoyama cabinet was reorganized on November 22, 1955, the institutional foundations for a Westminster-style parliamentary cabinet system had been put in place, if not in practice. Still, the cabinet system would be fundamentally shaped by an event that had taken place one week earlier, when the two major conservative parties merged to form the Liberal Democratic Party. While there was no exogenous shock comparable to Commodore Perry's uninvited visit or the arrival of MacArthur and his viceroys, the incremental changes effected under the "1955 system" and more than half a century of almost uninterrupted rule by the LDP would profoundly affect the evolution of Japan's cabinet system.

3

Corporatist Cabinets and the Emergence of the "1955 System," 1955–1972

The Cabinet is more than an agency of executive coordination. It is, above all, a body composed of parliamentary leaders. This circumstance has had definite consequences for its structure and place in the British political system.

—Hans Daalder, *Cabinet Reform in Britain, 1914–1963* (1963), 3

Cabinet officers don't have any time to make policy. They are new to their jobs and have to spend all their time boning up on answers to questions in the Diet. By the time they are experienced, they are out of office. The result is that policy is made by the bureaucrats.

—Miura Kineji quoted in Nathaniel B. Thayer, *How the Conservatives Rule Japan* (1969), 202–203

GENESIS OF LDP RULE

On November 15, 1955, the Liberal Democratic Party (*Jiyūminshutō*, or LDP) was born in a ceremony held on a university campus in Tokyo. Speeches were made, "*banzais*" were shouted under raised arms, and Ogata Taketora, Hatoyama Ichirō, Ōno Banboku, and Miki Bukichi emerged as the party's acting presidents. Although talk of a "conservative alliance" (*hoshū gōdō*) was not new, personal and partisan rivalries invariably stood in the way. The breakthrough had come six months earlier, the result of a telephone conversation between erstwhile enemies Ōno and Miki, the respective lieutenants in Ogata's Liberal and Hatoyama's Japan Democratic parties. This led to meetings of leaders of the rival parties, and, eventually, an agreement in principle to combine the main conservative parties into one (Thayer 1969, 13–14). Talk soon gave way to action when, in October, the left and right branches of the socialist movement merged to form the Japan Socialist Party. Fearful of the fate of business interests under a leftist regime, the captains of industry threatened to withhold campaign funding unless the major conservative parties united. This got the attention of Ogata, Hatoyama, and other leaders of the conservative parties, who put aside their differences and joined forces. With Hatoyama sitting in the prime minister's chair and the LDP in control of a comfortable majority in the Diet's lower house, the new LDP was a dominant force from the outset.

In this chapter, I trace the evolution of Japan's cabinet system from November 15, 1955, until July 6, 1972. During this period, new cabinet-related organs and government agencies were created, and a seniority system for cabinet ministers became established. Because LDP lawmakers all but monopolized ministerial portfolios, appointment to a cabinet post became simply another rung on the perpetually ruling party's internal promotional ladder. The LDP was, in essence, a "federation of factions" united for purposes of campaign and legislative strategy, rather than a unified national party (Scalapino and Masumi 1962, 18; Bowen 2003, 60). This ensured that Machiavellian machinations would play a role in deciding the party's president, who doubled as prime minister. Yet, under the surface, differences in style and outlook pitted rival camps of "ex-bureaucrats" and "career politicians," and the need to maintain balance among intraparty factions dictated frequent cabinet changes and, often, the appointment of ministers with dubious qualifications. At the same time, the autonomy of cabinets in executive affairs was challenged by a hegemonic party that demanded the right to preapprove all major policy departures and by an activist government bureaucracy. Finally, prime ministers and cabinets confronted a variety of challenges produced by high-speed economic growth and dissatisfaction with institutional arrangements put in place during the American-led occupation.

THE "1955 SYSTEM"

The creation of the LDP provided an opening for opportunistic leaders of the major conservative parties to rectify perceived flaws in the postwar institutional settlement, which in large measure had been imposed on a defeated nation by American military occupiers. Longtime premier Yoshida Shigeru was singled out as the principal domestic collaborator in forging these arrangements, symbolized in the 1947 "Peace Constitution" and the United States–Japan Mutual Security Treaty. These arrangements had permitted Japan to devote unfettered attention to economic recovery, but had constrained its diplomatic and military capabilities. An "anti-Yoshida alliance"—led by Hatoyama, Miki, Kōno Ichirō, Shigemitsu Mamoru, Kishi Nobusuke, and others, many of whom had been subject to the occupation-imposed purge of militarists and ultranationalists—was repulsed by the thought that a lightly armed Japan would have to depend forever on the United States for its national security. In December 1954, these conservative leaders ousted Yoshida and installed Hatoyama as prime minister. In so doing, their overarching aim was to bring about the "domestic counterpart" of Yoshida's "diplomatic opus" (Masumi 1985, 329).

The term "1955 system" denotes the political party system born from the creation of the JSP and the LDP as well as the "business first" economic strategy that defined the period (Masumi 1985, 16). Yet the two major parties were far from equipotent. The LDP was the party of preference for a solid majority of the electorate, while the JSP—with a weak grassroots base and a bad case of ideological division—played the part of permanent minority. In practice, therefore, Japan was governed under a "one-and-a-half-party system," in which the LDP did all the governing, while the JSP and the other parties could only oppose (Scalapino and Masumi 1962, 79).

Even though the first two LDP prime ministers—Hatoyama and Ishibashi Tanzan—were "career politicians," ex-bureaucrats sat in the prime minister's chair for the greater part of the period. Kishi Nobusuke, Ikeda Hayato, and Satō Eisaku were elite ex-bureaucrats who gravitated into "second careers" in elective politics. Meanwhile, other former officials occupied a disproportionate share of key ministerial posts. These leaders presided over an era of economic growth that catapulted Japan to the forefront of the industrialized world and, in so doing, enhanced the country's diplomatic stature. In 1961, the Ikeda cabinet launched a plan to double the country's GNP by the end of the decade; the goal was achieved in less than seven years, and Japan became the world's second largest economy. Policies to promote export-oriented "strategic industries" such as steel, shipbuilding, machine tools, and automobiles were crafted within the ministries and agencies of the central government (Johnson 1982).

Throughout this period, corporatist cabinets exerted a high degree of strategic choice in setting the agenda for executive decision-making and responding to domestic and international challenges. This was made possible by a pro-growth consensus among business and political leaders as well as by a rapidly expanding economic pie that raised the standard of living of the vast majority of Japanese citizens. It also legitimized a state of affairs in which the government bureaucracy took the lead in forging economic policy, while elite ex-bureaucrats occupied pivotal posts in government and in the hegemonic party. "Politicians from the bureaucracy have a firm grip on the Liberal Democratic leadership," explained a contemporary observer. "Bureaucratic politicians built up the status of power elite while they were in the Government Administration" (Sugimori 1968, 496). This meant that the ministerial elite possessed a stronger "bureaucratic" coloration than that expected in a Westminster system in which career politicians dominate. For the most part, the bureaucratically dominated governments adhered to the principle of balanced budgets prescribed under the Dodge Line (discussed in chapter 2). For the time being, therefore, career politicians were relegated to a supporting role in executive affairs, although the "shocks" of the 1970s would create conditions for a reversal of fortune.

THE CORPORATIST CABINET ELITE

Between November 1955 and July 1972, twenty-two cabinets were formed under five prime ministers. On average, a corporatist cabinet survived a mere 276 days. The longest-lived was the third Satō cabinet, which carried on for nearly eighteen months, while the shortest-lived was the Ishibashi cabinet, which collapsed along with the health of its premier after just sixty-four days. Meanwhile, the seven-and-a-half-year tenure of the Satō government is the longest in the history of Japan's cabinet system. Each of the prime ministers, who simultaneously served as LDP president, had previous ties to the Liberal Party, Japan Democratic Party, or both. Two held portfolios in prewar cabinets, and three had been purged under the American occupation. One had scarcely known a career other than elective politics, another had been a journalist, and three had risen to the apex of the career civil service before descending into "second careers" as MPs.

The Prime Ministers

As noted earlier, Hatoyama Ichirō (1883–1959) was born into a political family, and politics was his lifelong calling. In May 1946, Hatoyama had just been elected to an eleventh lower house term and, as leader of the largest party in the Diet's lower house, was preparing to form a cabinet when he was subjected to the U.S. occupation's purge of militarists. He reassumed his lower house seat in October 1952 but maintained an icy stance toward Liberal Party president Yoshida Shigeru, whom he suspected of delaying his rehabilitation. In March 1953, in the midst of a ruckus created by Yoshida's reference to a JSP lawmaker as a "fool" during Diet deliberations, Hatoyama helped establish the Japan Liberal Party. The following November he founded the Japan Democratic Party, and a year later became the LDP's inaugural president. He tried and failed to gerrymander the electoral system so that the LDP could acquire the requisite two-thirds of seats needed to revise the Constitution (Yamamuro 1995, 105). Although he could not secure the return of the disputed "Northern Territories," Hatoyama exited the premiership amid strong public approval for his role in restoring relations with the Soviet Union and negotiating the belated repatriation of Japanese prisoners of war (Ōkochi 1981, 354).

Ishibashi Tanzan (1884–1973) took his Waseda University diploma and set out on a journalistic career. He became editor in chief of the *Oriental Economic Journal* (*Tōyō keizai shinpō*), in whose pages he articulated liberal economic views and questioned Japan's colonial expansionism (Inoki 1995, 112–113). Ishibashi held several key posts in the first Yoshida cabinet but was purged shortly after winning a lower house seat in the 1947 general elections. He was rehabilitated in 1951 and three years later joined Hatoyama and others in founding the Japan Democratic Party. Kishi Nobusuke was considered the odds-on favorite to succeed Hatoyama when he resigned in 1956, but Ishibashi and rival Ishii Mitsujirō secretly agreed to join forces in the event that the LDP's presidential election required a second round of voting. When Kishi failed to obtain a majority on the first ballot, Ishii ordered members of his faction to vote for Ishibashi in the runoff. The result was the Ishibashi cabinet and the solidification of "eight private divisions" (*hachi-ko shidan*) that became the LDP's intraparty factions (*habatsu*) (Satō and Matsuzaki 1986, 240).[1] Ishibashi was a septuagenarian when he assumed the premiership, and his health quickly deteriorated owing to the heavy schedule of public speaking engagements.

Kishi Nobusuke's (1896–1987) birth name was Satō, but he adopted the family name of an uncle with whom he went to live. Legend has it that the young Kishi was so moved by the ideas of Kita Ikki, "the ideological *father of* Japanese fascism," that he hand-copied *An Outline Plan for the Reorganization of Japan* (*Nihon kaizō hōan taikō*) (Maruyama 1969,

28; Samuels 2003, 142). He chose to enter the Ministry of Agriculture and Commerce (MAC) rather than the mighty Home Ministry, as might have been expected of the top graduate of Tokyo Imperial University's Law Faculty (Kitaoka 1995, 125–126). Kishi rose through the ranks at MAC and its successor, the Ministry of Commerce and Industry (MCI), and in 1936 was posted to the powerful General Affairs Agency in the puppet state of Manchukuo, where he directed central economic planning (Samuels 2003, 144–145). After returning to Tokyo, Kishi became the leader of the technocratic "reform bureaucrats" who dominated government officialdom under the wartime regime (Mimura 2011, 3). In 1939, Kishi became administrative vice minister at MCI, and two years later he resigned to serve as a minister in the Tōjō cabinet. After Japan's surrender, Kishi was arrested as a "Class A" war criminal and imprisoned, but he was released in December 1948 and did not stand trial at the International Military Tribunal for the Far East. Kishi was rehabilitated in April 1952 and, a year later, was elected to the lower house. Shortly before the LDP's founding, Kishi began receiving funds from the U.S. Central Intelligence Agency to consolidate one-party rule in Japan and to press America's Cold War policies. These surreptitious payments, which were made using American businessmen as go-betweens and funneled to Kishi and other LDP MPs, continued for at least fifteen years (Weiner 2007, 119–120; Schaller 1996, 165).

Ikeda Hayato (1899–1965) was the son of a postmaster and sake brewer in Hiroshima Prefecture. It is not known why Ikeda chose to pursue his studies at Kyoto Imperial University—as opposed to Tokyo University, the institution of choice for aspiring government officials—in preparation for a career at the Ministry of Finance (Nakamura 1995, 150). In 1929, he contracted a rare skin disease that necessitated a five-year medical leave, during which he contemplated suicide (ibid., 150). After returning to the ministry, Ikeda ascended to the administrative vice minister post, from which he retired in 1948. Ikeda was just the sort of elite government official favored by Prime Minister Yoshida, who fast-tracked him into the coveted post of finance minister just one month after his election to the lower house. In November 1952, Ikeda was forced to resign the ministership after stating that he would not be troubled if a few small businessmen were driven to suicide as a result of his policies favoring large-scale heavy industries; he justified the policy by saying that "any major policy requires some unavoidable sacrifice" (ibid., 153). As premier, Ikeda promoted an "Income Doubling Plan" (*shotoku baizō keikaku*) emblematic of Japan's high-speed

Table 3.1. The Corporatist Cabinets, 1955 to 1972

Cabinet	Prime Minister	Established	Dissolved	PM's Background
3rd Hatoyama Cabinet	Hatoyama Ichirō	11/22/1955	12/23/1956	Career Politician
Ishibashi Cabinet	Ishibashi Tanzan	12/23/1956	2/25/1957	"
1st Kishi Cabinet	Kishi Nobusuke	2/25/1957	7/10/1957	Ex-Bureaucrat
Reorg'ed 1st Kishi Cabinet	"	7/10/1957	6/12/1958	"
2nd Kishi Cabinet	"	6/12/1958	6/18/1959	"
Reorg'ed 2nd Kishi Cabinet	"	6/18/1959	7/19/1960	"
1st Ikeda Cabinet	Ikeda Hayato	7/19/1960	12/8/1960	Ex-Bureaucrat
2nd Ikeda Cabinet	"	12/8/1960	7/18/1961	"
Reorg'ed 2nd Ikeda (1) Cabinet	"	7/18/1961	7/18/1962	"
Reorg'ed 2nd Ikeda (2) Cabinet	"	7/18/1962	7/18/1963	"
Reorg'ed 2nd Ikeda (3) Cabinet	"	7/18/1963	12/9/1963	"
3rd Ikeda Cabinet	"	12/9/1963	7/18/1964	"
Reorg'ed 3rd Ikeda Cabinet	"	7/18/1964	11/9/1964	"
1st Satō Cabinet	Satō Eisaku	11/9/1964	6/3/1965	Ex-Bureaucrat
Reorg'ed 1st Satō (1) Cabinet	"	6/3/1965	8/1/1966	"
Reorg'ed 1st Satō (2) Cabinet	"	8/1/1966	12/3/1966	"
Reorg'ed 1st Satō (3) Cabinet	"	12/3/1966	2/17/1967	"
2nd Satō Cabinet	"	2/17/1967	11/25/1967	"
Reorg'ed 2nd Satō (1) Cabinet	"	11/25/1967	11/30/1968	"
Reorg'ed 2nd Satō (2) Cabinet	"	11/30/1968	1/14/1970	"
3rd Satō Cabinet	"	1/14/1970	7/5/1971	"
Reorg'ed 3rd Satō Cabinet	"	7/5/1971	7/7/1972	"

Source: JCCM Database (Appendix A).

growth era, but was disparagingly referred to as a "transistor salesman" by French president Charles de Gaulle. Despite suffering from throat cancer, Ikeda delivered a speech to delegates of the International Monetary Fund and the World Bank and attended the opening ceremony of the 1964 Tokyo Olympic Games.

Satō Eisaku (1901–1975) followed in the footsteps of his biological brother, Kishi Nobusuke, by studying law at Tokyo Imperial University in preparation for a civil service career. He was promoted at the Ministry of Railways, which subsequently morphed into the Ministry of Transport, and in 1947 he became administrative vice minister. The following year Satō retired from the government bureaucracy and, like Ikeda, was fast-tracked into a ministerial post. Satō served as chief cabinet secretary in the second Yoshida cabinet and won a seat in the 1949 lower house elections. After Sato established himself as the "pillar" (*shichū*) of the Yoshida cabinet, his political career was jeopardized by allegations that he and Ikeda had received bribes in the 1954 Shipbuilding scandal (Johnson 1995b, 189). Thanks to the invocation of executive authority by Justice Minister Inukai Takeru, who acted on Yoshida's orders, Satō was spared prosecution (Mitchell 1996, 111). In 1964, he outmaneuvered Kōno Ichirō and Fujiyama Aiichirō to succeed the terminally ill Ikeda as prime minister (Masumi 1985, 137). Satō won the Nobel Peace Prize for his nuclear non-proliferation policies.

Departmental Ministers

Among the 308 individuals who held portfolios in the corporatist cabinets, the modal minister was an LDP MP who had been elected to six lower house terms and had spent more than a decade and a half treading the Diet's red-carpeted corridors. Chances are that this modal minister was a male university graduate who represented a district located outside the most highly urbanized centers. It is likely that he labored in the central state bureaucracy, prefectural or municipal politics, or worked as an MP's staff assistant or as a journalist before embarking on a career in national elective politics. This is to say that our modal minister claimed allegiance to the LDP's band of "ex-bureaucrats" or the rival contingent of "career politicians" (Sugimori 1968, 506).

Under the corporatist cabinets, ministerial portfolios were reserved almost exclusively for MPs. In fact, the lone nonparliamentarian was Fujiyama Aiichirō, a successful businessman who held the foreign minister's portfolio in the Kishi cabinet. Novice ministers had accumulated nearly fifteen years of parliamentary experience, more than four years longer than the previous ministerial cohort. These first-time ministers had been elected to 4.45 lower house terms (or 2.61 upper house terms), and the average for all ministers, novice and veteran, was the equivalent of 6.3 lower house terms. Moreover, seniority exceptions—in other words, ministers who had not been elected to the equivalent of at least five lower house terms—declined from two-thirds of comprador ministers to only one in five corporate cabinet ministers.

Ex-bureaucrats accounted for nearly half of all ministers (46 percent), and better than two-thirds of them separated from the civil service at the lofty rank of bureau chief or above. Prime Ministers Kishi, Ikeda, Satō, and Fukuda are numbered among these elite ex-bureaucrats, but even some of those who exited the civil service at a junior rank went on to spin out successful second careers as MPs. Ōhira Masayoshi (Finance), Nakasone Yasuhiro (Home), and Miyazawa Kiichi (Finance) separated from the civil service at junior ranks but went on to become prime ministers, while Ishii Mitsujirō and Funada Naka (Home Ministry officials) held important party leadership posts. Much has been made of the differences in political style between the LDP's rival contingents of ex-bureaucrats and career politicians, of whom many were former grassroots politicians (for example, prefectural assemblymen) or MPs' staff assistants (Scalapino and Masumi 1962, 54–59). Ex-bureaucrats were said to prefer centralized control and valued their ministry and school ties, while career politicians were more attuned to local interests and preferred decentralized control. Career politicians constituted a minority among corporatist cabinet ministers (in fact, they accounted for only 30 percent of ministers), so, at least for the time being, they were obliged to toil in the shadow of the ex-bureaucrats.

The vast majority of ministers were university-educated men who represented rural districts. Although the 1947 Constitution granted women the right to hold elective office, the ministerial elite remained an almost exclusively male preserve. In assuming the health and welfare portfolio in the first Ikeda cabinet on July 19, 1960, Nakayama Masa did for female ministerial aspirants what Jackie Robinson and Wat Misaka did for athletes of color in American professional baseball and basketball.[2] An alumna of Ohio Wesleyan University and wife of an MP, Nakayama was elected to the lower house in 1947, the first election in which women were allowed to vote. The only other female minister was Kondō Tsuruyo, who held the science and technology portfolio in the second Ikeda cabinet. Over 90 percent of ministers attended university, and nearly 60 percent of them held diplomas from either Tokyo University or Kyoto University, elite public universities whose graduates dominated the upper echelons of the career civil service. Four out of five of those who held portfolios represented districts outside the heavily urbanized Tokyo, Osaka, and Nagoya metropolitan areas.[3] This attests to the LDP's strong support among rural voters, who ensured that the party's candidates attained the requisite level of seniority to ascend the promotional ladder leading to coveted ministerial portfolios.

Finally, it is important to note the large number of ministers who held prewar and wartime leadership positions. Many of these individuals had been subject to the occupation-imposed purge of militarists and right-wingers. Among them were Prime Ministers Hatoyama, Ishibashi, and Kishi, as well as Kōno Ichirō (agriculture and construction minister in various cabinets), Makino Ryōzō (justice minister in the Hatoyama cabinet), Takasaki Tatsunosuke (MITI minister and director of the agencies for economic planning and science and technology in the Hatoyama and Kishi cabinets), Ōkubo Tomeijirō (chair of the National Public Safety Commission and director of the Administrative Management Agency in the Ishibashi and Kishi cabinets), and Narahashi Wataru (transport minister in the Kishi cabinet). As noted earlier, Hatoyama and Kishi held portfolios in prewar cabinets, which almost guaranteed that they would be purged. These leaders represented a human bridge linking the "undemocratic" techno-fascist cabinets with the "democratic" cabinets established under the 1947 Constitution. As Dower observes, "everywhere one looks, the corridors of power in postwar Japan are crowded with men whose talents had already been recognized during the war years, and who found the same talents highly prized in the 'new' Japan" (1993, 11).

Organizational Changes

A net increase of seven ministerial portfolios accrued under the corporatist cabinets, increasing the total number to twenty-eight portfolios. Since, by law, the maximum number of ministers was nineteen, it became necessary to award multiple portfolios. In the third Satō cabinet, for example, Nemoto Ryūtarō concurrently held the construction minister's portfolio as well as the portfolios for three cabinet-level regional development commissions. Still, the ministerial hierarchy associated with an established parliamentary cabinet system failed to appear. Based on ministers' parliamentary and social attributes, the most prestigious portfolios were economic planning, foreign affairs, administrative management, labor, and regional development (see Appendix C).[4] While the lofty ranking accorded the foreign affairs portfolio is to be expected, it is difficult to account for the fact that economic planning, administrative management, labor, and regional development ranked higher in the pecking order than the international trade and industry, finance, and prime minister portfolios.

A number of new ministerial portfolios were created. A cabinet-level Science and Technology Agency (*Kagakugijutsuchō*) was created on May 19, 1956, with Shōriki Matsutarō, a prewar Police Board (*Keishichō*) official who was briefly jailed as a "Class A" war criminal, as its director general. In July 1960, the Local Autonomy Agency (*Jichichō*), an external bureau of the Prime Minister's Office, became the Ministry of Home Affairs (*Jishishō*, or MOHA), and the title of its top administrator was upgraded from director general (*chōkan*) to minister (*daijin*). Ishihara Kan'ichirō, a former official of the Health and Welfare Ministry and a former governor of Fukushima Prefecture, became the inaugural minister of Home Affairs. Ishihara's successors included a pair of former Home Ministry officials, Yoshitake Eiichi and Yamazaki Iwao, and Sudō Hideo, an ex-official of MCI who had served on the powerful Cabinet Planning Board, one of the "superagencies" of the prewar state (Samuels 2003, 144). Many of those who had applauded the actions of American occupation authorities in dissolving the prewar Home Ministry (*Naimushō*), which housed the "Thought Police" and other organs of state repression, were troubled by the installation of former *Naimushō* officials at the helm of the new MOHA.

Ministerial portfolios were given to the directors general of the Prime Minister's Office and the newly created Environment Agency (*Kankyōchō*), as well as to the chairpersons of the three regional development commissions. In May 1965, Imamatsu Jirō, a former Home Ministry official who had been purged under the occupation, became the PMO's first minister-level director. The Environment Agency was established in January 1971 as part of the government's response to the environmental protest movement, and LDP lawmaker Yamanaka Sadanori was tapped to serve as director general (Reich 1984, 385). Meanwhile, the chairpersons of the commissions to oversee the development of the Capital Region (founded in June 1957) and the Kinki (July 1964) and Chūbu (July 1966) Regions assumed ministerial portfolios. In May 1972, following the reversion of sovereignty, the Okinawa Development Agency (*Okinawa kaihatsuchō*) was established with a cabinet-level director general as its head.

Several important cabinet-related auxiliary organs appeared. The National Defense Council (*Kokubō kaigi*) emerged in July 1956, with the prime minister as its chair and a membership that included the foreign minister, finance minister, and the directors general of defense and economic planning. A 1957 reform of the Cabinet Secretariat created three new offices—cabinet councilors, deliberation, and research. On May 15, 1972, the same day that sovereignty over Okinawa was restored, a Northern Territories Policy Headquarters (*Hoppō taisaku honbu*) was established within the PMO to coordinate efforts to regain sovereignty over the disputed islands. A 1956 overhaul of the Cabinet Secretariat created internal offices for general affairs (*naikaku sōmukan shitsu*), public relations (*naikaku kōdōkan shitsu*), and information research (*naikaku jōhō chōsa shitsu*). Although it bore scant likeness to its supposed American counterpart, the Cabinet Information Research Office was dubbed "Japan's CIA" (Hayao 1993, 175). Finally, although the chief cabinet secretary had attended cabinet meetings and served as the government's primary spokesperson since prewar times, it was not until 1966 that the occupant of the post was accorded formal ministerial status.

A BUREAUCRATIC CORE EXECUTIVE

Executive decision-making came to be dominated by the perpetually ruling party and the government bureaucracy. Although Hatoyama succeeded in normalizing relations with the Soviet Union and Kishi revised the Mutual Security Treaty, neither exhibited the focused, yet carefully calibrated and inclusive leadership style expected in prime ministerial government. Ikeda wisely chose to adopt a "low posture" leadership style to lower the political temperature following the security treaty crisis, and Satō's protracted tenure was more the result of good fortune (his three most serious rivals died soon after he took office) than of forceful prime ministerial leadership (Stockwin 2011, 11). Most of those who held ministerial portfolios were content to act as transitory figureheads who deferred to the career bureaucrats in the ministries they supervised (Thayer 1969, 203).

Mist-Enshrouded Party Government

In its role as ever-ruling party, the LDP exerted considerable influence over executive affairs. For one thing, the LDP's unyielding grasp on parliamentary power meant that its president would invariably double as prime minister and that its lawmaker members would virtually monopolize appointments to cabinet posts. This blurred the line between ruling party and cabinet, and appointment to a cabinet ministership became another step in the advancement of LDP MPs. As a result, the background characteristics of cabinet ministers became identical to those of senior LDP legislators. While that mirroring is expected, what is peculiar about the Japanese case is that LDP MPs all but monopolized ministerial portfolios for five and a half decades. Moreover, the internal politics of the ruling party—especially the need to maintain "factional balance"—determined who became cabinet ministers and how long they held office (Thayer 1969, 195). This process granted priority to factional affiliation over ability in selecting ministers. For example, Prime Minister Ikeda reshuffled his cabinet with craftsman-like precision, never allowing more than 365 days to pass without a change of ministers. The fact that five of Ikeda's seven reshufflings took place on July 18–19 and the other two on December 8–9 suggests that his chief aim was to obtain factional accord rather than to ensure that the most qualified MPs held ministerial posts (see table 3.1). Also, factionally unaffiliated MPs and those from smaller factions were routinely passed over in allocating portfolios. If these individuals were lucky enough to receive a portfolio at all, it is probable that it was one that offered limited prestige or pork-barreling opportunity (Cox et al. 1999, 47). In addition, the need to ensure harmony within the ruling party dictated rapid turnover of ministers, which made it difficult for elected politicians to acquire the policy expertise required to win the respect of senior bureaucrats and to effectively monitor the career civil servants in their ministries.

The LDP was in a position to require that all major legislative proposals be preapproved by internal party organs before being submitted for Diet deliberation. The Policy Affairs Research Council (*Seimuchōsakai*, or PARC) was the key intraparty organ in the preapproval process. During the era of corporatist cabinets, PARC was composed of around fifteen divisions (*bukai*), corresponding to the ministries and agencies of the central government and the Diet's standing committees (Satō and Matsuzaki 1986, 248). Each LDP MP was allowed to join up to three divisions, which attracted MPs with designs on becoming members of a particular "tribe" (*zoku*) of influential policy specialists (Inoguchi and Iwai 1987, 99). The most popular divisions were the "three noble houses" (*go-sanke*) of Agriculture (*Nōrin*), Commerce and Industry (*Shōkō*), and Construction (*Kensetsu*), whose magnetic appeal was a function of the cornucopia of distributive benefits (such as agricultural price supports, subsidies, and public works contracts) over which they held influence (Woodall 1996, 117). As early as 1962, the LDP was able to require that all policy and budgetary proposals be reviewed and debated within its internal organs before submission to the Diet (McCubbins and Noble 1995, 15; George Mulgan 2003a, 140). In this way, PARC became a sort of "shadow cabinet" in which a complex bargaining process ensured that members of the LDP's policy tribes could affect policy and budget proposals before they were debated in the Diet (Inoguchi and Iwai 1987, 20, 27–28).

Because LDP lawmakers virtually monopolized ministerial posts, instances of malfeasance involving ministers were perceived as the byproducts of protracted single-party rule. This was seen in the fallout over the Black Mist (*kurokiri*) scandals that erupted in 1966. The scandal was triggered by the arrest of LDP lower house MP Tanaka Shōji on charges that he accepted cash from businessmen in return for silence on faked government contracts (*Time Magazine*, November 4, 1966). Transport minister Arafune Seijurō then came under fire for allegedly using his influence to ensure that express trains stopped at a tiny railway station in his electoral district and for taking a pair of businessmen on a government-financed trip to South Korea. The opposition seized upon the scandal to lambast the Satō government. The scandal continued to expand, and Defense Agency director Kanbayashiyama Eikichi drew criticism for staging a lavish homecoming parade, replete with a Self-Defense Forces (SDF) band and senior SDF officers flown in on an official aircraft, when he visited his Kagoshima district. Agriculture Minister Matsuno Raizō came under scrutiny for funneling government loans to the ailing Kyōwa Sugar Refining Company, a loyal LDP contributor (Mitchell 1996, 117). Matsuno was also lambasted for ordering the installation of a private lavatory in the minister's office because he felt "sorry for the toilet guard, who had to salute him every time he entered the public rest room" (*Newsweek*, October 31, 1966).

The opposition argued that the Black Mist scandals were symptomatic of the LDP's spoils system, which awarded portfolios to party MPs recommended by their faction bosses rather than to qualified candidates. In most cases, prime ministers allocated cabinet posts according to a rank-ordered list of candidates proposed by each faction (Kyogoku 1987, 193). When the mist began to clear, popular approval of the Satō cabinet plummeted. Tanaka was expelled from the LDP as a result of his arrest, and Arafune resigned as transport minister, but Kanbayashiyama and Matsuno weathered the storm. The opposition turned up the heat on the Satō government by boycotting Diet deliberations, and Satō gave them what they wanted by dissolving the Diet and calling new elections for January 29, 1967. Despite the negative press and the emergence of the Soka Gakkai-sponsored Clean Government (*Kōmei*) Party, the LDP emerged from the 1967 lower house elections with 277 seats, a loss of only six.

The Kasumigaseki Shogunate

Japan's government bureaucrats were not mere value-neutral policy implementers; indeed, they initiated the majority of policy decisions, drafted bills, and explained government positions in Diet interpellations. Policy initiatives frequently emerged from "deliberation councils" (*shingikai*), official standing organs composed of civilian experts who advised the relevant ministers. The supposed autonomy of these councils was called into question, however, because their meetings were typically held in ministry offices, and ministry bureaucrats provided data for their deliberations (Johnson 1982, 36, 47). Moreover, in addition to drafting most government-sponsored bills (*seifu hōan*), bureaucrats were able to make policy incrementally by issuing cabinet ordinances (*seirei*), which did not require Diet approval. Under the corporatist cabinets, ordinances outnumbered enacted laws by a factor of better than two to one (387 to 164). The Cabinet Legislation Bureau (renamed from the Legislation Bureau in 1962) continued to play a role akin to that of a quasi-constitutional court concerning matters of constitutional interpretation. Although Hatoyama initially resisted the bureau's interpretations, he eventually came to see the light. As the bureau's director general of the time recalled, "Prime Minister Hatoyama was an amateur when it came to constitutional arguments and legal theory" (Samuels 2004, 6).

Although they were physically based in Tokyo's Kasumigaseki district, the government bureaucrats were able to make their influence felt through an expansive network of friends in high places. As noted, nearly half of all ministerial portfolios were given to ex-bureaucrats, and three of the five

prime ministers descended from the highest rank in the career civil service into second careers as MPs. In fact, Prime Ministers Kishi, Ikeda, and
Satō presided over twenty of the twenty-two cabinets formed during the
era of corporatist cabinets. Furthermore, ex-bureaucrats grabbed a disproportionate share of the most coveted cabinet posts. At various times, Kishi,
Ōhira Masayoshi, Shiina Etsusaburō, Aichi Kiichi, and Fukuda Takeo held
the foreign affairs portfolio, while Ikeda, Satō, Fukuda, and Ueki Koshirō
were among those who held the finance portfolio. The international trade
and industry portfolio went to Maeo Shigesaburō, Ikeda, Ishii Mitsujirō,
Shiina, Satō, Ōhira, Miyazawa Kiichi, and Nakasone Yasuhiro. In addition,
ex-bureaucrats held the portfolios of justice, education, posts and telecommunications, health and welfare, economic planning, and defense. It
is worth reiterating that two-thirds of these ex-bureaucrat ministers had
risen to the rarefied rank of bureau chief or above at the time they parted
ways with their ministries.

The bureaucracy consolidated its dominance over the executive branch
in the scrum to replace Kishi as prime minister. In June 1960, when Kishi
publicly announced his intention to resign, Ōno Banboku, Ishii Mitsujirō,
and Ikeda Hayato became the main candidates to replace him. Ōno and
Ishii were career politicians, as were most of their factional followers. Ikeda,
on the other hand, was the quintessential "Yoshida School" alumnus, and
many ex-bureaucrats were numbered among his followers. After enduring
Kishi's steamroller style of leadership (discussed below), the career politicians were eager to take the helm. As the date for the presidential election drew near, Ōno was confident that he could count on the support of
170 LDP MPs, but he needed the support of other factions to assemble
the 256 votes required for a majority. On the eve of the election, rumors
began circulating that Ishii's supporters and members of other factions
were being wooed away by a "last-ditch strategy" conjured up by Kishi to
ensure Ikeda's victory (Thayer 1969, 171). Ōno reluctantly ordered his followers to vote for Ishii, but Ikeda—backed by the "bureaucratic" Kishi and
Satō factions—prevailed in a 302 to 194 vote (with five invalid ballots).
After the election, Ōno cryptically observed, "Arrows broken, ammunition
spent, the battle ended in a defeat for the party politicians. Simply stated,
the reason we lost is that we ran out of money" (quoted in ibid., 173). It is
unclear whether or not "M-Fund" monies—a secret fund of money named
for General William F. Marquat, one of MacArthur's inner circle of advisers—funneled from the CIA to Kishi played a role in this triumph (John-

son 1995a; Schaller 1995). Ikeda's victory—which was followed by Sato's extended premiership—deepened the rift between the LDP's rival camps of ex-bureaucrats and career politicians.

Some ex-bureaucrats went on to become "muscle man ministers" who were able to shape policy (Thayer 1969, 203). For example, Finance Minister Ikeda Hayato was able to remove fiscally conservative officials at the ministry who opposed his high-speed growth policies (Johnson 1982, 53). Of course, ex-bureaucrats such as Ikeda had an advantage because they had firsthand knowledge of the inner workings and subject matter of their ministries. Yet, a few career politicians were able to dominate the irremovable career bureaucrats. For example, future prime minister Tanaka Kakuei was able to win the allegiance of bureaucrats with his impressive memory for details (including, as legend has it, the birthdays of all upper officials in the ministry) and his penchant for generous gift-giving (Johnson 1986b, 11). For the most part, though, political meddling in the internal affairs of the ministries produced little or no enduring change.[5]

THE CHALLENGES OF HIGH-SPEED GROWTH

The corporatist cabinets faced an array of domestic and international challenges. Conservative leaders such as Hatoyama and Kishi felt compelled to rectify the unequal and demeaning Japan-U.S. Mutual Security Treaty and to establish a more independent foreign policy by restoring relations with the Soviet Union. Domestically, these cabinets faced mounting public opposition to the large U.S. military presence on the mainland, protests against the Vietnam War, and a rising chorus of demands to secure the return of Okinawa. As they presided over an economic "miracle" that ushered Japan into the ranks of the world's most advanced countries, these executive leaders were forced to deal with the negative byproducts of high-speed growth that created trade friction and badly degraded air and waterways.

Steamrolling Revision

The rival camps in the "1955 system" were at odds over the Japan-U.S. Mutual Security Treaty (*Nichibei anzen hoshō jōyaku,* or *Anpo*), which had been agreed to by the Yoshida government in September 1951. Progressives opposed the *Anpo* because it allowed the United States to station its military forces on Japanese soil and to deploy those forces without having to receive approval from Tokyo. They feared that this could embroil the country in Cold War tensions of America's making, and they opposed the presumed existence of U.S. nuclear weapons at military bases in Japan. Meanwhile, the LDP and conservative elements believed that the *Anpo* perpetuated Japan's security dependence on the United States. While progressives advocated abrogation of the security treaty, the LDP and its allies tended to favor a revised treaty that was more equitable and gave Japan greater autonomy in providing for its own defense.

The revision of the *Anpo* became the Kishi cabinet's primary mission. Kishi was aware that any attempt to revise the treaty would provoke controversy, but he vowed to "brush such opposition aside and complete the task even if it meant putting his [political] life on the line" (quoted in Masumi 1985, 27). On September 11, 1958, Foreign Minister Fujiyama Aiichirō and U.S. secretary of state John Foster Dulles issued a joint communiqué pledging to revise the security treaty, and formal talks began the following month. Predictably, the opposition condemned the talks, but some elements within the LDP also took a dim view of treaty revision. With a party presidential election set for late January 1959, Kishi wished to avoid division within the ruling party. While Fujiyama and Dulles were in Washington hammering out the language of their communiqué, the Kishi cabinet sponsored a bill to modify the Police Duties Law to enhance the government's powers to curb mass demonstrations (Shiratori 1981, 208). Kishi viewed this as essential to maintaining public order in the chaos likely to be unleashed when the Diet took up treaty revision. Pacifists, socialists, and student groups wanted to reaffirm the Constitution's "no war" clause to rid Japan of American military bases. They viewed Kishi's obsession with treaty revision—which kept U.S. forces in Japan and strengthened the hand of Japanese militarists—as the worst of all worlds. Eventually the bill to modify the Police Duties Law evoked so much controversy that the Kishi cabinet allowed it to be shelved, but not before intraparty faction bosses Miki Takeo, Ikeda Hayato, and Nadao Hirokichi resigned their cabinet posts in protest. To hang on to the party presidency, Kishi had to make a secret pact with other faction bosses to resign as LDP president once a revised *Anpo* was enacted (Masumi 1985, 29; Kensei shiryō hensankai, ed. 1978, 42).

Despite an expansion of mass protests, Kishi and his cabinet pressed ahead with ratification. Anti-revision protests exploded in the spring of

1959, and a November 27 demonstration saw two hundred thousand protestors surround the Diet Building. On January 7, 1960, one day after bilateral talks produced an agreement, Kishi, Foreign Minister Fujiyama, and LDP Executive Council Chair Ishii Mitsujirō flew to Washington to sign the revised treaty, which they did on January 19. The Soviet Union responded by declaring that none of the islands in the disputed Northern Territories would be returned as long as American troops remained on Japanese soil. The treaty was submitted to the Diet for deliberation and ratification. Out in the streets, demonstrations continued, and in April a major clash occurred between police and members of *Zengakuren,* the radical All-Japan Federation of Students' Self-Governing Associations (Nihon Gakusei Jichikai Sō Rengō). On May 19, the Kishi government's decision to use the LDP's lower house majority to force an extension of the Diet session led JSP MPs to organize a sit-in to block House Speaker Kiyose Ichirō from entering the chamber. Kiyose called in the police, who proceeded to forcibly remove JSP MPs from the Diet corridor. Shortly after midnight, with JSP and Democratic Socialist Party lawmakers absent, Kiyose called a snap vote that resulted in lower house approval of the revised treaty.

Popular protests continued despite the fact that the Kishi government's steamroller tactics (*kyōkō saiketsu*) ensured the revised treaty's automatic ratification. Petitions were gathered, labor strikes were called, and protestors swarmed around the Diet Building on a daily basis. On June 11, a U.S. Marine helicopter had to be sent to rescue White House Press Secretary James Haggerty from several thousand protestors who surrounded the car in which he was riding. Haggerty had been sent to Tokyo to make final arrangements for President Dwight D. Eisenhower's planned visit, which, as it turned out, never took place. Four days later, a university coed was killed and hundreds were injured in a clash between students and police at a demonstration organized by *Zengakuren,* and large-scale demonstrations, complete with snake-dancing, continued in front of the Diet Building and in the streets of Tokyo (Packard 1966, 296). Nevertheless, the revised treaty was automatically ratified on June 19 and went into force on June 23, the same day the Kishi cabinet announced its intention to resign. On July 14, Kishi was stabbed by a member of a right-wing group who was incensed at his decision to endorse Ikeda Hayato, reputed to be a moderate, as his successor as LDP president. Although Kishi survived the attack, his progressive rival, JSP Chairman Asanuma Inejirō, was stabbed to death while delivering a speech on October 12.

Embracing Environmentalism

The success of Japan's high-speed growth policies legitimized a "business first" strategy that allowed companies to reap huge profits with little or no concern for the effects of the pollutants their factories dumped into the environment. By the mid-1960s, Japan's polluted air and waterways had become infamous. The willful disregard for the environment was symbolized in the "four great pollution diseases" (*yon-dai kōgyō byō*): Minamata disease, Itai-itai disease, Niigata Minamata disease, and Yokkaichi asthma. Yet policy-makers refused to acknowledge scientific evidence linking human deaths and disease to decades of unrestrained pollution. Furthermore, the government turned a blind eye when the polluters hired thugs to intimidate victims and physicians who initiated legal action.

An environmental protection movement emerged in the mid-1960s and coalesced around victims of pollution-related diseases and denizens of heavily industrialized urban areas (Reich 1984, 390). Buoyed by court rulings in favor of victims of the pollution-related diseases, several thousand citizens' groups sprouted up (McKean 1981, 17, 20; Mason 1999, 189). The Socialist, Japan Communist, and newly formed Clean Government (*Kōmei*) parties seized the opportunity to champion the environmental protection cause. Eventually, the anti-pollution movement became the dominant issue on the political agenda, making it impossible for the ruling LDP to go on with business as usual.

In contrast to the Kishi cabinet's steamroller approach to treaty revision, the Satō cabinet nimbly executed an about-face and embraced environmental protection. In 1967, the Basic Law on Environmental Pollution Control (which included a clause stating that the government would pursue pollution control as long as it was "in harmony with" the overall health of the economy) was enacted; two years later, the Diet passed a law to compensate the victims of pollution-related damage (Reich 1984, 383; McKean 1981, 21; Rosenbluth and Thies 1999, 11). The greatest burst of legislative action occurred in the "Pollution Diet" (*kōgai kokkai*) of 1970, in which the Satō cabinet orchestrated passage of fourteen bills related to environmental protection. In 1971, the Satō cabinet established a cabinet-level Environment Agency (*Kankyochō*) and charged it with producing monthly bulletins and an annual white paper on pollution (Reich 1984, 383–384). As a result, Japan came to possess "one of the most complete statutory frameworks for environmental policy in the world," transforming itself from environmental laggard to environmental leader almost overnight (ibid., 384). In so doing, the LDP-dominated Satō cabinet successfully undermined efforts to tie the plethora of citizens' groups into a unified national movement (Mason 1999, 189).

Selling Thread to Buy Rope

Securing the return of Okinawa became the Satō government's diplomatic magnum opus, but it extracted a high price. It is said that Satō "sold thread to buy rope" (*ito o utte nawa o kau*) at his 1969 summit with U.S. president Richard M. Nixon, which means that the Japanese prime minister was forced to accept voluntary restraints on Japanese textile exports (the character "*ito*" means thread in Japanese) to obtain the return of Oki*nawa* (the character "*nawa*" means rope) (Funabashi 1999, 132). While there would seem to be no connection between the return of Okinawa and textile exports, circumstances dictated that the two issues would be linked.

By the early 1950s, Japanese exports to the United States had become a source of contention. While Washington's official position was that a prosperous Japan was important in containing the Communist menace, it did not take long for American producers to feel threatened by products carrying the "Made in Japan" label. In 1951, the American tuna industry's complaints about unfair competition led the Japanese side to propose and implement temporary restraints on exports (McClenahan 1991, 181). Yet an economic boom stimulated by American procurements for the Korean War led to an increase in Japanese exports to U.S. markets. Japan's textile producers made some of the biggest gains, even though their products never captured more than 2 percent of the U.S. textile market (Mettler 2010, 217). American producers pointed with disdain to the Japanese-made "one dollar blouses" that were selling in U.S. department stores (ibid., 214). In December 1955, the Japanese side agreed to a one-year voluntary limit on exports of velveteens, cotton fabrics, and blouses. This did not appease the textile-producing states of Alabama, South Carolina, and Georgia, which enacted laws requiring businesses to display signs stating that they sold Japanese merchandise (ibid., 214–215; McClenahan 1991, 183). On January 16, 1957, Tokyo agreed to a five-year voluntary export restraint of cotton textile exports (McClenahan 1991, 183). Not surprisingly, this and subsequent concessions were deeply resented by Japan's textile manufacturers and their bureaucratic and political champions (Watanabe 1981b, 188; Johnson 1982, 249–252).

The textile issue continued to fester, leading presidential candidate Richard M. Nixon to promise textile producers in the southern states that, if elected in 1968, he would restrict imports of Japanese synthetic textiles. Shortly after becoming president, Nixon made it clear to National Security Adviser Henry Kissinger that he intended to keep his word (Kissinger 1979, 330). Meanwhile, Satō was keen to ensure that American displeasure over Japanese textile imports did not sidetrack efforts to secure the return of Okinawa, which was his government's top priority. Satō dispatched university professor Wakaizumi Kei to Washington to act as his secret emissary. Satō's decision to pursue back-channel diplomacy was motivated by his distrust of Foreign Minister Miki Takeo, a fellow faction leader and rival for the LDP presidency, and the justifiable assumption that MITI would torpedo any proposal to restrain textile exports. Kissinger and Wakaizumi—who referred to each other as "Mr. Jones" and "Mr. Yoshida" to maintain secrecy—began meeting in September 1969 (Wakaizumi 2002, 112). Wakaizumi signaled that his "friend" (Satō) was willing to accept comprehensive export limits on Japanese textiles in exchange for the return of Okinawa, with U.S. nuclear weapons removed. Kissinger relayed that his "friend" (Nixon) was amenable, but had some concerns regarding the nuclear weapons issue. Eventually, Kissinger and Wakaizumi agreed that the nuclear issue could be finessed by invoking language in the U.S.-Japan Mutual Security Treaty that called for prior consultation in emergencies. This allowed the Satō government to maintain its anti-nuclear stance, while the U.S. side could claim the right to use nuclear weapons in Okinawa even in advance of an emergency (Kissinger 1979, 334–335).

This back-channel deal nearly fell apart on the evening of Satō's arrival in Washington for his summit with Nixon. On November 17, Wakaizumi informed Kissinger that Satō was having second thoughts concerning an agreed-upon formula for comprehensive limits on textile exports (Kissinger 1979, 333; Watanabe 1981b, 190–191). Wakaizumi agreed to ask Satō to "sleep on it," and the next day the Japanese prime minister agreed to the planned scenario. However, Satō requested that the Okinawa communiqué contain no mention of the textile issue, thus revealing his justifiable fear that MITI and industry interests would vilify him for selling thread to buy rope. Satō wanted the textile deal to emerge seemingly out of the blue at separate bilateral talks going on in Geneva. Nixon and Kissinger were amenable, and the joint statement issued on November 21 contained no mention of the secret textile accord.

After their formal talks had concluded, Satō, Nixon, and Kissinger met privately. Nixon explained that the "nuclear-free" aspect of the Okinawa accord had been a tough sell for the American side and that, in return, he expected Satō to keep his part of the bargain by restraining Japanese textile exports (Schaller 1996, 219). The two heads of state shook hands, and Nixon walked away believing that Satō was a man of his word. Satō later claimed that he had not promised to curb textile exports, but had merely agreed to do his best to honor Nixon's request (Destler et al. 1979, 134–135; Watanabe 1981b, 191–192). Kissinger later conceded that Satō did not actually use the term "comprehensive" with regard to export limits, but claimed that Wakaizumi assured him on two occasions that Satō would honor his word (Kissinger 1979, 336–337; Wakaizumi 2002, 318). Whatever the case, the flow of Japanese textile exports continued unabated, and, in the minds of Nixon and Kissinger, textiles and Okinawa had become inextricably linked.

Tug of War over Okinawa

The United States had exercised military governance over the Ryūkyū Islands, including Okinawa, since June of 1945, although the San Francisco Peace Treaty designated them as United Nations Trust Territories. The U.S. military bases on Okinawa were viewed by the U.S. side as vital in supporting American forces fighting in Vietnam. At the same time, Okinawa was symbolically important to the Japanese, who viewed the restoration of sovereignty over this "homeland" territory and the Northern Territories as unresolved issues left over from the Pacific War. In fact, every postwar Japanese prime minister had made efforts to secure the reversion of sovereignty.

In January 1965, during his initial visit to Washington as Japan's prime minister, Satō broached the issue of the return of Okinawa. The Americans gave no response, although in a joint declaration Satō and President Lyndon B. Johnson reaffirmed Okinawa's importance for regional security. During an August visit to Okinawa, Satō famously declared that "the postwar era will not end until the return of Okinawa to the homeland is realized" (*Okinawa no fukki naku shite Nippon no sengo wa owaranai*) (Sarantakes 2000, 137). Satō tasked Cabinet Minister Mori Kiyoshi, director general of the Prime Minister's Office, with examining the Okinawa problem. Mori proposed an approach whereby Japan would negotiate for the reversion of control over Okinawa's functional administrative domains one at a time, beginning with education (ibid, 140; Watanabe 1981a, 167). Satō rejected Mori's approach and in August 1967 established the Okinawa Problems Council (*Okinawa mondai tō kondankai*) under the chairmanship of Kusumi Tadao, a former Imperial Navy officer and a military affairs commentator (Sarantakes 2000, 169). Satō's decision to create this extra-cabinet council was motivated, at least in part, by a distrust of Foreign Minister Miki, who was preparing to challenge him in the upcoming LDP presidential election.

Negotiations continued through 1967 and into 1968. On December 16, Satō and Johnson issued a joint declaration in Washington affirming that a decision concerning Okinawa's return would be made within three years. Meanwhile, back in Tokyo, LDP faction bosses Miki and Maeo Shigesaburō were gearing up for the party's presidential election by criticizing Satō's vague stance concerning the presumed existence of U.S. nuclear weapons on Okinawa (Watanabe 1981a, 169). At a December 11 meeting of the lower house budget committee, Satō deftly defanged his intraparty foes by declaring that "my responsibility is to achieve and maintain safety in Japan under the Three Non-Nuclear Principles [*hikaku san-gensoku*] of not possessing, not producing and not permitting the introduction of nuclear weapons, in line with Japan's Peace Constitution" (Ministry of Foreign Affairs, 1967). On November 27, 1968, Satō easily won a third term as the LDP president. Afterward, U.S. diplomat Richard L. Sneider returned from visiting Japan and Okinawa to report to Assistant Secretary of State for East Asian Affairs William Bundy that Satō "has put into office a cabinet, which is by far the ablest and most understanding of the vitals of U.S.-Japan relations," yet "by publicly committing his regime to solution of the Okinawa problem, he has given his rivals within the party and his foes outside the party a major test of success" ("Memorandum, Sneider to Bundy" 1968).

On March 3, 1969, Kusumi's Okinawa Problems Council recommended that a bilateral decision on Okinawa's return be agreed to by year's end, with reversion taking place no later than 1972 (Watanabe 1981a, 169). Two days later, at a meeting of the upper house Budget Committee, Satō affirmed that Okinawa must be returned all at once and with the understanding that this would be accompanied by the removal of nuclear weapons and a reduced American military presence (ibid., 170). At the

November 21 summit, Satō and Nixon agreed to proceed "with a view to accomplishing the reversion during 1972" and agreed that it would be carried out in a manner consistent with "the particular sentiment of the Japanese people against nuclear weapons and the policy of the Japanese Government reflecting such sentiment" (Joint Statement 1969). Satō and the LDP were rewarded with a landslide victory in December's lower house elections, and on March 31 the Satō cabinet agreed on basic policy measures for the return of Okinawa (*Okinawa fukki taisaku no kihon hōshin*). Japan assumed sovereignty over Okinawa on May 15, 1972.

Yet even as Satō and his associates were toasting the Okinawa accord, the seemingly insignificant textile dispute threatened to incite trade war. In March 1971, the Japan Textile Federation (*Nihon sen'i sangyō renmei*) proposed a plan to voluntarily limit textile exports to the United States. This came as a result of talks with Wilbur Mills, chairman of the U.S. House Ways and Means Committee and a leader in the Democratic Party (*Time Magazine*, March 29, 1971; Meyer interview 1996). Nixon was nonplussed at the thought that Mills would claim credit for bringing the Japanese to heel. With an election approaching, Nixon was eager to retain the backing of textile producers, who followed suit by claiming that the Mills-brokered proposal was overly generous to Japanese interests (Schaller 1996, 216).

On July 5, Satō reshuffled his cabinet and made the strategic decision to appoint Tanaka Kakuei as minister of international trade and industry. In so doing, Satō removed MITI minister Miyazawa Kiichi, a former Finance Ministry bureaucrat, who refused to accept comprehensive limits on Japanese textile exports (Kikuchi interview 1996). Tanaka was a rising star in the political world, with a reputation for getting results through sometimes ethically dubious means. Before Tanaka could tackle the textile problem, however, shock waves began emanating from the White House.

The Nixon "shocks" were a punch in the gut for the Satō government. On July 15, with little advance warning to Tokyo, Nixon announced plans to visit the People's Republic of China. This was viewed as an insult to Satō and the Japanese, who had loyally followed the American lead in recognizing the Republic of China on Taiwan as opposed to the Beijing government. In August, a second "Nixon shock" was administered in the form of the unilateral declaration that the dollar would no longer be convertible into gold and that a 10 percent surcharge would be imposed on all existing U.S. tariffs, a move that was seen as aimed at Japanese imports. Then, in September, Ambassador at Large David M. Kennedy delivered what was viewed as an "ultimatum" (*saigo tsūchō*) by setting a deadline of October 15 to reach an agreement on the textile issue (Ishii 2009, 443). With American officials threatening to invoke the "Trading with the Enemy Act," the Japanese side agreed to a three-year comprehensive limit on textile exports (Destler 1976, 44–45). In his trademark manner, Tanaka sealed the deal by arranging for a ¥200 billion payment to Japanese textile producers as compensation for the restrictions they were forced to bear (Johnson 1986b, 9; Kikuchi interview 1996). At the end of the day, Tanaka's deal gave the Americans the comprehensive export limitations they had insisted on all along.

FINDINGS

Between 1955 and 1972, corporatist cabinets sponsored the high-speed growth policies that gave birth to the "Japanese miracle" that became a source of pride for a nation not long removed from the sackcloth and ashes of defeat. This economic juggernaut, known to the world as "Japan, Inc.," was buoyed by a strong pro-growth consensus and legitimized by the success of the export-oriented, high-speed growth policies. Although the initial change agents were opportunistic party leaders, most of whom were "career politicians," the corporatist cabinets had a strong bureaucratic coloration. Indeed, three of the era's prime ministers were former high-ranking government officials, and ex-bureaucrats held a large share of ministerial posts. Although most of the key policy initiatives emerged from government ministries and agencies, the corporatist cabinets dutifully submitted government-sponsored bills that were rubber-stamped by the LDP-dominated Diet. In fact, the LDP was able to require that it preapprove all major policy and budgetary proposals before they could be submitted for Diet deliberation. As long as the economy grew and the budgetary pie expanded, the LDP and its leaders were content to claim credit for policy initiatives that emerged from the government ministries. LDP candidates were able to shower their supporters with patronage, especially in the form of public works projects and subsidies (Scheiner 2006, 2). In addition, the party's stranglehold over ministerial portfolios had the effect of creating a ministerial elite whose background characteristics mirrored those of its senior MPs. The combination of an activist bureaucracy and a perpetually ruling party ensured that cabinet government did not take root.

The corporatist cabinets responded with alacrity to some challenges and in a ham-handed manner to others. For example, Satō's duplicity in the textile dispute was the result of his failure to consult with the domestic government bureaucrats and industry groups whose compliance was necessary (Johnson 1982, 285). In the words of Armin Meyer, U.S. ambassador to Japan, "they're all sovereign bureaucracies and the Prime Minister cannot overrule them" (Meyer interview 1996). At the same time, Satō wanted to avoid distractions that might sidetrack the Okinawa talks, so he handed the international trade portfolio to someone he knew would buy off the domestic manufacturers. Satō ensured the return of Okinawa through back-channel diplomacy and the use of an extracabinet council. Meanwhile, Kishi and his ministers were determined to obtain treaty revision no matter what the cost, even if it meant steamrolling ratification. In the end, Kishi got a revised treaty, but at the cost of his government and an attempt on his life. Finally, the Satō cabinet deftly reversed course and embraced environmental protection by sponsoring a raft of laws and by creating a cabinet-level Environment Agency. This helped to ensure that the environmental movement did not coalesce into mass protest, as had been the case with the treaty revision crisis.

On June 7, 1972, Prime Minister Satō announced his resignation in a televised press conference from which all members of the press had been expelled. The scene of Satō, an elite ex-bureaucrat with little patience for impertinent reporters, speaking to the nation from a room filled with empty chairs symbolized the end of the era of corporatist cabinets. Satō's replacement, Tanaka Kakuei, the quintessential career politician, perceived the utility of the mass media and, more importantly, understood that political power was enhanced by expanding the number of one's followers and placing them in positions of influence in a range of important policy domains. The Nixon and oil "shocks" helped topple the Satō government and brought down the curtain on the era of high-speed economic growth with its constantly expanding budgetary pie. This ushered in the era of confederate cabinets and a fragmented policy-making environment dominated by "policy tribes."

4

Confederate Cabinets and the Demise of the "1955 System," 1972–1993

British government is essentially "ministerial government," although this is counter-balanced by a Cabinet whose collegiate ethos is stronger than in most countries.

 —Simon James, *British Cabinet Government*, 2nd ed. (2002), 12

Those legislators who wield influence in particular policy areas, the *zoku* politicians, are treated as lawmakers representing the various ministries and agencies. . . . Rather than going through the cabinet minister and the official chain of command, bureaucrats brief the ruling party's *zoku* politicians on a daily basis.

 —Iio Jun, *Nihon tōchi no Kōzō: Kanryō naikakusei kara giin naikakusei e* [*Japan's Structure of Governance: From Bureaucratic to Parliamentary Cabinet System*] (2007), 6.

Low Unseat the High

On July 7, 1972, at fifty-four years of age, Tanaka Kakuei became the youngest prime minister in the postwar era. His rise from humble origins to the pinnacle of the political executive conjured up images of a latter-day Toyotomi Hideyoshi (1537–1598), the peasant-turned-warlord who helped to establish a system of centralized governance that brought an end to the Warring States (*sengoku jidai*—1476–1615) period. Tanaka was proclaimed the "commoner premier" (*shōmin saishō*) because he displayed a populist style, liked to sing *naniwabushi* (traditional Japanese narrative songs), and lacked the elitist educational pedigree of his predecessors. He established a cabinet of "party men" (*tōjin ha*) dedicated to "the politics of decision and action" (*ketsudan to jikkō no seiji*) (Watanabe, ed. 1995, 210; Kensei shiryō hensankai, ed. 1978, 45). He assumed the premiership with a promise to visit the People's Republic of China, and fulfilled that promise just two months after taking office. He further stoked the public's imagination with a grandiose plan to "remodel" the Japanese archipelago through a bonanza of expressways, bullet train lines, and island-linking bridges. Tanaka's decision to dissolve the Diet and call new elections in December 1972 left the Liberal Democratic Party in control of a solid majority of seats in the Diet's lower house. The party's hegemonic control of the Diet seemed ensured with a dynamic, young, and popular party president sitting in the prime minister's chair.

Contrast this with the scene on August 9, 1993, when septuagenarian Miyazawa Kiichi was forced to turn over the premiership to Hosokawa Morihiro, a young former prefectural governor and the first non-LDP prime minister in nearly four decades. Miyazawa, an ex-Finance Ministry bureaucrat, had assumed leadership of the LDP in the midst of several high-profile scandals. His predecessor had gambled and lost in staking the future of his government on the passage of a package of bills to reform campaign finance and the system for electing lower house MPs. The reform bill proposed by the Miyazawa cabinet was torpedoed by the LDP's top leaders, resulting in plummeting public approval ratings for the cabinet and the secession of several party leaders and their followers. On June 18, an opposition-sponsored no-confidence vote against the Miyazawa cabinet had been approved as a result of the supporting votes cast by these disaffected former LDP MPs. The LDP emerged from the lower house election that followed in control of only 44 percent of the seats, paving the way for a non-LDP coalition government under the Hosokawa cabinet. With this, the curtain came down on nearly four decades of uninterrupted LDP predominance, bringing with it the demise of the "1955 system."

In this chapter, I explore the evolution of the cabinet system through the last days of the "1955 system." This was an era of "confederate cabinets," in which an already blurry distinction between ruling party and cabinet became even blurrier, and a succession of corruption scandals intensified demands for political reform. Measures were taken to enhance the prime minister's leadership powers, and yet these efforts failed to establish top-down executive leadership. At the same time, prime ministers and their cabinets struggled to provide coherent leadership in a context in which subgovernments dominated policy-making. Meanwhile, cabinets confronted an array of challenges that included reducing government debt in a slow-growth economy and responding to popular demands to reform a structurally corrupt political order. The story begins with the premiers and ministers who occupied center stage in the political drama that unfolded during the eventful 1970s and 1980s.

THE EMERGENCE OF CONFEDERATE CABINETS

Tanaka's triumphal rise signaled the advent of an age of confederate cabinets. The "Nixon shocks" dictated the demise of the fixed yen-dollar exchange rate and produced an unexpected thawing of relations between Washington and Beijing, while the "oil shocks" of 1973 and 1979 led to higher energy costs and the end of high-speed economic growth. This spelled the end to a constantly expanding economic pie and created fissures in the pro-growth consensus among government and business leaders. Influential lawmakers known as policy tribalists (*zoku giin*) assumed a leading role in the fief-like policy subgovernments that characterized a fragmented policy-making environment and exacerbated the difficulties faced by prime ministers and cabinets in pursuing their policy agendas. In contrast to the dramatic reconfigurations that followed the Meiji Restoration and the American occupation, institutional changes taken under the confederate cabinets were more akin to tectonic plate shifts. Ministerial portfolios came to be almost monopolized by career politicians who had ascended the LDP's promotional ladder and achieved the requisite level of seniority. In other words, the most coveted portfolios were no longer reserved for the likes of Kishi Nobusuke, Ikeda Hayato, and Satō Eisaku, who descended from the most senior posts in their respective ministries into second careers in elective politics. Predictably, the ascendency of the career politician was accompanied by increasing demands for pork barrel spending, a burgeoning black market for political "funds," and structural corruption that afflicted the entire body politic, producing a succession of corruption scandals that ultimately drove the LDP into the opposition pews (Woodall 2014).

Four factors combined to create conditions for the expanded influence of the LDP and its tribal politicians. One consequence of the slowed rate of economic growth that followed the 1973 oil shock (discussed below) was intensified competition among government ministries for a share of a government budget that was no longer expanding rapidly. The policy tribalists were called on to champion the positions of the various ministries in slicing up a static budgetary pie. In addition, changes in technology blurred distinctions among policy domains. For example, the Ministry of International Trade and Industry and the Ministry of Posts and Telecommunications—which, respectively, controlled the computer industry and electronic communications—fought sectionalist turf wars backed by tribalist champions to decide which would control telecommunications policy (Johnson 1986a). Third, the LDP's seemingly eternal parliamentary mastery—coupled with a well-established seniority system and an expansive system of policy-specific party committees and subcommittees—enabled ambitious MPs to specialize in particular policy areas. The expertise they acquired allowed them to more effectively monitor the career bureaucrats in the ministries. Finally, the LDP's factions continued to determine who occupied which ministerial post and for how long, with particular factions gaining disproportionate expertise in specific policy areas.[1] The downside of this was that, as the policy tribes developed their own strong ties to special interests and government bureaucrats, it became increasingly difficult for government and central party leaders to control their actions. In this sense, the rise of the policy tribes reflected "overinstitutionalization" in the political system (Kesselman 1970, 23).

THE RISE OF THE CAREER POLITICIAN

Between July 1973 and August 1993, twenty-five cabinets were organized under ten different prime ministers, and a total of 307 individuals held portfolios. The longest-lived of the confederate cabinets was the Miki cabinet, which held on for twenty-one months, while the most fleeting was the Reorganized second Tanaka cabinet, which collapsed after only twenty-eight days. This period witnessed an influx of career politicians into ministerial posts. The rise of once-marginalized MPs vis-à-vis traditionally elite bureaucrats can be likened to the phenomenon of "low unseating the high" (*gekokujō*), when vassals ousted their lords during the Warring States era that began in the fifteenth century (Conlan 2010).

The Prime Ministers

The majority of prime ministers were political careerists. Tanaka was the first career politician to hold the premiership since Ishibashi Tanzan more than a decade and a half earlier. Miki Takeo, Suzuki Zenkō, Takeshita Noboru, Uno Sōsuke, and Kaifu Toshiki also approached national elective politics as a primary career. Although Nakasone Yasuhiro briefly labored as a Home Ministry bureaucrat, most of his professional life was spent as a lower house MP, so he, too, deserves to be numbered among the career politicians. Even the three retired government bureaucrats Fukuda Takeo, Ōhira Masayoshi, and Miyazawa were a breed apart from their predecessors. In contrast to Kishi, Ikeda, and Satō—each of whom ascended to the pinnacle of the career civil service before embarking upon careers in elective politics—only Fukuda managed to gain promotion to a high-ranking bureaucratic post before running for election to the Diet. Kishi, Ikeda, and Satō held civil service positions for around two dozen years; the corresponding figure for Fukuda, Ōhira, and Miyazawa was just sixteen years. As Ōhira came to realize, a bureaucratic career did not offer the sort of "extraordinary adventure in which a man might give full rein to his vitality as an individual" (Satō et al. 1990, 128, 131).

The trio of ex-bureaucrats emerged from the powerful Finance Ministry. Fukuda Takeo received the coveted "silver watch" (*gin dokei*) recognizing the top graduate of Tokyo Imperial University's Law Faculty and ascended to the post of director of the Budget Bureau, making him a likely candidate for the coveted administrative vice ministership (Calder 1982, 3). However, his arrest on bribery charges (which were ultimately dropped) in the 1950 Shōwa Denkō scandal dictated an early departure from the civil service. Two years later, Fukuda was elected to a seat in the Diet's lower house, and he went on to serve as finance minister in five cabinets. Ōhira Masayoshi graduated from Tokyo University of Commerce (present-day Hitotsubashi University) and was chief of the Public Works Section at the Economic Stabilization Headquarters when, in 1949, Finance Minister Ikeda Hayato handpicked him to serve as his secretary. It was then that Ōhira began contemplating an "extraordinary adventure" in elective politics, which he launched in the 1952 general election. By 1976, Ōhira had inherited the reins of the Ikeda faction and was a contender for the premiership, but he agreed to support Fukuda on the condition that his "senior" (*senpai*) from the Finance Ministry step aside after "one term of two years" (Satō et al. 1990, 375). Fukuda's failure to do so resulted in a protracted feud between the rival faction bosses. Miyazawa Kiichi was born into a political family—his maternal grandfather held portfolios in two prewar cabinets and his father was a lower house MP—and graduated from Tokyo Imperial University's Law Faculty. In 1945, three years into his bureaucratic career, Miyazawa became one of Finance Minister Tsushima Jūichi's secretaries, the other being Ōhira. Miyazawa retired from the civil service in 1953 and was elected to an upper house seat, which he held until switching over to the lower house fourteen years later. Tanaka Kakuei famously referred to Miyazawa as an "English monger" (*eigoya*) in mockery of his impressive linguistic skills.

The seven remaining premiers were bona fide career politicians, having been elected to an average of twelve parliamentary terms and having accumulated more than three decades of parliamentary service at the time they formed their first cabinets. With the exception of Tanaka (who never completed high school) and Suzuki (who received instruction at the Agriculture Ministry's Fisheries Training Institute), all attended university. Nakasone graduated from Tokyo Imperial University, while Uno enrolled at the Kobe University of Commerce but failed to obtain a degree. Miki was a Meiji University alumnus who spent time studying at the University of Southern California, while Takeshita and Kaifu were Waseda University alumni who participated in the university's Oratorical Society (*Waseda daigaku yūbenkai*), which has served as a sort of prep school for aspiring political figures.

Tanaka, Suzuki, and Nakasone were young MPs at the time of the LDP's establishment, while Miki had earned the sobriquet of "Balkan Politician" (*barukan seijika*) for his frequent switches in party allegiance. Tanaka Kakuei employed the wealth he amassed in the construction business (augmented by wartime funds that remained in his possession for a never-to-be-completed project to relocate a piston ring factory to Korea) to launch a political career (Johnson 1986b, 5). After tasting defeat in 1946, he won a lower house seat the following year. Tanaka was arrested but not convicted in conjunction with the 1948 Coal Nationalization scandal and went on to become posts and telecommunications minister shortly after his thirty-ninth birthday. Miki Takeo was elected to the Diet in 1937 and was one of the relatively few successful candidates who won seats in the 1942 general election without the endorsement of the Imperial Rule Assistance Association. As communications minister in the JSP-led Katayama cabinet, Miki won kudos from the left for refusing to take part in the midnight snap vote called by the LDP to ratify the U.S.-Japan Security Treaty of 1960 (Calder 1988, 196). Suzuki Zenkō was elected to the Diet in 1947 running as a Socialist, which was logical given his background as a fisheries union leader. One year later he jumped to Yoshida Shigeru's Democratic Liberal Party and, after the conservative merger, joined Ikeda Hayato's faction. Nakasone Yasuhiro briefly held a post at the Home Ministry before becoming a junior officer in the Imperial Navy. He was elected to a lower house seat in 1947 and, later on, became a member of Kōno Ichirō's faction. He earned fame for being one side of the "Ron-Yasu" relationship with U.S. president Ronald Reagan, but evoked the ire of Japan's East Asian neighbors for being the first prime minister to make an official visit to the Yasukuni Shrine, where Japan's war dead, including fourteen "Class A" war criminals, are enshrined.

Takeshita, Uno, and Kaifu made their way to the Diet after first serving in local elective politics or as an MP's staff assistant. A one-time middle school English teacher, Takeshita Noboru served two terms as a prefectural assemblyman before winning a lower house seat in 1958. He became a protégé of Satō Eisaku and later Tanaka Kakuei. He parted ways with the latter in 1985 to establish his own faction (Itasaka 1987, 75). Takeshita perceived the benefits of pork barrel politics—as witnessed in his quip that "politics is roads, roads is politics" (*seiji izu dōro, dōro izu seiji*)—and was forced to resign the premiership as a result of his implication in the Recruit scandal, which involved insider trading and influence peddling (discussed below). But Takeshita retained his Diet seat and control of a mighty faction, which enabled him to play the role of kingmaker. Uno Sōsuke, a lieutenant in the Nakasone faction rather than a faction boss in his own right, was an unexpected selection to replace Takeshita. After being repatriated in 1947 following two years' detention in Siberia after the end of the Pacific War, Uno served as prefectural assemblyman and then as staff assistant to LDP faction leader Kōno Ichirō before gaining election to the lower house in 1960. Uno resigned the premiership after only sixty-seven days in office when it came to light that he had had an extramarital affair with a *geisha*. She had gone public because of her dissatisfaction with the pittance Uno paid to ensure her silence. Kaifu Toshiki served an apprenticeship as an MP's staff assistant in preparation for launching his own career in national elective politics. He was just twenty-nine years old at the time of his first election to the Diet in the 1960 general elections. Kaifu's appointment as prime minister was owed to the fact that he was one of the few rising leaders in the LDP not tainted by the Recruit scandal.

Table 4.1. The Confederate Cabinets, 1972 to 1993

Cabinet	Prime Minister	Established	Dissolved	PM's Background
1st Tanaka (Kakuei) Cabinet	Tanaka Kakuei	7/7/1972	12/22/1972	Career Politician
2nd Tanaka (Kakuei) Cabinet	"	12/22/1972	11/25/1973	"
Reorg'ed 2nd Tanaka (Kakuei) (1) Cabinet	"	11/25/1973	11/11/1974	"
Reorg'ed 2nd Tanaka (Kakuei) (2) Cabinet	"	11/11/1974	12/9/1974	"
Miki Cabinet	Miki Takeo	12/9/1974	9/15/1976	Career Politician
Reorg'ed Miki Cabinet	"	9/15/1976	12/24/1976	"
Fukuda Cabinet	Fukuda Takeo	12/24/1976	11/28/1977	Ex-Bureaucrat
Reorg'ed Fukuda Cabinet	"	11/28/1977	12/7/1978	"
1st Ōhira Cabinet	Ōhira Masayoshi	12/7/1978	11/9/1979	Ex-Bureaucrat
2nd Ōhira Cabinet	"	11/9/1979	7/17/1980	"
Suzuki (Zenkō) Cabinet	Suzuki Zenkō	7/17/1980	11/30/1981	Career Politician
Reorg'ed Suzuki (Zenkō) Cabinet	"	11/30/1981	11/27/1982	"
1st Nakasone Cabinet	Nakasone Yusuhiro	11/27/1982	12/27/1983	Career Politician[a]
2nd Nakasone Cabinet	"	12/27/1983	11/1/1984	"
Reorg'ed 2nd Nakasone (1) Cabinet	"	11/1/1984	12/28/1985	"
Reorg'ed 2nd Nakasone (2) Cabinet	"	12/28/1985	7/22/1986	"
3rd Nakasone Cabinet	"	7/22/1986	11/6/1987	"
Takeshita Cabinet	Takeshita Noboru	11/6/1987	12/27/1988	Career Politician
Reorg'ed Takeshita Cabinet	"	12/27/1988	6/3/1989	"
Uno Cabinet	Uno Sōsuke	6/3/1989	8/9/1989	Career Politician
1st Kaifu Cabinet	Kaifu Toshiki	8/9/1989	2/29/1990	Career Politician
2nd Kaifu Cabinet	"	2/29/1990	12/28/1990	"
Reorg'ed 2nd Kaifu Cabinet	"	12/28/1990	11/5/1991	"
Miyazawa Cabinet	Miyazawa Kiichi	11/5/1991	12/11/1992	Ex-Bureaucrat
Reorg'ed Miyazawa Cabinet	"	12/11/1992	8/9/1993	"

[a] Nakasone briefly served as a Home Ministry bureaucrat before becoming a naval officer.
Source: JCCM Database (Appendix A).

Departmental Ministers

The modal minister in the confederate cabinets was a sixtyish male MP serving a seventh term in the lower house (or a third term in the upper house). He was almost certainly affiliated with the LDP, and probably represented an electoral district located outside the country's most heavily urbanized areas. This modal minister was university educated, although, in contrast to earlier cohorts of ministers, it is much more likely that the diploma bore the name of an elite private university. There is better than a fifty-fifty chance our modal minister was a career politician, which, in most cases, meant that he gained experience as a local politician or as an MP's staff assistant before assuming a seat in the Diet. Those ex-bureaucrats given portfolios were more likely to have departed from the civil service at a junior rank than had been the case with previous ministerial cohorts. There is a better than one-in-three chance that our modal minister was a "hereditary politician," meaning that he was the offspring, adopted child, grandchild, or sibling of an MP.

Ninety-nine percent of all ministers in the confederate cabinets were male MPs, and 86 percent held seats in the lower house. The average minister had been elected to 6.7 lower house terms and accumulated two decades of parliamentary service. This meant that he was nearly three years older and had almost five years more parliamentary experience than the average minister in the corporatist cabinets. Four out of five ministers represented districts located in regions outside the largest metropolitan areas. Only four out of the 655 ministerial portfolios went to MPs not affiliated with the LDP. And all four of those portfolios went to MPs from the New Liberal Club (*Shin jiyū kurabu*), which split from the LDP in 1976. These New Liberal Club MPs were given entrée to the ministerial elite because the LDP had won only 49 percent of the seats in the 1983 lower house elections and needed to forge a coalition to manage the Diet.

Because of the LDP's unshakeable parliamentary majority, ministerial portfolios were reserved for party MPs. A novice MP could expect to be appointed to a supporting post in one of the party's headquarters bureaus, while a second- or third-term MP could acquire policy expertise in leadership positions in the Policy Affairs Research Council (*Seimuchōsakai*) or a Diet committee or subcommittee. A five-term MP was a ministerial candidate, while a seven- or eight-term MP was in line for a second portfolio or one of the top party leadership posts. An MP having even more parliamentary seniority would likely have become the boss or a senior lieutenant in one of the intraparty factions (Matsuzaki 1987, 22). Under the confederate cabinets, seniority violations became exceedingly rare. In fact, only 5 percent of ministers were selected for their posts before attaining the expected five-term norm (or two terms in the case of upper house MPs), as opposed to 20 percent of ministers in the corporatist cabinets. This suggests that a seniority system for recruiting cabinet ministers had become established.

Career politicians came to dominate the ministerial elite. Whereas ex-bureaucrats accounted for nearly half of all ministers in the corporatist cabinets, they accounted for less than 30 percent of ministers in the confederate cabinets. Moreover, a smaller percentage of these ex-officials—56 percent as opposed to 70 percent—had risen to a senior post before exiting the career civil service. At the same time, there was a steep jump in the number of ministers who had served in local elective office or as staff assistants to an MP. Specifically, 54 percent of ministers had served in local office or as staffers, as opposed to only 26 percent of ministers in the corporatist cabinets. All together, more than half of all ministers fit the description of career politicians, as opposed to less than one-third of corporatist cabinet ministers.

REMODELING THE CABINET SYSTEM

For the first time since Japan's modern cabinet system was established in 1885, the number of ministerial portfolios decreased, from a high of twenty-eight portfolios under the corporatist cabinets to twenty-one. Also for the first time ever, the Westminster-style ministerial hierarchy emerged with the prime minister stationed at the top of the pecking order followed by the holders of the finance, foreign affairs, and international trade and industry portfolios (see Appendix C).

Tanaka's plan to remodel the country with roads and bridges and railway lines created the need for a government agency to oversee land use policy. The Headquarters for Comprehensive Land Development (*Kokudo sōgō kaihatsu honbu*) was organized under the cabinet in July 1973, and one year later the National Land Agency (*Kokudochō*) was established as a cabinet-level organ. The new agency absorbed various functions from the Economic Planning Agency as well as the Construction and Home Affairs Ministries and assumed the functions of the Capital, Kinki, and

Chūbu regional development headquarters. Its main purpose was to over-see land use planning in the context of national and regional development and to coordinate the efforts of government agencies in developing water resources and guarding against natural disasters. The inaugural director was Nishimura Eiichi, a former Transport Ministry official, who, not sur-prisingly, was a senior leader in the LDP's Tanaka faction. Among the agen-cy's other directors were former Home Ministry bureaucrat Niwa Hyōsuke and Kanemaru Shin.

The Management and Coordination Agency (*Sōmuchō*, or MCA) was established on July 1, 1984, to implement the recommendations of the Sec-ond Ad Hoc Commission on Administrative Reform (discussed below). The agency absorbed functions scraped together from other government organs, including the Prime Minister's Office and the former Administra-tive Management Agency (*Gyōsei kanri chō*, or AMA). The MCA portfo-lio was given responsibility over the central government's organizational structure, coordination of policies and programs falling within the juris-dictions of multiple ministries or agencies, and the population census. Gotōda Masaharu, a former top official of the National Police Agency and a close confidant of former prime minister Tanaka Kakuei, was appointed as the MCA's inaugural director.

In 1986, three policy offices were created within the Cabinet Secretar-iat. The Office of Internal Affairs (*Naisei shingi shitsu*) was established under the directorship of a seconded official from the Finance Ministry, while a Foreign Ministry official supervised the Office of External Affairs (*Gaisei shingi shitsu*). Meanwhile, the Office of National Security Affairs (*Anzen hoshō kaigi*)—which, in 1998, changed its name to the Office of National Security Affairs and Crisis Management—was placed in the charge of a Defense Agency official (Shinoda 2005, 807; Hayao 1993, 168). Prime Min-ister Nakasone was the driving force behind these reforms, described as "the most ambitious and enduring postwar effort to strengthen the role of the prime minister and cabinet in Japan's national policy formulation and implementation processes" (Angel 1988–1989, 601).

POWER RELATIONS IN THE EXECUTIVE BRANCH

Power relations in the executive branch became more complicated during the 1970s and 1980s. Strong-willed prime ministers, immovable govern-ment bureaucrats, and influential policy tribalists (*zoku giin*) made claims for executive primacy. Cabinets struggled to impart purposeful direction in executive decision-making in a fragmented policy-making landscape.

The Advent of Twisted Diets

In a "Twisted Diet" (*nejire kokkai*)—or "Reverse Diet" (*gyakuten kokkai*)—the ruling party controls a majority of seats in the lower house but not in the upper house. This poses problems because, under Japan's Constitution, legislation requires approval of both houses of the Diet, and a two-thirds vote in the lower house is required to override an upper house rejection of one of its bills. In the event that a two-thirds lower house majority cannot be mustered or the upper house fails to take action, a joint committee of both houses will be created to seek reconciliation. If the joint committee fails to reconcile and the upper house does not act within sixty days, the lower house bill will be rejected (Constitution of Japan, Article 59). This enables the upper house to undermine the efforts of government to exercise policy leadership. In a Twisted Diet, the upper house can temporarily block passage of the government's budget, although the lower house bill becomes the decision of the Diet after thirty days (Article 60). In addition, if the two houses cannot agree on the choice of a prime minister, the lower house designee automatically becomes the decision of the Diet after ten days (Article 67). When the Diet is twisted, therefore, the opposition-controlled upper house is able to block the enactment of government bills and delay the passage of budgets and the appointment of prime ministers.

The 1989 upper house elections resulted in a somewhat Twisted Diet. Several factors accounted for the LDP's poor showing, including the party's sponsorship of an unpopular 3 percent consumption tax (enacted the previous December), opposition to the liberalization of agricultural markets, and fallout from the Recruit scandal. The knockout punch came in the form of Uno's geisha scandal, and the elections that followed left the LDP in control of only 109 upper house seats, well shy of the 127 required to maintain a majority. Uno accepted responsibility for the election fiasco and resigned, and the LDP-dominated lower house selected Kaifu to be the next prime minister. The opposition-controlled upper house chose JSP chairperson Doi Takako as its candidate, and a joint committee failed to resolve the impasse. Ultimately, Kaifu became prime minister on the basis of the primacy of the lower house vote, but the opposition had taken advantage of the Twisted Diet to delay his installation.

The opposition-controlled upper house in the Twisted Diet seldom missed a chance to torment the Kaifu cabinet. On March 26, 1990, the upper house rejected the government's supplementary budget proposal, which had been approved by the lower house four days earlier. Once again a joint committee failed to reconcile the bicameral discord, and the lower house's budget bill remained stalled for the requisite thirty days. Aside from the annoyance, the budget impasse resulted in delayed salary payments to more than 1 million national civil servants (Dolan and Worden, eds. 1994). Then, in December 1989, the upper house passed its own proposal to repeal the unpopular consumption tax—which had gone into effect the previous April—and sent it on to the lower house. Although this effort predictably came to naught, it contributed to the hubbub that led to the "consumption tax dissolution" (*shōhizei kaisan*) on January 24, 1990. As a result of the February 11 lower house elections, the JSP realized a net gain of 51 seats (going from 85 to 136 seats), while the LDP suffered a net loss of 25 seats (from 300 seats to 275). This was merely a preview of things to come in the tightly Twisted Diets that afflicted the body politic after the 2007 upper house election.

Prime Ministerial Government—Failure to Launch

Prime ministerial government is characterized by "a generalized ability [of the prime minister] to decide policy across all issue areas in which he or she takes an interest" and "by defining a governing 'ethos,' 'atmosphere,' or operating ideology which generates predictable and determinate solutions to most policy problems" (Dunleavy and Rhodes 1990, 5, 8). Of the ten premiers in the confederate cabinets, only two—Tanaka Kakuei and Nakasone Yasuhiro—displayed the sort of personal leadership that might be construed as prime ministerial government. In the early days of his administration, Tanaka enjoyed high levels of public support, and there was enthusiasm for his plan to remodel the Japanese archipelago. Tanaka's ability to parlay his policy initiatives into reality was made possible by his mammoth intraparty faction, referred to as the "Tanaka General Hospital" (*Tanaka sōgō byōin*) because it included "specialists" in every policy area. Tanaka's lavish gift-giving created numerous allies in the Diet and government bureaucracy (Johnson 1986b, 11). His excellent memory for names and details, coupled with a forceful, straight-ahead leadership style, earned him the nickname "computerized bulldozer."

Nakasone entered office with a weak power base and had to rely on the support of the Tanaka faction to gain and retain the premiership. Yet Nakasone's on-camera presence and close personal relationship with President Reagan helped make him appear "presidential." His influence peaked with the LDP's landslide victory in the 1986 "double elections," which left the party in control of nearly 60 percent of lower house seats and 57 percent of upper house seats. This granted Nakasone the political capital needed to privatize several debt-ridden state-owned enterprises (discussed below). In this effort, Nakasone deftly used personal advisory bodies to neutralize resistance from the government bureaucracy, appointed pro-privatization presidents of the new companies, and pressed companies to hire the public employees made redundant by privatization (Sakoh 1986, 2).

Yet neither Tanaka nor Nakasone was able to institutionalize prime ministerial government. Tanaka was toppled by scandal just two years after taking office and spent the remainder of his political career ruling from the shadows, which meant that none of his many factional followers could become prime minister (Fukui 1984, 430). This led to the breakup, in 1985, of the mighty Tanaka faction. Nakasone's influence derived, in large part, from his telegenic nature and the credit he could claim for the LDP's triumph in the 1986 elections. Yet despite his efforts to strengthen the premiership through establishing the Administrative Management Agency and reorganizing the Cabinet Secretariat, his successors did not exude a similar prime ministerial aura. As with most Japanese prime ministers, Takeshita Noboru's strong suit was that of a backroom deal-broker, while Uno Sōsuke was not in office long enough to do much of anything. Likewise, Kaifu Toshiki's tenure in office was possible only as long as the Tanaka faction supported him, while Miyazawa Kiichi was plagued by political scandal.

Eclipse of the Leviathan

The almighty powers of the bureaucratic Leviathan showed signs of withering away under the confederate cabinets. This was reflected in a drop in the share of government-sponsored bills that became enacted laws, which fell from 91 percent to 84 percent. The bureaucracy's enervated state was put on display in 1983 when Prime Minister Nakasone overruled the Cabinet Legislation Bureau in negotiating a Memorandum of Understanding with the United States; that agreement allowed Japan to sidestep the ban on the export of weapons by providing access to its dual-use military technology and other advanced research (Samuels 2004, 5). The bureaucracy's influence also declined as fewer ex-officials chose to pursue second careers in elective politics. As noted earlier, only three of the ten prime ministers who headed confederate cabinets were ex-bureaucrats, and only one had risen to a high post in his ministry. This contrasts with the state of affairs under the corporatist cabinets, when a succession of three elite ex-bureaucrats occupied the prime minister's chair. Most ex-bureaucrats who served as departmental ministers also separated from the career civil service at relatively junior rank.[2] In other words, the former government officials who held portfolios under the confederate cabinets were less steeped in the "way of the bureaucrat" than had been the case with their predecessors.

Nevertheless, the government bureaucracy continued to influence executive affairs. As Tanaka observed, "Eighty percent of a prime minister's job is getting the civil service to do what he wants" (quoted in Johnson 1986b, 6). The civil service was a traditionally elite career pathway, whose upper leadership was drawn disproportionately from alumni of the country's most prestigious universities. Bureaucrats continued to initiate and draft most policy proposals, and they did so under the oversight of, at most, three political appointees per ministry. They also performed the policy research function for understaffed MPs and drafted the answers read aloud by their ministers in Diet interpellations. Moreover, frequent cabinet reshufflings made it difficult for transitory ministers to effectively monitor the career officials in their ministries. In many cases, this ministerial turnover was done to reward LDP MPs rather than in response to an electoral mandate. Then there were the twice-weekly meetings of the administrative vice ministers of each ministry to set the agenda for cabinet meetings, and the institutional memory of the Cabinet Legislative Bureau, the bureaucracy's stronghold (*gajō*). In the fall of 1991, the CLB became the "mortal enemy" of LDP secretary general Ozawa Ichirō by declaring unconstitutional the proposed dispatch of Self-Defense Forces personnel to support the U.S.-led effort in the first Gulf War (Samuels 2004, 8).

Party High, Bureaucracy Low

In the aftermath of the first oil shock, the balance of power in executive affairs began to shift in favor of elected politicians, especially the "policy specialists" (*zoku giin*) who played the part of chieftains in the various "policy tribes" (*zoku*). "Thanks to prolonged immersion in their chosen field of specialization," Koh explains, tribal politicians were able to "boast more expertise in their field of specialization than senior bureaucrats, who are subject to frequent rotation in assignments" (Koh 1989, 213). In other words, the expertise and influence acquired as a result of long years of service in a specific policy area enabled the LDP's policy tribalists to "match and even dominate" their peers in the government bureaucracy (Schoppa 1991, 79). The term "*tōkō kantei*" (party high, bureaucracy low) was coined to denote this sea change (Inoguchi and Iwai 1987, 19–21; Koh 1989, 7, 212–213).

Policy tribes emerged in every major policy arena (Satō and Matsuzaki 1986, 216–229). The LDP's Policy Affairs Research Council (*Seimuchōsakai,* or PARC) became a training ground in which aspiring tribalists acquired policy expertise and forged links to allies in the bureaucracy (Inoguchi and Iwai 1987, 20, 27–28). Beginning in the early 1960s, the LDP required that all policy and budgetary proposals be reviewed within the relevant subunit of PARC before submission to the Diet, which ensured that the policy tribalists could exert their influence at the early stages of the policy-making process (McCubbins and Noble 1995, 15; George Mulgan 2003a, 78; Woodall 1996, 115). Each LDP MP was allowed to join a maximum of three PARC divisions (*bukai*) and an unlimited number of its investigation committees (*chōsakai*) and special committees (*tokubetsu iinkai*). Not surprisingly, the most popular PARC divisions were those with dominion over palpable distributive policy benefits, such as public works, agricultural subsidies, and tax breaks. The "three noble houses" (*go-sanke*) of commerce, agriculture, and construction—whose chairs were regarded as "cabinet ministers within the party"—attracted the largest numbers of members (Woodall 1996, 115, 117).

Tribalists brokered deals between the ruling party and the government ministries, mediated interministerial turf wars, and lobbied for policies and budget proposals desired by their ministries (ibid., 113). In return, the tribalists were rewarded with special policy briefings by ministry officials, early notification of actions that affected their constituents (which permitted them to credibly claim credit for those decisions), and a certain degree of leverage in steering distributive benefits to their districts and key supporters (ibid., 119–122; Iio 2004, 6).

The fact that the LDP was, in essence, a "federation of factions" rather than a unified political party imparted added drama to executive affairs

(Scalapino and Masumi 1962, 18). Particular factions wielded greater relative influence in certain policy domains (Inoguchi and Iwai 1987, 298,
296). For example, nearly half of the coveted agriculture portfolios distributed from 1955 to 1972 went to members of the Kishi faction and
its successor branches. Meanwhile, members of the Satō and Kōno factions and their successor branches dominated the porcine construction
portfolio (Woodall 1996, 109–110). Tanaka's attempt to build his mighty
faction into a "general hospital" with specialists on staff to treat every
conceivable policy malady posed a challenge to central party leaders
(Samuels 2003, 239).

Low Growth and Political Reform

The confederate cabinets confronted a range of challenges. The "Nixon
shocks" paved the way for the restoration of ties to Beijing, while the 1973
and 1979 oil shocks dictated dramatic changes in the country's energy policies. In addition, the historical interpretation given in Japanese school textbooks became a source of conflict with neighboring countries, while the
outbreak of the first Gulf War led to demands for Japan to play a greater
international security role. The ways in which a succession of governments
responded to the problem of a mushrooming public debt and demands to
reform a malfunctioning electoral system provide unique insights into the
adaptability of the cabinet system.

Trimming Debt in a Slow-Growth Economy

As career politicians came to dominate the political scene, so did demands
for increased government spending. From the late 1940s through the mid-
1960s, Japanese governments adhered to the policy of balanced budgets
dictated by the Dodge Line (discussed in chapter 2), but the slow-growth
economy and static government revenues that followed the 1973 oil shock
led to demands for Keynesian economic policies. As a result, total central
government debt as a percentage of GDP ballooned from 4.6 percent in
1964 to 50 percent by 1980. These massive government outlays financed
the bullet trains and island-linking bridges and a dramatic increase in
social spending that elevated Japan from "welfare laggard" to "welfare
superpower" (Nakagawa 1979). In this regard, Tanaka's "remodeling plan"
not only brought an end to balanced budgets, it also enhanced the relative

powers of MPs vis-à-vis civil servants in decisions concerning government spending (Vogel 1996, 54–55).

On October 17, 1973, six OPEC countries raised the producer price of oil by 21 percent and threatened an embargo against the United States and its allies as punishment for their support of Israel in the Yom Kippur War. As an American ally with a heavy addiction to petroleum, Japan was stunned by OPEC's action. Additional price hikes and production cuts followed, adding to the trepidation already felt in a country that depended on imports for 99 percent of its petroleum needs. The Tanaka cabinet responded with an Outline for Countermeasures for the Petroleum Crisis (*Sekiyu kinkyū taisaku yōko*), but bankruptcies surged and panic buying of toilet paper and other products ensued. One of the Miki cabinet's first acts was to announce that Japan had experienced its first negative economic growth in the postwar period.

The Ōhira cabinet proposed a general consumption tax to cut the deficit. Not surprisingly, the opposition denounced the plan, but some in the LDP camp were also opposed to it. Ōhira responded by dissolving the Diet and calling new elections, which left the LDP in control of only 49 percent of lower house seats. On May 17, 1980, after months of internecine warfare among the LDP's various factions, a JSP-sponsored non-confidence motion against the Ōhira cabinet passed by a 273 to 187 margin. The motion's passage was ensured by the strategic absence of sixty-nine members of the Fukuda and Miki factions. Ōhira and his cabinet resolved to remain in office, opting to dissolve the Diet and call new elections, which, for the first time ever, would simultaneously elect members of both Diet chambers. On May 31, while campaigning in an electoral contest that most pundits predicted would go badly for the LDP, Ōhira was hospitalized suffering from exhaustion. He succumbed to a heart attack less than two weeks later, but an unexpected "sympathy vote" gave the LDP absolute majorities in the lower and upper houses.

The takeaway lesson for Ōhira's successors was that proposing a consumption tax was risky business. Consequently, the Suzuki and Nakasone governments aimed to cut the deficit through administrative reform and spending cuts. Suzuki tasked the Second Ad Hoc Commission on Administrative Reform (*Daini rinji gyōsei chōsakai* or *Rinchō*) with setting the agenda for this delicate operation. Under the leadership of former Toshiba Corporation and Federation of Economic Organizations (*Keidanren*) president Dokō Toshio, the *Rinchō* (also known as the Dokō Commission) began operations on March 16, 1981 (Watanabe, ed. 1995, 321–322). Two days after the commission's launch, Suzuki pledged to "stake his political career"—hence, the fate of his cabinet—on the achievement of administrative reform (Elliott 1983, 773). As an extra-governmental advisory body, the *Rinchō* was in a position to make recommendations for reforms that shifted the blame away from the ruling LDP and its lawmakers, who were able to criticize the measures while at the same time voting them into law (Vogel 1996, 55–56). During the two years of its existence, the *Rinchō* issued five reports, the final two coming after Nakasone replaced Suzuki as prime minister. As Dokō and his colleagues eventually discovered, however, retired and incumbent bureaucrats who sat on the commission's committees were able to water down reform proposals that threatened to diminish their ministries' powers (ibid., 57; Watanabe, ed. 1995, 330).

Acting on the *Rinchō* recommendations, the Nakasone government set about privatizing debt-ridden public corporations. The biggest target of the privatization drive was the Japan National Railways (JNR), which by 1983 had accumulated in excess of $120 billion in debt and was losing $25 million per day (Vogel 1996, 56). JNR had become "one of the most inefficient and overstaffed railroads in the world," with 420,000 unionized workers on its payroll (Sakoh 1986). These workers understood that one aim of Nakasone's plan was to break the backs of their unions, while government bureaucrats and LDP MPs opposed JNR privatization out of fear of losing an important source of distributive benefits and votes (ibid.). The Nakasone government encountered similar resistance in attempting to privatize the Japan Tobacco and Salt Public Corporation (*Nippon senbai kōsha*), with its ninety thousand well-organized tobacco farmers—many of whom supported the LDP—and a Finance Ministry loath to lose $1.7 billion in annual tax revenues (ibid.). Privatization proceeded more smoothly in the case of Nippon Telephone and Telegraph (*Nippon denshin denwa*) and Japan Airlines. This is because NTT's 320,000 employees were allowed to remain with the company, and the government already owned only 35 percent of shares in the semipublic airline (ibid.; Vogel 1996, 56).

Reform Drama in Four Acts

The confederate cabinets had to respond to judicial rulings and popular demands to reform a malfunctioning electoral system. What was to become a four-part drama began to unfold following the July 1974 elections, in which the LDP lost its upper house majority. In an exposé published in the October 1974 issue of the *Bungei shunjū* magazine, journalist Tachibana Takashi trained a spotlight on Prime Minister Tanaka's shady business practices. Vice Prime Minister Miki Takeo openly criticized Tanaka and joined Foreign Minister Fukuda Takeo and Administrative Management Agency Director Hori Shigeru in resigning from their posts. Tanaka announced his resignation on November 26, and LDP vice president Shiina Etsusaburō brokered a deal to make Miki the next prime minister (Masumi 1985, 251). "Clean Miki" appointed a cabinet whose members publicly disclosed their finances and vowed to reform the electoral system (ibid., 265, 266). These efforts bore fruit in the passage of a significantly enhanced campaign finance law and in the adoption of a primary election system in which the LDP's MPs and general members voted to determine who would become party president (Woodall 1999, 37).

Act Two began in February 1976 with former Lockheed Corporation vice president A. Carl Kotchian's admission to a U.S. Senate subcommittee that he had dispensed millions of dollars in bribes to sell the Tristar passenger jet to airlines in Japan (Johnson 1986b, 13–14). This led Japanese prosecutors to follow Lockheed's money trail, which led to businessmen, right-wing fixers, and politicians, and then all the way to Prime Minister Tanaka. On August 16, the former prime minister was arrested on charges of violating the Foreign Exchange Law, while fifteen others were indicted on bribery and other charges (Mitchell 1996, 121). Prime Minister Miki was denounced by elements within the LDP for not halting the investigation of Tanaka (Watanabe, ed. 1995, 256; Johnson 1986b, 7). Miki was obliged to resign following the LDP's poor showing in the 1976 lower house elections, and, in a backstage deal, Fukuda agreed that he would serve a two-year term and then turn the premiership over to Ōhira. Fukuda's decision to renege on the deal by seeking a second term in 1978 led to warfare between the two faction leaders and their allies (Satō et al. 1990, 375–376, 384). Consequently, Ōhira's premiership was troubled from the outset, and it was left to Suzuki to restore public trust by promising political reform. On August 19, 1982, the Diet passed a cabinet-sponsored bill modifying the 1947 Public Election Law to create a proportional representation system to fill a portion of seats in the upper house. In October 1983, Tanaka's guilty verdict produced an uproar that led to new elections, in which the LDP failed to secure an absolute majority of seats, prompting

Prime Minister Nakasone to offer portfolios to an MP from the New Liberal Club, a splinter party.

Act Three in the reform drama was ushered in by the Supreme Court's ruling on July 17, 1985, that a five-to-one disparity between the most over- and underrepresented lower house districts was unconstitutional. The following June, the Nakasone cabinet secured passage of a bill to add one seat to the eight most underrepresented districts and take one seat away from the seven most overrepresented districts (Woodall 1999, 38). This brought the level of malapportionment just below the court-mandated disparity of three-to-one in time for the July 1986 "double elections," which gave Nakasone and the LDP a stunning victory. In late June 1988, though, it was revealed that Ezoe Hiromasa, chairman of the Recruit Company, had funneled gifts that included prelisted shares of stock in the real estate subsidiary of his company to politicians, bureaucrats, and others. Prime Minister Takeshita and former premier Nakasone Yasuhiro were among those implicated in the scandal, which led to the resignations of Foreign Minister Miyazawa Kiichi, Justice Minister Hasegawa Takashi, and Economic Planning Agency Director Harada Ken. In the end, no major politicians were arrested, but the scandal—coupled with the unpopular consumption tax— resulted in plunging public approval for the Takeshita cabinet. With all of the logical successors to the premiership sullied in the Recruit scandal, LDP leaders tapped Uno Sōsuke, a lieutenant in the Nakasone faction, to assume the party presidency (Watanabe, ed. 1995, 394–395). Uno was soon engulfed in his own geisha scandal, and he resigned to take responsibility for the LDP's defeat in the July 1989 upper house elections.

The selection of Kaifu Toshiki, who took office on August 25, 1989, was also owed to the fact that all of the other likely candidates carried the stench of the Recruit scandal. A lieutenant in the smallest of the LDP's five main factions, Kaifu would not have become party president (and, therefore, prime minister) without the support of the mighty Takeshita faction. That is why his cabinet came to be dubbed the "Cloistered Takeshita Cabinet" (*Takeshita insei naikaku*) and "remote-controlled cabinet" (*rimokon naikaku*) (Watanabe, ed. 1995, 409). Kaifu stated that "political reform is the mission of my cabinet" because "public opinion demands plain and clean politics" (Woodall 1999, 38). In August 1991, the Kaifu cabinet submitted a bill based on the recommendations of the nonpartisan Election System Deliberation Council calling for the creation of three hundred single-member districts and for 170 members to be elected from a national proportional representation district. While the opposition denounced the proposal, the most serious resistance came from LDP backbenchers, who feared that "rains of blood will fall if districts are tampered with" (cited in McElwain 2006, 34). In September 1991, the cabinet-sponsored bill stalled, leading Kaifu to consider dissolving the Diet. Party leaders convinced him to drop the idea, and on October 4 Kaifu announced that he would not seek another term as party president (Watanabe, ed. 1995, 411). The Takeshita faction threw its support behind Miyazawa, who was considered sufficiently rehabilitated to assume the premiership.

The protagonist in Act Four of the scandal-reform cycle was LDP vice president Kanemaru Shin. In the early months of 1992, the "shadow shogun" was accused of having underworld ties and peddling his influence to secure bureaucratic approval for additional trucking routes for the Sagawa Kyūbin express delivery company. Eventually, it was revealed that 130 MPs had received political contributions from Sagawa Kyūbin's generous owner. Kanemaru admitted his guilt on August 27 and resigned his party post, but the light fine he received—roughly equivalent to a parking ticket—drew public outcry. On October 14, Kanemaru resigned from his lower house seat, but prosecutors continued probing; they finally arrested the aging kingmaker on March 6. Searches of Kanemaru's residence and office uncovered $50 million in cash, gold bullion, and bonds (Mitchell 1996, 127). Subsequent investigations exposed a web of corruption involving bribes received from major general contractors (*zenekon*) for preferential intervention by politicians in the allocation of public works projects. It was rumored that Kanemaru himself received a kickback of 5 percent of the contracted price of each public works project he steered to a particular contractor (Woodall 1996, 40). The *zenekon* scandal exposed a vast network of influence peddling and bribery in which contractors funneled money to politicians or their intermediaries in exchange for public works contracts (ibid., 13).

With two major scandals raging, the Miyazawa cabinet had every reason to press for political reform to restore public approval. Its reform proposal—which bore a close resemblance to the Kaifu cabinet's proposal—was rejected by the LDP's Executive Council on June 15, 1993 (Woodall 1996, 39). Three days later, an opposition-sponsored no-confidence vote against the Miyazawa cabinet was approved, thanks to the support of Ozawa Ichirō, Hata Tsutomu, and a number of other disaffected former LDP legislators. The lower house elections of August 18 left the LDP in control of only 44 percent of the seats, paving the way for the establishment of the Hosokawa cabinet, founded on an eight-party coalition. This brought down the curtain on nearly four decades of LDP rule.

On August 10, in his first press conference as premier, Hosokawa Morihiro committed his government to the cause of political reform. After much debate and some compromise, the Hosokawa cabinet's reform bills were enacted into law on January 29, 1994. These laws created a lower house electoral system based on a mixture of single-member and proportional representation districts, and significantly strengthened the regulation of campaign finance. Ironically, the LDP, now in the unfamiliar role of opposition party, opted to support a lower house electoral system reform bill whose core provisions were almost identical to the proposal the party had rejected before it had self-destructed just eight months earlier.

FINDINGS

Tanaka Kakuei and Miyazawa Kiichi represented radically dissimilar bookends in an era of confederate cabinets that witnessed the zenith of LDP dominance and its inglorious fall from grace. During these two decades, the party's presidents continued to serve simultaneously as prime ministers, and only a handful of cabinet portfolios were allocated to non-LDP MPs. Because the LDP virtually monopolized the allocation of portfolios, ministerial appointment became a regular part of the ruling party's promotion process. In this way, the ministerial elite was shaped by the LDP's hegemonic mastery of the parliamentary realm; consequently, the characteristics of the ministerial elite came to mirror the narrow set of specific characteristics of the party's senior MPs.

At the end of the day, cabinet government did *not* become established under the corporate cabinets. Efforts to bolster the powers of the prime minister were not institutionalized, and, although the influence of the government bureaucracy declined, the advent of Twisted Diets made Diet management difficult for a succession of cabinets. Policy specialists came to rule over the fief-like subgovernments that dotted the policy-making landscape. Meanwhile, the oil shocks inflicted dramatically higher energy costs that brought an end to the high-speed growth era and its ever-expanding budgets. With a Diet dominated by career politicians with an insatiable appetite for pork barrel spending, the inevitable result was a mushrooming government deficit. Prime Minister Ōhira's disastrous experience with a proposed consumption tax prompted his successors to pursue deregulation and privatization. A series of corruption scandals and dangerously low public approval ratings forced a succession of LDP-led cabinets to try, but ultimately fail, to reform a malfunctioning electoral system. So it was that the LDP's protracted lordship over the parliamentary realm came to a temporary end.

Now Japan drifted aimlessly into consecutive "lost decades" of economic and political stagnation. With the end of LDP hegemony, coalition cabinets became the rule, and a once-toothless Diet became an irritation to a succession of governments. Disaffected former LDP MPs and the leaders of new parties played the role of change agents in the drama that unfolded. Surprisingly, an iconoclastic agent of change emerged from within a revitalized LDP and proceeded to declare war on a mighty policy lobby, whose chieftains were ruling party MPs.

5

Disjoined Cabinets—Act I

Coalition Governments and the Lost Decades, 1993–2006

At the broadest level it is possible to see that the demands of [the
Conservative-Liberal Democrat Coalition] have meant the restoration
of Cabinet government, and an end to the more informal style
of "government by sofa" that emerged under New Labour during
1997–2010.
      —Felicity Matthews, "Constitutional Stretching" (2011), 505–506

A cabinet should be a body that executes and realizes the policy of a
political party that won the support of a majority of voters. In Japan,
however, the policy of a cabinet often contradicts that of the ruling
party. The postal privatization by the Junichiro Koizumi cabinet was a
typical example.
      —Hideki Kato, "Political Reform of the Japanese
      System of Government" (2008), 3

Lost Decades, Lost Leadership

After enduring a seemingly interminable period of economic malaise, Japanese voters had all but lost hope that their democratically elected leaders could lead the country out of what came to be known as the "lost decade." Then, after a succession of faction bosses from the perpetually ruling Liberal Democratic Party (LDP) had taken turns as prime minister in cabinets composed of ministers recruited almost exclusively from the ranks of party lawmakers—and through half-baked policies, scandals, and gaffes had managed to drive popular support for the government to near historic lows—an unlikely leader emerged. In contrast to most of his predecessors, Koizumi Jun'ichirō did not command an internal faction, and he assembled his cabinet without consulting the faction bosses. He also pledged to refrain from engaging in the standard practice of frequent cabinet reshuffles that allowed LDP MPs to hold coveted cabinet posts but weakened political oversight of the government bureaucracy. He vowed to press through reforms to revitalize the economy. The Koizumi cabinet was welcomed with unprecedented public approval, and a majority of citizens continued to support it even as it pressed ahead with its tough-love reform agenda. Then, in August 2005, cabinet-sponsored postal privatization bills were defeated in the Diet's upper house as a result of the defection of a number of LDP MPs. Koizumi dissolved the Diet and called new elections to obtain a popular mandate for his cabinet's policies. Those elections revealed resounding public approval for the policies of the Koizumi cabinet, which quickly set about securing passage of the reform bills and punishing the "postal rebels." Finally, it seemed that maybe, just maybe, cabinet government had arrived on the Japanese scene.

In this chapter I assess the extent to which cabinet government became institutionalized during the period between August 1993 and September 2006. During these years, the already difficult task of providing tactical direction to government policy was magnified by the challenge of maintaining unity and focus in cabinets composed of ministers from multiple parties. As Koizumi and his cabinet learned through painful experience, the challenge was further magnified by a fragmented policy-making landscape dominated by powerful, self-serving subgovernments. These factors all came to the fore in the pitched battle led by Koizumi and his ministers to privatize postal services.

Renegade Reformers

It was the secession of a large number of LDP MPs in the run-up to the 1993 lower house election—*not* voter displeasure—that temporarily brought down the curtain on the LDP's hegemonic rule. While the leaders of the jailbreak claimed to be reformers, their motives were mixed (Reed and Scheiner 2003, 473–474). This was especially true of Ozawa Ichirō, the prized "disciple" of legendary wheeler-dealers Tanaka Kakuei and Kanemaru Shin (Samuels 2003, 326). An "opportunist" and a "child of the political machine," Ozawa began looking to abandon ship when Kanemaru became ensnared in a major corruption scandal (Gaunder 2007, 10). Ozawa's first move, in December 1992, was to gather forty-two loyal follow-ers and split from the Takeshita faction to establish the Reform Forum 21, with Hata Tsutomu as its titular head. In June of the following year, Ozawa and his followers used the LDP's rejection of a political reform bill as the pretext to establish the Japan Renewal Party (*Shinseitō*) (Woodall 1996, 144). Henceforth, Ozawa would be the leader—or shadow shōgun—in a succession of parties. When the Japan Renewal Party merged into the New Frontier Party (*Shinshintō*) in 1994, Ozawa became its president. When that party disbanded four years later, he established the Liberal Party (*Jiyūtō*), which became a partner in an LDP-led coalition. Ozawa seized the opportunity to settle an old score by downgrading the formal status of the director general of the Cabinet Legislation Bureau, who had blocked his proposal to dispatch SDF forces to participate in the first Gulf War. Never-theless, the CLB director general was allowed to continue answering ques-tions on behalf of the government in Diet deliberations (Samuels 2004, 10).

Other change agents emerged from new parties created around the time of the LDP's fall. Hosokawa Morihiro founded the Japan New Party (*Nihon shintō*) in May 1992 and became prime minister in the first non-LDP cabinet in nearly four decades. Future prime minister Noda Yoshi-hiko was one of the thirty-five candidates endorsed by the Japan New Party to win a Diet seat in the 1993 lower house elections. The New Party Sakigake (*Shintō sakigake*), founded by LDP defector Takemura Masayoshi in June 1993, produced a pair of future prime ministers—Hatoyama Yukio and Kan Naoto. Hata Tsutomu was cofounder of the Japan Renewal Party, which also nurtured Okada Katsuya, Nikai Toshihiro, and other future leaders. In addition, Koizumi Jun'ichirō should be numbered among the change agents. Although he never left the LDP, Koizumi was always an outsider in the long-ruling party. As mentioned, he was not the boss of his own faction—which set him apart from most LDP prime ministers—and, as we shall see, he refused to play by the party's rules. Ever the maverick, Koizumi dared to declare war on LDP MPs and key party support groups that opposed his policies.

The eight parties that formed the coalition that made up the Hoso-kawa cabinet vowed to "smash the union of legislators, bureaucrats, and industrialists" and to enact a political reform bill (Woodall 1996, 100). While the coalition made little headway in smashing the unholy union, it managed to enact a new system for electing lower house MPs. Even after the LDP reassumed the reins of power—albeit in coalition governments—pressure for reform continued. This was evident in the October 1996 lower house election campaign—which took place in the shadow of several highly publicized corruption scandals involving government officials (discussed below)—when all of the major parties called for administrative reform (Nakano 1998, 303; Mishima 1998, 969). In response, Prime Minister Hashimoto Ryūtarō tasked his Administrative Reform Council (*Gyōsei kaikaku iinkai,* or ARC) with proposing measures to strengthen the cabinet's functions, streamline government, and make administration more transparent. In June 1998, the Diet passed a bill to streamline government that, when implemented in January 2001, cut the number of government ministries almost in half, established a Cabinet Office, and bolstered political oversight of the government bureaucracy.[1] Yet this institutional upheaval did *not* give birth to cabinet government. On the contrary, this period saw the rise of disjoined cabinets that failed to restore economic growth or to respond effectively to domestic and international challenges.

THE MINISTERIAL ELITE

Between August 9, 1993, and September 26, 2006, seven prime ministers presided over twenty-one cabinets. The average life expectancy of these cabinets was just over seven months (228 days), making them three months shorter than the confederate cabinets that preceded them. However, the Reorganized first Koizumi cabinet, which held office for 722 days, stands as one of the longest-lived cabinets. As for prime ministerial tenure, the Koizumi government endured for nearly five and a half years (1,979 days), while the Hata government lost vital signs after just over two months (63 days) in office.

Prime Ministers

The prime ministers were career politicians one and all. Each held a seat in the Diet's lower house, and, on average, had been elected to an average of nine and a half lower house terms and had accumulated nearly twenty-seven years of parliamentary experience. Two of them built local bases of support as grassroots politicians, four learned the trade as lawmakers' staff assistants, two were journalists, and one was a labor union leader. Five of them emerged from political families.

The 1993 elections opened the door for three non-LDP prime min-

Table 5.1. Disjoined Cabinets and Coalition Governments, 1993 to 2006

Cabinet	Prime Minister	Established	Dissolved	Coalition Parties
Hosokawa Cabinet	Hosokawa Morihiro	8/9/1993	4/28/1994	JNP, JSP, JRP, CGP, DSP, NPS, SDF, DRP
Hata Cabinet	Hata Tsutomu	4/28/1994	6/30/1994	JRP, CGP, JNP, LP, DSP, SDF, KK
Murayama Cabinet	Murayama Tomiichi	6/30/1994	8/8/1995	JSP, LDP, NPS
Reorg'ed Murayama Cabinet	"	8/8/1995	1/11/1996	JSP, LDP, NPS
1st Hashimoto Cabinet	Hashimoto Ryūtarō	1/11/1996	11/7/1996	LDP, JSP, NPS
2nd Hashimoto Cabinet	"	11/7/1996	9/11/1997	LDP
Reorg'ed 2nd Hashimoto Cabinet	"	9/11/1997	7/30/1998	LDP
Obuchi Cabinet	Obuchi Keizō	7/30/1998	1/14/1999	LDP
Reorg'ed Obuchi (1) Cabinet	"	1/14/1999	10/5/1999	LDP, LP
Reorg'ed Obuchi (2) Cabinet	"	10/5/1999	4/5/2000	LDP, LP, CGP
1st Mori Cabinet	Mori Yoshirō	4/5/2000	7/4/2000	LDP, CGP, NCP
2nd Mori Cabinet	"	7/4/2000	12/5/2000	LDP, CGP, NCP
Reorg'ed 2nd Mori (1) Cabinet	"	12/5/2000	1/6/2001	LDP, CGP, NCP
Reorg'ed 2nd Mori (2) Cabinet	"	1/6/2001	4/26/2001	LDP, CGP, NCP
1st Koizumi Cabinet	Koizumi Jun'ichirō	4/26/2001	9/30/2001	LDP, CGP, NCP
Reorg'ed 1st Koizumi (1) Cabinet	"	9/30/2001	9/22/2003	LDP, CGP, NCP
Reorg'ed 1st Koizumi (2) Cabinet	"	9/22/2003	11/19/2003	LDP, CGP, NCP
2nd Koizumi Cabinet	"	11/19/2003	9/27/2004	LDP, CGP
Reorg'ed 2nd Koizumi Cabinet	"	9/27/2004	9/21/2005	LDP, CGP
3rd Koizumi Cabinet	"	9/21/2005	10/31/2005	LDP, CGP
Reorg'ed 3rd Koizumi Cabinet	"	10/31/2005	9/26/2006	LDP, CGP

Key: CGP: Clean Government Party   JSP: Japan Socialist Party   NCP: New Conservative Party
        DRP: Democratic Reform Party   KK: Reform Party   NPS: New Party Sakigake
        DSP: Democratic Socialist Party   LDP: Liberal Democratic Party   PNP: People's New Party
        JNP: Japan New Party   LP: Liberal Party   SDF: Socialist Democratic Federation
        JRP: Japan Renewal Party

Source: JCCM Database (Appendix A).

isters. Hosokawa Morihiro was a descendent of a feudal lord and grandson of former premier Konoe Fumimaro, Hata Tsutomu was the son of a lower house MP, and Murayama Tomiichi was a fisherman's son. All three graduated from private universities—Hosokawa from Sophia, Hata from Seijō, and Murayama from Meiji. Hosokawa worked as a newspaper reporter before winning an upper house seat, which he relinquished to run for prefectural governor. Hata worked at a bus company prior to serving as an MP's staff assistant, while Murayama was a labor union leader before going into grassroots politics. In 1992 Hosokawa founded the Japan New Party (*Nihon shintō*), and the following year Hata cofounded the Japan Renewal Party. Hosokawa and Hata headed coalition governments composed of all of the former opposition parties except the Japan Communist Party. Murayama's cabinets made "oddly coupled coalition partners" of his Japan Socialist Party and the LDP, its longtime nemesis in the "1955 system" (Samuels 2004, 5). Hosokawa resigned amid accusations that he failed to repay a loan from an express delivery company. The JSP's decision to withdraw from the coalition left Hata at the helm of a minority government that was replaced by a JSP-LDP alliance with Murayama in the prime minister's chair. But, as a condition for its partnership in the coalition, the LDP insisted that the JSP renounce its opposition to the U.S.-Japan security alliance, a central element in the JSP's branding.

The next three prime ministers were LDP faction bosses. All three graduated from famous private universities—Hashimoto Ryūtarō was a Keiō man, while Obuchi Keizō and Mori Yoshirō were Waseda alumni. Hashimoto's father was a minister in the Yoshida and Kishi cabinets, and Obuchi was also an MP's son. Hashimoto briefly served as staff assistant to Health and Welfare Minister Nishimura Eiichi. Mori worked as a newspaper reporter before becoming an MP's staff assistant. Both Hashimoto and Obuchi were first elected to the Diet in 1963; Mori joined them in the lower house pews half a dozen years later. Hashimoto and Obuchi were members of the Tanaka faction, and Mori enlisted in the Fukuda faction. The first Hashimoto cabinet was founded on a coalition with the Japan Socialist and Sakigake parties, but the LDP's strong showing in the 1996 lower house elections temporarily eliminated the need for a coalition partner. Obuchi assumed the premiership after Hashimoto resigned to take responsibility for the LDPs' dismal showing in the 1998 upper house elections. When Obuchi suffered a stroke in April 2000, Mori took the helm, but his premiership was marred by microscopic approval ratings and a series of gaffes, one of which occurred in an exchange with U.S. president Bill Clinton at the G8 summit in 2000. When introduced to the American president, Mori blurted out, "Who are you?"—instead of "How are you?"—to which Clinton jokingly replied, "I'm Hillary's husband." An oblivious Mori responded, "Me too."[2]

Koizumi Jun'ichirō was a third-generation cabinet minister who, at the time he became prime minister, had occupied a lower house seat for nearly three decades. In August 1969, a twenty-seven-year-old Koizumi was studying at London University when his lawmaker father passed away unexpectedly. He returned to Japan but failed in his bid to "inherit" his father's seat in the December elections, so he went to work as staff assistant to Finance Minister Fukuda Takeo, whose faction he joined upon winning a Diet seat three years later. Koizumi served several stints as health and welfare minister, and held the posts and telecommunications portfolio at the time of the LDP's fall from grace in 1993. In 1995 and 1997 Koizumi declared his candidacy for the LDP presidency, but he was defeated each time. When he finally managed to win the post in April 2001, pundits predicted that his tenure in office would be short-lived. Koizumi defied the naysayers and went on to occupy the presidency and premiership for nearly five and a half years.

Departmental Ministers

Of the 214 individuals who held portfolios in these cabinets, the modal minister was a sixty-two-year-old male university graduate who had spent nearly two decades as an MP. (While the ministerial elite remained a largely male affair, the fact that women now accounted for one in ten ministers marked a major change. In contrast, only 1 percent of ministers in the previous ministerial cohort were female.) Chances are that this modal minister held a lower house seat and was serving a sixth term in that Diet chamber, or a fourth term in the case of upper house MPs. There is a four-in-five chance that our modal minister was an alumnus of one of only eight public or private universities: Tokyo, Kyoto, or Hitotsubashi universities (the publics) and Keiō, Waseda, Chūō, Meiji, or Nihon universities (the privates). Keiō alumni alone claimed 17 percent of all portfolios. There is a high probability that this modal minister was a career politician.

The changing composition of the ministerial elite is reflected in the continued influx of career politicians and further institutionalization of a seniority system for recruiting ministers. Forty-three percent of ministers were first elected to the Diet before their fortieth birthdays, which suggests that ministerial aspirants understood that an early start was sine qua non for a successful career in national elective politics. The average ministerial appointee had spent nineteen years treading upon the Diet's fabled red carpet (*aka jūtan*), while the average novice minister arrived with nearly sixteen years of accumulated parliamentary service. Fifty-seven percent of ministers emerged from preparliamentary apprenticeships typically pursued by aspiring political careerists, including MP's staff assistant (which, by itself, accounted for 36 percent of ministerial appointees), grassroots politician, journalist, and attorney. While ex-bureaucrats accounted for one-quarter of ministers, three out of four of them had exited the civil service before attaining senior rank. In other words, they too perceived that politics was no longer an amateur avocation to be taken up later in life. Forty percent of ministers seemingly inherited the "political gene" as second-generation (or in some cases third- or fourth-generation) politicians.

With the advent of coalition governments came additional changes. For one thing, only 78 percent of ministers were affiliated with the prime minister's party. This was a major change from the days of single-party rule, when 99 percent of ministers were LDP lawmakers. The most extreme case was that of the Hosokawa cabinet, in which the prime minister himself was the only MP with ties to the Japan New Party. Less extreme were the Murakawa cabinets—which were JSP-LDP joint ventures—in which only a quarter of ministers were numbered among Socialist Party MPs. In a related vein, the advent of coalition governments brought a surge in the presence of ministers from the urbanized areas surrounding Tokyo, Nagoya, and Osaka. These urban or suburban ministers claimed one in three portfolios, as opposed to the one in five figure for ministers appointed during the LDP's hegemonic reign. Thus, ministers in coalition cabinets brought a broader range of policy perspectives and interests to executive decision-making than had been the case with LDP-dominated cabinets.

REORGANIZING GOVERNMENT

All of the major parties called for administrative reform during the campaign for the July 1996 general elections. The New Party Sakigake firmly embraced the issue and insisted that it be placed on the political agenda as a condition for its participation in an LDP-led coalition government. Upon forming his cabinet, Prime Minister Hashimoto pledged to "consume himself to ashes" in pursuing the cause of reform (Nakano 1998, 291–292). By establishing and serving as chair of the Administrative Reform Council, Hashimoto signaled that his cabinet took the issue seriously. In its final report, issued on December 3, 1997, the ARC recommended that the number of major central government organs be reduced and that the powers of the prime minister and cabinet be bolstered. At an extraordinary cabinet meeting convened the following day, Hashimoto and his ministers pledged "firm resolve" to bring about the recommended reforms by 2001 (Administrative Reform Council 1997). The successor Obuchi and Mori cabinets continued to press for the enactment of the reforms, and on January 7, 2001, a dramatically reconfigured central government organization was unveiled.

As a result of the restructuring, the Prime Minister's Office, a dozen ministries, two commissions, and eight agencies were recast into a Cabinet Office, ten ministries, a commission, and an agency. In a single stroke, twenty-four major administrative organs were reduced to thirteen. Some changes were essentially cosmetic. For example, the Ministry of Finance's name was changed from *Ōkurashō* to *Zaimushō*—meaning "Treasury Ministry"—presumably to signal its rebirth following a series of embarrassing scandals, while the Ministry of International Trade and Industry became the Ministry of Economy, Trade, and Industry (*Keizai sangyō shō*, or METI). At the same time, a Westminster-style ministerial hierarchy became firmly established. Before and after the restructuring, the prime minister, finance, economy, and foreign affairs portfolios attracted high-status MPs (see Appendix C).

Five ministries were created through the amalgamation of existing governmental organs. The Ministry of Education, Culture, Sports, Science, and Technology (*Monbukagakushō*) arose from the merger of the Education Ministry and the Science and Technology Agency (*Kagakugijutsuchō*), while the Ministry of Health, Labor, and Welfare (*Kōseirōdōshō*) was produced by the union of the Health and Labor Ministries. The Ministry of Internal Affairs and Communications (*Sōmushō*—known as the Ministry of Public Management, Home Affairs, Posts and Telecommunications until 2004) was brought forth from the amalgamation of the Home Affairs and Telecommunications Ministries and the transfer of functions of the Management and Coordination Agency (*Sōmuchō*), while the Ministry of Land, Infrastructure, and

Transport (*Kokudokōtsūshō*) was created through the amalgamation of the Transport and Construction Ministries and the Hokkaidō Development Agency. Meanwhile, the Environment Agency was upgraded to the Ministry of the Environment (*Kankyōshō*) and assumed the waste recycling functions of the former Health Ministry.

The Cabinet Office (*Naikakufu*) combined the functions of the Prime Minister's Office and the agencies for economic planning, Okinawa development, management and coordination, science and technology, and national land. It was also given supervisory power over the National Public Safety Commission as well as the Defense and Financial Services agencies, and, at least in theory, was accorded a status superior to that of the ten regular government ministries. The Cabinet Office's administrative staff were placed under the direct supervision of the prime minister and chief cabinet secretary, who were assisted by three senior vice ministers (*naikakufu fukudaijin*) and three parliamentary secretaries (*naikakufu daijin seimujikan*). This meant that the Cabinet Office was supervised by eight political appointees, as opposed to the maximum of six in other government ministries.[3] As with other government ministries, however, the post of administrative vice minister—who was in charge of its day-to-day operations—was filled by a senior career civil servant.

Steps were taken to strengthen the leadership role of the cabinet and prime minister. Four "important policy councils" (*jūyō seisaku kaigi*) were established as "places of wisdom" (*chie no ba*) to assist in "the planning and drafting, and comprehensive coordination needed for the integration of the policies of administrative branches" (Headquarters for the Administrative Reform of the Central Government 2000). They included the Council on Economic and Fiscal Policy (*Keizai zaisei shimon kaigi,* or CEFP), the Council for Science and Technology Policy (*Chūō kagaku gijutsu kaigi*), the Central Disaster Prevention Council (*Chūō bōsai kaigi*), and the Council for Gender Equality (*Danjo kyōdō sankaku kaigi*). Council members included ministers of state as well as individuals from the private sector, academia, NGOs, labor unions, quasi-governmental bodies, and local government. In addition, the Cabinet Secretariat was given charge of the "comprehensive coordination" of the "important policies" relating to foreign affairs and national security, administrative and financial management, economic policy and budgetary planning, and governmental affairs. To assist in this, three new positions were established within the Secretariat—assistant cabinet secretary, cabinet secretary for public relations, and cabinet secretary for information research (ibid.). The prime minister was empowered to appoint as many as five special advisers (the previous maximum had been three) and to fill key posts in the Cabinet Secretariat with officials from the various ministries and specialists from outside government.

The post of "minister of state for special missions" (*tokumei tantō daijin*) was created to boost the prime minister's power to focus on high-value policy priorities (Headquarters for the Administrative Reform of the Central Government 2000). Although there was no limit to the number of special minister portfolios, cabinets formed between January 2001 and September 2008 allocated between six and twenty-six of them. According to the revised Cabinet Law, prime ministers were obliged to appoint special ministers for financial services, problems concerning Okinawa and the Northern Territories, and consumer and food safety. In practice, most cabinets included special ministers for disaster management, economic and fiscal policy, science and technology policy, regulatory reform, and gender equality and social affairs. In addition, special ministers were appointed to oversee a variety of other issues, including civil service reform, regional revitalization, global environmental problems, ocean policy, the abduction of Japanese citizens by North Korea, and the possible transfer of the functions of the capital. Because the Cabinet Law limited the maximum number of ministers to eighteen, special missions ministers frequently held as many as five portfolios.

EXECUTIVE RIVALS

At least on paper, the government restructuring enhanced the powers of the prime minister and cabinet. Although the government bureaucracy had lost much of its luster, it remained a force in executive affairs. Koizumi's "presidential" leadership style led to speculation that prime ministerial government might become the rule, but his successors "failed miserably to come even close to Koizumi's successes" (Krauss and Pekkanen 2010, 250). While maintaining solidarity among coalition partners caused a few headaches, the fractured policy-making environment—which was, as Samuels aptly put it, "characterized by excessively diffused power guarded tenaciously within narrow policy silos"—proved far more troublesome (2013, 53). In this feudalistic arrangement, policy specialists (*zoku giin*), government bureaucrats, and special interests defended their policy fiefs from all

challengers. This revealed the essential nature of the LDP as a confedera-
tion of policy tribes that put narrow vested interests above the broader
interests of ruling party and country.

Bureaucratic Inertia

The establishment of the Cabinet Office gave ministers greater voice in
shaping policy proposals, and the appointment of state secretaries and parliamentary vice ministers meant that additional "political eyes" were now
dedicated to the task of monitoring bureaucrats in the ministries. Prior
to the 2001 restructuring, the maximum number of political appointees
supervising any given ministry was three, including the minister and one
or two parliamentary vice ministers, while the cabinet-level agencies were
supervised by a politically appointed director general and a parliamentary
vice minister. This meant that fifty-five elected politicians were responsible
for monitoring nearly eight hundred thousand government bureaucrats.
As a result of the 2001 restructuring, sixty-three political appointees now
supervised a government bureaucracy that was in the process of being
"slimmed down" (*surimuka*) through privatization and staff reductions.
As part of the restructuring, a measure was taken to reduce bureaucratic
influence by allowing only four "special government assistants" to testify in
Diet debates (Kyodo News, January 11, 1999). Prior to this, it was common
for senior bureaucrats to take the podium for their ministers in legislative
interpellations.

Yet the bureaucracy continued to influence executive affairs through
the institutional memory embodied in the Cabinet Legislation Bureau and
the position of deputy chief cabinet secretary for administrative affairs,
who chaired the biweekly gatherings of administrative vice ministers to set
the agenda for cabinet meetings. For instance, Deputy Secretary Ishihara
Nobuo, a former administrative vice minister of home affairs known as the
"Don of Kasumigaseki," was able to block initiatives taken by the Hosokawa and Murayama governments (Shimizu 2005, 33). As the CLB's director general explained to Murayama following the 1995 Kōbe earthquake,
"it is problematic to amend the law to enable the prime minister to control
and supervise the ministries and agencies—even during an emergency"
(Samuels 2004, 5).

Corruption scandals and incompetence, however, combined to shat-
ter whatever remained of the myth of bureaucratic infallibility (Koh 1989,

205). The Ministry of Health and Welfare was vilified in 1996 when it came to light that more than one thousand hemophiliacs and others had contracted HIV through the use of non-heat-treated blood products, even though safe products were available (Feldman and Bayer 1999). By the late 1990s, the Finance Ministry's once pristine image was in tatters as a result of officials receiving bribes and illegal benefits, and for the ministry's role in a controversial $6.5 billion bailout for troubled credit unions (*jūsen*) (Laurence 2001, 174). Then, in 2001, the Foreign Ministry took a reputational hit when the media reported that one of its officials had used more than ¥50 million in embezzled funds to purchase racehorses and to finance an extravagant lifestyle (Berkofsky 2002).

As a result, government ministries found it increasingly difficult to recruit and retain the best and brightest university graduates. Until the early 1990s, nearly two hundred graduates each year from Tokyo University's prestigious Faculty of Law elected to become career bureaucrats. In 2006, only sixty-eight Tōdai law graduates accepted civil service posts (Nariai 2007). While this was partly the result of an overall cut in the number of civil service positions (discussed below), growing numbers of young bureaucrats were moving on to greener pastures with private-sector companies or in the legal profession. In fact, between 2001 and 2006, nearly three hundred career civil servants chose to take early retirement from government positions, a 3.5-fold increase over the corresponding figure from the 1980s (ibid.). It is likely that the bureaucracy's tarnished image contributed to these recruiting and retention problems, and the allure of a civil service career was weakened as a result of the diminution of powers and prerogatives dictated by deregulation.

Threshold of Cabinet Government

The 2001 restructuring elevated the status of the Cabinet Office to that of "comprehensive coordinator" of interministerial affairs, which meant that the Cabinet Office was *primus inter pares* among government ministries. Other ministries responded by seconding their rising stars to the Cabinet Office and the Cabinet Secretariat (*Yomiuri Shimbun,* May 31, 2005). Moreover, while the ministries and agencies eliminated nearly two hundred thousand staff positions between 2000 and 2007, there was an increase in the number of employees assigned to the Cabinet Office (2,202 to 2,337) and the Cabinet Secretariat (338 to 612).

However, policy failures, gaffes, and scandal negated efforts to establish cabinet government. While every cabinet has its share of slips, the Mori cabinet set a new standard for dim-wittedness. In a speech delivered in May 2000, Mori referred to Japan as "the nation with the Emperor at its heart in the land of deities" (*tennō o chūshin to suru kami no kuni*), which conjured up images of the militaristic prewar regime under a divine-right ruler ("Statement," May 16, 2000). This sent public support for the cabinet into a tailspin (dropping to a low of 7.2 percent in April 2001) and led to a no-confidence bill, to which Mori responded by dissolving the Diet and calling new elections. October found Mori with his foot in his mouth again, this time for suggesting to North Korean officials that the abductee problem could be resolved by having the kidnapped Japanese pop up in a third country (*The Independent,* October 25, 2000). Later that month, Chief Cabinet Secretary Nakagawa Hidenao was forced to resign after being implicated in a sex scandal and for reputed ties to the underworld. All of these gaffes and scandals might have been overlooked had the cabinet's economic policies produced results. In a general sense, the descriptions of Mori as having "the heart of a flea and the brain of a shark" and as "an embarrassment" corresponded with the popular perception of the prime ministers and cabinets at the country's executive helm (BBC, November 20, 2000; *Guardian,* November 6, 2000).

A Maverick Stakes His Claim

Of the dozen individuals to sit in the prime minister's seat between 1993 and 2006, only Koizumi displayed the type of forceful leadership associated with prime ministerial government. While Koizumi's *"kantei* style" approach was different from the traditional, understated leadership associated with Japanese prime ministers, some measure of his success in effecting policy change was owed to the longevity of his government. In fact, Koizumi's five-and-a-half-year premiership ranks as the third longest among postwar prime ministers (behind only Satō Eisaku and Yoshida Shigeru). This gave Koizumi considerable time to pursue his policy agenda, which included rectifying the bad debt crisis, trimming pork barrel spending, and privatizing postal services (Shimizu 2005). In addition, his government brought Japan into the U.S.-led War on Terror and dispatched Self-Defense Forces personnel to Iraq, the first such mission to an active war zone since the end of the Pacific War.

Nicknamed the "Lone Wolf Prime Minister" (*ippiki ōkami no shushō*) because of his go-it-alone tendencies—and, more famously, "Lionheart" (*raion haato*) because of his tenacity and leonine hairstyle—Koizumi was unusually assertive for a Japanese prime minister (Maeda 2006, 623). His refusal to consult with faction leaders in making cabinet appointments and threats to eliminate pork barrel spending ruffled feathers within the ruling party (Takenaka 2008, 19–21; Scheiner 2006, 34). By keeping his first cabinet intact for 611 days, Koizumi went against the norm of frequent cabinet reshuffles to maintain factional balance. He claimed that his selection of ministers was based on merit rather than factional ties, and he took the unusual step of appointing Takenaka Heizō, an economics professor who did not hold a Diet seat, to take the lead in resolving the bad debt crisis and privatizing postal services. Koizumi also went outside the cabinet to make use of specially created organs, such as the Council on Economic and Fiscal Policy, to avoid the difficulties and delays that would have arisen by working through established channels (Takenaka 2008, 5).

A self-styled maverick, Koizumi was willing to attack party structures and vested interests that obstructed pursuit of his policy agenda. He eliminated some of the perks enjoyed by postmasters, organized farmers, and construction contractors, and endeavored to expand the LDP's support base in urban areas. Koizumi appealed to female voters by giving a record number of portfolios to women. However, his support rating went into a free fall after he sacked popular foreign minister Tanaka Makiko, Tanaka Kakuei's daughter, for causing a stir at the ministry (Uriu 2003, 81). By calling snap elections following the upper house rejection of his postal privatization package, Koizumi employed a style of leadership seldom seen on Japan's political stage. In the words of one observer, "Koizumi really challenged the traditional machinations of domestic politics to achieve his reform agenda. . . . He decided that he was going to push ahead with his agenda and sweep tradition aside" (Nicholas Szechenyi quoted in Fogarty 2006).

Still, Koizumi failed to firmly establish prime ministerial government. As time would tell, none of the half-dozen LDP and DPJ prime ministers who followed him was similarly telegenic or suited to "*kantei*-style" leadership. Moreover, despite Koizumi's vow to break the ties binding the political, bureaucratic, and business worlds, he failed to vanquish the subgovernments that dominated the fragmented policy-making environment, including the dreaded postal family. In fact, Koizumi's powers peaked following the referendum on postal privatization, which left him barely more than one year in the prime minister's seat. At the end of the day, Koizumi— like Tanaka Kakuei and Nakasone Yasuhiro before him—was unable to establish a system of top-down prime ministerial leadership.

Coping with the Fragmented Policy-Making Environment

Cabinets were forced to deal with a variety of challenges. The Murayama cabinet had to respond to the deadly Kōbe earthquake and the sarin gas attack unleashed by Aum Shinrikyō cultists on the Tokyo subway system. The Hashimoto cabinet was forced to apologize for the government's failure to recall blood products that carried the virus that causes AIDS, while the Obuchi cabinet had to deal with the "financial big bang" (kin'yū biggu ban) that resulted in major changes in banking and financial services. The Mori cabinet was forced to address public concerns about food safety when fifteen thousand citizens became ill after consuming Snow Brand milk, and the Koizumi cabinet took steps to repatriate citizens abducted by North Korean agents. Above all those, the Koizumi government's efforts to privatize postal services provide a unique lens through which to assess the challenges cabinets faced in providing executive leadership in a policy-making landscape dominated by powerful subgovernments.

Postal Privatization Armageddon

On April 26, 2001, Koizumi assumed the premiership, vowing to revitalize the economy through liberalization and deregulation. He and his ministers understood that they would have to do battle with powerful subgovernments whose core members included influential LDP lawmakers, government bureaucrats, and the leaders of well-organized special interests. As one cabinet minister observed, "after the collapse of the [asset] bubble there was a rush to implement a variety of reforms. . . . Nonetheless, because policy decisions were driven by the bureaucracy and zoku giin (Diet members who act in the interest of certain government ministries and the industries they regulate), the necessary reforms were all postponed to another day" (Takenaka 2008, 12–13). In many ways, the postal lobby epitomized the fragmented system of subgovernments that dominated the political landscape and subordinated the national interest to vested interests. Koizumi vowed to "smash" obstructionist elements in the LDP and boldly committed his government to the cause of privatizing the debt-ridden postal service, repeatedly vowing to dissolve the Diet if his reform efforts were thwarted (ibid. 2008, 16; Maeda 2006, 623).

The Koizumi cabinet's opponent was the "postal family" (*yūsei ikka*), a legendarily powerful subgovernment. Its chieftains included members of the LDP's postal tribe (*yūsei zoku*), officials of the Ministry of Internal Affairs and Communications (formerly the Ministry of Posts and Tele-communications, or MPT), and the heads of two postmasters' organizations.[4] It was said that postmasters could mobilize 1 million votes at election time, and MPT bureaucrats often directed postmasters to support specific candidates, some of whom were retired postal officials (MacLachlan 2004, 307–308). The family's influence was enhanced by the fact that post offices were located in every locality and offered government-insured, tax-free interest on deposits up to a certain amount. In other words, post offices performed some of the functions served by banks and financial institutions in other countries. By the time the Koizumi cabinet took office, the postal savings system boasted ¥224 trillion in household deposits, and postal life insurance services claimed holdings of ¥126 trillion. This meant that Japan's postal savings system was the world's largest bank, while government borrowing through the issuance of bonds drawn from the Fiscal Investment and Loan Plan (FILP) accounted for a significant slice of the national debt.

The Koizumi Cabinet's Reform Bill

Calls for the reform of postal services began as early as the late 1960s, but the issue did not gain traction in policy circles until the 1990s (MacLachlan 2004, 282). In its September 2007 interim report, Hashimoto's ARC called for a dramatic overhaul of mail delivery, postal savings, and insurance. MPT officials counterpunched by mobilizing postmasters to lobby members of the postal tribe and other LDP politicians to oppose the ARC's recommendations (Kawabata 2004, 28). Nevertheless, in December the council issued a final report recommending that postal delivery, savings, and insurance be managed by an independent public corporation. Hashimoto went further, proposing to allow private companies to enter the postal business and to sever the link between the postal savings system and the FILP (Porges and Leong 2006, 387). However, the Hashimoto government was forced to resign as a result of the LDP's poor showing in the 1998 upper house elections, and the postal privatization debate fell into semihibernation.

Koizumi realized that the biggest obstacle to postal privatization would come from members of his own political party, which is why he assembled a cabinet that "transcended factional and tenure balance" (Takenaka 2008, 21). Among his ministers were five women and three individuals from the private sector, including Takenaka Heizō, a Keiō University economist who was given the economic and fiscal policy portfolio. "We have a really tough fight ahead," said Koizumi to Takenaka, "please join my cabinet as a minister and fight with me" (ibid., 2). At the cabinet's inaugural meeting, Koizumi declared that "without structural reforms there can be no economic recovery" (*kōzō kaikaku nakushite keiki kaifuku nashi*) ("Statement by Prime Minister Junichiro Koizumi" 2001). Boosted by an 81 percent public approval rating, Koizumi threw down the gauntlet at a May 9 plenary session of the lower house, declaring that "the nonsensical logic of the ex-Ministry of Posts and Telecommunications does not work for the Koizumi cabinet. . . . [The impediment of private-sector activities by postal businesses] will not be tolerated by the Koizumi cabinet" (Kawabata 2004, 21; Takenaka 2008, 26).

Acting on cabinet orders, the Internal Affairs Ministry dutifully produced two draft bills in March 2002. The first bill proposed to open the letter delivery market to private firms. However, the fact that it required participating firms to install mailboxes in the ninety-nine thousand localities nationwide extinguished whatever interest there might have been among private-sector firms (Kawabata 2004, 29). The second bill called for the establishment of the Japan Postal Services Corporation (*Nihon yusei kōsha*)—or "Japan Post"—to replace the Postal Services Agency (ibid.; "Statement by Prime Minister Junichiro Koizumi" 2001). In April, the Koizumi cabinet unilaterally approved and sent the bills to the Diet without having gone through the LDP's preapproval system (Kawabata 2004, 29). Naturally, this did not please senior LDP leaders, leading to anxious moments for Koizumi and his ministers, especially as the bills appeared to be stalled in a Diet session set to close at the end of June. Then Policy Affairs Research Council chairman Asō Tarō stepped in and persuaded the postal tribe to allow the establishment of Japan Post in exchange for an amended letter delivery service bill (ibid., 30). The Diet approved both bills in July.

In a September 2003 address to the Diet, Koizumi stated his government's goal of realizing the privatization of postal services within four years. "Soon we will arrive at the heart of hearts," the prime minister observed. "Privatization of the postal service has now become a *cabinet issue*" (Takenaka 2008, 134; italics added). The CEFP was tasked with devising a plan to submit the privatization bills to the Diet the following year. In the meantime, Koizumi dissolved the lower house and called new elections, observing in his email magazine that he did so to gauge popular support for his reform agenda (Koizumi Cabinet E-mail Magazine 2003). The 2003 general elections left the LDP and its coalition partners, the New Kōmei and New Conservative parties, in control of 57 percent of lower house seats. In the aftermath, DPJ president Kan Naoto conceded that the "Koizumi administration won public trust through this election" (*Nikkei Net,* November 10, 2003).

In early 2004, the Koizumi cabinet shifted into overdrive. A Preparatory Office for Privatization of Postal Services was established in April, and four months later the CEFP unveiled the outline of a basic plan for privatizing the Japanese postal system (Takenaka 2008, 142, 144). The council's plan called for the establishment of independent corporations to handle counter services, mail delivery, postal banking, and postal insurance. A holding corporation would be set up to control shares of the four corporate subsidiaries, but the national government would continue to own more than one-third of the issued corporate stock (Porges and Leong 2006, 388). The following month, the cabinet approved the plan, once again without securing preapproval from the LDP's top leaders (Takenaka 2008, 154). In late September, Koizumi reshuffled his cabinet, giving Takenaka the postal privatization and economic/fiscal policy portfolios to guard against sabotage by Ministry of Internal Affairs and Communications bureaucrats (ibid., 155).

Defeat in the Diet

In early January 2005, Takenaka began to feel that "there was a distinct possibility that the situation surrounding postal privatization could take a turn for the worse, and sound the death knell of the Koizumi Cabinet" (2008, 165). Later that month, at the opening session of the Diet, Koizumi reaffirmed his determination to privatize postal services along the lines outlined in a plan proposed by the CEFP (ibid., 166–167). In early April, Koizumi asked Takenaka to obtain a unified cabinet position on postal reform, which he endeavored to achieve by convening a marathon meeting of ministers (ibid., 171). Reflecting on the meeting, Takenaka mused, "I doubt there has ever been another administration that experienced having its ministers stuck in a room to debate intensively for two full days" (ibid., 173). The ordeal produced a unified cabinet proposal that was passed along for approval by the LDP's five top leaders and the six concerned cabinet ministers. On April 25, the party leaders approved the reform bills over the objections of upper house secretary general Katayama Toranosuke (ibid., 178). Two days later, at an extraordinary cabinet meeting, the Koizumi cabinet approved the package of bills and sent them to the LDP's Executive Council for review (ibid.).

The lower house began deliberating the bills on May 26, with the DPJ refusing to participate on the grounds that "postal privatization is . . . irresponsible and unwise, and the increasing pressure for private management is of concern" (Takenaka 2008, 180). Although the DPJ later joined the debate, the Koizumi cabinet faced a far greater challenge dealing with the chieftains of the postal tribe. One of them, Watanuki Tamisuke, was in the process of mobilizing about seventy LDP MPs to vote against the cabinet-sponsored bills (ibid., 191). Nevertheless, on July 4, after 109 hours of debate, the lower house approved the bills in a 233 to 228 vote. The narrow margin of victory was owed to the fact that fifty-one LDP MPs either voted against or refrained from voting on the cabinet-sponsored bills (ibid., 194).

The bills were then sent to the upper house, which commenced deliberations on July 13. About this time, Takenaka, who had been elected to the upper house in 2004, began noticing large groups of postmasters from rural areas descending upon the upper house members' office building to lobby for rejection of the privatization bills (ibid., 198). On August 5, after eighty hours of question-and-answer debate in the Diet, the upper house rejected the Koizumi cabinet's reform package in a 125 to 108 vote (ibid., 199). This time, twenty-two LDP MPs voted "no," while eight abstained (Maeda 2006, 622). Koizumi immediately convened an emergency cabinet meeting at which he proposed to dissolve the Diet and call new elections. Initially only three ministers supported the plan, but eventually all except Agriculture Minister Shimamura Yoshinobu came around to the prime minister's point of view (Takenaka 2008, 200). When Shimamura refused to go with the flow, Koizumi fired him.[5] Koizumi conveyed the cabinet's decision to the emperor, who then formally dissolved the lower house and called new elections (Porges and Leong 2006, 891).

The Koizumi Cabinet Prevails

At a press conference on August 8, Koizumi observed that: "the Diet has reached the conclusion that there is no need to privatize the postal services. Still, I intend to once again ask the people whether it really is the case that only civil servants can handle the work of the post office and if we really cannot allow the private sector to take it on" (Koizumi Press Conference 2005). Ignoring the fact that eighty MPs from his own party had voted against or abstained from voting on the privatization bills, Koizumi declared that "now that we have become the party of reform, the LDP will face the DPJ straight on and turn to the people to ask them to pass their judgment. That is why I choose to dissolve the Diet" (ibid.). Koizumi vowed to punish the "postal rebels" by denying them party backing and by dispatching "assassins" (*shikaku*)—including female candidates whom the foreign media dubbed "lipstick *ninjas*"—to run against them in the districts.[6]

The general elections of September 11 brought forth the highest voter turnout since 1990 (69.3 percent) and delivered an electoral mandate for the Koizumi cabinet's policies. Candidates of the LDP and the Clean Government Party, its coalition partner, combined to win 68 percent of lower house seats. Meanwhile, the DPJ suffered a net loss of sixty-four seats. The new Diet convened on September 21 and took only three weeks to approve the postal reform bills. To prevent bureaucratic sabotage, Koizumi handed the internal affairs and communications and postal privatization portfolios in his reshuffled cabinet to the trusted Takenaka (Takenaka 2008, 210). Koizumi continued to punish the postal rebels, expelling former agriculture minister Norota Hōsei and pressuring ex-cabinet ministers Horiuchi Mitsuo, Hiranuma Takeo, Noda Seiko, and others to leave the party (*Japan Times,* October 29, 2005).

FINDINGS

Coalition governments became the norm following the tumultuous 1993 lower house elections. With the exception of the period from July 1998 through January 1999, when the LDP ruled alone, coalition governments defined the period. The eight-party coalition that established the Hosokawa cabinet survived less than nine months, while the Hata cabinet collapsed after only sixty-three days. In June 1994, the LDP returned to power as senior partner in a series of coalitions with the JSP and other parties. A central objective of the 2001 government restructuring was to enhance the leadership role of the cabinet and prime minister. The newly established Cabinet Office enhanced the cabinet's oversight and coordination functions, while the appointment of special missions ministers granted greater discretion to the prime minister in pursuing high-priority policies. The establishment of state secretary and parliamentary secretary posts augmented the cabinet's ability to oversee and coordinate the policy activities of the government ministries and agencies.

Even though on the surface Japan's cabinet system was more "Westminsterian" than ever, cabinet government failed to take root. Although the relative influence of the government bureaucracy continued to decline—a consequence of rising public distrust, reduced bureaucratic powers, and fewer ex-officials among the ministerial elite—cabinets did not fill the void. Although the Koizumi cabinet's victory in the battle to privatize postal services led some pundits to believe that Japan was on the threshold of an era of prime ministerial government, this, too, did not materialize. While the Koizumi cabinet prevailed in the postal privatization battle, the postal family would live to fight another day. The challenge of providing effective executive leadership would become even more vexing in an era of Twisted Diets.

6

Disjoined Cabinets—Act II

Twisted Diets and Lost Leadership Opportunity, 2006–2013

[Under the Westminster model,] the executive is in a powerful
position to lead government and pass the legislation it wishes. British
government is usually *strong government.*
—Stuart McAnulla, *British Politics* (2006), 14

Governments facing Twisted Diets propose fewer laws, they suffer more
changes to and failures of the legislative proposals they do submit, and
they must adapt the scope and . . . content of their programs to the
exigencies of extra-governmental legislative coalition building.
—Michael F. Thies and Yuki Yanai,
"Divided Parliaments and Lawmaking" (2012), 28

THE RETURN OF THE PRINCE

On December 26, 2012, Abe Shinzō became the first former premier to
return to form a government since Yoshida Shigeru had done so sixty-
four years earlier. Known as the "prince of the political realm" (*seikai no
purinsu*) because both his father and grandfather had been royalty in parliamentary circles, Abe had formed his first cabinet on September 26, 2006.
Despite strong public approval, Abe's predecessor, Koizumi Jun'ichirō, had
been obliged to step aside to comply with the rule that limited the tenure
of the LDP's president to two three-year terms. Abe's first stint as prime
minister, which began with high hopes, endured just one troubled year,
and similar fates befell the governments of Fukuda Yasuo and Asō Tarō,
the LDP leaders who followed him. In the general elections held on August
30, 2009, voters demonstrated their displeasure with the ineptitude and

corruption associated with LDP-led cabinets by installing a new ruling party that promised meaningful reform. Yet, despite great expectations, the average length of tenure for the three DPJ-led governments—under Hatoyama Yukio, Kan Naoto, and Noda Yoshihiko—was barely more than one trouble-filled year. As a consequence, scarcely any of the promised changes were actually accomplished. So it was that Prince Abe reassumed the throne amid popular optimism that his "Abenomics" policies—which assumed that aggressive monetary easing and public works spending would revive the economy—might finally bring an end to the lost decades (*Wall Street Journal,* May 9, 2013).

In this chapter, I focus on the seven governments that occupied the executive helm from September 2006 through late 2013. During this period of controversy and crisis, the difficulties of dealing with "Twisted Diets"— in which the ruling coalition did not control an upper house majority— created countless headaches for prime ministers and their cabinets. Once portrayed as the essentially functionless "appendix of the Diet" (*kokkai no mōchō*), the upper house became hostile and obstructed the appointment of prime ministers and passage of the national budget, and determined what policy objectives governments could and could not pursue. In the same way that acute appendicitis causes intense physical discomfort, the angst caused by dealing with Twisted Diets was palpable, and it led to a succession of ephemeral cabinets. Finally, I assess the extent to which a Westminster-style cabinet system had become established by exploring the controversy over the proposed relocation of the U.S. Marine Corps Air Station at Futenma.

RESTORATIONISTS AND REFORMISTS

Koizumi's aggressive reform efforts brought forth two types of detractors: *restorationists* and *reformists.* The trio of post-Koizumi LDP premiers attempted to restore intraparty factionalism and shore up the fragmented policy-making system dominated by powerful subgovernments. Although Abe was seen as Koizumi's protégé, his decision to readmit the postal rebels to the LDP seemed to signal a return to old-school politics (Kabashima and Steel 2010, 119). This, along with the disappearance of millions of pension payment records (discussed below) and several corruption scandals, sent the Abe cabinet's public approval rating plummeting. Thus, it came as no surprise that the LDP lost its upper house majority in the July 2007 elections. Citing health concerns, Abe resigned about a month later, leaving it to Fukuda and Asō to tussle with a DPJ-dominated upper house. Fukuda attempted to end the policy gridlock caused by a Twisted Diet by proposing a grand coalition to DPJ leader Ozawa Ichirō, but other DPJ leaders objected. When his turn came, Asō installed a cabinet of cronies and unleashed a torrent of old-fashioned LDP pork barrel spending in a fruitless effort to jump-start the economy (ibid., 125).

The August 2009 lower house elections propelled reformist DPJ-led cabinets into power, but the Hatoyama cabinet did not control a majority of seats in the upper house, a situation that obliged him to include MPs from two minor coalition partners in his cabinet. One of them, the Social Democratic Party (*Shakai minshutō*, or SDP)—formerly known as the Japan Socialist Party—had long advocated the removal of U.S. military bases from Japanese soil. Although the DPJ's "Manifesto" and Hatoyama's campaign pledges clearly indicated that the party wished to see the American bases moved elsewhere, the reality of being at the executive helm, as opposed to sitting in the opposition pews, led to equivocation. When Hatoyama finally agreed to relocate the U.S. Marine Corps Futenma Air Base to another location on Okinawa, the Social Democratic Party minister publicly announced her refusal to abide by the cabinet's decision. With sagging approval ratings and upper house elections on the horizon, the Hatoyama cabinet was obliged to resign. The July 2010 upper house elections produced an even more tightly Twisted Diet, which became a perpetual thorn in the sides of the subsequent DPJ-led Kan and Noda cabinets.

So it was that, despite alternation in ruling party and promises to reform the executive branch, cabinet government did not materialize. The three LDP-led governments that followed Koizumi's required resignation attempted to restore features of the *ancien regime*, while the three DPJ-led governments put forward reform agendas. Whenever the Diet became twisted, a hostile upper house could be counted on to block government-proposed bills and to delay the passage of the national budget and the selection of a prime minister. Dealing with Twisted Diets made governing difficult and led to rapid turnover of prime ministers and cabinets.

THE MINISTERIAL ELITE

Between September 2007 and December 2013, seven prime ministers presided over fourteen cabinets. A total of 135 individuals held ministerial portfolios. The average life span of these cabinets was less than six months (178 days), making them the shortest-lived of those of any era in the evolution of Japan's parliamentary cabinet system. With a life of just thirty days, the Reorganized Abe cabinet was Japan's second shortest.

Prime Ministers

The trio of LDP prime ministers who came after Koizumi were portrayed as "spoiled sons" (*obotchan*) of famous political families. Abe Shinzō was the son of a veteran foreign minister and LDP faction boss (Abe Shintarō), and his maternal grandfather was Kishi Nobusuke. Fukuda Yasuo was the son of Fukuda Takeo, while Asō Tarō was an MP's son and the grandson of legendary premier Yoshida Shigeru. Fukuda was a Waseda University alumnus, while Abe graduated from Seikei University and Asō from Gakushūin University. Both Abe and Fukuda worked in the private sector—for Kobe Steel and Maruzen Petroleum, respectively—and apprenticed as staff assistants to their MP fathers before "inheriting" their Diet seats. Prior to becoming prime minister, Abe had held only one ministerial appointment, as chief cabinet secretary in the Koizumi government, although he gained fame for his role in negotiating the release of Japanese citizens abducted by North Korean agents. Fukuda had the misfortune of having to deal with a Twisted Diet that blocked his cabinet's efforts to renew a bill to continue Japan's role in refueling American warships engaged in the War on Terror. Asō's tenure in office was plagued by a sluggish economy and, ultimately, met its demise in the LDP's defeat in the 2009 lower house elections.

The DPJ prime ministers presented a mixed bag. Like the three LDP premiers who preceded him, Hatoyama Yukio was seen as an *obotchan*. The son of a foreign minister, grandson of a prime minister, and great grandson of a Meiji-era lower house speaker, Hatoyama was a rare *fourth*-generation MP. Kan Naoto was the son of a "salary man," and Noda Yoshihiko's grandparents were farmers. Hatoyama's mother was heiress to the Bridgestone Tire Company fortune, while Noda's parents were so poor that they could not afford to pay for him to have a wedding reception (Bloomberg.net, August 30, 2011). Hatoyama was educated at the prestigious Peers School, while Kan and Noda attended public schools. Hatoyama matriculated to Tokyo University and received his doctorate from Stanford University, while Kan studied at the Tokyo Institute of Technology and Noda at Waseda University. Hatoyama was an assistant professor before entering

Table 6.1. Disjoined Cabinets and Twisted Diets, 2006 to 2013

Cabinet	Prime Minister	Established	Dissolved	Lower House	Upper House	Diet Status
1st Abe Cabinet	Abe Shinzō	9/26/2006	8/27/2007	LDP-Led Coalition	DPJ-Led Coalition	Twisted
Reorg'ed Abe Cabinet	"	8/27/2007	9/26/2007	"	"	"
Fukuda Cabinet	Fukuda Yasuo	9/26/2007	8/1/2008	"	"	"
Reorg'ed Fukuda Cabinet	"	8/1/2008	9/24/2008	"	"	"
Asō Cabinet	Asō Tarō	9/24/2008	9/16/2009	"	"	"
Hatoyama Cabinet	Hatoyama Yukio	9/16/2009	6/8/2010	DPJ-Led Coalition	DPJ-Led Coalition	Unified
Kan Cabinet	Kan Naoto	6/8/2010	9/17/2010	DPJ-Led Coalition	LDP-Led Coalition	Twisted
1st Reorg'ed Kan Cabinet	"	9/17/2010	1/14/2011	"	"	"
2nd Reorg'ed Kan Cabinet	"	1/14/2011	9/2/2011	"	"	"
Noda Cabinet	Noda Yoshihiko	9/2/2011	1/13/2012	"	"	"
1st Reorg'ed Noda Cabinet	"	1/13/2012	6/4/2012	"	"	"
2nd Reorg'ed Noda Cabinet	"	6/4/2012	10/1/2012	"	"	"
3rd Reorg'ed Noda Cabinet	"	10/1/2012	12/26/2012	"	"	"
2nd Abe Cabinet	Abe Shinzō	12/26/2012	–	LDP-Led Coalition	LDP-Led Coalition	Unified

Note: In these cabinets, the largest party held a solid Lower House majority but opted to retain coalition partners.
Source: JCCM Database (Appendix A). Some data in this table were adapted from Thies and Yanai (2012).

the family business, which he did by winning a lower house seat in 1986. Kan worked as a patent attorney (*benrishi*) and as a campaign strategist before winning election to the lower house in 1980 on his fourth attempt. Noda entered politics at the grassroots level as a member of the Chiba Prefectural Assembly and was elected to the Diet in 1993 as a member of Hosokawa Morihiro's Japan New Party. Hatoyama's extraterrestrial looks earned him the nickname of "ET" or "The Alien" (*uchūjin*), while Noda compared himself to a *dojō* loach, a plain-looking bottom-feeding fish whose tireless efforts keep the pond livable for all its inhabitants. As health minister, Kan famously ordered ministry officials to open up internal files on decisions that allowed tainted blood products to infect more than one thousand Japanese citizens with HIV.

Departmental Ministers

The modal minister was a sixty-year-old male university graduate in his fifth lower house term (or third upper house term in the case of the one-quarter of ministers who held seats in that chamber). He had spent nearly nineteen years in national elective politics, which he approached as a life-long career. There is a better than two-in-three chance that this modal minister studied at one of three elite public universities (Tokyo, Kyoto, or Hitotsubashi) or five elite private universities (Waseda, Keiō, Chūō, Nihon, or Meiji). Yet while these eight universities continued to groom the greatest number of ministers, it is worth noting that they produced 87 percent of ministers in the previous cohort.

The composite background of ministers demonstrates that career politicians continued to climb the parliamentary ladder. In fact, nearly two-thirds of ministers emerged from pre-parliamentary occupations that facilitate the pursuit of a political career, such as parliamentary staffer (29 percent), local elective politics (22 percent), law (13 percent), and the mass media (8 percent). At the same time, fewer ex-bureaucrats were awarded portfolios, and most of those who received portfolios had exited the civil service from low-level posts. Ex-bureaucrats accounted for one minister in every five (as opposed to one in every four in the previous cohort), and only 10 percent of them retired from high-level civil servant posts (as opposed to 22 percent in the previous group). In addition, ministers were a bit younger (by 1.8 years) and assumed their seats in the Diet at a more youthful age (by 1.2 years) than the previous ministerial cohort.

Even though Hatoyama was a fourth-generation MP, the DPJ's 2009 election manifesto promised to put an end to hereditary Diet seats. Perhaps as a result, there was a marked drop in the presence of hereditary politicians among ministerial appointees (from 42 percent to 30 percent). Because of the DPJ's relatively stronger base of support in urban areas, there was an increase in the number of ministers representing districts located in the Tokyo, Osaka, and Nagoya metropolitan areas (from 33 percent to 38 percent).

RECONSTRUCTING THE CABINET SYSTEM

The cabinet system was modified in several ways. In January 2007, the Abe cabinet supervised the transformation of the Defense Agency into the Defense Ministry (*Bōeishō*). Not surprisingly, the move to convert a dependent agency under the Prime Minister's Office into a free-standing Ministry of Defense with its own budget was portrayed by opponents as a step toward Japanese remilitarization. Veteran LDP lawmaker Kyūma Fumio was given the inaugural defense minister's portfolio, but he had to resign in July after opining that the atomic bombings of Japanese cities had been necessary to end the Pacific War (*Washington Times*, July 1, 2007). His successor, Koike Yuriko, was forced to stand down after only fifty-four days amid controversy sparked by her attempt to replace the ministry's administrative vice minister without having first consulted with the chief cabinet secretary (*Japan Times*, July 14, 2007). Despite the alternation in ruling party, high-status ministers continued to hold the finance, prime minister, foreign affairs, and economy portfolios (see Appendix C).

The DPJ assumed power vowing to end "government delegated to the bureaucracy" by founding a "unitary system of Cabinet-centered policy-making" (Democratic Party of Japan 2009). On September 18, 2009, the newly formed Hatoyama cabinet created a National Policy Unit (*Kokka senryaku shitsu*, or NPU), subsequently renamed the National Policy Bureau, to facilitate interministerial coordination and strengthen political oversight of the bureaucracy. The NPU aimed to "strengthen the functions of the Prime Ministership" by bringing together "talented people from both the public and the private sector to shape a national vision for the new era, and formulate the budget framework with politicians taking the lead" (ibid.). One of Kan Naoto's first tasks as inaugural state minister for national policy (*Kokka senryaku tantō*) was to supervise the compilation of a supplementary budget for fiscal year 2009 and a general budget for fiscal year 2010. One month later, in October, the Hatoyama cabinet established the Government Revitalization Unit (*Gyōsei sasshin kaigi*) to propose ways to eliminate budgetary waste and improve government administration. Hatoyama himself chaired the body, whose inaugural members included state minister Sengoku Yoshito, Inamori Kazuo (former CEO of Kyocera Corporation), and others.

The DPJ resolved to establish a fully functional Westminster-style cabinet system. During the summer of 2009, party leaders Kan Naoto and Ozawa Ichirō took study trips to Britain to observe a Westminster system in action (Noble 2011, 257). Upon taking power, the DPJ declared that the policy-making influence of government bureaucrats would be dramatically curtailed, and the resulting void would be filled by expanding the role of ministers, senior vice ministers, and parliamentary secretaries in intra-ministry affairs. In addition, Ozawa seized the opportunity to pursue his vendetta with the Cabinet Legislation Bureau for vetoing his effort to send SDF personnel to participate in the first Gulf War (Samuels 2004, 8). At the urging of the DPJ strongman, the CLB's director general was excluded from testifying on behalf of the government in Diet interpellations (Kyodo News, January 14, 2010). The Noda cabinet subsequently lifted the exclusion (*MSN Sankei News,* January 20, 2012).

The DPJ aimed to establish a "unified system of Cabinet-centred policy-making" by abolishing its Policy Affairs Research Council (*Seimuchōsakai*) to enable the cabinet to assume its rightful role as policy initiator (Noble 2011, 257). "Policy decisions will be made by the Cabinet," explained Secretary General Ozawa, "with the opinion of lawmakers being heard in policy committees within each ministry" (*Japan Times,* October 21, 2009). To this end, the DPJ established "policy conferences" (*seisaku kaigi*) to correspond with the Cabinet Office and the government ministries, and all DPJ MPs were allowed to attend. The relevant state secretaries and parliamentary secretaries were tapped to chair the policy conferences tasked with coming up with proposals for ministers to use in drawing up bills for cabinet approval.

The DPJ's promise to bring the bureaucracy to heel was immediately put to the test. An ex-bureaucrat was second in command at the new Consumer Affairs Agency (*Shōhisha chō*), which had begun operations just two weeks before the Hatoyama cabinet took office. The cabinet-level agency was created to allay public concerns over faulty product labeling and food safety. These issues had become front-page news as a result of scandals involving the importation of American-grown beef products that held the potential of causing mad cow disease, water heaters that emitted lethal levels of carbon monoxide, and the sale of Chinese-made "*gyōza*" dumplings that contained pesticides. Although the Hatoyama cabinet fulminated, it did not remove the ex-bureaucrat from his post (*Japan Times,* September 11, 2009).

The March 2011 disasters led to the establishment of the Reconstruction Agency (*Fukkōchō*) as a cabinet-level "control tower" (Samuels 2013, 142). On June 27, DPJ lawmaker Matsumoto Ryū became minister of state in charge of recovery from the disasters. Matsumoto's tenure was brief, as eight days later he was forced to resign as a result of gaffes made during a visit to the badly damaged region. He offended residents by confessing his ignorance of local geography and publicly dressing down the Miyagi Prefecture governor for keeping him waiting in a reception room. Matsumoto sealed his fate by explaining to the Iwate Prefecture governor that the Kan government "will try to help those places that come up with ideas to help themselves, but not those that don't" (*New York Times,* July 5, 2011). Matsumoto was replaced by Hirano Tatsuo, an upper house MP from Iwate Prefecture who became minister of reconstruction following the agency's formal establishment on February 10, 2012. After the December 2012 elections returned the LDP to power, the portfolio was given to Nemoto Takumi, a lower house MP from Fukushima Prefecture.

Finally, in May 2013, the second Abe cabinet began laying the groundwork to establish a National Security Council (*Kokka anzen hosho kaigi,* or NSC) patterned after the American model. The advent of a Twisted Diet frustrated the first Abe cabinet's initial quest to establish an NSC by reorganizing the Security Council of Japan. Soon after reassuming the premiership, however, Abe focused his administration on establishing an NSC with the prime minister, chief cabinet secretary, foreign minister, and defense minister as core members to decide national security and diplomatic strategies. In emergency situations such as the March 2011 disasters, the group would expand to nine members, including four ministers (land, infrastructure, and transport; finance; economy, trade, and industry; and internal affairs and communications) and the commissioner of national public safety (*Yomiuri Shimbun,* May 23, 2013). In late November 2013, soon after the Diet passed the bill establishing the NSC, the new body was called into

action to respond to China's unilateral imposition of an air defense iden-
tification zone over the disputed Senkaku/Diaoyu Islands (*Japan Times*,
November 27, 2013).

EXECUTIVE RIVALS

Despite efforts to reinforce structural supports for a Westminster system,
cabinets competed with government bureaucrats and Twisted Diets for
executive primacy. While subgovernments continued to lord over fief-like
policy domains, no government attempted to throw down the gauntlet as
Koizumi had done in the battle with the "postal family." Prime ministers
and cabinets failed to take decisive action even after the Fukushima Daiichi
nuclear disaster exposed the dangerous realities of the so-called nuclear
village (*genshi mura*), which imperiled public safety in serving the narrow interests of a tightly knit policy community of government regulators,
lawmakers, and the regulated firms (Kushida 2012, 39–40; Samuels 2013,
111). While the coalitional nature of cabinets created difficulties in getting
everyone on the same policy page, a succession of scandal-ridden cabinets
and oblivious prime ministers ensured that cabinet government would not
take hold.

Clueless Prime Ministers

Japanese young people use the colloquialism "cannot read the air" (*kūki
yomenai,* or simply KY) to describe someone who is "out of touch" or "clueless." To be dubbed "KY" is especially bad in Japan's political realm, where
the ability to pick up on unspoken social signals is highly valued. Unfortunately for those who hoped that Koizumi's top-down *kantei*-style leadership would take root, each of the next six men to serve as prime minister
demonstrated varying degrees of obtuseness when it came to "reading the
air" of public opinion and political reality.

   Abe set the stage by promoting patriotic education, enhanced military
status, and constitutional reform when what the public really wanted was
economic recovery and a solution to a fiasco involving lost pension records
(*New York Times*, August 28, 2007). An oblivious Fukuda followed by failing to display sufficient concern for the missing pension records (discussed
below) and by proposing a substantial hike in health insurance premiums
paid by senior citizens (BBC, June 11, 2008). Asō earned the moniker "Tri-

ple KY" for his inability to revive the economy, his indecisiveness when it came to dissolving the Diet, and his problems in pronouncing certain Chinese characters used in written Japanese (Shiota 2011, 316; Reuters, January 21, 2009). Not to be outdone, Hatoyama displayed "KY" in pledging that Japan would cut greenhouse gas emissions on the order of 25 percent by the year 2020 even though he had not first discussed the matter with the government bureaucrats who would have to implement what many believed was an unfeasible policy (Duffield and Woodall 2011, 3743). Kan earned his "KY" stripes by repeatedly flip-flopping on the future of nuclear power, prompting cabinet ministers to complain about his habit of making off-the-cuff policy proclamations (Woodall 2013). Noda jumped on the "KY" bandwagon by ordering the restart of two idled nuclear reactors despite strong public opposition, flip-flopping on a pledge to eliminate reliance on nuclear power by the 2030s, and pressing on with a bill to raise taxes (*New York Times*, December 17, 2012).

For almost a year after returning to the premiership, Prince Abe did not experience a major "KY" relapse. However, his popularity nose-dived in December 2013 following the forced enactment of a controversial bill imposing stiff penalties for leaking "state secrets" (*Mainichi Shinbun*, December 17, 2013). Coming amid the hubbub over Edward Snowden's revelation of the U.S. National Security Agency's secret data gathering, Abe's forced passage of the state secrets bill, with little Diet deliberation, rekindled images of Kishi Nobusuke—his grandfather—steamrolling ratification of the revised U.S.-Japan Mutual Security Treaty in 1960. While there may be a fine line between forceful and clueless leadership, the fact that the economy remained healthy may have earned Abe a free pass from a citizenry with fresh memories of the lost decades.

Resilient Leviathan

Any lingering belief in bureaucratic infallibility was extinguished once and for all with the revelation that sloppy record keeping at the Social Insurance Agency (SIA) made it impossible to verify as many as 50 million pension records. Prime Minister Abe appeared to not take the "pension records problem" (*nenkin kiroku mondai*) seriously when early disclosures began to appear. When the full extent of the bureaucratic bungling was revealed in May 2007, droves of distraught senior citizens descended on government offices and demanded assurances about their retirement nest eggs.

The resulting hubbub contributed to the defeat of the LDP in the July 2007 upper house elections and ensured the collapse of the Abe cabinet. As one observer explained, "Government officials in Japan used to be regarded as the best and brightest, and thus too much reliance on bureaucracy was observed. . . . The general public was under the illusion that government officials were able to do and did everything correctly without committing any errors" (Takayama 2009).

In the DPJ's 2009 election manifesto, the party vowed to move away "from government delegated to the bureaucracy, to politician-led government in which the ruling party holds full responsibility" (Democratic Party of Japan 2009). To this end, the party proposed to abolish the administrative vice ministers meetings, believed to be the "real decision-making organ in the executive branch" and the venue at which the top career bureaucrats set the agenda for cabinet meetings (Koh 1989, 202). These meetings, which were chaired by the deputy chief cabinet secretary for administrative affairs, had been held each Monday and Thursday to coordinate issues prior to the regular Tuesday and Friday cabinet meetings (*Yomiuri Shimbun*, September 15, 2009). What was supposed to have been the last vice ministers meeting was held on September 14, 2009, just two days before the Hatoyama cabinet took office (*Kyōdō Tsūshin*, September 14, 2009). However, the vice ministers meeting did not stay abolished for long, as just two years later the Noda cabinet repackaged the institution under the new guise of "ministerial liaison meetings" (*kaku fu-shō renraku kaigi*) (*Asahi Shimbun Globe*, September 10, 2011).

Still, the government bureaucracy was able to influence executive affairs. Ex-bureaucrats continued to rotate through the post of deputy chief cabinet secretary for administrative affairs, and the Cabinet Secretariat continued to be "largely dominated by bureaucrats" (Shinoda 2005, 821). Despite the efforts of Prime Minister Kan, the Cabinet Legislation Bureau continued to ensure that the country's time-honored "bureaucratic cabinet system" (*kanryō naikakusei*) did not devolve into a "parliamentary cabinet system" (*kokkai naikakusei*) (*Asahi Shimbun Globe*, June 14, 2010). Bureaucrats in the ministries continued to do their jobs with relatively few "political" eyes trained on them. In 2008, for example, a total of sixty-eight MPs monitored Japan's historically activist government bureaucracy, as opposed to the nearly one thousand political appointees supervising the executive branch of the U.S. government.[1] This meant that only five political appointees monitored the Ministry of Agriculture, while 184 political appointees supervised the U.S. Department of Agriculture (U.S. Government 2008). The fact that Japanese MPs were afforded few legislative staffers also meant that they had to rely on bureaucrats for policy expertise (Takenaka 2008, 51). In addition, Japan's government bureaucrats continued to wield significant regulatory and approval powers and exerted influence through the issuance of cabinet orders (which do not require Diet approval) and exercising discretion in implementing policies. As Takenaka observed, "government administration really is the accumulation of many minute legal actions. It is precisely because bureaucrats control each of those that they wield such great power" (ibid., 81).

Painfully Twisted Diets

The 2007 upper house elections produced the first truly Twisted Diet (*nejire kokkai*) in Japan's political history. In contrast to the mildly Twisted Diets that prevailed from 1989 to 1993 and 1998 to 1999, when the governing party remained the largest group in the upper house, the 2007 elections produced a state of affairs more prone to policy paralysis. In fact, for all but one year between 2007 and 2012, the governing party confronted an upper house controlled by the opposition. "In this scenario," Thies and Yanai explain, "opposition coalition building is the easier task and it is the government that would have to assemble a broad, incoherent menagerie in order to deny the opposition control over the chamber" (2012, 8). As a consequence, post-2007 governments proposed markedly fewer laws, suffered more changes to and failures of the legislative bills they did submit, and had to adapt their programs to enlist legislative coalition partners (ibid., 28). The resulting gridlock and frustration led to a succession of short-lived governments.

In Hobbesian terms, Twisted Diets dictated a "solitary, poor, nasty, brutish and short" existence for LDP- and DPJ-led governments alike. In 2007, the DPJ flexed its upper house muscles to deny passage of proposals from the Abe and Fukuda cabinets to extend a law that allowed the Maritime Self-Defense Force to refuel U.S. and allied warships in the Indian Ocean. The original law had been passed as a show of support in the aftermath of the 9/11 terrorist attacks, but the DPJ objected to renewal of the law on the grounds that the refueling mission had no United Nations mandate. Having failed to get the DPJ to back down, Abe abruptly announced his resignation on September 12.[2] Still, the DPJ refused to concede, and the anti-terrorism law was allowed to expire on November 1, forcing a cessation of MSDF refueling activities. This embarrassed the Fukuda cabinet, as it seemed to signal Japan's unwillingness to participate in the U.S.-led War on Terror. In early January, the Fukuda government employed its two-thirds majority to force through a one-year extension of the bill. The only prior instance of the use of a supermajority in this manner was in 1951, when the Diet awarded a monopoly over motorboat racing and gambling to an untried "Class A" war criminal (Samuels 2003, 244). Later on, in June 2008, the upper house approved the first-ever censure motion against a postwar prime minister for Fukuda's role in the vanishing pensions records fiasco. When Fukuda resigned three months later, the upper house nominated DPJ leader Ozawa Ichirō in a nose-thumbing gesture aimed at Asō Tarō, the lower house's nominee to be prime minister.

When the DPJ-led Hatoyama cabinet stepped down in June 2010, party strategists hoped that the July upper house elections would un-twist the Diet. But this was not to be, and the de facto minority government of Kan Naoto was forced to seek support from other parties on a policy-by-policy basis. By February of the following year, the Kan government was under siege as a result of the LDP-led upper house's approval of censure motions against two ministers for their mishandling of the fallout from the collisions between a Chinese trawler and Japan Coast Guard vessels off the disputed Senkaku/Diaoyu Islands (*Yomiuri Shimbun*, November 28, 2010). The triple disasters of March 2011 granted Kan a temporary reprieve, but he was able to cling to power only by promising the Twisted Diet that he would step down if it approved his energy reform bills (Woodall 2013, 24). Noda Yoshihiko staked the survival of his cabinet on gaining passage of a bill that aimed to curb Japan's sovereign debt crisis by doubling the national income tax. The LDP-led opposition agreed to allow the bill to pass only on Noda's assurance that the lower house would be dissolved and new elections called at an early date (Thies and Yanai 2012, 9).

Cabinet Government Postponed

Those who hoped for the emergence of cabinet government were disappointed. While ministers' gaffes and scandals had been familiar fare throughout the evolution of Japan's parliamentary cabinet system, the 2006 to 2013 period was especially rife with folly and tragedy. Health Minister Yanagisawa Hakuo unwisely referred to women as "birthing machines" in a January 2007 speech, while Defense Minister Kyūma Fumio was obliged to resign later that year for remarks that seemed to justify the U.S. atomic bombing of Hiroshima and Nagasaki. Long the subject of corruption accusations, Agriculture Minister Matsuoka Toshikatsu committed suicide in May 2007, just hours before having to explain his padded office expenses before a Diet committee (George Mulgan 2006; Kabashima and Steel 2010, 121). Less than two months later, Matsuoka's successor, Akagi Norihiko, was forced to resign on charges of expense padding; he added fuel to the fire by refusing to explain why he appeared at a cabinet meeting with two large bandages plastered to his face (*New York Times*, July 28, 2007). Yet another agriculture minister, Ōta Seiichi, resigned in September 2008 to take responsibility for his ministry's failure to prevent imported rice meant for industrial purposes from being sold for human consumption. In February 2009, Finance Minister Nakagawa Shōichi, reputed to be a heavy drinker, was forced to step down after delivering a slur-laden speech following a meeting with counterparts from the G7 countries.

Five and a half decades of LDP dominance created a vacuum that the DPJ was unequipped to fill. Because almost all ministerial portfolios allocated between 1955 and 2009 had gone to LDP MPs, the DPJ-led cabinets had relatively few ministerial veterans from whom to choose. Indeed, only five of the nineteen ministers in the Hatoyama cabinet arrived with any prior experience. Further, the DPJ's distrust of government bureaucrats created difficulties when it came to getting on the same page with the Captains of Kasumigaseki. This was plainly evident in Kan's refusal to believe what bureaucrats were telling him about the situation at the crippled Fukushima Daiichi Nuclear Power Plant (Kushida 2012, 60). This lent credence to accusations that the DPJ was "a group of 'amateurs' who were insufficiently aggressive in implementing the changes they had promised in their 2009 party manifesto and too slow to respond" to the March 2011 disasters (Samuels 2013, 33).

COPING WITH CONTROVERSY

Cabinets were forced to respond to a variety of challenges, including the disappearing pension records scandal, food safety concerns, renewal of the bill to extend the SDF's refueling mission in the Indian Ocean, the collapse of the Lehman Brothers global financial services firm, and territorial conflicts with China, South Korea, and Russia. The proposed relocation of an American military air base in Okinawa provoked a controversy that spanned the entire period and provides a lens through which to view the domestic and foreign policy challenges that cabinets confronted.

The Futenma Fiasco

Although opposition to the American military presence on Okinawa had been simmering for years, concrete steps to reduce the burden of hosting the bulk of U.S. forces in Japan did not crystallize until 1995. The pivotal event was the kidnap and rape of a twelve-year-old Japanese girl by three U.S. servicemen. The barbarity of the incident—the perpetrators duct-taped the girl's eyes and mouth shut, bound her hands, and took turns raping her on a deserted beach—shocked and disgusted Okinawans (*Time Magazine*, October 2, 1995). In preparation for the February 1996 summit meeting with President Bill Clinton, Prime Minister Hashimoto met with Okinawa governor Ōta Masahide, who explained that "the emotions of the Okinawan people would be soothed if the Futenma base is returned to Okinawans and the Marine presence reduced" (Eda 2010). When he sat down with Clinton, however, Hashimoto could not get himself to broach the matter. At the end of the meeting Clinton turned to the prime minister and said, "If there are any problems with Okinawa, please tell me." "I know this is difficult," a suddenly emboldened Hashimoto replied, "but we would be grateful if you could return Futenma" (ibid.). Three days later, Clinton instructed Secretary of Defense William Perry to explore the possibility of returning the air base. Soon thereafter, Washington secretly conveyed to Tokyo that the return of Futenma was possible as long as a suitable replacement site could be found. As an aide to Hashimoto observed, "for us Japanese, it was a success we couldn't have dreamed of hoping for" (ibid.).

On April 12, Hashimoto and U.S. ambassador Walter Mondale announced that the two sides had reached an understanding concerning relocation of the air base. Three days later, the interim report of the Special Action Committee on Okinawa (SACO) proposed to explore ways to "reduce the impact of the activities of U.S. forces on communities in Okinawa, while fully maintaining the capabilities and readiness of U.S. forces in Japan" (SACO 1996a). The two governments agreed that the United States would return a substantial portion of land from its military facilities on Okinawa and called for the "return of Futenma Air Station within the next five to seven years, after adequate replacement facilities are completed." Four days later, the Hashimoto cabinet agreed to promote solutions to problems involving U.S. military bases in Okinawa. This whirlwind of diplomatic and governmental activity was carefully timed to set the stage for Clinton's visit to Japan, which produced the Japan-U.S. Joint Declaration on Security. SACO's final report, issued on December 2, proposed that twelve thousand acres at eleven U.S. military facilities be returned and that Futenma Air Station be relocated to a sea-based facility to be constructed "off the east coast of the main island of Okinawa" (SACO 1996b).

Although Tokyo and Washington were on the same page concerning the Futenma issue, politicians and citizens' groups in Okinawa were sending mixed signals. On January 15, 1996, the Okinawa Prefectural Assembly passed a motion calling for a reduction of bases on the island (Eldridge 1997, 889). In a nonbinding plebiscite taken a year later, a majority of Nago City voters expressed their opposition to the construction of an offshore heliport for the relocated Futenma Air Station. Three days later, Higa Tetsuya, Nago's mayor, traveled to Tokyo, where he told Hashimoto that he was committing political "*seppuku*" by agreeing to accept the heliport (Eda 2010). Higa's prophecy was fulfilled on February 8, 1998, when a pro-base candidate was elected to succeed him. In early April, after the central and prefectural governments proposed a ¥100 billion economic stimulus package for Okinawa, residents of the Henoko district in Nago City sent a request to the prefectural assembly inviting the construction of an offshore heliport. Then, on November 15, Okinawan voters replaced Governor Ōta with Inamine Keiichi, who announced that the prefecture would accept the proposed heliport.

Attention now turned to deciding what type of facility to build. On November 22, 1999, Governor Inamine proposed the construction of a large-scale offshore airport in Nago City to be used for dual military-civilian purposes for fifteen years, at which time the airport would revert to civilian use. The Obuchi cabinet endorsed Inamine's plan without informing Washington, which, unsurprisingly, was not keen on the idea of restrictions on military use of the airport. In 2002, the national, prefectural, and municipal governments settled on a plan to build a dual-use airport with a two thousand-meter runway to be constructed on reclaimed land some two kilometers off Henoko's coast. This infuriated environmentalists, who, beginning in 2004, launched a prolonged sit-in campaign to obstruct efforts to conduct an environmental impact assessment. The protestors opposed relocation of the airport, which threatened to damage a coral reef and the habitat of the dugong, an endangered relative of the manatee. Tensions soared in August 2004 after the crash of a Marine helicopter on the grounds of a university campus adjacent to Futenma Air Station. Fortunately no one was killed or injured in the accident. These environmental and safety concerns prompted Tokyo and Washington to abandon the idea of an offshore dual-use airport in favor of an L-shaped runway jutting out from the Henoko Peninsula at Camp Schwab.

Finally, on May 1, 2006, the United States–Japan Roadmap for Realignment Implementation (*Saihen jisshi no tame no nichibei rōdo mappu*) was signed by the two countries' foreign and defense ministers. The Roadmap called for the construction of a V-shaped runway to be located partially on-shore and partially off-shore on reclaimed land. Assurances were made that the new facility would permit the U.S. military to maintain operational capabilities "while at the same time addressing issues of safety, noise, and environmental impact." A target date of 2014 was set for its completion. In addition, the American side agreed to relocate approximately eight thousand Marines and their nine thousand dependents from Okinawa to Guam. The Koizumi cabinet approved the plan on May 30.

The Cabinet Implodes

From the opposition pews, the DPJ demanded that the Futenma Air Station be moved out of Okinawa. In July 1999, the party released its "DPJ Okinawa Policy." DPJ MPs submitted two Okinawa-related bills to the Diet the following year. One bill called for the return of land used by the U.S. military, while the other proposed revisions to the Status of Forces Agreement. In May 2002, the party established its Okinawa Vision Council, which called for a reduced U.S. military presence in Okinawa. During the summer of 2008, the DPJ began forging a platform for lower house elections that, by law, had to be held no later than September 11, 2009. In its "Okinawa Vision 2008," the party proposed an action program to "achieve closure of the Futenma base" and other U.S. military facilities (Minshūtō 2008). In May 2010, DPJ president Hatoyama Yukio stated that he expected that "at the very least [the Futenma airstrip] would be relocated outside [Okinawa] prefecture" (*Yomiuri Shimbun*, May 28, 2010). The DPJ's 2009 election manifesto pledged to establish an "autonomous foreign policy strategy for Japan" and to "move in the direction of re-examining the realignment of the U.S. military forces in Japan and the role of U.S. military bases in Japan" (Democratic Party of Japan 2009, 28).

As a result of the August 30 general elections, the DPJ-led Hatoyama cabinet assumed the executive helm, with the Social Democratic Party and the People's New Party as coalition partners. The three parties pledged to "move in the direction of reexamining the realignment of the U.S. military forces in Japan and the role of U.S. military bases in Japan so as to reduce the burden on Okinawa residents" (Kyodo News, September 10, 2009). While the agreement echoed pledges enumerated in the DPJ election manifesto, the SDP maintained its hard-line opposition to the presence of U.S. military forces in Japan. At a September 25 press conference, Hatoyama stated that the inability to resolve the Futenma relocation issue "is a big failure on the part of previous [LDP-led] governments." He continued, "We need to address this matter within the overall review of the question [of the realignment of U.S. forces in Japan], without drawing out the matter for very long. . . . We need to draw a conclusion bearing fully in mind the feelings of the Okinawan people, not just those of the Japanese and U.S. governments" ("Hatoyama Statement" 2009).

With the arrival of fall, Hatoyama began to equivocate. At a press conference on October 7, he admitted that reevaluation of the situation concerning U.S. bases on Okinawa might necessitate changes in the government's position (*Yomiuri Shimbun*, May 28, 2010). Two weeks later, U.S. Defense Secretary Robert Gates reminded Foreign Minister Okada Katsuya that the bilateral plan for relocating the Futenma base had been reached "after consideration of various options over a long period of time" by both parties and was, therefore, "the only viable option." Okada begged Gates to understand "the difficult political situation in Japan" ("Meeting Between" 2009). On November 14, Hatoyama and President Barack Obama established a working group to consider the Futenma issue, and in early December Okada traveled to Okinawa to plead with residents to understand the "crisis of the alliance" and the "difficulty" of the negotiations (McCormack 2010). At a news conference on December 15, Hatoyama explained that he was "groping to find a site other than Henoko" for the airstrip. Ten days later he vowed to "devote his maximum effort" to resolve the controversy by a self-imposed deadline of May 31, 2010 (*Yomiuri Shimbun*, May 28, 2010). On several occasions Hatoyama reaffirmed his determination to adhere to the deadline.

With the arrival of spring, Hatoyama flipped over to Washington's point of view (*Yomiuri Shimbun,* April 30, 2010). On May 1, the cabinet decided to propose that a runway be built in almost the same location as the site agreed upon by the Japanese and U.S. governments in 2006, leading to predictions that it would "trigger a barrage of criticism of Hatoyama and his administration from the [SDP], a junior coalition partner . . . and people and local governments of Okinawa Prefecture" (*Yomiuri Shimbun,* May 1, 2010). Three days later, during his first visit to Okinawa since taking office, Hatoyama explained to Governor Nakaima Hirokazu that it would be difficult to move Futenma out of Okinawa without straining bilateral relations. In early May, the Hatoyama cabinet's public approval rating plunged to 24 percent, the "danger zone," and intracabinet schisms soon became public (*Yomiuri Shimbun,* May 11, 2010). Consumer Affairs Minister—and Social Democratic Party chairperson—Fukushima Mizuho stated that "[Hatoyama] does not have to stick to the deadline. It will be better [for Hatoyama] to seek a true solution [to the problem] rather than reach a terrible conclusion at the end of May." Meanwhile, Defense Minister Kitazawa Toshimi called on coalition partners to reach an accord as soon as possible (*Yomiuri Shimbun,* May 12, 2010).

On May 24, the Hatoyama cabinet decided to relocate the Futenma Air Station to the agreed-upon site in Nago City. Hatoyama knew that this would alienate the SDP and negatively impact the DPJ's prospects in anticipated lower house elections. Two days later, Fukushima announced her refusal to sign a cabinet order approving the cabinet's decision (*Yomiuri Shimbun,* May 27, 2010). In so doing, she violated the norm of collective solidarity, by which ministers are expected to publicly support cabinet policy—or else resign—so as to avoid the confusion that inevitably would arise "if ministers contradict each other in public and abide by some decisions and not others" (James 2002, 6; Rose 1971, 412). Hatoyama made a final effort to resolve the impasse by calling an extraordinary cabinet meeting, to be followed by talks with the coalition party leaders. He ordered Chief Cabinet Secretary Hirano Hirofumi to ensure that all concerned cabinet members, including Fukushima, would be on standby until midnight in the vicinity of the Prime Minister's Official Residence. After meeting with DPJ power broker Ozawa Ichirō, however, Hatoyama cancelled the order (*Yomiuri Shimbun,* May 28, 2010). Sometime around 8:00 the following morning, Hatoyama spoke on the telephone with Obama, who addressed the Japanese prime minister by his given name and thanked him for agreeing to the Futenma plan. Hatoyama then fired Fukushima and telephoned

Governor Nakaima to offer a "heartfelt apology" for causing confusion and for failing to keep his promise to move the Futenma base out of the prefecture (*Japan Times*, May 24, 2010).

Tokyo and Washington issued a joint statement on May 29 confirming their intention to relocate Futenma Air Station to "the Camp Schwab Henokosaki area and adjacent waters." Four days later, Hatoyama announced his resignation, saying, "I sincerely hope people will understand the agonizing choice I had to make. I knew we had to maintain a trusting relationship with the U.S. at any cost" (*Guardian*, June 2, 2010). Later that day, Ozawa resigned as DPJ secretary general, although his decision may have had less to do with the Futenma fiasco than with unrelated allegations of campaign finance irregularities (Woodall 2014). Reflecting on this, Eda Kenji, an aide to Prime Minister Hashimoto during the 1996 negotiations, observed that Hatoyama and his ministers were "too thoughtless, saying whatever popped into their heads about the country's foundation—national security—and the agreement [concerning Futenma] that is as delicate as a layered glass sculpture. They've fallen into a grave they've dug for themselves" (Eda 2010).

Unresolved Controversy

Yet the base relocation controversy continued to smolder. In September 2012, protests followed the announcement that MV-22B Osprey aircraft—with a reputation of being accident-prone—were to be deployed to Futenma (*New York Times*, September 14, 2012). The following February, a newly recrowned Abe initiated negotiations with Governor Nakaima to win approval for the base relocation plan. Shortly thereafter, Abe asked President Obama to arrange for the early return of the U.S. Marine Corps' Camp Kinser, which had been agreed to in bilateral talks, as a tangible sign that efforts were being made to ease Okinawa's burden of hosting U.S. military forces (*Yomiuri Shimbun*, March 24, 2013). Behind the scenes, negotiations continued between the Abe government and Okinawan officials. On December 25, Abe and Nakaima met for talks in Tokyo amid media speculation that a deal was imminent. The following day, Abe's unannounced visit to Yasukuni Shrine elicited outrage from the governments of China and South Korea, and disappointment from the Obama administration. On December 27, Governor Nakaima announced his decision to approve land reclamation in Henoko in exchange for large outlays of development funds from the national budget and Abe's promise to revise the Status of Forces Agreement to allow Japanese authorities to enter U.S. bases to conduct environmental surveys (*Mainichi Shimbun,* December 27, 2013). Although Abe produced a breakthrough in a controversy that spanned eighteen years, the deal he brokered did little to reduce Okinawa's burden, ensuring that the issue would remain a Damoclean sword for future prime ministers and their cabinets.

FINDINGS

The cabinets formed between 2007 and 2012 dealt with Twisted Diets that produced policy gridlock. Under constant harassment by a hostile upper house, these cabinets proposed fewer laws and endured frequent compromise and defeat of their legislative proposals (Thies and Yanai 2012, 28). As a result, the average life span of these governments was barely more than one year. While the rigors of doing battle with Twisted Diets extracted a toll, it did not help that each of the men who sat in the prime minister's chair displayed varying degrees of "KY" dyslexia when it came to "reading the air" of public opinion and political common sense. The manner in which the Futenma fiasco brought down the Hatoyama cabinet revealed the absence of a well-established norm of collective solidarity.

Despite temporarily unseating the LDP as governing party, the DPJ failed to bring forth a fully functional Westminster system. Even though the government bureaucracy was a shell of its once supposedly infallible self, the Captains of Kasumigaseki continued to shape executive affairs. It mattered not whether the DPJ or LDP controlled the upper house; the result was the same—policy gridlock. If nothing else, the era of Twisted Diets demonstrated that the upper house was hardly the innocuous "appendix" of the legislative branch that pundits portrayed it to be. As one of the LDP's first actions, Prime Minister Abe restored the party's system of preapproving policy proposals. Henceforth, before any bill could be submitted to the Diet, it would have to be precleared by the LDP's Policy Affairs Research Council, Executive Council, and Government/Ruling Party Liaison Conference, at which point the coalition partner Clean Government Party would get a chance to weigh in (*Nihon Keizai Shimbun,* December 28, 2012). In the final analysis, therefore, it is clear that cabinet government failed to take root.

Conclusion

The Cabinet is the core of the British constitutional system. It is the supreme directing authority. It integrates what would otherwise be a heterogeneous collection of authorities exercising a vast variety of functions. It provides unity to the British system of government.
—Ivor Jennings, *Cabinet Government* (1936), 1

With the Kan Cabinet running about like a chicken with its head cut off—in stark contrast to the calm, stoical demeanor that . . . earned the . . . victims [of the March 2011 disasters] worldwide admiration—the public can scarcely feel reassured about the future.
—Hiroshi Izumi, *Post-Earthquake Politics* (2011), 1

FAILURE OF THE SECOND ATTEMPT?

Why has cabinet government failed to develop in Japan? The failure is puzzling because the 1947 Constitution established Westminster-style parliamentary institutions, and more surprising given the fact that the seedlings of parliamentary democracy began to sprout under the *anti*-Westminsterian prewar order. Most would agree that postwar Japan has established a stable system of democratic governance; but it has yet to produce the effective executive leadership—in the form of cabinet government, strong prime ministerial leadership, or other structures—that is needed to respond to the panoply of challenges faced by advanced industrialized democracies. After all these years, why has Japan produced parliamentary democracy in form but failed to do so in practice? The shorthand solution to this puzzle is that cabinet government has not become institutionalized in the Japanese context. To get a sense for the degree to which institutionalization has progressed, it is useful to compare the Japanese system with an idealized Westminster model.

Focusing first on the *internal* orientation of institutionalization—in other words, the *cohesiveness* of the cabinet as an executive actor—it is clear that Japan's cabinet system has approached, but never achieved, the Westminster ideal. Since the mid-1950s, over 95 percent of ministers have

212 GROWING DEMOCRACY IN JAPAN

been recruited from the ranks of elected MPs, just as expected in a Westminster system. Moreover, on average, ministers in the post-1955 cabinets embarked on political careers before reaching their mid-forties and had spent more than eighteen years as MPs upon assuming their portfolios. Seniority violations—the awarding of portfolios to MPs who had not been elected to a minimum of five lower house (or two upper house) terms—decreased as the cabinets formed between 1946 and 1955 (in which nearly two-thirds of ministers violated the seniority norm) gave way to those formed between 1955 and 1972 (13 percent) and the cabinets of 1972 to 1993 (3 percent). The instability associated with coalition governments and Twisted Diets is reflected in the fact that 11 percent of ministers in the cabinets formed between 1993 and 2013 did not meet the seniority standard. From the early 1970s on, a majority of ministers were career politicians who had emerged from preparliamentary occupations, such as local elective politics, parliamentary staffer, law, media, and academia. Ex-bureaucrats represented a significant presence among ministers in the cabinets formed between 1946 and 1955 (37 percent) and those formed between 1955 and 1972 (46 percent), and the majority of them left senior posts in the career civil service.

Meanwhile, cabinets became increasingly complex. On the one hand, a Westminster-style ministerial hierarchy appeared in the early 1970s and remains in place. As in other advanced parliamentary democracies, the prime ministership and the portfolios of finance, foreign affairs, and economy are almost exclusively reserved for ministers with elite parliamentary and social background attributes. Yet, to the extent that cabinets formed between 1972 and 1993 performed suboptimally, the blame might lie in appointing too many ministers, resulting in "overinstitutionalization" (Klimek et al. 2008; Kesselman 1970, 26). Indeed, the expansion of portfolios, especially under the cabinets formed between 1993 and 2011 (which averaged over twenty-seven portfolios distributed among nineteen ministers) raises questions as to whether or not a minister can effectively carry out the duties of multiple portfolios.

Japanese cabinets clearly came up short in exercising *strategic choice* in executive decision-making, the *external* dimension of institutionalization. Pre-1947 cabinets were never able to exercise strategic choice, as they were, in essence, tools in the hands of the Sat-Chō oligarchs, technocrats, and unfettered generals and admirals. Although postwar prime ministers were empowered to appoint and dismiss ministers, they and their cabinets were constrained when it came to setting the policy agenda, overseeing government ministries, and authorizing policy initiatives. Until the government restructuring in 2001, no more than three transitory political appointees were responsible for monitoring the activities of each ministry's legions of immovable career civil servants. Even a doubling in the number of political "eyes" monitoring bureaucrats in streamlined ministries did not bring the bureaucrats to heel. From 1886 until 2009, the government's agenda was set at gatherings of the top career civil servants who met on the day prior to regular cabinet meetings. In addition, from the early 1960s until it was ousted from power in 2009, the LDP approved all major policy and budgetary proposals before they were decided upon in cabinet meetings. While, in theory, cabinets were collectively responsible to the Diet, in reality their collective solidarity could not be ensured. This was demonstrated by the inability of the Koizumi cabinet to obtain party discipline in the postal privatization brouhaha and in the fact that a lone dissenting minister from a small coalition partner was able to bring down the Hatoyama cabinet in the Futenma Air Station relocation fiasco.

As for their durability and adaptability, which also relate to institutionalization's external dimension, once again the performance of Japanese cabinets fell short of the Westminster ideal. On the one hand, by continuing through 141 cabinet formations from July 1871 through April 2013, the cabinet system proved to be a durable and accepted presence in the central state executive. Despite the assassination of three prewar prime ministers and the passage of non-confidence votes against four postwar cabinets, there was no lapse in prime ministerial leadership succession. However, cabinets displayed an uneven record when it came to adapting to major challenges. Although they were sometimes able to exploit GHQ's bipolar tendencies, the early postwar cabinets did nothing to prevent the pernicious growth of "structural corruption." Even as the Satō cabinet deftly reversed course to embrace environmental protection and managed to secure the return of Okinawa, it was unable to prevent a bilateral textile imbroglio. The Kishi cabinet's strong-arm tactics in pressing forward with ratification of a revised security treaty poisoned relations with the opposition and generated widespread public protest. The cabinets formed between 1972 and 1993 responded effectively to the challenge of government deregulation in a slow-growth economy, yet failed miserably in addressing demands for electoral reform. Finally, to privatize postal services, the Koizumi cabinet had to fight a civil war against a powerful subgovernment that had been numbered among the party's key support groups, while the DPJ-led Hatoyama cabinet imploded over its flip-flop on the Futenma issue. It is worth pointing out that prime ministers found it necessary to work through back-channel diplomacy or extracabinet committees to achieve favorable resolution of the Okinawa reversion, government deregulation, and postal privatization issues.

In sum, more than six decades after erecting the institutional framework for a parliamentary cabinet system—and more than twelve decades since the birth of its modern cabinet system—Japan has failed to institutionalize cabinet government. The greatest deficiency lies in factors that inhibit the cabinet's ability to exercise strategic choice. The cabinet has never become the foremost executive organ, as expected in a Westminster system, and this has contributed to its mixed record in responding to critical challenges. The autonomy of post-1947 cabinets was never ensured, as the American military dictatorship, an activist economic bureaucracy, self-governing "policy tribes," and the uncertainties of coalition governments and Twisted Diets kept the cabinet from assuming its prescribed role. Although on the surface Japan's cabinet system resembles the Westminster model, in practice it does not. While Japan deserves praise for establishing a stable and broadly accepted democratic order, thus far efforts to establish cabinet government have not succeeded. At least in a limited sense, the postwar experience can be viewed as a failed second attempt at parliamentary democracy, the prewar flirtation with democratic governance that came to a bloody end on May 15, 1932, being the first.[1]

INSTITUTIONALIZATION AND INSTITUTIONS

To understand why Japan has established a parliamentary system in form but not in practice, one must appreciate the role of institutions and institutional change. This prompts a second puzzle. Since institutionalization is a ubiquitous process, why has Japan's cabinet system assumed its characteristic form and function? This draws attention to the shaping influence of institutions, which requires that we account for the significant roles played by context and history in determining institutional change. It also highlights the distributional consequences of institutions and the role of critical junctures and tipping points as strategic openings for institutional change.

By viewing institutions as humanly devised constraints that structure behavior and carry power-distributional consequences, we can perceive their shaping effect and the role they play in bringing forth bold as well as incremental change. Seen in this light, it is evident that the distinctive organizational structures, roles, and relationships that give form to Japan's cabinet system were forged in a matrix composed of laws, ordinances, political structures, norms, and unwritten codes of conduct.

The pre-1947 cabinet system was forged in a matrix cobbled together out of an assortment of institutions. When it came to designing the institutions of a central state executive, the Sat-Chō oligarchs went to great lengths to create an *anti*-Westminsterian system. Shortly after the cabinet system was created in 1885, the top career civil servants in the various ministries began holding weekly meetings to set the agenda for cabinet sessions; those bureaucratic meetings would continue for the next 123 years. Measures were taken to prevent partisan meddling in bureaucratic personnel matters, although the people's parties would challenge this. The purpose of cabinet meetings, whose decisions were based on the principle of unanimity, was to adopt state policies and engage in discussion "to ensure that such policies were consistent with those of the state" ("Naikaku seido to rekidai naikaku," accessed May 23, 2013). The Meiji Constitution of 1890 made "ministers of state" individually responsible for advising a divine-right emperor, but it did not make cabinets collectively responsible to the Imperial Diet. The prime minister was not empowered to appoint and dismiss ministers, as this was the prerogative of the divine-right emperor. Naturally, there was no expectation that the prime minister would be the leader of the largest party in the lower house or that ministers would be recruited from the ranks of elected MPs. In addition, the Meiji Constitution established a Privy Council with veto power over all policy and budgetary proposals, and created a dual system of government by allowing the military branches to select their own ministers (thus empowering them to topple cabinets with whose policies they disagreed) and authorizing them to bypass the cabinet in reporting directly to the emperor. Like a "fatal thread" running through the history of the late 1920s and early 1930s, maintaining the prerogatives and prestige of the armed forces became "the standard by which decisions affecting the whole course of the nation's policy were taken" (Maxon 1957, 29).

The post-1947 cabinet system was shaped in a matrix fashioned out of imposed and indigenous institutions. When the first two postwar Japanese cabinets proved unwilling to democratize the Meiji Constitution, American officials produced a document that became the basis for the Constitution of

Japan. The 1947 Constitution made the cabinet collectively responsible to the House of Representatives, whose continuing confidence was required to remain in office. It mandated that the prime minister and the majority of ministers be elected MPs and that all must be civilians. The prime minister was empowered to appoint and dismiss ministers, whose maximum number was specified in the Cabinet Law. That law dictated that the cabinet "shall perform its functions through cabinet meetings," which was, in keeping with long-standing tradition, informally interpreted to mean that collective decisions must be unanimous. The decision of occupation planners to occupy a defeated Japan indirectly enhanced the influence of an already powerful government bureaucracy, and for a quarter-century Japanese governments embraced the balanced budget principle proposed in the Dodge Line.

Other institutions shaped the development of the cabinet system. Institutions such as the deputy chief cabinet secretary for administration and the Cabinet Legislation Bureau ensured that bureaucratic interests were reflected in executive actions. Referred to as the "bureaucrat of the bureaucrats" (kanryō naka no kanryō), the deputy chief cabinet secretary presided over the biweekly meetings of administrative vice ministers that set the agenda for cabinet meetings, while the CLB proved to be an especially significant source of institutional inertia. Between May 1946 and December 2012, for example, a total of seventeen men held the powerful post of CLB director general—dubbed the country's foremost "policy technician" (hōritsu gijutsuya) and the prime minister's "in-house lawyer"—while thirty-two governments and ninety-three cabinets came and went (Naikaku Hōsei Kyoku 1985, 141; Samuels 2004, 2). This meant that the average length of tenure for a CLB director general was double that of the average prime minister.[2] In addition, under the LDP's protracted dominance the system for electing lower house MPs through a single nontransferable vote (SNTV) in multimember constituencies produced intraparty factionalism, which led to frequent cabinet reshufflings and the appointment of ministers with sometimes dubious qualifications (Grofman et al. 1999, 14–15). The fact that voters favored candidates who could bring home the bacon in the form of delivered policy benefits reduced the significance of policy-based issues and provided fertile ground for money politics.

Thus, while the post-1947 cabinet system was similar to the Westminster model in form, the institutional matrix in which it was forged ensured that in practice it bore little resemblance. The perpetuation of an activ-

ist government bureaucracy that operated under minimal political supervision meant that the relative autonomy of cabinets in carrying out their
executive responsibilities could not be ensured and that ministers would
struggle to be more than mere figureheads. The byproducts of a lower
house election system founded upon SNTV in multimember districts dictated that the central leaders of the perpetually ruling LDP (whose presidents doubled as prime ministers and whose MPs virtually monopolized
ministerial portfolios) could not effectively discipline the intraparty factions, veteran MPs (especially members of the policy tribes), or even the
party's backbenchers. In addition, the perpetuation of certain informal
institutions, such as the twice-weekly meetings of top bureaucrats and the
unanimity principle, worked at cross-purposes with the strong executive
role and collective solidarity required for effective cabinet government.

CRITICAL JUNCTURES AND INSTITUTIONAL CHANGE

But where do institutions come from and when do they change? The answer
is found in the spurts of institutional innovation that cluster around critical junctures in history, when "institutional configurations are upended
and replaced by fundamentally new ones," as well as in the gradual evolution of established institutions (Mahoney and Thelen 2010, 2). The Kan
cabinet and its support staff, whose responsibility it was to provide executive leadership in the wake of the triple disasters of March 2011, was itself
the product of evolutionary institutional change. While the foundations of
Japan's parliamentary cabinet system were set in place under an American-
led occupation, that system inherited genetic material from a central state
executive that took shape in the latter half of the nineteenth century. In
other words, the parliamentary democratic system established under the
1947 Constitution inherited institutions, structures, personnel, and norms
from an authoritarian prewar order. Viewed in this light, Japan's present
parliamentary cabinet system evolved through eight distinct stages.

The pre-1947 cabinet system was forged in three historical stages. An
exogenous shock in the form of an uninvited port call by a small squadron
of American warships in 1853 led to the collapse of the Tokugawa shōgunate
and the putative restoration of power to the Emperor Meiji. In 1868, an
alliance of feudal lords and lower-ranking samurai toppled a shōgunate
whose once mighty control structures had atrophied to the point that it
could not fend off the insurgency. As a result of the Meiji Restoration, a

cabal of leaders from Satsuma and Chōshū—the feudal domains that led the charge against the shōgunate—came to dominate the organs of the central state executive. The "cabal cabinets" that congealed under a central state executive inspired by an eighth-century Chinese model dominated the scene for three decades. In response to demands for a representative assembly and expanded popular rights, the Sat-Chō oligarchs established a modern cabinet system and granted a constitution designed to prevent the emergence of parliamentary democracy. Nevertheless, beginning in 1898, an era of "quasi-party cabinets" was born as a result of endogenous pressure exerted by renegade former government insiders. On three occasions, the leader of the largest party in the lower house sat in the prime minister's chair, and by the late 1920s elected MPs routinely held half of all portfolios. This brief flirtation with democracy abruptly ended on May 15, 1932, with the assassination of Prime Minister Inukai. The young naval officers who fired the fatal shots simultaneously killed Inukai and the era of party cabinets and opened the door to a decade and a half of rule under a union of "reform bureaucrats," "control officers," and the leaders of fascist-inspired groups. Under the techno-fascist cabinets, anti-government voices were suppressed and priority was given to rational planning that employed all of the economic, political, and spiritual resources of the Empire of Japan.

While the 1947 Constitution established a Westminster-style cabinet system, much of the material used in its construction was left over from the prewar system. Even after the new Constitution went into effect and the Home Ministry and military ministries had been dissolved, much of the government structure remained intact; in fact, twelve ministerial portfolios traced their roots to the prewar order. Moreover, twenty-six individuals who held portfolios in postwar cabinets—including five prime ministers—brought with them skills acquired as prewar cabinet ministers. Many of these carry-overs and other postwar ministers had been deemed unfit to hold public office under the occupation-inspired purge of militarists and rightists. Meanwhile, the Cabinet Secretariat, Cabinet Legislation Bureau, and other support organs for the cabinet system continued to perform their functions. In addition, the unanimity principle in cabinet decision-making lived on, enabling lone-wolf dissenters to continue to undermine the prime minister's leadership role. The resurrection of the SNTV system, under which an average of four MPs were elected in each lower house district, created conditions for intraparty factionalism and "money power politics" (*kinken seiji*) that would shape the evolution of the cabinet system. Finally, the tradition of cabinet subordination lived on, especially when it came to the career civil servants who continued to initiate and draft the vast majority of government proposals. These elite bureaucrats—many of whom would choose to descend into second careers in elective politics—continued to be monitored by no more than three sets of political eyes per ministry.

The evolution of the post-1947 parliamentary cabinet system can be subdivided into five stages. In the initial postwar stage, the blunt trauma of total defeat and unconditional surrender paved the way for sweeping reforms under General MacArthur and the American military dictator-ship. Yet continuities from the prewar order shaped the evolution of Japan's parliamentary cabinet system. The leadership vacuum created by the purge of militarists and right-wingers enhanced the relative influence of the civil bureaucrats, who represented the best pool of experienced administrative talent. Prime Minister Yoshida actively recruited elite ex-bureaucrats and fast-tracked them into ministerial posts. Meanwhile, as MacArthur ruled from his headquarters in the Dai-Ichi Mutual Life Insurance Building, a succession of figurehead cabinets under leaders who functioned as go-betweens with the American occupiers reigned. Although these compra-dor cabinets were sometimes able to get their way by playing factions at GHQ against one another, at the end of the day they danced to an Ameri-can tune. This was displayed in the "essentially American" origins of the 1947 Constitution, for which the Japanese side dutifully claimed author-ship. It was also seen in the government's willingness to adhere to the balanced budget policy dictated by the Dodge Line and the tax reforms pressed by the Shoup mission.

In November of 1955, the leaders of the major conservative parties put aside their differences to establish the Liberal Democratic Party. These lead-ers found common cause in the specter of a unified Socialist Party and in the perception that many occupation-inspired reforms had gone too far and needed to be rolled back. Many key leaders in the corporatist cabinets that emerged under the "1955 system," including three of the five prime minis-ters, were ex-government officials who took politics as a second career and who approached their ministerial responsibilities with a bureaucratic men-tality and style. Yet, thanks to a national consensus supporting the high-speed growth policies they sponsored (which were, incidentally, initiated by bureaucrats), the corporatist cabinets were able to play a symbolic role in imparting strategic direction to government policy. This enabled them to claim credit for a constantly expanding economic pie while for the most part maintaining balanced budgets. Nevertheless, because of its ongoing mastery of the parliamentary realm, the LDP was in a position to demand that it be allowed to preapprove all policy and budgetary proposals before they were taken up by the cabinet or Diet.

The exogenous "shocks" of the early 1970s were a tipping point in the cabinet system's evolution. In particular, OPEC's threatened embargo of petroleum exports in October 1973 brought dramatically higher energy costs that dictated an end to the high-speed growth era. But modest economic growth was not accompanied by reduced demand for government spending. On the contrary, the "policy specialists" who now played a protagonist's role in policy-making subverted the balanced budget policy through increased spending on pork barrel projects and social welfare programs. These veteran MPs vigorously defended the interests of their subgovernments in what devolved into a fragmented policy-making environment. Consequently, the confederate cabinets at the executive helm were challenged to provide tactical direction to government policy, even though the career politicians who dominated their ministerial rosters exuded a more "Westminsterian" persona than their ex-bureaucrat predecessors. In its role as permanent ruling party, the LDP was able to ensure that its lawmakers virtually monopolized appointments to cabinet posts; as a consequence, the background characteristics of cabinet ministers became identical to those of senior LDP MPs.

Finally, the LDP's fall from grace in August 1993 raised the curtain on an era of coalition governments and Twisted Diets. The principal agents of change in the ensuing drama were renegade former LDP lawmakers who now led new political parties and a self-proclaimed "maverick" who managed to become LDP president and prime minister during the party's temporary resurgence. They succeeded in reforming the lower house electoral system, restructuring government administrative organs, creating a Cabinet Office, and privatizing postal services. In August 2009, the Democratic Party of Japan came to power promising to bolster the powers of the cabinet and to bring bureaucrats under the control of politicians. As one of its first acts, the DPJ abolished the twice-weekly gatherings of the top career bureaucrats from each ministry on the day before regular cabinet meetings. On the surface, Japan's parliamentary cabinet system was now more Westminsterian than ever; in reality, cabinet government still failed to materialize. In fact, a combination of factors—among them coalition governments, Twisted Diets, inexperienced ministerial leadership, and an enervated government bureaucracy—produced disjoined cabinets. These cabinets occupied the executive helm as the nation drifted aimlessly through two decades of economic malaise and failed to provide effective leadership in response to the cascading disasters of March 2011.

IMPLICATIONS

Important theoretical and policy implications emerge from the analysis presented in the pages of this book. As Marx observed in *The Eighteenth Brumaire of Louis Bonaparte*, "Men make their own history, but they do not make it as they please; they do not make it under self-selected circumstances, but under circumstances existing already, given and transmitted from the past. The tradition of all dead generations weighs like a nightmare on the brains of the living." Indeed, the tradition of earlier Japanese cabinets and the institutional changes that shaped them weigh down on today's prime ministers and their cabinets. Although institutionalization is a universal process, the manner in which a particular organization institutionalizes—or *fails* to do so—is shaped by the institutional matrix in which it operates. The specific institutions from which that matrix is fabricated are given under "circumstances already existing." This draws attention to the role of path dependency, the determination of solutions as a consequence of small events that, once those solutions prevail, lead down a particular path from whence it is difficult to exit (North 1990, 94). Thus, to understand the capabilities and limitations of today's Japanese parliamentary cabinet system, it is essential to trace the long-lasting process through which it evolved, which leads back to institutional solutions rendered by renegade reformers in the 1990s, American occupation planners, technocrats in the superagencies of the late 1930s, and, ultimately, the cabal that ruled in the aftermath of the Meiji Restoration. In other words, it is essential "to distinguish between long-lasting movements and short bursts, the latter detected from the moment they originate, the former over the course of a distant time" (Braudel 1982, 34).

The domestic implications are plain to see. Indeed, six and a half decades after establishing a parliamentary system *in form*, Japan has yet to establish parliamentary government *in practice*. At the very least, it is clear that the system of cabinet government associated with the Westminster model has not been firmly planted. While cabinet government is an elusive ideal and not necessarily the only possible solution to Japan's problems, the perpetual lack of direction from the country's political executive is taking a toll on the citizenry's confidence. In fact, the ineffective executive leadership displayed throughout the "lost decades" and the policy gridlock produced by Twisted Diets led to increased popular disillusionment and cynicism. Prime Minister Kan's much-criticized performance in responding to the disasters of March 2011 deepened these doubts, although blame should have been ascribed to a malfunctioning cabinet system. In fact, the cabinet system did not provide the essential infrastructural support and corporate solidarity required to impart coherent direction to government policy. The Japanese people deserve better than this, and if the country is going to prosper and avoid the possibility of constitutional crisis they must demand and expect systemic reform of the executive branch.

The most meaningful lesson taught by the evolution of Japan's parliamentary system is that growing democracy is not easy. Establishing the requisite institutional framework is difficult enough, but it is orders of magnitude more difficult to create a system of democracy that functions properly in practice. Would-be reformers must consider the broader institutional and historical context in which they seek to implant democratic institutions. For example, American planners never understood the power of Japan's career civil service; consequently, the bureaucracy emerged from the occupation stronger than ever. For this reason, the first cohort of postwar prime ministers and their cabinets not only labored under the institutional inertia built up as a result of decades of authoritarian rule, they had to learn how to perform their expected role in the shadow of not one, but two, mandarinates: the domestic government bureaucracy and the American military dictatorship. As the DPJ-led cabinets learned the hard way, it is exceedingly difficult to break bonds that congealed over the course of nearly fifty-five years of single-party rule. Indeed, set patterns do not break down easily and, however illogical, are a "long time in dying" (Braudel 1982, 32).

By tracing the evolution of Japan's parliamentary cabinet system, it is clear that a properly functioning system of democratic governance is not likely to appear swiftly or spontaneously, nor can it be imposed by the sword or simply snapped together on the ground using parts from an imported model.[3] If democracy is to take root in a political setting—be it in Japan or elsewhere—it has to grow from within, shaped by carefully crafted institutions and institutionalizing by degrees until the essential processes and values become well established and broadly embraced by an empowered citizenry.

Acknowledgments

Epiphanies can strike in the unlikeliest of places. The epiphany that led to this book occurred on a Scandinavian cruise ship flying the Bahamian flag as it sailed the inside passage en route to Alaska. It occurred during a casual chat with a Japanese friend about the effects of the 2001 government reorganization that established Japan's Cabinet Office. When I asked my friend—a savvy guy who happens to be the retired president of a major Japanese corporation—what he thought about the prospects for "cabinet government," he said that Japan's cabinet would never amount to anything more than a political sideshow performed by anemic premiers and parvenu ministers. And yet, I asserted, Japan's Constitution vests executive power in the cabinet, which means that it is *supposed* to be the country's supreme executive organ. This flipped a cerebral switch. Why is it that Japan has developed parliamentary democracy *in form* but not *in practice*? It struck me that the development of the cabinet system can be seen as a proxy for Japan's experiment with democratic governance in the protracted, mostly gradual unfolding of change that the French *Annalistes* refer to as the "*longue durée.*" So it is fitting that an epiphany that took place aboard a cruise ship would lead to a voyage of discovery that traces the evolution of Japan's parliamentary cabinet system.

Many people and institutions helped make this book happen. Among those who read and commented on the entire manuscript or draft chapters are J.A.A. Stockwin, John Creighton Campbell, Aurelia George Mulgan, Steven K. Vogel, John Duffield, John Garver, Kirk Bowman, William J. Long, Jarrod Hayes, Lawrence Rubin, Liz Dallas, Jason Landrum, and Vince Pedicino. Their suggestions contributed to the refinement of the argument and the avoidance of many factual errors. And yet the finished product would be better had I not stubbornly refused to heed all of the excellent advice proffered. The capable and good-natured research assistance provided by Tomoko Ohta, Yukihiko Osaka, Mieko Matsui, and Adrienne Smith eased my burden. I am especially grateful to Shūji and Yukie Hashimoto for many kindnesses showered upon my family and me, which included keeping my bookshelf stocked with the latest edition of

Seikan yōran. And I am thankful to Kristina Troost of Duke University's Perkins Library for generously providing access to key research materials, and to the Georgia Tech Library for tracking down many of the works that populate this book's bibliography. Richard Matthews lent the skilled eye of a former newspaper editorial writer to improving my prose and presentation, and Leslie Woodall helped prepare the figures and tables. It was a pleasure working with the good people at the University Press of Kentucky, especially Stephen M. Wrinn, Shiping Hua, and Allison B. Webster. Derik Shelor did a superb job of copyediting. Finally, I am much obliged to Georgia Tech's Sam Nunn School of International Affairs and Ivan Allen College for sundry forms of support.

As with many of life's endeavors, particularly those that require prolonged gestation, this book was forged within a family. The women in my life—Joyce, Leslie, and Melissa—provided warmth, tenderness, and innumerable smiles. They are my bedrock. I am honored to dedicate this book to my mother and the memory of my father, who, together, provided a joyful childhood and instilled the basic values that, like a trusty sextant, guide my daily navigation through life's unmapped seas.

Appendix A

Japanese Cabinets and Cabinet Ministers Database

The Japanese Cabinets and Cabinet Ministers (JCCM) Database contains a wide range of data pertaining to the 141 cabinets formations, 1,350 individuals appointed to ministerial posts, and 3,612 portfolios allocated between July 1871 and May 2013. In delineating cabinet formations and dissolutions, I followed the system employed by the Government of Japan, which provides a complete listing of cabinets, portfolios allocated, and the names and the dates of appointment and dismissal of all ministers from December 22, 1885, to the present (http://www.kantei.go.jp/jp/rekidai/index .html). My JCCM Database deviates from that system in that it begins with the *de facto* cabinets that emerged within the Grand Council (*Dajōkan*) beginning in July 1871.

By tracing ministers' changing parliamentary and social frame attributes, the JCCM Database illuminates the "cohesiveness" aspect of cabinet institutionalization (explained in chapter 1). The "parliamentary" data distinguish MPs from non-MPs, and in the case of the former specify the Diet chamber in which the minister held a seat, number of elective terms, length of parliamentary service (since first election to the Diet), age (at time of appointment, first election to the Diet, and initial ministerial posting), partisan and factional affiliation, factors related to the electoral district (for example, urban or rural character, etc.), and prior ministerial service. The "social frame" attributes include ministers' gender, family background (in other words, whether or not she or he is a "hereditary politician"), geographic origin (by region and prefecture), educational attainment (for example, university attended, type of university, whether or not it was among the eight elite institutions, etc.), and occupational background (subdivided into upper-level or junior grade ex-government bureaucrat, local politician, legislative staffer, attorney, journalist, labor union leader, local government official, and entertainer/celebrity).

The JCCM Database was forged of data mined from various sources. I dug especially deeply into *Seikan yōran* (various years), Miyagawa, ed. (1990), Shiratori (1979), and "Naikaku seido to rekidai naikaku" (http://www.kantei.go.jp/jp/rekidai/index.html; last accessed May 26, 2013). In addition, I found valuable data in Kensei shiryō hensankai (1978), Naikaku seido hyakunenshi henshū iinkai (1980), *Jinjikōshinroku* (various years), Kodama et al. (1983), Satō and Matsuzaki (1986), Naka (1980), Nihonkoku kokkai zengiin meikan hensan iinkai (1986), Naikaku seido hyakujūchōnen kinenshi henshū iinkai (1995), Naikaku seido hyakunenshi henshū iinkai (1980), Naikaku shisei chōsakai (1980), and the National Diet Library's "Portraits of Modern Japanese Historical Figures" website (http://www.ndl.go.jp/portrait/e/contents/#nameNavi; last accessed May 26, 2013). In addition, Steven R. Reed's "Japan MMD Data Set" (http://www.fps.chuo-u.ac.jp/~sreed/DataPage.html; last accessed May 26, 2013) provides data for candidates in every Diet election held from 1947 to 1993. Constructing the JCCM Database was made immeasurably easier thanks to the efforts of these researchers, who sifted through mountains of raw data to extract valuable ore.

Appendix B

Ministers' Parliamentary and Social Attributes

Table A.1. Ministers' Parliamentary Traits by Cabinet Era

Parliamentary Trait	1871-1898	1898-1932	1932-1946	1946-1955	1955-1972	1972-1993	1993-2006	2006-2013
Member of Parliament (%)	1.5	25.3	15.9	89.3	99.8	98.9	94.9	97.0
• Lower House MP (%)	1.5	25.3	15.9	75.7	85.0	85.6	78.5	74.77
• Upper House MP (%)	–	–	–	13.6	14.7	13.3	18.6	25.1
Parliamentary Terms								
• # Lower House Terms	0.6	4.897	6.574	3.645	5.352	6.702	5.653	5.34
• # Upper House Terms	–	–	–	0.915	2.799	3.493	3.332	2.197
• < 5 Lower House Terms (%)	100	39.8	13.8	64.6	21.0	5.2	13.7	15.7
Parliamentary Service								
• MP Service (# years)	3.026	16.708	19.21	10.639	15.87	20.331	19.318	18.75
• < 15 Years of MP Service (%)	100	47.4	25.1	69.1	48.7	27.2	29.6	26.7
Age								
• Age at Cabinet Appt.	46.831	55.641	58.294	58.674	60.146	62.988	61.922	60.149
• Age at 1st Diet Election	40.872	41.449	40.422	47.965	44.272	42.674	42.63	41.47
• Age < 40 at 1st Diet Election (%)	10.0	31.4	44.6	25.1	28.7	38.5	43.0	51.1
• Age 1st Cabinet Appt.	41.076	51.052	55.238	56.551	54.716	57.551	57.7	56.907
"Urban" District[a] (%)	13.2	21.5	32.5	32.2	21.6	21.2	32.7	37.9
Prior Ministerial Appt. (%)	65.4	57.5	50.6	51.9	67.2	53.3	65.0	67.1
Member of PM's Party (%)	0	50.5	56.0	76.9	100	99.6	78.1	81.6

[a] Minister hails from relatively "urbanized" prefecture (Tokyo, Saitama, Chiba, Kanagawa, Aichi, Osaka, Kyoto, or Hyōgō).
Source: JCCM Database.

Table A.2. Ministers' Social Frame Attributes by Cabinet Era (%)

Social Frame Attribute	1871-1898	1898-1932	1932-1946	1946-1955	1955-1972	1972-1993	1993-2006	2006-2013
Male	100	100	100	100	99.5	99.1	90.3	91.4
"Hereditary Politician"	0	0	1.5	6.5	1.9	35.0	42.3	30.2
Attended University	3.0	60.6	95.2	91.0	91.6	85.6	91.9	98.9
• Military Academy	0	10.2	22.9	0	0	0	0	0.8
• Tokyo University	0.5	38.1	52.1	41.7	46.4	32.9	33.8	29.7
• Waseda University	0	1.4	4.2	10.5	12.3	13.0	13.7	14.9
• Keiō University	0.7	3.8	1.8	0.8	4.5	7.6	17.1	7.7
• Kyoto University	0	0	5.3	14.2	4.0	4.0	2.1	7.7
• Chūō University	0	1.7	1.8	3.2	9.3	3.7	7.7	5.3
• Nihon University	0	0	0.7	4.1	2.1	3.8	0.9	1.8
• Hitotsubashi University	0	0	2.6	4.1	3.0	4.0	2.5	1.5
• Meiji University	0	0	0.3	3.88	0.9	3.5	1.1	1.1
Previous Occupation								
• Military	30.4	21.2	24.6	0	0	0	0	1.9
• Government Official	70.2	51.6	50.3	37.4	11.4	29.5	25.3	19.8
• (% high-level official)	(88.7)	(80.8)	(86.0)	(55.5)	(45.6)	(55.5)	(21.8)	(9.8)
• MP's Staffer	1.8	3.8	3.4	7.1	7.3	26.7	35.9	28.7
• Local Politician	0	6.0	1.1	15.1	14.5	27.3	17.7	22.4
• Attorney	0	3.7	5.3	10.4	3.8	2.2	7.2	13.2
• Journalist	1.7	8.8	7.0	13.4	11.2	8.7	9.7	8.0
• Union Leader	0	0	0.4	3.0	0	1.8	3.0	3.1
• Local Government	0.5	0.8	2.1	0	2.6	1.6	1.7	1.5
• Celebrity	0	0	0	0	0	0.5	1.8	1.5

Source: JCCM Database.

Appendix C

Ministerial Hierarchy

Table A.3. Ministerial Hierarchy

Ministerial Portfolio	Ministers' Parliamentary and Social Frame Attributes Score[a]				
	1955-1972	1972-1993	1993-2001	2001-2006	2006-2013
Finance	5.4545	7.6552	8.3542	8.75	10
Prime Minister	5.4091	8.0150	8.4176	9.8571	7.7857
Foreign Affairs	6.0823	7.7368	7.8462	6.8	7.2667
Justice	5.3465	6.0552	5.2923	4.5	6.7692
Agriculture, Forestry, & Fisheries	5.7950	6.4214	5.9026	7.0571	6.5625
Economy, Trade, & Industry	5.8182	7.5385	7.3923	7.0536	6.5310
Chief Cabinet Secretary	5.6491	6.9872	5.9881	6.5556	6.1099
Internal Affairs & Communications	–	–	–	6.125	6.0643
Environment	–	4.9286	3.5513	5.1270	6.0615
Land, Infrastructure, & Transport	–	–	–	6.125	5.9810
National Public Safety	5.5833	5.9933	5.7568	5.2381	5.9018
Defense	5.7308	6.3036	6.4359	6.1429	5.7884
Education	5.5505	6.0038	4.8951	4.6310	5.1758
Health, Welfare, & Labor	–	–	–	7.25	4.7857
Administrative Management	6.1255	6.4615	–	–	–
Regional Development	5.9091	5.6667	–	–	–
Prime Minister's Office	5.6316	5.0000	–	–	–
Special Missions	–	–	–	–	–
Construction	5.8217	6.0292	6.7778	–	–
Management & Coordination	–	5.9679	6.4256	–	–
Health & Welfare	4.9583	5.8796	6.2867	–	–
Financial Revitalization	–	–	6.1250	–	–
Science & Technology	4.7554	5.2475	5.9077	–	–
Transport	5.3460	6.2600	5.8042	–	–
Labor	6.1739	5.2873	5.6667	–	–
Home Affairs	5.2092	5.9548	5.6224	–	–

Table A.3. Ministerial Hierarchy *(continued)*

Ministerial Portfolio	Ministers' Parliamentary and Social Frame Attributes Score[a]				
	1955-1972	1972-1993	1993-2001	2001-2006	2006-2013
Posts & Telecommunications	4.3750	5.6806	5.5192	–	–
Okinawa Development	–	5.4056	5.5167	–	–
Hokkaidō Development	5.1667	5.7436	5.1571	–	–
Economic Planning	5.9249	6.4087	4.3965	–	–

[a] The Parliamentary and Social Frame Attributes (PSFA) Score is the sum of ten dummy variables (1 or 0) for ministers who held each respective portfolio: (1) MP; (2) <40 years old at first election; (3) ≥5 terms; (4) >7 terms; (5) >20 years of MP service; (6) prior ministerial service; (7) male (alas, few women become ministers); (8) attended university; (9) pursued pre-MP "preparatory" occupation (attorney, journalist, local government official, union leader, MP's staffer, or local politician); and (10) close relative of an elected MP. In this table, the PSFA scores for ministers were summed and averaged for the time periods indicated. The assumption here is that the most prestigious portfolios will go to high-status MPs.
Source: JCCM Database.

Notes

INTRODUCTION

1. As a result of the 1995 Kōbe earthquake, the posts of Minister of State for Disaster Management and Deputy Chief Cabinet Secretary for Crisis Management were created to coordinate disaster response policies.

2. The "lost decades" refers to the prolonged economic stagnation and absence of effective political leadership that followed the bursting of the "bubble economy" in the early 1990s. It left Japanese financial institutions buried under a mountain of nonperforming loans and produced a succession of governments that proved unable to enact fruitful policy solutions.

3. The symbolic powers of Japan's head of state are constitutionally defined, while in Britain those powers developed through historical convention. Australia's constitution grants extensive powers to its head of state, although those powers are not actually used. Aurelia George Mulgan kindly pointed this out to me.

4. Members of the press corps were allowed to observe cabinet meetings in December 1985, September 1993, and April 2002 (Naikaku seido hyakunen shi henshū iinkai 1980, 22 and 24).

5. Tent villages became a fixture on the scene around the time of the formation of the Okada cabinet in July 1934 (Naikaku seido hyakujūchōnen 1995, 130).

6. For purposes of this study, the Imperial Household Office, Fair Trade Commission, Financial Services Agency, and the National Personnel Authority are not considered part of the cabinet system.

7. Of the forty-nine non-confidence motions submitted between May 1947 and May 2013, only four were approved—December 23, 1948 (second Yoshida cabinet), March 14, 1953 (fourth Yoshida cabinet), May 16, 1980 (second Ōhira cabinet), and June 18, 1993 (Miyazawa cabinet).

8. Australia, Austria, Canada, the Czech Republic, Denmark, Finland, Germany, Greece, Hungary, Iceland, Ireland, Italy, Korea, New Zealand, Poland, Spain, Turkey, and the United Kingdom also permit ministers to retain their parliamentary seats.

9. By traditional convention, British ministers are expected to be MPs (Rose 1971, 401, 411). Many of the isolated instances in which non-MPs have been awarded portfolios occurred during wartime, and came with the expectation that these individuals would win a seat in the House of Commons in a subsequent by-election. Peacetime examples are rare. In October 1964, Prime Minister Har-

235

old Wilson gave the foreign secretary portfolio to Patrick Gordon Walker and the technology portfolio to Frank Cousins even though neither held seats in the Commons. Walker and Cousins agreed to accept peerages, and were expected to win seats as "carpetbaggers" in by-elections held several months later. Cousins emerged victorious, but Walker was defeated and had to surrender his portfolio (Brazier 1997, 64–65). More recently, in October 2008, Prime Minister Gordon Brown gave the business secretary portfolio to Peter Mandelson, a veteran of Tony Blair's cabinet who did not currently hold a seat in Commons, but Mandelson was immediately elevated to the House of Lords (*Telegraph,* October 3, 2008). I am grateful to Arthur Stockwin for pressing me to clarify this point.

10. Britain's "government" consists of about one hundred members who are nominated by the prime minister and appointed by the monarch; the "cabinet" itself consists of only about fourteen of these individuals (Curtis 1997a, 68). In contrast, Japan's government in late December 2012 consisted of seventy-four individuals—nineteen cabinet ministers, three deputy chief cabinet secretaries, twenty-five state secretaries, and twenty-seven parliamentary secretaries.

11. A study of Canadian provincial governments found that larger cabinets complicate decision-making and erode teamwork (White 1994, 262).

12. The types of cabinet decisions are explained at "Naikaku seido to rekidai naikaku," www.kantei.go.jp/jp/rekidai/1-2-5.html; accessed May 23, 2013.

13. Since May 7, 2002, cabinet meetings have been held in a room on the fourth floor of the Prime Minister's Official Residence (*Kantei*), except during parliamentary sessions, when they are held in a special chamber in the National Diet Building. Prior to this, the cabinet met in a room on the second floor of the old *Kantei,* a Frank Lloyd Wright-inspired structure that opened in March 1929. In the closing days of the Pacific War, cabinet meetings were held behind two-meter-thick reinforced walls in the National Defense Telephone Bureau (Naikaku seido hyakujūchōnen 1995, 99).

14. The term "government" denotes the continuous period from the appointment of a prime minister until his or her dismissal.

15. As Heasman observed, "the relative importance of any office . . . [depends] in large measure on the influence and character of the incumbent as well as on conditions of the time" (1962a, 309).

16. Mahoney and Thelen (2010) associate *symbionts* with institutional drift.

1. The Anti-Westminsterian Roots of Japan's Parliamentary Cabinet System, 1868–1946

1. Ming Dynasty (1368–1644) emperor Hongwu initially modeled his government on the centralized T'ang model, but by 1380 he was relying on a small group of loyal mid-level officials for advice and assistance. Eventually this inner court came to be known as the "Nèigé," or cabinet.

2. Shidehara Kijūrō, Yoshida Shigeru (the former diplomat, *not* the prewar

"reform" bureaucrat of the same name), Ashida Hitoshi, Hatoyama Ichirō, and Kishi Nobusuke were prewar ministers who went on to become postwar prime ministers. The other members of this human bridge are Saitō Takao, Kanamori Tokujirō, Obara Naoshi, Uchida Nobuya, Funada Naka, Kaya Okinori, Yoshino Shinji, Karasawa Toshiki, Ino Hiroya, Ōasa Tadao, Shigemitsu Mamoru, Miura Kunio, Ogata Taketora, Ōdachi Shigeo, Tsushima Juichi, Sakomizu Hisatsune, Matsumura Kenzō, Yamazaki Iwao, Murakami Giichi, Ogasawara Sankurō, and Narahashi Wataru.

3. Seven of these men—whose average life span was just forty-five years—met violent ends through assassination (Ōkubo Toshimichi, Ōmura Masajirō, Hirosawa Saneomi, and Yokoi Shonan), execution (Etō Shinpei and Maehara Issei), or suicide (Saigō Takamori). Only three died of natural causes (Kido Kōin, Komatsu Tatewaki, and Iwakura Tomomi).

4. The "Three Departments and Six Ministries System" was a centralized model of government administration established during the Sui Dynasty (561–618). Under that system, the senior official (*zaixiang*) in each department performed the functions of a prime minister, while a senior secretary supervised each of the six ministries (Civil Affairs, Revenue, Rites, War, Justice, and Public Works). Together with the emperor and a few dignitaries, the zaixiang and the senior secretaries composed the Grand Council of State (Gernet 1996, 242; Asakawa 1903, 223–225). This system was modified during the T'ang Dynasty (618–907).

5. The Taika Reform (646) established a system of government that allowed the Imperial Court to exercise centralized control of the entire country. The Taihō Code (702) introduced suitably adapted Chinese political institutions to the Japanese context (Varley 1974a, 34). Nara was selected as the site for a capital patterned after the T'ang capital at Chang'an (present-day Sian), and the imperial court moved there in 710.

6. The Imperial Household Ministry (*Kunaishō*) had no equivalent in the original T'ang model.

7. A central state executive based upon "three posts and seven departments" (*sanshoku, nanaka*) was established on January 11, 1868. The three posts—minister president (*sōsai*), legislators (*gitei*), and councilors (*san'yo*)—were occupied by imperial princes and court nobles, who had the right of direct access to the emperor on matters of state. Beneath them were seven functional "departments" (*ka*, later recast as administrative bureaus) for religious rites, finance, justice, administration, and domestic, foreign, military affairs, and, later on, a minister president's bureau (*sōsai kyoku*).

8. The only non-*hanbatsu* councilor was Katsu Kaishū, a former Tokugawa naval officer.

9. In this and subsequent reorganizations of government organs, the Imperial Household Ministry existed apart from other governmental ministries and agencies.

10. The number of cabinet-related officials—including those attached to the

Board of Audit—varied from 434 (1895) to 1,006 (1886) (Ministry of Internal Affairs and Communications 2012a).

11. The cabinet's powers and functions were clarified in "Cabinet Decisions" (*Naikaku giketsusho*) and "Cabinet Rules" (*Naikaku kisoku*), documents inspired by Itō Hirobumi and drafted by Itō Miyoji.

12. Note: the analysis presented throughout this book does not take account of caretaker premierships (for example, Sanjō Sanetomi, who served as acting prime minister from October 25, 1889, to December 24, 1889). In addition to Sanjō, the other caretaker and acting premiers were Kuroda Kiyotaka, Saionji Kinmochi, Uchida Yasuya (twice), Wakatsuki Reijirō, Shidehara Kijūrō, Takahashi Korekiyo, Gotō Fumio, Kishi Nobusuke, and Itō Masayoshi.

13. Iwakura was assisted by Ōkubo Toshimichi, Kido Kōin, Yamaguchi Nao-yoshi, and Itō Hirobumi. Kido and Ōkubo were senior leaders of the respective Chōshū and Satsuma cliques. The mission was composed of 108 people, including forty-three students being sent abroad to study ("Iwakura shisetsudan" 2004/2005).

14. Ravina argues that Saigō did not necessarily want his assassination to pro-voke war with Korea, but, rather, to "determine the Koreans' true intentions and to ascertain whether they intended to impugn the Japanese imperial house" (2004, 185).

15. Although Ōki also hailed from Hizen, his opposition to constitutional gov-ernment was in line with the views of the Sat-Chō councilors.

16. The key posts in the Grand Council were prime minister (*dajōdaijin*), minister of the left (*sadaijin*), minister of the right (*udaijin*), cabinet adviser (*nai-kaku kōmon*), imperial councilor (*sangi*), director general of colonization (*kaitaku chōkan*), and the home (*naimukyō*), foreign affairs (*gaimukyō*), finance (*ōkurakyō*), army (*rikugunkyō*), navy (*kaigunkyō*), justice (*shihōkyō*), education (*kyōbukyō* and *monbukyō*), industry (*kōbukyō*), and agriculture and commerce (*nōshōmukyō*) ministerships.

17. Suematsu Kenchō (a former journalist) and Shimazu Hisamitsu (the last daimyō of Satsuma domain) were the only ministers who did not emerge from the government bureaucracy or the armed forces.

18. They were Iwakura Tomomi, Itō Hirobumi, Kaneko Kentarō, Ōkubo Toshi-michi, Kido Kōin, Tanaka Fujimarō, Yamada Akiyoshi, Sasaki Takayuki, Tanaka Mitsuaki, and Nomura Yasushi.

19. Until 1893, graduates of Tokyo Imperial University were exempted from taking the Higher Civil Service Examination (Tanaka 1976, 43).

20. Between 1891 and 1898, the bureaucracy issued 2,264 imperial ordinances and treaties, while the Diet passed only 266 laws (calculated from data in Naikaku seido 1995, 170).

21. Once again, Ōki Takatō was the lone outsider.

22. The council was empowered to approve Imperial ordinances during the nine months out of the year when the Diet was not in session (*Japan Times Year-book* 1933, 30). In contrast to cabinet ministers, who advised the emperor and

headed a ministry, Privy Councilors had "no other function than to debate in an irresponsible consultative body" (Colegrove 1931a, 596).

23. This requirement was modified on several occasions. It was revised in 1900 to allow only active-duty officers to hold the military portfolios, but modified three years later to allow reserve-duty officers to supervise the military branches. The active-duty requirement was reinstated in 1936.

24. In fact, only Katsu Kaishū and Enomoto Takeaki were not *hanbatsu* figures.

25. South Sakhalin was under the administrative purview of the Karafuto Office (*Karafuto chō*).

26. The characters in Yamamoto's given name are sometimes given as "Gonnohyōe."

27. The regional- and prefectural-level population data are taken as an average of the eighteen censuses conducted between 1898 and 1932.

28. Some ministers, such as Home Minister Hara Kei, were able to promote cooperative bureaucrats and demote the uncompliant (Sims 2001, 95; Ramseyer and Rosenbluth 1995, 10, 62, 73).

29. The undersecretaries' titles were later changed to administrative vice minister (*seimujikan*) and parliamentary councilor (*san'yokan*) (Colegrove 1936a, 906).

30. The Taishō emperor, who reigned from 1912 to 1926, suffered from the effects of meningitis contracted during childhood. In 1921 his health deteriorated, and Crown Prince Hirohito (the future Shōwa emperor) was appointed regent.

31. The consequences of SNTV in multi-member districts—devised by Yamagata to weaken the people's parties—would become apparent after the system was revived in 1947 (Woodall 1999, 26).

32. In firing the shots that killed Inukai, the young naval officers effectively "killed the 'party cabinet system'" (Tanaka 1976, 640).

33. On average, 327 days elapsed between the dissolution or establishment of cabinets and the next lower house election.

34. Mimura uses the term "techno-fascism" to denote a "radical, authoritarian form of technocracy" whose advocates "sought to realize a productive, hierarchical, organic, national community based on the cultural and geographical notions of Japanese ethnic superiority and the managerial principles of 'fusing private and public' and 'separating capital and management'" (2011, 3–4). While I agree with Mimura about the origins and orientations of the technocrats, I believe that the mystical, backward-looking ideologies of conservative rightists, such as Hiranuma and Konoe, emerged from a separate conduit. In my opinion, it is essential to understand that the rational strategies of the technocrats were justified by mystical, emperor-centric "national essence" ideologies. That said, it is important to note that use of the term "fascist" as a label for Japan's prewar political order is hotly contested (e.g., Tansman 2009, 3; Lederer 1934; Maruyama 1969; Moore 1966; Forman 1974; Duus and Okimoto 1979; and Kasza 1984).

35. The term "Versailles-Washington System" denotes an amalgamation of ele-

ments from the Versailles Treaty, Washington Conference on Naval Limitations, and the Kellogg-Briand Pact (Hata 1989, 282; Schlichtmann 2009, 7).

36. The Resources Bureau's organizational predecessor was the Equipment Bureau, established in 1925 (Mimura 2011, 20).

37. Even veteran cabinet ministers with ties to political parties—for example, Yamazaki Tatsunosuke, Maeda Yonezō, Ogawa Gotarō, Shimada Toshio, and Machida Chūji—accepted portfolios as IRAPA affiliates.

38. The February 26 Incident was inspired by the Aizawa Incident, which was precipitated by the dismissal of Imperial Way leader Mazaki Jinzaborō from the post of Inspector General of Military Education. This action was seen as a calculated move by the rival Control faction to dominate the army's supreme high command. On August 12, 1935, Imperial Way officer Lieutenant Colonel Aizawa Saburō avenged the trespass by assassinating General Nagata Tetsuzan, the supposed "evil genius" behind Mazaki's removal (Crowley 1962, 322, 325).

2. COMPRADOR CABINETS AND DEMOCRACY BY THE SWORD, 1946–1955

1. The compradors, also known as "*cohong*" or "*hong*" merchants, were "authorized merchants" who acted as authorized brokers for foreign trade (Mazumdar 1998, 302).

2. After consenting to serve as foreign minister in the Higashikuni cabinet, Yoshida Shigeru consulted former prime minister Suzuki Kantarō, who told him to be a "good loser." "It was good advice," Yoshida recalled, "and I decided then and there to follow it throughout my dealings with GHQ" (Nara, ed. 2007, 49).

3. Many of the same U.S. officials worked together at the Inter-Divisional Area Committee on the Far East (est. October 1943), the Post War Program Committee (est. July 1944), the SWNCC and its Subcommittee on the Far East, and, finally, the Far Eastern Commission (est. 1945) (Borton 1966, 205).

4. Draft constitutions were proposed by private groups and individuals, among them former prime minister Konoe Fumimaro. Konoe committed suicide the day before he was to be taken into custody as an accused war criminal.

5. For example, GHQ's translation of Article 2 of the Matsumoto draft reads, "The Emperor is the monarch and *exercises the rights of sovereignty* according to the present constitution" (NDL "Birth" 3-7).

6. The Constitution Investigation Association's (*Kenpō kenkyūkai*) "Outline of Constitution Draft" (*Kenpō sōan yōkō*)—submitted to the Shidehara cabinet on December 26, 1945, and translated in full by GHQ—made the cabinet collectively responsible to the Diet and tasked the speakers of the Diet's two chambers with recommending the prime minister (NDL "Birth" 2-16).

7. Because Esman's refusal to concur with the Constitution Steering Committee's perspective threatened to delay completion of the GHQ draft, Kades sent him to Nikkō to get some "rest and rehabilitation." For this reason, Esman's sig-

nature does not appear on the letter that accompanied the GHQ draft (McNelly 2000, 72).

8. The remaining cut-and-paste articles are: Article 3 of the final draft (compare with Article 3 of the GHQ draft), Article 63 (Article 56), Article 70 (Article 63), Article 72 (Article 64), Article 74 (Article 66), Article 75 (Article 67), Article 79 (Article 71), Article 80 (Article 72), Article 86 (Article 79), Article 87 (Article 81), Article 90 (Article 84), and Article 91 (Article 85).

9. Article 57 of the GHQ draft became two separate articles in the Constitution, but the upshot remains the same. That is, the cabinet must resign en masse or dissolve the Diet within ten days of passage of a non-confidence resolution or rejection of a confidence resolution (Article 69) and a general election must be held within forty days in the event of Diet dissolution (Article 54).

10. For the record, the Philippines did not become an independent state until July 4, 1946. Because the FEC was home-based in Washington, D.C., it was deemed prudent to set up an "outpost in Tokyo"—the Allied Council for Japan—to monitor occupation policy.

11. Yoshida claimed that Whitney and Kades conveyed to him that GHQ had no objection to this interpretation as long as the principle of civilian control was firmly established (Lu 1997, 471).

12. The Soviet, British, Canadian, Australian, Dutch, and New Zealand representatives also insisted that the "civilian" clause be included in an amended Constitution (NDL "Birth" 4-11).

13. Hatoyama recalled that Yoshida had a fourth condition, which was that Hatoyama would retain control over party personnel decisions (Itoh 2003, 105). In 1952, a group of Japanese nationals—at least some of whom may have worked for G2's intelligence-gathering operation—plotted to assassinate Yoshida to pave the way for his replacement by the more hawkish Hatoyama. The plot collapsed because of intelligence leaks, insufficient personnel, and internal rivalries ("CIA Papers Reveal Japan Coup Plot," Associated Press, March 1, 2007).

14. MacArthur also noted the significance of the emergence of Christian heads of government in China (Ch'iang Kai-shek) and the Philippines (Manuel Roxas).

15. In December 1948, Izumiyama created a hubbub by hugging and planting an unwanted kiss on the cheek of Yamashita Harue, a female MP. When Yamashita resisted his advance, the finance minister allegedly bit her on the cheek (Togawa 1983, 280). Although Izumiyama was forced to surrender his portfolio and resign from the Diet, he earned the moniker "Tiger Minister" (*Tora daijin*) and easily won election to the upper house in 1953.

16. Home Ministry officials accounted for thirteen hundred of the eighteen hundred civil bureaucrats who were purged (Johnson 1982, 41–2; Calder 1988, 151).

17. As evidence of the "reverse course," in July 1950, shortly after the outbreak of hostilities on the Korean peninsula, MacArthur sent a letter to Prime Minister Yoshida authorizing him to establish a seventy-five thousand-man national police reserve.

18. This meant that the justice minister was seated on the premier's immediate right, while the foreign minister was seated to the immediate left of the chief cabinet secretary, with the remaining ministers seated sequentially in the following order: finance, education, health and welfare, agriculture, international trade and industry, transport, posts and telecommunications, labor, construction, and home affairs.

19. When asked how many students passed through his "School," Yoshida jokingly replied, "I don't know how many, since I do not receive tuition" (Masumi 1985, 279).

20. Japanese servility is also evident in the Yoshida government's agreement to diplomatically recognize the Republic of China, rather than the Peoples' Republic of China, in acceding to the terms of the San Francisco Peace Treaty.

21. For example, Nishio Suehiro, vice prime minister in the Ashida cabinet, was forced to resign amid allegations that he accepted bribes from a construction company. The Coal Nationalization scandal (which resulted in the conviction, subsequently reversed, of Tanaka Kakuei), the MCI Textile scandal, and the Tōyō Milling scandal were among the other high-profile corruption incidents of the early postwar period (Satō et al. 1990, 119; Mitchell 1996, 92–108).

3. Corporatist Cabinets and the Emergence of the "1955 System," 1955–1972

1. In addition, a schism emerged between the "mainstream" (*shuryū*) factions that supported the party president and the "non-mainstream" (*hi-shuryū*) factions.

2. While Jackie Robinson's story is well-known, few are aware that Japanese American Wataru (Wat) Misaka broke the National Basketball Association's color barrier when he suited up for the New York Knicks in 1947.

3. For purposes of this study, the "urban" prefectures include Tokyo, Saitama, Chiba, Kanagawa, Aichi, Osaka, Hyōgo, and Kyoto.

4. The "Regional Development" portfolio is taken as an average of the amalgamated characteristics of the directors-general portfolios for the Capital Region (created in 1957), Kinki Region (1964), and Chūbu Region (1966) development commissions.

5. For instance, Construction Minister Kōno Ichirō's heavy-handed appointment of handpicked officials to serve in key ministry posts temporarily disturbed the delicate balance among the ministry's "generalist" (*jimukan*) and "technical specialist" (*gikan*) bureaucrats (Woodall 1996, 61–63).

4. Confederate Cabinets and the Demise of the "1955 System," 1972–1993

1. In the mid-1980s, for example, Tanaka faction MPs accounted for 69 percent and 56 percent of the respective memberships of the construction and postal tribes (Inoguchi and Iwai 1987, 295–304).

2. As Park explains, it is not surprising that ambitious bureaucrats would exit the civil service at midcareer "to enter the 'all-powerful' . . . LDP Diet contingent . . . rather than try to reach the pinnacle of the bureaucratic hierarchy . . . only to toil under . . . often much younger LDP ministers" (1986, 180).

5. DISJOINED CABINETS—ACT I

1. The Law for Basic Reform of Central Government (*Chūō shōchō to kaikaku kihon hō*) was enacted on June 9, 1998, while the Law to Establish the Cabinet Office (*Naikakufu setchi hō*) received Diet approval the following week.

2. The Japanese government denies that this exchange took place, although it was reported in the media (for example, *Shūkan bunshun*, August 5, 2000). A different version of the story has it that Mori was instructed to greet Clinton with "How are you?" to which the U.S. president would reply, "Fine, thanks," and then Mori would respond, "Me too." In fact, however, Clinton replied, "I've come with Hillary," and then Mori replied, "Me too." Arthur Stockwin alerted me to this alternative version of Mori's famous gaffe.

3. Beginning in February 2012, the number of political appointees attached to the Cabinet Office increased with the inclusion of three senior vice ministers and parliamentary secretaries with concurrent appointments in other agencies (for example, the Reconstruction Agency). The number of political appointees does not include the Assistants to the Prime Minister (*Naikaku sōridaijin hosakan*), of whom the prime minister may appoint a maximum of five.

4. The National Association of Private Postmasters (*Zenkoku tokutei yūbinkyokuchō kai*) is the principal lobby for nearly three hundred thousand postal service employees, while the Liaison Association for the Promotion of the Commissioned Postmasters' Duties (*Tokutei Yūbinkyokuchō Gyōmu Suishin Renrakukai*) provides a bridge to the government bureaucracy (MacLachlan 2004, 300–301).

5. Prime Minister Nakasone sacked Education Minister Fujio Masayuki in 1986 for refusing to apologize for remarks he made justifying Japan's actions during the Pacific War. In 1953, Prime Minister Yoshida fired Agriculture Minister Hirozawa Kōzen for participating in a Diet boycott protesting the prime minister's reference to a JSP MP as a "fool" during parliamentary interpellations (discussed in chapter 3).

6. Of the thirty-seven postal rebels, three chose to not seek reelection, seven joined other parties, while all the rest ran as independents (Maeda 2006, 623).

6. DISJOINED CABINETS—ACT II

1. The DPJ's 2009 election manifesto proclaimed that "real responsibility for drafting and deciding the policies of the central government and agencies" should

be given to the one hundred or so MPs who hold the posts of minister, senior vice minister, and parliamentary secretary (Democratic Party of Japan 2009).

2. Although Abe was admitted to a hospital with a stomach issue, many believed that he resigned to secure the DPJ's agreement to extend the anti-terrorism law (BBC News On-line, September 12, 2007).

Conclusion

1. "The failure of the first attempt" is the subtitle of Scalapino's *Democracy and the Party Movement in Prewar Japan* (1953).

2. From June 1947 through December 2012, the average length of tenure for CLB directors general was 1,413 days, as opposed to the 760-day life span of the average government.

3. Some of these same points are emphasized in "Current Challenges to Democracy," a statement issued in 2008 by the World Movement for Democracy (http://www.wmd.org/about/current-challenges/current-challenges-democracy; accessed May 28, 2013).

Selected References

Abbott, Wilbur C. 1906. "The Long Parliament of Charles II." *English Historical Review* 21: 21–56.

Aberbach, Joel D., Robert D. Putnam, and Bert A. Rockman. 1981. *Bureaucrats and Politicians in Western Democracies*. Cambridge, Mass.: Harvard Univ. Press.

Administrative Management Bureau. 2007. *Organization of the Government of Japan*. Tokyo: Administrative Management Bureau.

Administrative Reform Council. 1997. "Saishū hōkoku" ["Final Report"]. http://www.kantei.go.jp/jp/gyokaku/index.html. Accessed May 21, 2013.

Akimoto Shunkichi. 1933. *Manchuria Scene*. Tokyo: Taisho Eibun Sha.

Akita, George. 1967. *The Foundations of Constitutional Government in Modern Japan, 1868–1900*. Cambridge, Mass.: Harvard Univ. Press.

Amakawa Akira. 1995. "Shidehara Kijūrō: 'saigo no o hōkō' to shin kenpō sōan" ["Shidehara Kijūrō: 'Last Honorary Apprenticeship' and the New Draft Constitution"]. In Watanabe, ed., 17–28.

Amyx, Jennifer A. 2004. *Japan's Financial Crisis: Institutional Rigidity and Reluctant Change*. Princeton: Princeton Univ. Press.

Anderson, Stephen J. 1993. *Welfare Policy and Politics in Japan: Beyond the Developmental State*. St. Paul, Minn.: Paragon House.

Andeweg, Rudy B., and Wilma Bakema. 1994. "The Netherlands: Ministers and Cabinet Policy." In Laver and Shepsle, eds., 56–72.

Angel, Robert C. 1988–1989. "Prime Ministerial Leadership in Japan." *Pacific Affairs* 61: 583–602.

Asakawa Kan'ichi. 1903. *The Early Institutional Life of Japan: A Study in the Reform of 645 A.D.* Tokyo: Tokyo Shueisha.

Ashford, Douglas. 1986. *The Emergence of the Welfare States*. Oxford: Basil Blackwell.

Awaya Kentarō. 1993. "Naikaku jōhō kyoku" ["Cabinet Information Bureau"]. In *Nihonshi daijiten* [*Encyclopedia of Japanese History*]. Tokyo: Heibonsha. 292–293.

Baerwald, Hans H. 2003. "The Occupation of Japan as an Exercise in 'Regime Change': Reflections after Fifty Years by a Participant." JPRI Occasional Paper No. 29. http://www.jpri.org/publications/occasionalpapers/op29.html. Accessed April 26, 2013.

Bagehot, Walter. (1867) 1925. *The English Constitution*. London: Kegan Paul, Trench, Trubner.

Bailey, Jackson H. 1983. "Matsukata Masayoshi." In Harry Wray and Hilary Con-
    roy, eds., *Japan Examined: Perspectives on Modern Japanese History*, 104–111.
    Honolulu: Univ. of Hawai'i Press.
Banno Junji. 1992. *The Establishment of the Japanese Constitutional System*. Trans-
    lated by J.A.A. Stockwin. London: Routledge.
Barnhart, Michael A. 1987. *Japan Prepares for Total War: The Search for Economic
    Security, 1919-1941*. Ithaca, N.Y.: Cornell Univ. Press.
Baxter, James C. 1994. *The Meiji Unification through the Lens of Ishikawa Prefec-
    ture*. Cambridge, Mass.: Harvard University Asia Center.
Beasley, W. G. 1989. "Meiji Political Institutions." In Marius B. Jansen, ed., *The Cam-
    bridge History of Japan*, vol. 5, 618–673. Cambridge: Cambridge Univ. Press.
———. 1995. *The Rise of Modern Japan: Political, Economic, and Social Change
    since 1850*. New York: St. Martin's Press.
Beckmann, Gordon M. 1957. *The Making of the Meiji Constitution: The Oligarchs
    and the Constitutional Development of Japan*. Lawrence: Univ. of Kansas Press.
Berger, Gordon Mark. 1974. "Japan's Young Prince: Konoe Fumimaro's Early Polit-
    ical Career, 1916–1931." *Monumenta Nipponica* 29: 451–475.
———. 1977. *Parties Out of Power in Japan, 1931-1941*. Princeton: Princeton Univ.
    Press.
———. 1989. "Politics and Mobilization in Japan, 1931–1945." In John Whitney
    Hall, ed., *The Cambridge History of Japan: The Twentieth Century*, 97–153.
    Cambridge: Cambridge Univ. Press.
Berkofsky, Axel. 2002. "Corruption and Bribery in Japan's Ministry of Foreign
    Affairs: The Case of Muneo Suzuki." JPRI Working Paper No. 86. http://www.
    jpri.org/publications/workingpapers/wp86.html. Accessed April 26, 2013.
Bix, Herbert P. 2000. *Hirohito and the Making of Modern Japan*. New York:
    Harper-Collins.
Blaker, Michael. 1977. "Japan 1976: The Year of Lockheed." *Asian Survey* 17: 81–90.
Blondel, Jean. 1977. "The Government of France." In Curtis, ed., 1997b, 99–152.
Borton, Hugh. 1955. *Japan's Modern Century*. New York: Ronald Press.
———. 1966. "Preparation for the Occupation of Japan." *Journal of Asian Studies*
    25: 203–212.
———. 2002. *Spanning Japan's Modern Century: The Memoirs of Hugh Borton*. Lan-
    ham, Md.: Lexington Books.
Bowen, Roger. 2003. *Japan's Dysfunctional Democracy: The Liberal Democratic
    Party and Structural Corruption*. Armonk, N.Y.: M. E. Sharpe.
Braudel, Fernand. 1982. *On History*. Translated by Sarah Matthews. Chicago: Univ.
    of Chicago Press.
Brazier, Rodney. 1997. *Ministers of the Crown*. Oxford: Oxford Univ. Press.
Buckley, Roger. 1978. "Britain and the Emperor: The Foreign Office and Constitu-
    tional Reform in Japan, 1945–1946." *Modern Asian Studies* 12: 553–570.
Buckley, Stephen. 2006. *The Prime Minister and Cabinet*. Edinburgh, UK: Edin-
    burgh Univ. Press.

Butow, Robert J. C. 1969. *Tojo and the Coming of War.* Stanford: Stanford Univ. Press.

Byas, Hugh. 1942. *Government by Assassination.* New York: Knopf.

Cabinet Office (United Kingdom). 2010. "Cabinet Office Structure Charts." https:// www.gov.uk/government/organisations/cabinet-office/series/cabinet-office-structure-charts. Accessed April 27, 2013.

Calder, Kent E. 1982. "Kanryō vs. Shomin: Contrasting Dynamics of Conservative Leadership in Postwar Japan." In Terry Edward MacDougall, ed., *Political Leadership in Contemporary Japan,* 1–28. Ann Arbor: Michigan Papers in Japanese Studies.

———. 1988. *Crisis and Compensation: Public Policy and Political Stability in Japan, 1949–1986.* Princeton: Princeton Univ. Press.

Campbell, John Creighton. 1977. *Contemporary Japanese Budget Politics.* Berkeley: Univ. of California Press.

———. 1984. "Policy Conflict and Its Resolution within the Governmental System." In Ellis S. Krauss, Thomas P. Rohlen, and Patricia G. Steinhoff, eds., *Conflict in Japan,* 294–334. Honolulu: Univ. of Hawai'i Press.

Campbell, John Creighton, and Ethan Scheiner. 2008. "Fragmentation and Power: Reconceptualizing Policy Making under Japan's 1955 System." *Japanese Journal of Political Science* 9: 89–113.

Campbell, Kenneth J. 1998. "Major General Charles A. Willoughby: A Mixed Performance." Unpublished paper. http://intellit.muskingum.edu/wwii_folder/wwiifepac_folder/wwiifepacwilloughby.html. Accessed December 26, 2006.

Carlson, Matthew. 2008. "Japan's Postal Privatization Battle: The Continuing Reverberations for the Liberal Democratic Party of Rebels-Assassins Conflicts." *Asian Survey* 48: 603–625.

Central Intelligence Agency. 2010. "Chiefs of State and Cabinet Members of Foreign Governments." https://www.cia.gov/library/publications/world-leaders-1/. Accessed December 23, 2010.

Cheng, Peter P. 1974. "The Japanese Cabinets, 1885–1973: An Elite Analysis." *Asian Survey* 14: 1055–1071.

Chihō giin to shimin no seisaku kenkyūkai, ed. 1998. *Chihō jichi riken to akirame ni shūshifu o [To Give Up Local Rights].* Kagoshima: Tosho shuppan/Nanpō shinsha.

Clark, Gregory. 2005. "Japan-Russia Dispute over Northern Territories Highlights Flawed Diplomacy." *Japan Focus.* www.japanfocus.org/-Gregory-Clark/2018. Accessed April 27, 2013.

Cohen, Jeffrey E. 1988. *The Politics of the U.S. Cabinet: Representation in the Executive Branch, 1789–1984.* Pittsburgh: Univ. of Pittsburgh Press.

Cohen, Jerome B. 1949. "Tax Reform in Japan." *Far Eastern Survey* 18: 307–311.

Colegrove, Kenneth. 1931a. "The Japanese Privy Council." *American Political Science Review* 25: 589–614.

———. 1931b. "The Japanese Privy Council." *American Political Science Review* 25: 881–905.

———. 1936a. "The Japanese Cabinet." *American Political Science Review* 30: 903–923.

———. 1936b. *Militarism in Japan.* New York: World Peace Foundation.

Conlan, Thomas. 2010. "Instruments of Change: Organizational Technology and the Consolidation of Regional Power in Japan, 1333–1600." In John A. Ferejohn and Frances McCall Rosenbluth, eds., *War and State Building in Medieval Japan,* 124–158. Stanford: Stanford Univ. Press.

Coox, Alvin D. 1990. *Nomonhan: Japan against Russia, 1939.* Vols. 1 and 2. Stanford: Stanford Univ. Press.

Cox, Gary, Frances McCall Rosenbluth, and Michael F. Thies. 1999. "Electoral Reform and the Fate of Factions: The Case of Japan's LDP." *British Journal of Political Science* 29 (1): 33–56.

Craig, Albert M. 1961. *Chōshū in the Meiji Restoration.* Cambridge, Mass.: Harvard Univ. Press.

Cronin, Thomas E. 1980. *The State of the Presidency,* 2nd ed. Boston: Little, Brown.

Crowley, James B. 1962. "Japanese Army Factionalism in the Early 1930s." *Journal of Asian Studies* 21: 309–326.

Cullen, Louis M. 2003. *A History of Japan, 1582–1941.* London: Cambridge Univ. Press.

Curtis, Gerald L. 1988. *The Japanese Way of Politics.* New York: Columbia Univ. Press.

Curtis, Michael. 1997a. "The Government of Great Britain." In Curtis, ed., 1997b, 27–98.

———, ed. 1997b. *Western European Government and Politics.* New York: Longman.

Daalder, Hans. 1963. *Cabinet Reform in Britain, 1914–1963.* Stanford: Stanford Univ. Press.

Democratic Party of Japan. 2009. "2009 Change of Government: The Democratic Party of Japan's Platform for Government" and "Manifesto." ikjeld.com/file_download/5/dpj_manifesto_2009.pdf. Accessed April 27, 2013.

Destler, I. M. 1976. *Managing an Alliance: The Politics of U.S.-Japanese Relations.* Washington, D.C.: Brookings Institution Press.

Destler, I. M., Haruhiro Fukui, and Hideo Satō. 1979. *The Textile Wrangle: Conflict in Japanese-American Relations, 1969–1971.* Ithaca, N.Y.: Cornell Univ. Press.

Dolan, Ronald E., and Robert L. Worden, eds. 1994. *Japan: A Country Study.* Washington, D.C.: Government Printing Office. http://countrystudies.us/japan/114.htm. Accessed April 26, 2013.

Domínguez, Jorge I., and Christopher N. Mitchell. 1977. "The Roads Not Taken: Institutionalization and Political Parties in Cuba and Bolivia." *Comparative Politics* 9: 173–195.

Dower, John W. 1993. *Japan in War and Peace.* New York: New Press.

———. 1999. *Embracing Defeat: Japan in the Wake of World War II.* New York: Norton.

———. 2003. "Democracy in Japan." Asia Program Special Report #109. Woodrow Wilson International Center for Scholars. 4–8.

Duffield, John S., and Brian Woodall. 2011. "Japan's New Basic Energy Plan." *Energy Policy* 39: 3741–3749.

Dunleavy, Patrick, and R.A.W. Rhodes. 1990. "Core Executive Studies in Britain." *Public Administration* 68: 3–28.

Dunn, Christopher J. C. 1995. *The Institutionalized Cabinet: Governing the Western Provinces.* Montreal: McGill-Queen's Univ. Press.

Durkheim, Emile. (1893) 1984. *The Division of Labor in Society.* New York: Free Press.

Duus, Peter. 1968. *Party Rivalry and Political Change in Taishō Japan.* Cambridge, Mass.: Harvard Univ. Press.

———. 1969. *Feudalism in Japan,* 2nd ed. New York: Knopf.

———. 1998. *Modern Japan,* 2nd ed. Boston: Houghton Mifflin.

Duus, Peter, and Kenji Hasegawa. 2011. *Rediscovering America: Japanese Perspectives on the American Century.* Berkeley: Univ. of California Press.

Duus, Peter, and Daniel I. Okimoto. 1979. "Comment: Fascism and the History of Pre-War Japan: The Failure of a Concept." *Journal of Asian Studies* 39: 65–76.

Eda Kenji. 2010. "Futenma at the Beginning." *Ampontan.* ampontan.wordpress. com/2010/05/05/eda-kenji-futenma-at-the-beginning/. Accessed April 27, 2013.

Eldridge, Robert D. 1997. "The 1996 Okinawa Referendum on U.S. Base Reductions: One Question, Several Answers." *Asian Survey* 37: 879–904.

Elgie, Robert. 1997. "Models of Executive Politics: A Framework for the Study of Executive Power Relations in Parliamentary and Semi-Presidential Regimes." *Political Studies* 45: 217–231.

Elliott, James. 1983. "The 1981 Administrative Reform in Japan." *Asian Survey* 23: 765–779.

Estevez-Abe, Margarita. 2006. "Japan's Shift toward a Westminster System: A Structural Analysis of the 2005 Lower House Election and Its Aftermath." *Asian Survey* 46: 632–651.

Evans, David C., and Mark R. Peattie. 1997. *Kaigun: Strategy, Tactics, and Technology in the Imperial Japanese Navy, 1887–1941.* Annapolis, Md.: Naval Institute Press.

Evans, Peter. 1996. "The Role of Theory in Comparative Politics: A Symposium." *World Politics* 48: 2–10.

Fairbank, John K. 1992. *China: A New History.* Cambridge, Mass.: Harvard Univ. Press.

Falk, Stanley L. 1961. "Organization and Military Power: The Japanese High Command in World War II." *Political Science Quarterly* 76: 503–518.

Farrell, Brian. 1994. "The Political Role of Cabinet Ministers in Ireland." In Laver and Shepsle, eds., 73–87.

Feldman, Eric A., and Ronald Bayer. 1999. *Blood Feuds: AIDS, Blood, and the Politics of Medical Disaster.* Oxford: Oxford Univ. Press.

Finn, Richard B. 1992. *Winners in Peace: MacArthur, Yoshida, and Postwar Japan.* Berkeley: Univ. of California Press.

Fogarty, Philippa. 2006. "Koizumi's Unique Legacy of Change." BBC News. news. bbc.co.uk/2/hi/asia-pacific/5346460.stm. Accessed April 27, 2013.

Forman, James D. 1974. *Fascism: The Meaning and Experience of Reactionary Revolution.* New York: Franklin Watts.

Fraser, Andrew. 1967. "The Osaka Conference of 1875." *Journal of Asian Studies* 26: 589–610.

Fukui Haruhiro. 1984. "The Liberal Democratic Party Revisited: Continuity and Change in the Party's Structure and Performance." *Journal of Japanese Studies* 10: 385–435.

Funabashi Yōichi. 1999. *Alliance Adrift.* New York: Council on Foreign Relations Press.

Furuya Tetsuo. 1991. *Teikoku gikai no seiritsu—seiritsu katei to seido no gaiyō* [*Establishment of the Imperial Diet—An Overview of the Formation Process and Institutions*]. Tokyo: Daiichi Hōki.

Gaunder, Alicia. 2007. *Political Reform in Japan: Leadership Looming Large.* Abingdon: Taylor and Francis.

——, ed. 2011. *Routledge Handbook of Japanese Politics.* London: Routledge.

Gayn, Mark. (1946) 1973. "Drafting the Japanese Constitution." In Jon Livingston, Joe Moore, and Felicia Oldfather, eds., *Postwar Japan: 1945 to the Present,* 20–24. New York: Random House.

——. 1981. *Japan Diary.* Rutland: Tuttle.

George Mulgan, Aurelia. 2003a. *Japan's Failed Revolution: Koizumi and the Politics of Economic Reform.* Canberra: Asia Pacific Press.

——. 2003b. "Japan's 'Un-Westminster' System: Impediments to Reform in a Crisis Economy." *Government and Opposition* 38: 73–91.

——. 2006. *Power and Pork: A Japanese Political Life.* Canberra: Australia National University.

——. 2009. "Decapitating the Bureaucracy in Japan." *East Asia Forum.* http://www.eastasiaforum.org/2009/12/10/decapitating-the-bureaucracy-in-japan/. Accessed April 27, 2013.

——. 2011. "The Politics of Economic Reform." In Gaunder, ed., 261–272.

Gernet, Jacques. 1996. *A History of Chinese Civilization.* Cambridge: Cambridge Univ. Press.

Gibney, Alex. 1996. "Six Days to Reinvent Japan." *Wilson Quarterly* 20: 72–80.

Gordon, Andrew. 2003. *A Modern History of Japan: From Tokugawa Times to the Present.* New York: Oxford Univ. Press.

Grofman, Bernard, Sung-Chull Lee, Edwin Winckler, and Brian Woodall. 1999. "Introduction." In *Elections and Campaigning in Japan, Korea, and Taiwan,* edited by Grofman et al., 1–20. Ann Arbor: Univ. of Michigan Press.

Hackett, Roger F. 1971. *Yamagata Aritomo in the Rise of Modern Japan, 1838–1922.* Cambridge, Mass.: Harvard Univ. Press.

———. 1974. "The Era of Fulfillment: 1877–1911." In Tiedemann, ed., 181–216.

Hao, Yen-p'ing. 1970. "A 'New Class' in China's Treaty Ports: The Rise of the Comprador-Merchants." *Business History Review* 44: 446–459.

Hara Takeshi. 2008a. "The 'Great Emperor' Meiji." In Shillony, ed., 213–226.

———. 2008b. "Taishō: The Enigmatic Emperor and His Influential Wife." In Shillony, ed., 227–240.

Harada Kumao. 1968. *Fragile Victory: Prince Saionji and the 1930 London Treaty Issue from the Memoirs of Baron Harada Kumao.* Translated by Thomas Francis Mayer-Oakes. Detroit: Wayne State Univ. Press.

Hata Ikuhiko. 1989. "Continental Expansion, 1905–1941." In *The Cambridge History of Japan: The Twentieth Century,* edited by John Whitney Hall, 271–314. Cambridge: Cambridge Univ. Press.

"Hatoyama Statement." 2009. Press Conference by Prime Minister Yukio Hatoyama, December 25. http://www.kantei.go.jp/jp/hatoyama/statement/200912/25kaiken.html. Accessed April 27, 2013.

Hayao, Kenji. 1993. *The Japanese Prime Minister and Public Policy.* Pittsburgh: Univ. of Pittsburgh Press.

Hayashi Shigeru and Tsuji Kiyoaki, eds. 1981. *Nihon no naikaku shiroku* [*History of Japan's Cabinets*]. 6 vols. Tokyo: Daiichi Hōki.

Headquarters for the Administrative Reform of the Central Government. 2000. "Central Government Reform of Japan." www.kantei.go.jp/foreign/central_government/index.html. Accessed April 26, 2013.

Heasman, D. J. 1962a. "The Ministerial Hierarchy." *Parliamentary Affairs* 15: 307–330.

———. 1962b. "Parliamentary Paths to High Office." *Parliamentary Affairs* 16: 315–330.

Hein, Laura Elizabeth. 1990. *Fueling Growth: The Energy Revolution and Economic Policy in Postwar Japan.* Cambridge, Mass.: Harvard University Asia Center.

Holliday, Ian, and Tomohito Shinoda. 2002. "Governing from the Centre: Core Executive Capacity in Britain and Japan." *Japanese Journal of Political Science* 3: 91–111.

House of Commons, Public Administration Select Committee. 2010. *Goats and Tsars: Ministerial and Other Appointments from Outside Parliament.* London: Stationery Office.

Hrebiniak, Lawrence G., and William F. Joyce. 1985. "Strategic Choice and Environmental Determinism." *Administrative Science Quarterly* 30: 336–349.

Hsu, Immanuel C. Y. 1983. *The Rise of Modern China,* 3rd ed. Oxford: Oxford Univ. Press.

Huber, John D., and Cecilia Martinez-Gallardo. 2004. "Cabinet Instability and the Accumulation of Experience in the Cabinet: The French Fourth and Fifth Republics in Comparative Perspective." *British Journal of Political Science* 34: 27–48.

Huntington, Samuel P. 1965. "Political Development and Political Decay." *World Politics* 17: 386–430.

Ienaga Saburō. 1978. *The Pacific War, 1931–1945: A Critical Perspective on Japan's Role in World War II*. New York: Pantheon Books.

Iio Jun. 2004. "Zaisei ni okeru Nihon kanryōsei no futatsu no kao" ["The Two Faces of Japanese Bureaucracy in Financial Reconstruction"]. RIETI Discussion Paper 04-J-007. www.rieti.go.jp/jp/publications/dp/04j007.pdf. Accessed April 26, 2013.

———. 2007. *Nihon no tōchi kōzō: kanryō naikakusei kara giin naikakusei e* [*Japan's Structure of Governance—From Bureaucratic to Parliamentary Cabinet System*]. Tokyo: Chūō kōron shinsha.

Inoguchi Takashi. 1983. *Gendai Nihon seiji keizai no kōzu* [*The Structure of the Contemporary Japanese Political Economy*]. Tokyo: Tōyō keizai shinpōsha.

Inoguchi Takashi and Iwai Tomoaki. 1987. *"Zoku giin" no kenkyū: Jimintō seiken o gyūjiru shuyakutachi* [*Research on Policy Tribalists: Protagonists of the LDP Regime*]. Tokyo: Nihon Keizai Shinbunsha.

Inoki Takenori. 1995. "Ishibashi Tanzan—tōtetsu shita jiyūshugi shisōka" ["Hatoyama Ichirō—Clear-Minded Liberal Political Thinker"]. In Watanabe, ed., 109–120.

Inoue Kyoko. 1991. *MacArthur's Japanese Constitution*. Chicago: Univ. of Chicago Press.

Ishi Hiromitsu. 1989. *The Japanese Tax System*, 3rd ed. Oxford: Oxford Univ. Press.

Ishida Takeshi and Ellis S. Krauss, eds. 1989. *Democracy in Japan*. Pittsburgh: Univ. of Pittsburgh Press.

Ishii Osamu. 2009. "Dainiji nichibei sen'i funsō, 1969–1971: meisō no sen-nichi" ["The Second Japan-US Textile Dispute, 1969–1971: 1000 Days of Wandering"]. Departmental Bulletin Paper, Hitotsubashi Daigaku. http://hermes-ir.lib.hit-u.ac.jp/rs/items-by-author?author=ISHII%2C+Osamu. Accessed April 27, 2013.

Ishii Ryosuke. 1980. *A History of Political Institutions in Japan*. Tokyo: Univ. of Tokyo Press.

Itasaka Hidenori. 1987. *Zoku no kenkyū* [*Research on Tribes*]. Tokyo: Keizaikai.

Ito Hirobumi. 1889. *Commentaries on the Constitution of Japan*. Tokyo: Igirisu Hōritsu Gakkō.

Itoh, Mayumi. 2003. *The Hatoyama Dynasty: Japanese Political Leadership through the Generations*. New York: Palgrave Macmillan.

"Iwakura shisetsudan" ["Iwakura Mission"]. 2004/2005. Japan Center for Asian Historical Records. www.jacar.go.jp/iwakura/sisetudan/main.html. Accessed April 27, 2013.

Iwasaki Uichi. 1921. *The Working Forces in Japanese Politics: A Brief Account of Political Conflicts, 1867–1920*. New York: Columbia University.

Iyenaga, T. 1917. "Parties and the Cabinet System in Japan." *American Political Science Review* 11: 381–383.

Izumi Hiroshi. 2011. "Post-Earthquake Politics: A New Paradigm?" The Tokyo Foundation. www.tokyofoundation.org/en/articles/2011/post-quake-politics. Accessed December 17, 2013.

James, Simon. 2002. *British Cabinet Government*, 2nd ed. London: Routledge.

Jansen, Marius B. 2002. *The Making of Modern Japan*. Cambridge, Mass.: Harvard Univ. Press.

Janssens, Rudolf V. A. 1995. *"What Future for Japan?" U.S. Wartime Planning for the Postwar Era, 1942–1945*. Atlanta: Rodopi.

The Japan Times Year Book. 1933. Tokyo: Japan Times.

Jennings, Ivor. 1936. *Cabinet Government*. Cambridge: Cambridge Univ. Press.

Jinjikōshinroku [*Who's Who*]. Various years. Tokyo: Jinji Kōshinroku Henshū Iinkai.

Johnson, Chalmers. 1982. *MITI and the Japanese Miracle: The Growth of Industrial Policy, 1925–1975*. Stanford, Calif.: Stanford Univ. Press.

———. 1986a. "MITI, MPT, and the Telecom Wars: How Japan Makes Policy for High Technology." Berkeley Roundtable on the International Economy. escholarship.org/uc/item/8fd1m9cr.pdf%3Borigin=repeccitec.   Accessed   April   26, 2013.

———. 1986b. "Tanaka Kakuei, Structural Corruption, and the Advent of Machine Politics in Japan." *Journal of Japanese Studies* 12: 1–28.

———. 1995a. "The 1955 System and the American Connection: A Bibliographic Introduction." JPRI Working Paper, No. 11. http://www.jpri.org/publications/workingpapers/wp11.html. Accessed May 21, 2013.

———. 1995b. *The Rise of the Developmental State*. New York: Norton.

Joint Statement by President Nixon and Prime Minister Satō. Washington, D.C., November 21, 1969.

Kabashima Ikuo and Gill Steel. 2010. *Changing Politics in Japan*. Ithaca, N.Y.: Cornell Univ. Press.

Kades, Charles L. 1989. "The American Role in Revising Japan's Imperial Constitution." *Political Science Quarterly* 104: 215–247.

Kanechika Teruo. 1979. "Tanaka Giichi naikaku kara Hayashi Sejūrō naikaku made" ["From the Tanaka Giichi Cabinet to the Hayashi Senjūrō Cabinet"]. In Shiratori, ed., 1981, 63–90.

Kasza, Gregory J. 1984. "Fascism from Below: A Comparative Perspective on the Japanese Right, 1931–1936." *Journal of Contemporary History* 19: 607–629.

Kato Hideki. 2008. "Political Reform of the Japanese System of Government." The Tokyo   Foundation.   www.tokyofoundation.org/en/articles/2008/political-reform-of-the-japanese-system-of-government-symposium-report-2. Accessed March 28, 2012.

Kato Junko. 1994. *The Problem of Bureaucratic Rationality: Tax Politics in Japan*. Princeton: Princeton Univ. Press.

Kato Junko and Michael Laver. 1998. "Theories of Government Formation and the 1996 General Election in Japan." *Party Politics* 4: 229–252.

Katzenstein, Peter J., and Nobuo Okawara. 2001/2002. "Japan, Asian-Pacific Security, and the Case for Analytical Eclecticism." *International Security* 26: 153–185.

Kavanaugh, Dennis. 2000. *British Politics—Continuities and Change*, 4th ed. Oxford: Oxford Univ. Press.

Kawabata Eiji. 2004. "Dual Governance: The Contemporary Politics of Posts and Telecommunications in Japan." *Social Science Japan Journal* 7: 21–39.

Keene, Donald. 2005. *Emperor of Japan: Meiji and His World, 1852–1912.* New York: Columbia Univ. Press.

Keith, Arthur Berriedale. 1939. *The British Cabinet System, 1830–1938.* London: Stevens and Sons.

Kensei shiryō hensankai, ed. 1978. *Rekidai kakuryō to kokkai giin meikan* [*Directory of Cabinets and Diet Members*]. Tokyo: Raifu.

Kesselman, Mark. 1970. "Overinstitutionalization and Political Constraint: The Case of France." *Comparative Politics* 3: 21–44.

Kikuchi interview. 1996. Kiyoaki Kikuchi interviewed by Robert A. Wampler, U.S.-Japan Project's Oral History Program, George Washington University. www.gwu.edu/~nsarchiv/japan/ohpage.htm. Accessed January 2, 2012.

King, Anthony. 1981. "The Rise of the Career Politician in Britain—And Its Consequences." *British Journal of Political Science* 11: 249–285.

Kissinger, Henry A. 1979. *White House Years.* Boston: Little, Brown.

Kitaoka Shin'ichi. 1993. "The Army as a Bureaucracy: Japanese Militarism Revisited." *Journal of Military History* 57: 67–86.

———. 1995. "Kishi Nobusuke—yashin to zasetsu" ["Kishi Nobusuke—Ambition and Frustration"]. In Watanabe, ed., 121–147.

Kitazawa Naokichi. 1929. *The Government of Japan.* Princeton: Princeton Univ. Press.

"Kiyoaki Kikuchi." 1996. U.S.-Japan Project's Oral History Program, George Washington University. http://www.gwu.edu/~nsarchiv/japan/ohpage.htm. Accessed January 2, 2012.

Klimek, Peter, Stefan Thurner, and Rudolf Hanel. 2008. "Parkinson's Law Quantified: Three Investigations on Bureaucratic Inefficiency." Santa Fe Institute Working Paper 08-12-055. www.santafe.edu/media/workingpapers/08-12-055.pdf. Accessed April 26, 2013.

Kodama Kōta, Konishi Shirō, and Takeuchi Rizō. 1983. *Nihon shi sōran* [*Survey of Japanese History*], vols. 6 and 9. Tokyo: Shin Jinbutsu Ōraisha.

Koh, B. C. 1989. *Japan's Administrative Elite.* Berkeley: Univ. of California Press.

Koizumi Cabinet E-mail Magazine. 2003. Shūshō Kantei. http://www.kantei.go.jp/jp/m-magazine/backnumber/2003/1016.html. Accessed April 27, 2013.

Koizumi Press Conference. 2005. Shūshō Kantei. www.kantei.go.jp/foreign/koizumispeech/2005/08/08kaiken_e.html. Accessed April 27, 2013.

Kommers, Donald. 1997. "The Government of Germany." In Curtis, ed., 1997b, 153–221.

Koseki Shoichi. 1997. *The Birth of Japan's Postwar Constitution.* Translated by Ray A. Moore. Boulder, Colo.: Westview Press.

Koyama Hironari. 1979. "Meiji no naikaku" ["Cabinets of the Meiji Era"]. In Shiratori, ed., 1981, 9–34.

Krauss, Ellis S. 1989. "Politics and the Policymaking Process." In Ishida and Krauss, 39–64.

———. 2007. "Has Japanese Politics Really Changed? My Views." *Keizai Kōhō* (December). www.kkc.or.jp/english/activities/views/0712.html. Accessed October 21, 2010.

Krauss, Ellis S., and Benjamin Nyblade. 2005. "'Presidentialization' in Japan? The Prime Minister, Media and Elections in Japan." *British Journal of Political Science* 35: 357–368.

Krauss, Ellis S., and Robert J. Pekkanen. 2010. *The Rise and Fall of Japan's LDP: Political Party Organizations as Historical Institutions*. Ithaca, N.Y.: Cornell Univ. Press.

Krook, Mona Lena, and Diana Z. O'Brien. 2012. "All the President's Men? The Appointment of Female Cabinet Ministers Worldwide." *Journal of Politics* 74: 840–855.

Kuroda Yasumasa and Takayoshi Miyagawa. 1990. "Changing Leadership Profile in the Japanese House of Representatives, 1890–1990." Paper presented at the Annual Meeting of the American Political Science Association. Chicago, August 30, 1990.

Kushida, Kenji E. 2012. "Japan's Fukushima Nuclear Disaster: Narrative, Analysis, and Recommendations." Stanford: Shorenstein APARC Working Paper Series.

Kyogoku Jun-ichi. 1987. *The Political Dynamics of Japan*. Tokyo: Tokyo Univ. Press.

Lancaster, Thomas. 1997. "The Government of Spain." In Curtis, ed., 1997b, 282–340.

Large, Stephen S. 2009. "Oligarchy, Democracy, and Fascism." In *A Companion to Japanese History*, edited by William M. Tsutsui, 156–171. Malden, Mass.: Wiley-Blackwell.

Larsson, Torbjorn. 1994. "Cabinet Ministers and Parliamentary Government in Sweden." In Laver and Shepsle, eds., 169–186.

Laurence, Henry. 2001. *Money Rules: The New Politics of Finance in Britain and Japan*. Ithaca, N.Y.: Cornell Univ. Press.

Laver, Michael, and Ben W. Hunt. 1992. *Policy and Party Competition*. New York: Routledge.

Laver, Michael, and Kenneth A. Shepsle. 1994a. "Cabinet Government in Theoretical Perspective." In Laver and Shepsle, eds., 285–310.

———. 1994b. "Cabinet Ministers and Government Formation in Parliamentary Democracies." In Laver and Shepsle, eds., 3–14.

———, eds. 1994. *Cabinet Ministers and Parliamentary Government*. Cambridge: Cambridge Univ. Press.

Lebra, Joyce Chapman. 1959. "Okuma Shigenobu and the 1881 Political Crisis." *Journal of Asian Studies* 18: 475–487.

———. 1973. *Okuma Shigenobu: Statesman of Meiji Japan*. Canberra: Australian National Univ. Press.

Lederer, Emil. 1934. "Fascist Tendencies in Japan." *Pacific Affairs* 7: 373–385.

Lee, Maurice. 1965. *The Cabal.* Urbana: Univ. of Illinois Press.

Lijphart, Arend J. 1999. *Patterns of Democracy: Government Forms and Performance in Thirty-Six Countries.* New Haven, Conn.: Yale Univ. Press.

Lowi, Theodore J., and Benjamin Ginsburg. 1998. *American Government: Freedom and Power,* 5th ed. New York: Norton.

Lu, David John. 1973. *Japan: A Documentary History,* vol. 1. Armonk, N.Y.: M. E. Sharpe.

———. 1997. *Japan: A Documentary History,* vol. 1. New York: M. E. Sharp.

———. 2002. *Agony of Choice: Matsuoka Yōsuke and the Rise and Fall of the Japanese Empire, 1880–1946.* Lanham, Md.: Lexington Books.

MacLachlan, Patricia L. 2004. "Postal Office Politics in Modern Japan: The Postmasters, Iron Triangles, and the Limits of Reform." *Journal of Japanese Studies* 30: 281–313.

Maeda, Ko. 2006. "The General Election in Japan, September 2005." *Electoral Studies* 25: 621–627.

Mahoney, James. 2001. *The Legacies of Liberalism: Path Dependence and Political Regimes in Central America.* Baltimore, Md.: Johns Hopkins Univ. Press.

Mahoney, James, and Kathleen Thelen. 2010. "A Theory of Gradual Institutional Change." In *Explaining Institutional Change: Ambiguity, Agency, and Power,* edited by James Mahoney and Kathleen Thelen, 1–37. Cambridge: Cambridge Univ. Press.

Maruyama Masao. 1969. *Thought and Behavior in Modern Japanese Politics.* London: Oxford Univ. Press.

Marx, Karl. (1852) 1978. "The Eighteenth Brumaire of Louis Bonaparte." In *The Marx-Engels Reader,* edited by Robert C. Tucker, 594–617. New York: Norton.

Mason, Robert J. 1999. "Whither Japan's Environmental Movement? An Assessment of Its Problems and Prospects at the National Level." *Pacific Affairs* 72: 187–207.

Masumi Junnosuke. 1985. *Contemporary Politics in Japan.* Translated by Lonnie Carlile. Berkeley: Univ. of California Press.

———. 1988. "The 1955 System and Its Subsequent Development." *Asian Survey* 28: 286–306.

Matsuzaki Tetsuhisa. 1987. "Jimintō seiji" ["LDP Politics"]. In *Jimintō to iu chie* [*Wisdom on the LDP*], edited by Ishii Shinji, 9–28. Tokyo: JICC.

Matthews, Felicity. 2011. "Constitutional Stretching: Coalition Government and the Westminster Model." *Commonwealth and Comparative Politics* 49: 486–509.

Maxon, Yale Candee. 1957. *Control of Japanese Foreign Policy: A Study of Civil-Military Rivalry, 1930–1945.* Berkeley: Univ. of California Press.

Mayer-Oakes, Thomas Francis. 1968. *Fragile Victory: The Saionji-Harada Memoirs.* Detroit: Wayne State Univ. Press.

Mazumdar, Sucheta. 1998. *Sugar and Society in China: Peasants, Technology, and the World Market.* Cambridge, Mass.: Harvard University Asia Center.

McAnulla, Stuart. 2006. *British Politics: A Critical Introduction*. London: Continuum.

McClenahan, William. 1991. "The Growth of Voluntary Export Restraints and American Foreign Economic Policy, 1956–1969." *Business and Economic History* 20: 180–190.

McCormack, Gavan. 2010. "The US-Japan 'Alliance,' Okinawa, and Three Looming Elections." *Asia-Pacific Journal*. www.japanfocus.org/-gavan-mccormack/3407. Accessed April 28, 2013.

McCubbins, Matthew D., and Gregory W. Noble. 1995. "The Appearance of Power: Legislators, Bureaucrats, and the Budget Process in the United States and Japan." In *Structure and Policy in Japan and the United States*, edited by Matthew D. McCubbins and Peter F. Cowhey, 56–80. Cambridge: Cambridge Univ. Press.

McElwain, Kenneth Mori. 2006. "Explaining Suboptimal Institutional Frameworks: The Effect of Intra-Party Conflict on Electoral Rule Stasis in Japan." Occasional Paper Series of the Program on US-Japan Relations, Harvard University. www.wcfia.harvard.edu/us-japan/research/pdf/06-08.mcelwain.pdf. Accessed April 28, 2013.

McGovern, William Montgomery. 1920. *Modern Japan: Its Political, Military, and Industrial Organization*. London: Fisher Unwin.

McKean, Margaret A. 1981. *Environmental Protest and Citizen Politics in Japan*. Berkeley: Univ. of California Press.

McNelly, Theodore. 1959. "The Japanese Constitution: Child of the Cold War." *Political Science Quarterly* 74: 176–195.

———. 2000. *The Origins of Japan's Democratic Constitution*. Lanham, Md.: Univ. Press of America.

"Meeting between Minister for Foreign Affairs Katsuya Okada and Secretary of Defense of the United States Robert Gates." 2009. Ministry of Foreign Affairs. www.mofa.go.jp/region/n-america/us/security/meet0910.html. Accessed April 28, 2013.

"Memorandum, Sneider to Bundy, 12/24/68." 1968. National Security Archive, George Washington University. http://www.gwu.edu/~nsarchiv/japan/okinawa/oki12_a.htm. Accessed April 28, 2013.

Mettler, Meghan Warner. 2010. "Gimcracks, Dollar Blouses, and Transistors: American Reactions to Imported Japanese Products, 1945–1964." *Pacific Historical Review* 79: 202–230.

Meyer interview. 1996. Armin Meyer interviewed by Robert A. Wampler, U.S.-Japan Project's Oral History Program, George Washington University, 1995–1996. http://www.gwu.edu/~nsarchiv/japan/ohpage.htm. Accessed January 2, 2012.

Meyer, John W., and Brian Rowan. 1977. "Institutionalized Organizations: Formal Structure as Myth and Ceremony." *American Journal of Sociology* 83: 340–363.

Michels, Robert. (1911) 1962. *Political Parties*. New York: Free Press.

Miller, John. 1991. *Charles II.* London: Weidenfeld and Nicolson.

Mimura, Janis. 2011. *Planning for Empire: Reform Bureaucrats and the Japanese Wartime State.* Ithaca, N.Y.: Cornell Univ. Press.

Ministry of Foreign Affairs. 1967. "Three Non-Nuclear Principles." http://www.mofa.go.jp/policy/un/disarmament/nnp/. Accessed May 11, 2013.

Ministry of Internal Affairs and Communications. 2012a. Historical Statistics of Japan. http://www.stat.go.jp/english/data/chouki/index.htm. Accessed April 26, 2013.

———. 2012b. Japan Statistical Yearbook. http://www.stat.go.jp/english/data/nenkan/. Accessed July 14, 2013.

Minshūtō. 2008. "Minshūtō Okinawa bijon" ["DPJ Okinawa Vision"]. July 8, 2008. http://www.dpj.or.jp/news/files/okinawa(2).pdf. Accessed December 17, 2013.

Mishima Ko. 1998. "The Changing Relationship between Japan's LDP and the Bureaucracy: Hashimoto's Administrative Reform Effort and Its Politics." *Asian Survey* 38: 968–985.

Mitchell, Richard H. 1996. *Political Bribery in Japan.* Honolulu: Univ. of Hawaiʻi Press.

Miyagawa Takayoshi, ed. 1990. *Rekidai kokkai giin keireki meikan* [*Directory of Diet Members' Careers*]. Tokyo: Seiji Jōhō Sentaa.

Mochizuki, Mike M. 2007. "Japan's Long Transition: The Politics of Recalibrating Grand Strategy." In *Domestic Political Change and Grand Strategy,* edited by Ashley J. Tellis and Michael Wills, 69–112. Washington, D.C.: National Bureau of Asian Research.

Moore, Barrington. 1966. *The Social Origins of Dictatorship and Democracy: Lord and Peasant in the Making of the Modern World.* Boston: Beacon Press.

Moore, Ray A., and Donald L. Robinson. 2002. *Partners for Democracy: Crafting the New Japanese State under MacArthur.* New York: Oxford Univ. Press.

Murai Ryōta. 2002. "Who Should Govern: The Political Reformation after the First World War in Japan." *Kobe University Law Review* 36: 19–43.

———. 2005. *Seitō naikakusei no seiritsu, 1918–27* [*The Establishment of Party Cabinets, 1918–27*]. Tokyo: Yuhikaku.

Muramatsu Michio and Ellis S. Krauss. 1984. "Bureaucrats and Politicians in Policymaking: The Case of Japan." *American Political Science Review* 78: 126–146.

———. 1987. "The Conservative Policy Line and the Development of Patterned Pluralism." In *The Political Economy of Japan,* vol. 1, *The Domestic Transformation,* edited by Kozo Yamamura and Yasukichi Yasuba, 56–554. Stanford: Stanford Univ. Press.

Murota, Y., and Y. Yano. 1993. "Japan's Policy on Energy and the Environment." *Annual Review of Energy and the Environment* 18: 89–135.

Naikaku hōsei kyoku shi henshū iinkai, ed. 1985. *Naikaku hōsei kyoku hyakunenshi* [*One Hundred-Year History of the Cabinet Legislation Bureau*]. Tokyo: Ōkurashō Insatsu Kyoku.

Naikaku seido hyakujūchōnen kinenshi henshū iinkai, ed. 1995. *Rekidai naikaku to sōri kantei* [*Cabinets and the Prime Minister's Residence*]. Tokyo: Taiko.

Naikaku seido hyakunenshi henshū iinkai, comp. 1980. *Naikaku seido hyakunenshi* [*One Hundred-Year History of the Cabinet System*]. 2 vols. Tokyo: Ōkurashō Insatsu Kyoku.

"Naikaku seido to rekidai naikaku" ["Cabinet System and Historical Cabinets"]. 2013. Shūshō kantei [Office of the Prime Minister and Cabinet]. www.kantei. go.jp/jp/rekidai/1.html. Accessed April 26, 2013.

Naikaku shisei chōsakai, comp. 1980. *Naikaku no rekishi* [*A History of the Cabinet*]. Tokyo: Akatsuki.

Najita Tetsuo. 1967. *Hara Kei in the Politics of Compromise.* Cambridge, Mass. Harvard Univ. Press.

Naka Hisarō, ed. 1980. *Kokkai giin no kōsei to henka* [*Composition and Changes in the Members of Parliament*]. Tokyo: Seiji Kōhō sentaa.

Nakagawa Yatsuhiro. 1979. "Japan, the Welfare Super-Power." *Journal of Japanese Studies* 5: 5–51.

Nakamura Takafusa. 1995. *The Postwar Economy.* Tokyo: Univ. of Tokyo Press.

Nakamura Yoshihisa and Tobe Ryoichi. 1988. "The Imperial Japanese Army and Politics." *Armed Forces and Society* 14: 511–525.

Nakano Koichi. 1998. "The Politics of Administrative Reform in Japan, 1993–1998: Toward a More Accountable Government." *Asian Survey* 38: 291–309.

Nara Hiroshi, ed. 2007. *Yoshida Shigeru: Last Meiji Man.* Lanham: Rowman and Littlefield.

Nariai Osamu. 2007. "A New Business Model for the Civil Service." *Japan Echo* 34. http://www.japanecho.com/sum/2007/340507.html. Accessed April 28, 2013.

NDL "Birth." 2013. National Diet Library. "Birth of the Constitution of Japan." http://www.ndl.go.jp/constitution/e/etc/list.html. Accessed April 29, 2013. Documents cited:

———. 2-16. Constitution Investigation Association. "Outline of Constitution Draft." December 26, 1945.

———. 3-2. "Reform of the Japanese Governmental System (SWNCC 228)." January 7, 1946.

———. 3-5. "Report of Preliminary Studies and Recommendations of Japanese Constitution." December 6, 1945.

———. 3-7. "Courtney Whitney's Memorandum regarding Constitutional Reform." February 1, 1946.

———. 3-10. "MacArthur Notes (MacArthur's Three Basic Points)." February 3, 1946.

———. 3-14. "Drafts of the Revised Constitution" and "Original Drafts of Committee Reports." February 4, 1946.

———. 3-16. "Record of Events on 13 February 1946 when Proposed New Constitution for Japan was Submitted to the Prime Minister, Mr. Yoshida, in Behalf of the Supreme Commander." February 13, 1946.

———. 4-6. Far Eastern Commission. "Basic Principles for a New Japanese Constitution." July 2, 1946.

———. 4-11. "Transcript of Twenty-Seventh Meeting of the Far Eastern Commission." September 21, 1946.

———. Hussey Papers-1. "Summary Report on Meeting of the Government Section." February 4, 1946.

———. Hussey Papers-2. "Ellerman Notes on Minutes of Government Section, Public Administration Division Meetings and Steering Committee Meetings." February 5 to 12, 1946.

NDL "Modern." 2013. National Diet Library. "Modern Japan in Archives." http://www.ndl.go.jp/modern/e/utility/list.html. Accessed April 30, 2013. Documents cited:

———. 1-10-1. "Blueprint for Governmental Reform." January–February 1875.

———. 5-9-2. "General MacArthur's Statement." May 24, 1947.

Nihonkoku kokkai zengiin meikan hensan iinkai, comp. 1986. *Nihonkoku kokkai zengiin meikan* [*Directory of Japanese Parliamentarians*]. 3 vols. Tokyo: Kokutai Kenkyūin.

Nishi Toshio. 2004. *Unconditional Democracy: Education and Politics in Occupied Japan, 1945–1952*. Stanford, Calif.: Hoover Press.

Nitobe Inazō. 1931. *Japan: Some Phases of Her Problems and Development*. New York: Scribner's Sons.

Noble, Gregory W. 2011. "The Evolution of the Japanese Policymaking System." In Gaunder, ed., 249–260.

North, Douglass C. 1990. *Institutions, Institutional Change and Economic Performance*. Cambridge: Cambridge Univ. Press.

Nouisiainen, Jaakko. 1994. "Finland: Ministerial Autonomy, Constitutional Collectivism, and Party Oligarchy." In Laver and Shepsle, eds., 88–105.

Office for National Statistics (United Kingdom). 2010. www.statistics.gov.uk/statbase/. Accessed December 22, 2010.

Ōkochi Shigeo. 1981. "Daisanji Hatoyama naikaku" ["The Third Hatoyama Cabinet"]. In Hayashi and Tsuji, eds., 6:335–356.

Ono Yoshikuni. 2012. "Portfolio Allocation as Leadership Strategy: Intraparty Bargaining in Japan." *American Journal of Political Science* 56: 553–567.

Packard, George. 1966. *Protest in Tokyo: The Security Treaty Crisis of 1960*. Princeton: Princeton Univ. Press.

Palmer, Matthew S. R. 1994. "Collective Cabinet Decision Making in New Zealand." In Laver and Shepsle, eds., 226–250.

Park, Yung H. 1986. *Bureaucrats and Ministers in Contemporary Japanese Government*. Berkeley, Calif.: Institute of East Asian Studies.

Parkinson, C. Northcote. 1955. "Parkinson's Law." *The Economist*. http://www.economist.com/node/14116121. Accessed April 28, 2013.

Peattie, Mark R. 1984. "Japanese Attitudes toward Colonialism, 1895–1945." In *The Japanese Colonial Empire, 1895–1945*, edited by Ramon H. Myers and Mark R. Peattie, 80–127. Princeton: Princeton Univ. Press.

Pempel, T. J. 1974. "The Bureaucratization of Policymaking in Postwar Japan." *American Journal of Political Science* 18: 647–664.

———. 1982. "The National Bureaucracy." In *Kodansha Encyclopedia of Japan,* edited by Gen Itasaka, 218. Cambridge: Kodansha.

———. 1986. "Uneasy toward Autonomy: Parliament and Parliamentarians in Japan." In *Parliaments and Parliamentarians in Democratic Politics,* edited by Ezra N. Suleiman, 106–153. New York: Holmes and Meier.

———. 1998. *Regime Shift: Comparative Dynamics of the Japanese Political Economy.* Ithaca, N.Y.: Cornell Univ. Press.

Pierson, Paul. 2000. "Increasing Returns, Path Dependence, and the Study of Politics." *American Political Science Review* 94: 251–268.

Pierson, Paul, and Theda Skocpol. 2002. "Historical Institutionalism in Contemporary Political Science." In *Political Science: State of the Discipline,* edited by Ira Katznelson and Helen V. Milner, 693–721. New York: Norton.

Polsby, Nelson W. 1968. "The Institutionalization of the U.S. House of Representatives." *American Political Science Review* 62: 144–168.

Porges, Amelia, and Joy M. Leong. 2006. "The Privatization of Japan Post: Ensuring Both a Viable Post and a Level Playing Field." In *Progress toward Liberalization of the Postal and Delivery Sector,* edited by Michael A. Crew and Paul R. Kleindorfer, 385–400. New York: Springer Science+Business Media.

Pyle, Kenneth B. 1996a. *The Japanese Question: Power and Purpose in a New Era.* Washington, D.C.: American Enterprise Institute.

———.1996b. *The Making of Modern Japan,* 2nd ed. Lexington. D. C. Heath.

Pyle, Kenneth B., Michael Finnegan, Michael J. Green, Kent E. Calder, Andrew L. Oros, and Yuki Tatsumi. 2010. "Roundtable: A New Stage for the U.S.-Japan Alliance?" *Asia Policy,* no. 10 (July): 1–41.

Quigley, Harold S. 1931. "Privy Council vs. Cabinet in Japan." *Foreign Affairs* 9: 501–505.

———. 1932. *Japanese Government and Politics: An Introductory Study.* New York: Century Company.

Quo, F. Q. 1972. "Democratic Theories and Japanese Modernization." *Modern Asian Studies* 6 (1): 17–31.

Ragsdale, Lyn, and John J. Theis III. 1997. "The Institutionalization of the American Presidency, 1924–92." *American Journal of Political Science* 41: 1280–1318.

Ramseyer, Mark, and Frances McCall Rosenbluth. 1993. *Japan's Political Marketplace.* Cambridge, Mass: Harvard Univ. Press.

———. 1995. *The Politics of Oligarchy: Institutional Choice in Imperial Japan.* Cambridge: Cambridge Univ. Press.

Ravina, Mark. 2004. *The Last Samurai: The Life and Battles of Saigo Takamori.* Hoboken: Wiley.

Reed, Steven R. 1991. "Jiyūminshutō no kōteika" ["The Institutionalization of the LDP"]. *Leviathan* 9: 80–103.

Reed, Steven R., and Ethan Scheiner. 2003. "Electoral Incentives and Policy Preferences: Mixed Motives behind Party Defections in Japan." *British Journal of Political Science* 33: 469–490.

Reich, Michael R. 1984. "Mobilizing for Environmental Policy in Italy and Japan." *Comparative Politics* 16: 379–402.

Rhodes, R.A.W., John Wanna, and Patrick Weller. 2009. *Comparing Westminster.* Oxford: Oxford Univ. Press.

Rose, Richard. 1971. "The Making of Cabinet Ministers." *British Journal of Political Science* 1: 393–414.

Rosenbluth, Frances, and Michael F. Thies. 1999. "The Political Economy of Japanese Pollution Regulation." Paper presented at the Annual Meetings of the American Political Science Association. Atlanta, September 2–5, 1999. www.yale.edu/leitner/resources/docs/1999-01.pdf. Accessed April 28, 2013.

Saikō hōki toshite no kenpō no arikata ni kansuru chōsa koiinkai. 2003. *Meiji kenpō to Nipponkoku kenpō nikansuru kiso-teki shiryō [Basic Materials concerning the Meiji Constitution and Constitution of Japan].* Tokyo: Shūgiin kenpō chōsa-kai jimu-kyoku. www.shugiin.go.jp/itdb_kenpou . . . /shukenshi027.pdf. Accessed April 26, 2013.

Sakoh Katsuro. 1986. "Privatizing State-Owned Enterprises: A Japanese Case Study, Heritage Foundation Asian Studies Backgrounder." No. 51. http://www.heritage.org/research/reports/1986/09/privatizing-state-owned-enterprises-a-japanese-case-study. Accessed April 26, 2013.

Samuels, Richard J. 2003. *Machiavelli's Children: Leaders and Their Legacies in Italy and Japan.* Ithaca, N.Y.: Cornell Univ. Press.

———. 2004. "Politics, Security Policy, and Japan's Cabinet Legislation Bureau: Who Elected These Guys Anyway?" JPRI Working Paper No. 99. www.jpri.org/publications/workingpapers/wp99.html. Accessed April 26, 2013.

———. 2013. *3.11: Disaster and Change in Japan.* Ithaca, N.Y.: Cornell Univ. Press.

Sarantakes, Nicholas Evan. 2000. *Keystone: The American Occupation of Okinawa and U.S.-Japanese Relations.* College Station: Texas A&M Univ. Press.

Satō Seizaburō and Matsuzaki Tetsuhisa. 1986. *Jimintō seiken [LDP Rule].* Tokyo: Chūō kōronsha.

Satō Seizaburō, Koyama Kenichi, and Kumon Shunpei. 1990. *Postwar Politician: The Life of Former Prime Minister Masayoshi Ohira.* Translated by William R. Carter. Tokyo: New York: Kodansha International.

Savage, James D. 2002. "The Origins of Budgetary Preferences: The Dodge Line and the Balanced Budget Norm in Japan." *Administration and Society* 34: 261–284.

Scalapino, Robert A. 1953. *Democracy and the Party Movement in Prewar Japan: The Failure of the First Attempt.* Berkeley: Univ. of California Press.

Scalapino, Robert A., and Junnosuke Masumi. 1962. *Parties and Politics in Contemporary Japan.* Berkeley: Univ. of California Press.

Schaller, Michael. 1995. "America's Favorite War Criminal: Kishi Nobusuke and the Transformation of U.S.-Japan Relations." JPRI Working Paper No. 11.

http://www.jpri.org/publications/workingpapers/wp11.html. Accessed May 21, 2013.

———. 1996. "The Nixon 'Shocks' and U.S.-Japan Strategic Relations, 1969–74." Washington, D.C.: National Security Archive, Working Paper No. 2. www.gwu.edu/~nsarchiv/japan/schaller.htm. Accessed April 26, 2013.

Scheiner, Ethan. 2006. *Democracy without Competition: Opposition Failure in a One-Party Dominant State*. Cambridge: Cambridge Univ. Press.

Schlichtmann, Klaus. 2009. *Japan in the World: Shidehara Kijūrō, Pacifism, and the Abolition of War*. Lanham, Md.: Lexington Books.

Schoppa, Leonard J. 1991. "Zoku Power and LDP Power: A Case Study of the Zoku Role in Education Policy." *Journal of Japanese Studies* 17: 79–106.

———. 1997. *Bargaining with Japan: What American Pressure Can and Cannot Do*. Ithaca, N.Y.: Cornell Univ. Press.

Searing, Donald D. 1994. *Westminster's World: Understanding Political Roles*. Cambridge, Mass.: Harvard Univ. Press.

Seikan yōran [*Politics-Bureaucracy Handbook*]. Various years. Tokyo: Seisaku jihōsha.

Sekiguchi Yasushi. 1938. "The Changing Status of the Cabinet in Japan." *Pacific Affairs* 11: 5–20.

Shillony, Ben-Ami. 1973. *Revolt in Japan: The Young Officers and the February 26, 1936 Incident*. Princeton: Princeton Univ. Press.

———, ed. 2008. *The Emperors of Modern Japan*. Leiden: Koninklijke Brill.

Shimizu Masato. 2005. *Kantei shudō: Koizumi Jun'ichirō no kakumei* [*Prime Ministerial Leadership: Koizumi Jun'ichirō's Revolution*]. Tokyo: Tōyō keizai shinbunsha.

Shinoda Tomohito. 2000. *Leading Japan: The Role of the Prime Minister*. Westport, Conn.: Praeger.

———. 2005. "Japan's Cabinet Secretariat and Its Emergence as Core Executive." *Asian Survey* 45: 800–821.

———. 2007. *Koizumi Diplomacy: Japan's Kantei Approach to Foreign and Defense Affairs*. Seattle: Univ. of Washington Press.

Shiota Ushio. 2011. *Nihon no naikaku sōridaijin jiten* [*Encyclopedia of Japan's Prime Ministers*]. Tokyo: Tatsumi Shuppan.

Shiratori Rei, ed. 1979. *Gekidō no nihon seijishi: Meiji, Taishō, Shōwa rekidai kokkai giin shiroku* [*Japan's Tumultuous Political History: Meiji, Taishō, and Shōwa Era Diet Members*]. Tokyo: Asaka Shobō.

———, ed. 1981. *Nihon no naikaku* [*Japan's Cabinets*]. 3 vols. Contributing authors: Horie Fukashi, Fukuoka Masayuki, Iizuka Shigetarō, Iwami Takao, Senda Hisashi, Tomita Nobuo, and Yamakawa Katsumi. Tokyo: Shinpyōron.

Shugart, Matthew Soberg. 2005. "Semi-Presidential Systems: Dual Executive and Mixed Authority Patterns." *French Politics* 3: 323–351.

Silberman, Bernard S. 1967. "Bureaucratic Development and the Structure of Decision-Making in the Meiji Period: The Case of the Genrō." *Journal of Asian Studies* 27 (1): 81–94.

———. 1970. "Bureaucratic Development and the Structure of Decision-Making in Japan: 1868–1925." *Journal of Asian Studies* 29 (2): 347–362.

———. 1976. "Bureaucratization of the Meiji State: The Problem of Succession in the Meiji Restoration, 1868–1900." *Journal of Asian Studies* 35 (3): 421–430.

———. 1993. *Cages of Reason: The Rise of the Rational State in France, Japan, the United States, and Great Britain.* Chicago: Univ. of Chicago Press.

Sims, Richard. 1982. "Japanese Fascism." *History Today* 32: 10–13.

———. 2001. *Japanese Political History since the Meiji Renovation, 1868–2000.* New York: Palgrave.

Skocpol, Theda. 1995. "Why I Am a Historical Institutionalist," *Polity* 28: 103–106.

Smith, Thomas C. 1988. *Native Sources of Japanese Industrialization, 1750–1920.* Berkeley: Univ. of California Press.

Sodei Rinjirō. 2001. "The Double Conversion of a Cartoonist: The Case of Katō Etsurō." In *War, Occupation, and Creativity: Japan and East Asia, 1920–1960,* edited by Marlene J. Mayo and J. Thomas Rimer, with H. Eleanor Kerkham, 235–268. Honolulu: Univ. of Hawai'i Press.

Special Action Committee on Okinawa (SACO). 1996a. "The Japan-U.S. Special Action Committee (SACO) Interim Report, April 15, 1996." www.mofa.go.jp/region/n-america/us/security/seco.html. Accessed December 17, 2013.

———. 1996b. "The SACO Final Report, December 2, 1996." www.mofa.go.jp/region/n-america/us/security/96saco1.html. Accessed December 17, 2013.

"Statement by Prime Minister Junichiro Koizumi at the First Meeting of the New Cabinet." 2001. Shūshō Kantei. http://www.kantei.go.jp/foreign/koizumispeech/2001/0426setuji_e.html. Accessed April 28, 2013.

"Statement by Prime Minister Yoshiro Mori at the Press Conference." 2000. Shūshō Kantei. http://www.kantei.go.jp/foreign/souri/mori/2000/0526press.html. Accessed April 28, 2013.

Steinhoff, Patricia G. 1989. "Protest and Democracy." In Ishida and Krauss, eds., 171–198.

Stockwin, J.A.A. 1999. *Governing Japan: Divided Politics in a Major Economy,* 3rd ed. Oxford: Blackwell.

———. 2011. "Political Leadership in Japan: Are Effective Leaders Possible?" Paper presented to the Biennial Conference of the Japanese Studies Association of Australia, Melbourne University. June 2011. http://japaninstitute.anu.edu.au/japanese_studies/issue_04/Issue_4_2011.pdf. Accessed December 23, 2011.

Stratton, Samuel S. 1948. "The Far Eastern Commission." *International Organization* 2: 1–18.

Strom, Kaare. 1994. "The Political Role of Norwegian Cabinet Ministers." In Laver and Shepsle, eds., 35–55.

Strom, Kaare, Ian Budge, and Michael J. Laver. 1994. "Constraints on Cabinet Formation in Parliamentary Democracies." *American Journal of Political Science* 38: 303–335.

Sugimori Kōji. 1968. "The Social Background of Political Leadership in Japan." *Developing Economies* 6 (4): 487–509.

Supreme Commander for the Allied Powers, Government Section. 1949. *Political Reorientation of Japan*, vol. 1. Washington, D.C.: Government Printing Office.

Takayama Noriyuki. 2009. "On Fifty Million Floating Pension Records in Japan." www.ier.hit-u.ac.jp/pie/stage2/Japanese/d_p/dp2009/ . . . /text.pdf. Accessed April 12, 2012.

Takemae Eiji. 2002. *Inside GHQ: The Allied Occupation of Japan*. New York: Continuum International Publishing Group.

Takenaka Heizo. 2008. *The Structural Reforms of the Koizumi Cabinet: An Insider's Account of the Economic Revival of Japan*. Translated by Jillian Yorke. Tokyo: Nihon Keizai Shinbun Shuppansha.

Takeuchi Tatsuji. 1967. *War and Diplomacy in the Japanese Empire*. New York: Russell and Russell.

Tanaka Akihiko. 2000. "The Domestic Context of the Alliances: The Politics of Tokyo." Asia-Pacific Research Center Working Paper. iis-db.stanford.edu/pubs/11376/Tanaka.pdf. Accessed April 26, 2013.

Tanaka Hiroshi. 1976. *The Japanese Legal System: Introductory Cases and Materials*. Tokyo: Univ. of Tokyo Press.

Tansman, Alan. 2009. "Introduction: The Culture of Japanese Fascism." In *The Culture of Japanese Fascism*, edited by Alan Tansman, 1–28. Durham, N.C.: Duke Univ. Press.

Tehan, William J., III. 2002. "Douglas MacArthur: An Administrative Biography." Ph.D. diss., Virginia Polytechnic Institute and State University. scholar.lib.vt.edu/theses/available/etd-09292002-133302/ . . . /Tehan.pdf. Accessed April 26, 2013.

Thayer, Nathaniel B. 1969. *How the Conservatives Rule Japan*. New York: Columbia Univ. Press.

———. 1996. "The Japanese Prime Minister and His Cabinet." *SAIS Review* 16: 71–86.

Thies, Michael F., and Yuki Yanai. 2012. "Divided Parliaments and Lawmaking: Japan's Twisted Diet." Social Science Research Network. papers.ssrn.com/s013/Delivery.cfm?abstractid=2128993. Accessed April 26, 2013.

Thomas, Graham P. 1998. *Prime Minister and Cabinet Today*. Manchester, UK: Manchester Univ. Press.

Tiedemann, Arthur E., ed. 1974. *An Introduction to Japanese Civilization*. Lexington, Mass.: D. C. Heath.

Togawa Isamu. 1983. *Shosetsu Yoshida Shigeru* [*Yoshida Shigeru—The Novel*]. Tokyo: Kadokawa Shoten.

Tolbert, Pamela S., and Lynne G. Zucker. 1996. "The Institutionalization of Institutional Theory." In *Handbook of Organization Studies*, edited by Stewart Clegg, Cynthia Hardy, and Walter R. Nord, 175–189. Thousand Oaks, Calif.: Sage.

Tomita Nobuo, Hans Baerwald, and Akira Nakamura. 1981. "Prerequisites to Ministerial Careers in Japan 1885–1980." *International Political Science Review* 2: 235–256.

Totman, Conrad D. 1967. *Politics in the Tokugawa Bakufu, 1600–1843*. Cambridge, Mass.: Harvard Univ. Press.

———. 1974. "Tokugawa Japan." In Tiedemann, ed., 97–130.

Uriu, Robert. 2003. "Japan in 2002: An Up-and-Down Year, but Mostly Down." *Asian Survey* 43: 78–90.

U.S. Government. 2008. *Policy and Supporting Positions*. Washington, D.C.: Government Printing Office.

Uyehara, George Etsujiro. 1910. *The Political Development of Japan*. London: Constable and Company.

Uzawa Yoshiyuki. 1981. "Daiichiji Konoe naikaku kara Shidehara Kijūrō naikaku made" ["From the First Konoe Fumimaro Cabinet to the Shidehara Kijūrō Cabinet"]. In *Nihon seiji no jitsuryokushatachi: riidaa no jōken* [*Japan's Political Powerbrokers: Conditions of Leaders*], vol. 3, edited by Uchida Kenzō, Nakamura Katsunori, Tomita Nobuo, Watanabe Akio, and Andō Jinbei, 91–121. Tokyo: Yuhikaku.

Van Wolferen, Karel G. 1989. *The Enigma of Japanese Power: People and Politics in a Stateless Nation*. New York: Knopf.

———. 2001. "Yamagata's Legacy." www.karelvanwolferen.com/wp-content/uploads/pdf/Yamaga.pdf. Accessed April 28, 2013.

Varley, H. Paul. 1974a. "The Age of the Court Nobles." In Tiedemann, ed., 33–59.

———. 1974b. "Early Japan." In Tiedemann, ed., 4–32.

Vlastos, Stephen. 1990. *Peasant Protests and Uprisings in Tokugawa Japan*. Berkeley: Univ. of California Press.

Vogel, Steven K. 1996. *Freer Markets, More Rules: Regulatory Reform in Advanced Industrial Countries*. Ithaca, N.Y.: Cornell Univ. Press.

Wakaizumi Kei. 2002. *The Best Course Available: A Personal Account of the Secret U.S.-Japan Okinawa Reversion Negotiations*. Edited by John Swenson-Wright. Honolulu: Univ. of Hawai'i Press.

Ward, Robert E. 1956. "The Origins of the Present Japanese Constitution." *American Political Science Review* 50: 980–1010.

———. 1987. "Conclusion." In Robert E. Ward and Sakamoto Yoshikazu, eds., *Democratizing Japan*, 392–433. Honolulu: Univ. of Hawai'i Press.

Watanabe Akio. 1981a. "Dainiji Satō naikaku" ["The Second Satō Cabinet"]. In Hayashi and Tsuji, eds., vol. 6, 139–174.

———. 1981b. "Daisanji Satō naikaku" ["The Third Satō Cabinet"]. In Hayashi and Tsuji, eds., vol. 6, 175–211.

———. ed. 1995. *Sengō Nihon no saishōtachi* [*Postwar Japan's Prime Ministers*]. Tokyo: Chūō kōron sha.

Weber, Max. 1946. "Bureaucracy." In *From Max Weber: Essays in Sociology*, edited by H. H. Gerth and C. Wright Mills, 196–244. Oxford: Oxford Univ. Press.

Weller, Patrick, Herman Bakvis, and R.A.W. Rhodes, eds. 1997. *The Hollow Crown: Countervailing Trends in Core Executives*. New York: St. Martin's Press.

Weiner, Tim. 2007. *Legacy of Ashes: The History of the CIA*. New York: Doubleday.

White, Graham. 1994. "The Interpersonal Dynamics of Decision Making in Canadian Provincial Cabinets." In Laver and Shepsle, eds., 251–269.

Whitney, Courtney. 1956. *MacArthur: His Rendezvous with History*. New York: Knopf.

Wildavsky, Aaron. 1978. "A Budget for All Seasons: Why the Traditional Budget Lasts." *Public Administration Review* 38: 501–510.

Woodall, Brian. 1992. "The Politics of Land in Japan's Dual Political Economy." In *Land Issues in Japan: A Policy Failure*, edited by John O. Haley and Kozo Yamamura, 113–148. Seattle, Wash.: Society for Japanese Studies.

———. 1996. *Japan Under Construction: Corruption, Politics, and Public Works*. Berkeley: Univ. of California Press.

———. 1999. "The Politics of Reform in Japan's Lower House Electoral System." In Grofman et al., eds., 23–50.

———. 2013. "Japan: Energy Efficiency Paragon, Green Growth Laggard." In *Can Green Sustain Growth? From the Religion to the Reality of Sustainable Prosperity*, edited by Mark Huberty and John Zysman, 150–169. Stanford, Calif.: Stanford Univ. Press.

———. 2014. "The Unshakable Money Base of Japanese Politics: Parties, Candidates, Donors and Corruption." In *Party Politics in Japan: Political Chaos and Stalemate in the 21st Century*, edited by Ronald J. Hrebenar and Akira Nakamura. London: Routledge.

Yamamuro Kentoku. 1995. "Hatoyama Ichirō—nisso kokkō kaifuku to kenpō kaisei e no shūnen" ["Hatoyama Ichirō—Restoring Japan-USSR Relations and Tenaciously Pursuing Constitutional Revision"]. In Watanabe, ed., 91–108.

Yoshida Shigeru. 1962. *The Yoshida Memoirs: The Story of Japan in Crisis*. Translated by Kenichi Yoshida. Boston: Houghton Mifflin.

Zucker, Lynne. 1991. "The Role of Institutionalization in Cultural Persistence." In *The New Institutionalism in Organizational Analysis*, edited by Walter Powell and Paul DiMaggio, 83–107. Chicago: Univ. of Chicago Press.

Index

References to specific cabinets (e.g., Miki cabinet) are listed under the name of the prime minister (e.g., Miki Takeo), and ministerial portfolios (e.g., finance minister) are listed under the name of the relevant ministry or agency (e.g., Ministry of Finance).

Abe Genki, 73, 76
Abe Nobuyuki, 74; cabinets of, 75
Abe Shinzō, 189–91, 192, 197, 198, 199–200, 201, 209–10, 244n2; cabinets of, 8, 11, 189, 190, 192, 193, 195, 197, 200, 201
Administrative Evaluation Department, 102
Administrative Management Agency, 102, 124, 153, 162; portfolio, 102, 125, 232
Administrative Reform Council, 170, 175
administrative vice ministers' meeting, 25, 157, 178, 200, 216
Aichi Kiichi, 106, 130
Aikoku Kōtō, 45–46
Aizawa Saburō, 240n38
Akagi Norihiko, 203
Akahata, 113
Allied Council of Japan, 241n10
All-Japan Federation of Students' Self-Governing Associations, 133
alternate attendance (*sankin kōtai*) system, 34
Aoki Kazuo, 73, 76
Arab Spring, 21, 30
Arafune Seijurō, 128
Arita Jirō, 110
Asanuma Inejirō, 133

Ashida Hitoshi, 95–97, 237n2; cabinets of, 97, 242n21
Ashikaga shōgunate, 39
Asō Tarō, 184, 189, 192, 198–99, 202; cabinets of, 191, 193
Atcheson, George, 86
Attlee, Clement, 85
Aum Shinrikyō. *See* sarin gas attack
Ayukawa Yoshisuke, 78

Baerwald, Hans, 112
Bank of Taiwan controversy, 65
Basic Law on Environmental Pollution Control. *See* environmental protection movement
Bix, Herbert, 55, 58, 66, 77, 78, 79
Black Mist scandals, 128–29
Blakeslee, George H., 85
Board of Audit, 238n10
Borton, Hugh, 85–86, 87, 90, 94, 240n3
Boshin War, 36–37
bubble economy, 3, 235n2
Bundy, William, 138
bureaucratic government, 24–26
Byrnes, James F., 86, 94

Cabal Cabinet. *See* cabinet system (United Kingdom)
cabal cabinets, 51–57; Sat-Chō cabal, 31–32, 37, 43, 44, 45, 46, 47, 48, 50–53, 54, 55, 56–57, 58, 59–60, 61, 65, 67, 81, 212, 215, 218, 238n13
cabinet councilor, 73
Cabinet Deliberation Council, 74
cabinet government, 3, 4, 13, 18, 24, 25, 27, 29, 84, 109, 114, 140, 165, 167, 168, 170, 179–80, 188, 191,

ASIA IN THE NEW MILLENNIUM

SERIES EDITOR: Shiping Hua, University of Louisville

Asia in the New Millennium is a series of books offering new interpretations of an important geopolitical region. The series examines the challenges and opportunities of Asia from the perspectives of politics, economics, and cultural-historical traditions, highlighting the impact of Asian developments on the world. Of particular interest are books on the history and prospect of the democratization process in Asia. The series also includes policy-oriented works that can be used as teaching materials at the undergraduate and graduate levels. Innovative manuscript proposals at any stage are welcome.

ADVISORY BOARD

William Callahan, University of Manchester, Southeast Asia, Thailand
Lowell Dittmer, University of California at Berkeley, East Asia and South Asia
Robert Hathaway, Woodrow Wilson International Center for Scholars, South
  Asia, India, Pakistan
Mike Mochizuki, George Washington University, East Asia, Japan and Korea
Peter Moody, University of Notre Dame, China and Japan
Brantly Womack, University of Virginia, China and Vietnam
Charles Ziegler, University of Louisville, Central Asia and Russia Far East

BOOKS IN THE SERIES

The Future of China-Russia Relations
Edited by James Bellacqua

Contemporary Chinese Political Thought: Debates and Perspectives
Edited by Fred Dallmayr and Zhao Tingyang

The Mind of Empire: China's History and Modern Foreign Relations
Christopher A. Ford

State Violence in East Asia
Edited by N. Ganesan and Sung Chull Kim

Korean Democracy in Transition: A Rational Blueprint for Developing Societies
HeeMin Kim

www.ingramcontent.com/pod-product-compliance
Lightning Source LLC
Chambersburg PA
CBHW031545260326
41914CB00002B/273